Quality assurance of pharmaceuticals

A compendium of guidelines
and related materials

Volume 2, 2nd updated edition

Good manufacturing practices
and inspection

World Health
Organization

WHO Library Cataloguing-in-Publication Data

Quality assurance of pharmaceuticals : a compendium of guidelines and related materials. Vol. 2, Good manufacturing practices and inspection. – 2nd ed.

1.Drug and narcotic control – standards 2.Drug industry – standards
3.Pharmaceutical preparations – standards 4.Biological products – standards
5.Quality control 6.Guidelines I.World Health Organization
II.Title: Good manufacturing practices and inspection

ISBN 92 4 154708 1
ISBN 978 92 4 154708 6

(NLM classification: QV 33)

Printed in India

Contents

Introduction 1

1. WHO good manufacturing practices: main principles for pharmaceutical products 7

Quality management in the drug industry: philosophy and essential elements (update on sampling) (new) 7

Heating Ventilation and air-conditioning systems for non-sterile pharmaceutical dosage forms (new) 58

Validation (new) 101

Water for pharmaceutical use (new) 170

2. WHO good manufacturing practices: starting materials 188

Active pharmaceutical ingredients (bulk drug substances) 188

Pharmaceutical excipients 196

3. WHO good manufacturing practices: specific pharmaceutical products 215

Sterile pharmaceutical products 215

Biological products 232

Investigational pharmaceutical products for clinical trials in humans 242

The manufacture of herbal medicines (updated) 254

Radiopharmaceutical products 276

4. Inspection 285

Pre-approval inspections 285

Inspection of pharmaceutical manufacturers 291

Inspection of drug distribution channels 303

Quality systems requirements for national good manufacturing practice inspectorates 322

Guidance on good manufacturing practices: inspection report 338

Model certificate of good manufacturing practices 347

5. Hazard and risk analysis in pharmaceutical products 346

Application of hazard analysis and critical control point (HACCP) methodology to pharmaceuticals 346

6. Sampling operations (new) 359

Sampling of pharmaceutical products and related materials (new) 359

Index 389

Introduction

The quality of pharmaceuticals has been a concern of the World Health Organization (WHO) since its inception. The setting of global standards is requested in Article 2 of the WHO Constitution, which cites as one of the Organization's functions that it should "develop, establish and promote international standards with respect to food, biological, pharmaceutical and similar products."

Every government allocates a substantial proportion of its total health budget to medicines. This proportion tends to be greatest in developing countries, where it may exceed 40%.

Without assurance that these medicines are relevant to priority health needs and that they meet acceptable standards of quality, safety and efficacy, any health service is evidently compromised. In developing countries considerable administrative and technical effort is directed to ensuring that patients receive effective medicines of good quality. It is crucial to the objective of health for all that a reliable system of medicines control be brought within the reach of every country.

The supply of essential medicines of good quality was identified as one of the prerequisites for the delivery of health care at the International Conference on Primary Health Care in Alma-Ata in 1978. Similarly, the Conference of Experts on the Rational Use of Drugs, held in Nairobi in 1985, and WHO's Revised Drug Strategy, adopted by the World Health Assembly in May 1986, identified the effective functioning of national drug regulation and control systems as the only means to assure safety and quality of medicines. Yet the World Health Assembly continues to express great concern about the quality, safety and efficacy of medicines, particularly those products or active pharmaceutical substances imported into, or produced in, developing countries. In recent years counterfeit products have infiltrated certain markets in disquieting proportions. Since the founding of WHO, the World Health Assembly has adopted many resolutions requesting the Organization to develop international standards, recommendations and instruments to assure the quality of medicines, whether produced and traded nationally or internationally.

In response to these resolutions, the WHO Expert Committee on Specifications for Pharmaceutical Preparations, which was originally created to prepare *The International Pharmacopoeia*, has made numerous recommendations relevant to quality assurance and control. Most of these recommendations, even though they were made several years ago, are still valid. Thus far, however, most have been available only as separate sets of recommendations contained in annexes to various *WHO Technical Reports*. The recommendations are essential to all concerned with the quality assurance of medicines, but separate publications over a period of years has made it difficult to recognize them as complementary parts of a comprehensive system of quality assurance.

To provide easy access to this information, the appropriate annexes and updates are reproduced in the volumes of this publication. They are supplemented with other material relevant to the quality assurance of pharmaceuticals, some already issued in the form of WHO documents. The information is presented in logical sequence as a series of administrative instruments and technical elements of an overall quality assurance system. Readers should bear in mind that, in certain previously published texts, reference is made to WHO guidelines and other documents that have since been updated. Some of these updated texts are themselves included in the compendium.

Volume 1 of *Quality assurance of pharmaceuticals: a compendium of guidelines and related materials* was published by WHO in 1997. Material relating to national drug regulations, product assessment and registration, *The International Pharmacopoeia* and related activities, quality control laboratories, international trade in pharmaceuticals and their distribution, counterfeit products, basic tests for pharmaceutical products and training of technical personnel is collected and reproduced in Volume 1. Volume 2, first published by WHO in 1999, reproduces guidelines related to good manufacturing practices (GMP) and to the inspection of pharmaceutical manufacturers and drug distribution channels. This volume was updated in 2004, and the current version constitutes the second updated edition of Volume 2 including new texts and revisions adopted to date as WHO guidelines.

Both for manufacturers and at national level, GMP are an important part of a comprehensive system of quality assurance. They also represent the technical standard upon which is based the WHO Certification Scheme on the Quality of Pharmaceutical Products Moving in International Commerce. The first GMP text published by WHO was developed during 1967–69 upon request by WHO's Member States and was revised in 1975. In the 1980s and early 1990s, several national and regional drug regulatory authorities issued or revised guidelines reflecting the ongoing elaboration of the concept of GMP. In addition, the WHO Certification Scheme on the Quality of Pharmaceutical Products Moving in International Commerce was extended in 1988. Together, these developments necessitated an update of the existing guidelines on GMP published by WHO.

Revised and expanded GMP guidelines were prepared during 1989–90, approved by the WHO Expert Committee on Specifications for Pharmaceutical Preparations in late 1990 and subsequently published by WHO. At that time, Part One of these revised and expanded guidelines set out the philosophy and essential elements of GMP; Part Two dealt with good practices in production and quality control. These two parts together represented the "core" of the GMP guidelines published by WHO.

Their provisions were and still are fully consonant with those of other internationally recognized texts on GMP. GMP guidelines published by WHO are to be regarded as advisory in nature and may need to be adapted to address specific conditions in individual countries. However, if any departures from recommended practices are introduced, the equivalence of such alternative approaches should be validated.

In 1996, GMP guidelines were published by WHO for the validation of manufacturing processes. These guidelines were prepared to explain and promote the concept of validation embedded in the core GMP texts, and to assist in establishing priorities and selecting approaches when a validation programme is being developed. In 1997, the WHO Expert Committee on Specifications for Pharmaceutical Preparations approved an explanatory text on the role and functions of the "authorized person" at manufacturing establishments in the medicines industry. The core GMP guidelines define the authorized person as the person responsible for the release of batches of finished products for sale. The explanatory text is intended to assist manufacturers wishing to strengthen their quality assurance systems. These concepts were integrated in its revised text in 2003. The guidance on validation has been extensively revised and expanded. The new text has been adopted in 2005 and is now included in its revised form.

GMP guidelines published by WHO in 1992–2006 constitute in the first instalment an ongoing series of applications of the principles of GMP to various specialized areas. The series of the "main" GMP texts on the manufacture of pharmaceutical active substances and excipients, were approved by the WHO Expert Committee on Specifications for Pharmaceutical Preparations in 1992, 1997, and therafter.

Chapter 1 ("Main principles for pharmaceutical products") includes the core GMP guidelines, as well as GMP guidance texts for the heating, ventilation and air-conditioning systems; validation; and water for pharmaceutical use in their updated forms.

The two texts in Chapter 2 constitute the existing body of GMP guidance for pharmaceutical starting materials. As strict application of full GMP is not always practical or necessary for such materials, these texts outline the procedures and practices that manufacturers should employ to ensure that the methods, facilities and controls used for their production are operated or managed so that pharmaceutical starting materials have the quality and purity appropriate for use in finished pharmaceutical products.

On the other hand, certain specific kinds of pharmaceutical products demand practices or procedures not described in the core GMP guidelines. For example, section 17 in Part Three of the 1992 guidelines, updated in 2002 (to be found in Chapter 3) stresses additional points necessary to minimize the risks of microbiological, particulate and pyrogen contamination in sterile pharmaceutical products. Other specialized GMP guidelines were subsequently published by WHO for biological products, investigational pharmaceutical products, herbal medicinal products, radiopharmaceuticals, etc.

The GMP guidelines for biological products have been approved by both the WHO Expert Committee on Biological Standardization and the WHO Expert Committee on Specifications for Pharmaceutical Preparations. Unlike conventional pharmaceutical products which are normally produced and controlled by means of reproducible chemical and physical techniques, biological products are manufactured with biological materials and processes, such as the cultivation of cells or the extraction of materials from living organisms. As such materials and processes display inherent variability, the range and nature of manufacturing by-products in biological products are likewise variable. For such products, including allergens, antigens, vaccines, hormones, cytokines, enzymes, human whole-blood and plasma derivatives, immune sera, immunoglobulins, products of fermentation and diagnostic agents for in vitro use, full adherence to the GMP guidelines for biological products is recommended for all production steps, including those from which active ingredients are produced.

The GMP guidelines for the manufacture of investigational pharmaceutical products for clinical trials in humans supplement both the core GMP guidelines for pharmaceutical products and "Guidelines for good clinical practice (GCP) for trials on pharmaceutical products" (WHO Technical Report Series, No. 850, 1995, pp. 97–137). These specialized GMP guidelines specifically address those manufacturing practices that may be different for investigational products (which are not usually manufactured in accordance with a set routine), and which may be incompletely characterized during the initial stages of clinical development.

The specialized GMP guidelines for the manufacture of herbal medicinal products address the manufacture of products from material of plant origin, which may be subject to contamination and deterioration and vary in its composition and properties. Furthermore, in the manufacture and quality control of herbal medicinal products, procedures and techniques are often used that are substantially different from those employed for conventional pharmaceutical products. The newly revised text was adopted by the Expert Committee in 2005 (WHO Technical Report Series, No. 937, 2006, pp. 85–116).

The text on radiopharmaceuticals has been developed in close collaboration with the International Atomic Energy Agency (IAEA). The text covers radiopharmaceutical products that are prepared in hospital radiopharmacies, centralized radiopharmacies, nuclear centres and insititutes or by industrial manufacturers, as well as in positron emission tomography (PET) centres.

These five sets of specialized guidelines—for sterile, biological, investigational and herbal products and for radiopharmaceuticals—are reproduced in Chapter 3 (Specific pharmaceutical products).

Inspection is closely related to other elements of the overall medicines quality assurance system: GMP, licensing of manufacturing facilities, product registration, etc. Without a competent inspectorate operating to high professional standards, neither GMP compliance nor licensing provisions can be effectively enforced. In addition, inspection of manufacturing facilities is pivotal to the operation of the WHO Certification Scheme on the Quality of Pharmaceutical Products Moving in International Commerce, which provides for the issuance of an attestation that a given product is manufactured under GMP conditions as established by periodic inspections.

A text on pre-approval inspections was developed to complement the text on inspections, described below. These guidelines apply to the inspection of manufacturing and quality control facilities prior to the issuing of a marketing authorization for a pharmaceutical product.

A text entitled “Provisional guidelines on the inspection of pharmaceutical manufacturers” was published by WHO in 1992 along with the core GMP guidelines on pharmaceutical products. The provisional guidelines were intended to promote the harmonization of inspection practices among WHO Member States, and the Expert Committee noted that they would be of particular value to government inspectors operating within small national regulatory authorities.

In general, the objective of inspecting pharmaceutical manufacturing facilities is either to enforce general GMP compliance or to provide authorization for the manufacture of specific pharmaceutical products, usually in relation to an application for registration. The provisional guidelines are applicable mostly to inspections of the first type, whether performed before a manufacturing authorization is issued, or on a periodic, routine basis.

A further aspect of pharmaceutical inspection is monitoring the quality of pharmaceutical products in distribution channels, that is, from the point of manufacture to delivery to the recipient. In recent years the hazard posed by the infiltration of counterfeit products has been identified in addition to problems related to the inadequate stability of drug products and their improper handling and storage. The text “Guidelines for inspection of drug distribution channels”, part of the Thirty-fifth report of the WHO Expert Committee on Specifications for Pharmaceutical Preparations, is included in this volume and provides detailed advice to national drug regulatory authorities on the inspection of distribution channels.

The provisional guidelines on the inspection of pharmaceutical manufacturers and the guidelines for inspection of drug distribution channels are reproduced in Chapter 4 (“Inspections”).

With the worldwide acceptance of the ISO 9000-series standards addressing quality management and quality systems, a trend has emerged in some Member States for non-commercial institutions such as certification bodies, testing laboratories and the like to introduce principles of quality systems into their internal operations. The same principles have begun to be applied to governmental pharmaceutical inspectorates and medicines control laboratories. The WHO Expert Committee on Specifications for Pharmaceutical Preparations recently recommended that further guidance in this area should address the introduction of quality systems principles in the practice of pharmaceutical inspections.

Following the publication of the guidance texts on inspections, additional guidelines dealing with the quality system requirements for national good manufacturing practice inspectorates were adopted by the Expert Committee. This guidance is one important tool when implementing GMP. The establishment and operation of a quality system is an essential element in the mutual recognition among inspectorates. The quality system should include all activities involved in the inspection.

To complement the set of guidance texts in this area, the Expert Committee adopted a model layout for an inspection report, as well as a model certificate of GMP for a manufacturing site.

Hazards affecting quality are to a certain extent covered and controlled through the validation of critical operations and processes in the manufacture of finished pharmaceutical products in accordance with GMP. However, GMP do not cover the safety of the personnel engaged in manufacture, whereas the application of hazard analysis and critical control point (HACCP) methodology does. Traditionally, this concept has been applied to food safety management systems. The same principles have increasingly also been adopted in other industries. The guidance reproduced in this volume, in Chapter 5 (Hazard and risk analysis in pharmaceutical products), suggests their use also in the area of pharmaceuticals.

Sampling is an essential element when surveying the national markets for the quality of drug products in accordance with national drug quality surveillance programmes of marketed products, whether registered for sale or compounded in pharmacies. The Expert Committee adopted a revised guideline in 2004 primarily intended to assist governmental organizations, such as drug control authorities (including inspectorates), quality control laboratories, customs and police officials, but some of the general principles may also be appropriate for procurement agencies, manufacturers and customers. The guidance text is reproduced in Chapter 6 ("Sampling operations").

An alphabetical index of subjects covered in Volume 2 of *Quality assurance of pharmaceuticals: a compendium of guidelines and related materials* is included at the end of this volume.

1.

WHO good manufacturing practices: main principles for pharmaceutical products[1]

Quality management in the drug industry: philosophy and essential elements

Introduction 9
General considerations 10
Glossary 10
Quality management in the drug industry 15
1. Quality assurance 16
2. Good manufacturing practices for pharmaceutical products (GMP) 17
3. Sanitation and hygiene 18
4. Qualification and validation 18
5. Complaints 19
6. Product recalls 20
7. Contract production and analysis 21
   General 21
   The contract giver 21
   The contract accepter 22
   The contract 22
8. Self-inspection and quality audits 23
   Items for self-inspection 23
   Self-inspection team 24
   Frequency of self-inspection 24
   Self-inspection report 24
   Follow-up action 24
   Quality audit 24
   Suppliers' audits and approval 24
9. Personnel 25
   General 25
   Key personnel 25
10. Training 28

---

[1] Good manufacturing practices for pharmaceutical products: main principles. In: *WHO Expert Committee on Specifications for Pharmaceutical Preparations. Thirty-seventh report.* Geneva, World Health Organization, 2003 (WHO Technical Report Series, No. 908), Annex 4.

11. Personal hygiene 29
12. Premises 30
 General 30
 Ancillary areas 31
 Storage areas 31
 Weighing areas 32
 Production areas 32
 Quality control areas 33
13. Equipment 33
14. Materials 34
 General 35
 Starting materials 35
 Packaging materials 36
 Intermediate and bulk products 37
 Finished products 37
 Rejected, recovered, reprocessed and reworked materials 37
 Recalled products 38
 Returned goods 38
 Reagents and culture media 38
 Reference standards 38
 Waste materials 39
 Miscellaneous 39
15. Documentation 39
 General 40
 Documents required 41
16. Good practices in production 48
 General 48
 Prevention of cross-contamination and bacterial contamination during production 49
 Processing operations 50
 Packaging operations 51
17. Good practices in quality control 52
 Control of starting materials and intermediate, bulk and finished products 54
 Test requirements 55
 Batch record review 56
 Stability studies 57
References 57

Introduction

The first WHO draft text on good manufacturing practices (GMP) was prepared in 1967 by a group of consultants at the request of the Twentieth World Health Assembly (resolution WHA20.34). It was subsequently submitted to the Twenty-first World Health Assembly under the title "Draft requirements for good manufacturing practice in the manufacture and quality control of drugs and pharmaceutical specialities" and was accepted.

The revised text was discussed by the WHO Expert Committee on Specifications for Pharmaceutical Preparations in 1968 and published as an annex to its twenty-second report. The text was then reproduced (with some revisions) in 1971 in the Supplement to the second edition of *The International Pharmacopoeia*.

In 1969, when the World Health Assembly recommended the first version of the WHO Certification Scheme on the Quality of Pharmaceutical Products Moving in International Commerce in resolution WHA22.50, it accepted at the same time the GMP text as an integral part of the Scheme. Revised versions of both the Certification Scheme and the GMP text were adopted in 1975 by resolution WHA28.65. Since then, the Certification Scheme has been extended to include the certification of:

— veterinary products administered to food-producing animals;
— starting materials for use in dosage forms, when they are subject to control by legislation in both the exporting Member State and the importing Member State;
— information on safety and efficacy (resolution WHA41.18, 1988).

In 1992, the revised draft requirements for GMP were presented in three parts, of which only Parts One and Two are reproduced in this document (*1*).

"Quality management in the drug industry: philosophy and essential elements" outlines the general concepts of quality assurance as well as the principal components or subsystems of GMP, which are joint responsibilities of top management and of production and quality control management. These include hygiene, validation, self-inspection, personnel, premises, equipment, materials and documentation.

"Good practices in production" (section 16) and "Good practices in quality control" (section 17), provide guidance on actions to be taken separately by production and by quality control personnel for the implementation of the general principles of quality assurance.

These two parts were subsequently supplemented by further guidelines which are integral parts of these good manufacturing practices for pharmaceutical products. All these texts are available on the web page of the World Health Organization http://www.who.int/medicines/areas/quality_safety/quality_assurance/production/en/index.html.

Considerable developments in GMP have taken place in the intervening years, and important national and international documents, including new revisions, have appeared (*2, 3, 4, 5*). Thus the necessity to revise the main principles and incorporate the concept of validation.

General considerations

Licensed pharmaceutical products (marketing authorization) should be manufactured only by licensed manufacturers (holders of a manufacturing authorization) whose activities are regularly inspected by competent national authorities. This guide to GMP shall be used as a standard to justify GMP status, which constitutes one of the elements of the WHO Certification Scheme on the Quality of Pharmaceutical Products Moving in International Commerce, through the assessment of applications for manufacturing authorizations and as a basis for the inspection of manufacturing facilities. It may also be used as training material for government drug inspectors, as well as for production, quality control and quality assurance personnel in the industry.

The guide is applicable to operations for the manufacture of drugs in their finished dosage forms, including large-scale processes in hospitals and the preparation of supplies for use in clinical trials.

The good practices outlined below are to be considered general guides,[1] and they may be adapted to meet individual needs. The equivalence of alternative approaches to quality assurance, however, should be validated. The guide as a whole does not cover safety aspects for the personnel engaged in manufacture or environmental protection: these are normally governed by national legislation. A new concept of hazard analysis related to the risks in production and personnel safety is also newly recommended (Chapter 5). The manufacturer should assure the safety of workers and take the necessary measures to prevent pollution of the external environment. International Nonproprietary Names (INNs) for pharmaceutical substances designated by WHO should be used when available, together with other designated names.

Glossary

The definitions given below apply to the terms used in this guide. They may have different meanings in other contexts.

active pharmaceutical ingredient (API)
Any substance or mixture of substances intended to be used in the manufacture of a pharmaceutical dosage form and that, when so used, becomes an active ingredient of that pharmaceutical dosage form. Such substances are intended to furnish pharmacological activity or other direct effect in the diagnosis, cure, mitigation, treatment, or prevention of disease or to affect the structure and function of the body.

---

[1] The word "should" in the text means a strong recommendation.

airlock
An enclosed space with two or more doors, which is interposed between two or more rooms, e.g. of differing classes of cleanliness, for the purpose of controlling the airflow between those rooms when they need to be entered. An airlock is designed for use either by people or for goods and/or equipment.

authorized person
The person recognized by the national regulatory authority as having the responsibility for ensuring that each batch of finished product has been manufactured, tested and approved for release in compliance with the laws and regulations in force in that country.

batch (or lot)
A defined quantity of starting material, packaging material, or product processed in a single process or series of processes so that it is expected to be homogeneous. It may sometimes be necessary to divide a batch into a number of sub-batches, which are later brought together to form a final homogeneous batch. In the case of terminal sterilization, the batch size is determined by the capacity of the autoclave. In continuous manufacture, the batch must correspond to a defined fraction of the production, characterized by its intended homogeneity. The batch size can be defined either as a fixed quantity or as the amount produced in a fixed time interval.

batch number (or lot number)
A distinctive combination of numbers and/or letters which uniquely identifies a batch on the labels, its batch records and corresponding certificates of analysis, etc.

batch records
All documents associated with the manufacture of a batch of bulk product or finished product. They provide a history of each batch of product and of all circumstances pertinent to the quality of the final product.

bulk product
Any product that has completed all processing stages up to, but not including, final packaging.

calibration
The set of operations that establish, under specified conditions, the relationship between values indicated by an instrument or system for measuring (especially weighing), recording, and controlling, or the values represented by a material measure, and the corresponding known values of a reference standard. Limits for acceptance of the results of measuring should be established.

clean area
An area with defined environmental control of particulate and microbial contamination, constructed and used in such a way as to reduce the introduction, generation, and retention of contaminants within the area.

consignment (or delivery)
The quantity of a pharmaceutical(s), made by one manufacturer and supplied at one time in response to a particular request or order. A consignment may comprise one or more packages or containers and may include material belonging to more than one batch.

contamination
The undesired introduction of impurities of a chemical or microbiological nature, or of foreign matter, into or on to a starting material or intermediate during production, sampling, packaging or repackaging, storage or transport.

critical operation
An operation in the manufacturing process that may cause variation in the quality of the pharmaceutical product.

cross-contamination
Contamination of a starting material, intermediate product or finished product with another starting material or product during production.

finished product
A finished dosage form that has undergone all stages of manufacture, including packaging in its final container and labelling.

in-process control
Checks performed during production in order to monitor and, if necessary, to adjust the process to ensure that the product conforms to its specifications. The control of the environment or equipment may also be regarded as a part of in-process control.

intermediate product
Partly processed product that must undergo further manufacturing steps before it becomes a bulk product.

large-volume parenterals
Sterile solutions intended for parenteral application with a volume of 100 ml or more in one container of the finished dosage form.

manufacture
All operations of purchase of materials and products, production, quality control, release, storage and distribution of pharmaceutical products, and the related controls.

manufacturer
A company that carries out operations such as production, packaging, repackaging, labelling and relabelling of pharmaceuticals.

marketing authorization (product licence, registration certificate)
A legal document issued by the competent drug regulatory authority that establishes the detailed composition and formulation of the product and the pharmacopoeial or other recognized specifications of its ingredients and of the final product itself, and includes details of packaging, labelling and shelf-life.

master formula
A document or set of documents specifying the starting materials with their quantities and the packaging materials, together with a description of the procedures and precautions required to produce a specified quantity of a finished product as well as the processing instructions, including the in-process controls.

master record
A document or set of documents that serve as a basis for the batch documentation (blank batch record).

packaging
All operations, including filling and labelling, that a bulk product has to undergo in order to become a finished product. Filling of a sterile product under aseptic conditions or a product intended to be terminally sterilized, would not normally be regarded as part of packaging.

packaging material
Any material, including printed material, employed in the packaging of a pharmaceutical, but excluding any outer packaging used for transportation or shipment. Packaging materials are referred to as primary or secondary according to whether or not they are intended to be in direct contact with the product.

pharmaceutical product
Any material or product intended for human or veterinary use presented in its finished dosage form or as a starting material for use in such a dosage form, that is subject to control by pharmaceutical legislation in the exporting state and/or the importing state.

production
All operations involved in the preparation of a pharmaceutical product, from receipt of materials, through processing, packaging and repackaging, labelling and relabelling, to completion of the finished product.

qualification
Action of proving that any premises, systems and items of equipment work correctly and actually lead to the expected results. The meaning of the word "validation" is sometimes extended to incorporate the concept of qualification.

quality assurance
See page 16.

quality control
See page 17.

quarantine
The status of starting or packaging materials, intermediates, or bulk or finished products isolated physically or by other effective means while a decision is awaited on their release, rejection or reprocessing.

reconciliation
A comparison between the theoretical quantity and the actual quantity.

recovery
The introduction of all or part of previous batches (or of redistilled solvents and similar products) of the required quality into another batch at a defined stage of manufacture. It includes the removal of impurities from waste to obtain a pure substance or the recovery of used materials for a separate use.

reprocessing
Subjecting all or part of a batch or lot of an in-process drug, bulk process intermediate (final biological bulk intermediate) or bulk product of a single batch/lot to a previous step in the validated manufacturing process due to failure to meet predetermined specifications. Reprocessing procedures are foreseen as occasionally necessary for biological drugs and, in such cases, are validated and pre-approved as part of the marketing authorization.

reworking
Subjecting an in-process or bulk process intermediate (final biological bulk intermediate) or final product of a single batch to an alternate manufacturing process due to a failure to meet predetermined specifications. Reworking is an unexpected occurrence and is not pre-approved as part of the marketing authorization.

self-contained area
Premises which provide complete and total separation of all aspects of an operation, including personnel and equipment movement, with well established procedures, controls and monitoring. This includes physical barriers as well as separate air-handling systems, but does not necessarily imply two distinct and separate buildings.

specification
A list of detailed requirements with which the products or materials used or obtained during manufacture have to conform. They serve as a basis for quality evaluation.

standard operating procedure (SOP)
An authorized written procedure giving instructions for performing operations not necessarily specific to a given product or material (e.g. equipment operation, maintenance and cleaning; validation; cleaning of premises and environmental control; sampling and inspection). Certain SOPs may be used to supplement product-specific master and batch production documentation.

starting material
Any substance of a defined quality used in the production of a pharmaceutical product, but excluding packaging materials.

validation
Action of proving, in accordance with the principles of GMP, that any procedure, process, equipment, material, activity or system actually leads to the expected results (see also *qualification*).

Quality management in the drug industry

In the drug industry at large, quality management is usually defined as the aspect of management function that determines and implements the "quality policy", i.e. the overall intention and direction of an organization regarding quality, as formally expressed and authorized by top management. The basic elements of quality management are:

— an appropriate infrastructure or "quality system", encompassing the organizational structure, procedures, processes and resources;
— systematic actions necessary to ensure adequate confidence that a product (or service) will satisfy given requirements for quality. The totality of these actions is termed "quality assurance".

Within an organization, quality assurance serves as a management tool. In contractual situations, quality assurance also serves to generate confidence in the supplier. The concepts of quality assurance, GMP and quality control are interrelated aspects of quality management. They are described here in order to emphasize their relationship and their fundamental importance to the production and control of pharmaceutical products.

1. Quality assurance

1.1 *Principle.* "Quality assurance" is a wide-ranging concept covering all matters that individually or collectively influence the quality of a product. It is the totality of the arrangements made with the object of ensuring that pharmaceutical products are of the quality required for their intended use. Quality assurance therefore incorporates GMP and other factors, including those outside the scope of this guide such as product design and development.

1.2 The system of quality assurance appropriate to the manufacture of pharmaceutical products should ensure that:

(a) pharmaceutical products are designed and developed in a way that takes account of the requirements of GMP and other associated codes such as those of good laboratory practice (GLP)[1] and good clinical practice (GCP);
(b) production and control operations are clearly specified in a written form and GMP requirements are adopted;
(c) managerial responsibilities are clearly specified in job descriptions;
(d) arrangements are made for the manufacture, supply and use of the correct starting and packaging materials;
(e) all necessary controls on starting materials, intermediate products, and bulk products and other in-process controls, calibrations, and validations are carried out;
(f) the finished product is correctly processed and checked, according to the defined procedures;
(g) pharmaceutical products are not sold or supplied before the authorized persons (see also sections 9.11 and 9.12) have certified that each production batch has been produced and controlled in accordance with the requirements of the marketing authorization and any other regulations relevant to the production, control and release of pharmaceutical products;
(h) satisfactory arrangements exist to ensure, as far as possible, that the pharmaceutical products are stored by the manufacturer, distributed, and subsequently handled so that quality is maintained throughout their shelf-life;

[1] This is a code governing the testing of chemicals to obtain data on their properties and ensuring safety with respect to human health and the environment. It is different from that described in "Good laboratory practices in governmental drug control laboratories" in the Thirtieth report of the WHO Expert Committee on Specifications for Pharmaceutical Preparations (WHO Technical Report Series, No. 748, 1987, Annex 1).

(i) there is a procedure for self-inspection and/or quality audit that regularly appraises the effectiveness and applicability of the quality assurance system;
(j) deviations are reported, investigated and recorded;
(k) there is a system for approving changes that may have an impact on product quality;
(l) regular evaluations of the quality of pharmaceutical products should be conducted with the objective of verifying the consistency of the process and ensuring its continuous improvement.

1.3 The manufacturer must assume responsibility for the quality of the pharmaceutical products to ensure that they are fit for their intended use, comply with the requirements of the marketing authorization and do not place patients at risk due to inadequate safety, quality or efficacy. The attainment of this quality objective is the responsibility of senior management and requires the participation and commitment of staff in many different departments and at all levels within the company, the company's suppliers, and the distributors. To achieve the quality objective reliably there must be a comprehensively designed and correctly implemented system of quality assurance incorporating GMP and quality control. It should be fully documented and its effectiveness monitored. All parts of the quality assurance system should be adequately staffed with competent personnel, and should have suitable and sufficient premises, equipment, and facilities.

2. Good manufacturing practices for pharmaceutical products (GMP)

2.1 Good manufacturing practice is that part of quality assurance which ensures that products are consistently produced and controlled to the quality standards appropriate to their intended use and as required by the marketing authorization. GMP are aimed primarily at diminishing the risks inherent in any pharmaceutical production. Such risks are essentially of two types: cross-contamination (in particular of unexpected contaminants) and mix-ups (confusion) caused by, for example, false labels being put on containers. Under GMP:

(a) all manufacturing processes are clearly defined, systematically reviewed in the light of experience, and shown to be capable of consistently manufacturing pharmaceutical products of the required quality that comply with their specifications;
(b) qualification and validation are performed;
(c) all necessary resources are provided, including:
    (i) appropriately qualified and trained personnel;
    (ii) adequate premises and space;

   (iii) suitable equipment and services;
   (iv) appropriate materials, containers and labels;
   (v) approved procedures and instructions;
   (vi) suitable storage and transport;
   (vii) adequate personnel, laboratories and equipment for in-process controls;

(d) instructions and procedures are written in clear and unambiguous language, specifically applicable to the facilities provided;
(e) operators are trained to carry out procedures correctly;
(f) records are made (manually and/or by recording instruments) during manufacture to show that all the steps required by the defined procedures and instructions have in fact been taken and that the quantity and quality of the product are as expected; any significant deviations are fully recorded and investigated;
(g) records covering manufacture and distribution, which enable the complete history of a batch to be traced, are retained in a comprehensible and accessible form;
(h) the proper storage and distribution of the products minimizes any risk to their quality;
(i) a system is available to recall any batch of product from sale or supply;
(j) complaints about marketed products are examined, the causes of quality defects investigated, and appropriate measures taken in respect of the defective products to prevent recurrence.

3. Sanitation and hygiene

3.1 A high level of sanitation and hygiene should be practised in every aspect of the manufacture of drug products. The scope of sanitation and hygiene covers personnel, premises, equipment and apparatus, production materials and containers, products for cleaning and disinfection, and anything that could become a source of contamination to the product. Potential sources of contamination should be eliminated through an integrated comprehensive programme of sanitation and hygiene. (For *personal hygiene* see section 11, and for *sanitation* see section 12, "Premises".)

4. Qualification and validation

4.1 In accordance with GMP, each pharmaceutical company should identify what qualification and validation work is required to prove that the critical aspects of their particular operation are controlled.

4.2 The key elements of a qualification and validation programme of a company should be clearly defined and documented in a validation master plan.

4.3 Qualification and validation should establish and provide documentary evidence that:

(a) the premises, supporting utilities, equipment and processes have been designed in accordance with the requirements for GMP (design qualification, or DQ);
(b) the premises, supporting utilities and equipment have been built and installed in compliance with their design specifications (installation qualification, or IQ);
(c) the premises, supporting utilities and equipment operate in accordance with their design specifications (operational qualification, or OQ);
(d) a specific process will consistently produce a product meeting its predetermined specifications and quality attributes (process validation, or PV, also called performance qualification, or PQ).

4.4 Any aspect of operation, including significant changes to the premises, facilities, equipment or processes, which may affect the quality of the product, directly or indirectly, should be qualified and validated.

4.5 Qualification and validation should not be considered as one-off exercises. An ongoing programme should follow their first implementation and should be based on an annual review.

4.6 The commitment to maintain continued validation status should be stated in the relevant company documentation, such as the quality manual or validation master plan.

4.7 The responsibility of performing validation should be clearly defined.

4.8 Validation studies are an essential part of GMP and should be conducted in accordance with predefined and approved protocols.

4.9 A written report summarizing the results recorded and the conclusions reached should be prepared and stored.

4.10 Processes and procedures should be established on the basis of the results of the validation performed.

4.11 It is of critical importance that particular attention is paid to the validation of analytical test methods, automated systems and cleaning procedures.

5. Complaints

5.1 *Principle.* All complaints and other information concerning potentially defective products should be carefully reviewed according to written procedures and the corrective action should be taken.

5.2 A person responsible for handling the complaints and deciding the measures to be taken should be designated, together with sufficient supporting staff to assist him or her. If this person is different from the authorized person, the latter should be made aware of any complaint, investigation or recall.

5.3 There should be written procedures describing the action to be taken, including the need to consider a recall, in the case of a complaint concerning a possible product defect.

5.4 Special attention should be given to establishing whether a complaint was caused because of counterfeiting.

5.5 Any complaint concerning a product defect should be recorded with all the original details and thoroughly investigated. The person responsible for quality control should normally be involved in the review of such investigations.

5.6 If a product defect is discovered or suspected in a batch, consideration should be given to whether other batches should be checked in order to determine whether they are also affected. In particular, other batches that may contain reprocessed product from the defective batch should be investigated.

5.7 Where necessary, appropriate follow-up action, possibly including product recall, should be taken after investigation and evaluation of the complaint.

5.8 All decisions made and measures taken as a result of a complaint should be recorded and referenced to the corresponding batch records.

5.9 Complaints records should be regularly reviewed for any indication of specific or recurring problems that require attention and might justify the recall of marketed products.

5.10 The competent authorities should be informed if a manufacturer is considering action following possibly faulty manufacture, product deterioration, counterfeiting or any other serious quality problems with a product.

6. Product recalls

6.1 *Principle.* There should be a system to recall from the market, promptly and effectively, products known or suspected to be defective.

6.2 The authorized person should be responsible for the execution and coordination of recalls. He/she should have sufficient staff to handle all aspects of the recalls with the appropriate degree of urgency.

6.3 There should be established written procedures, which are regularly reviewed and updated, for the organization of any recall activity. Recall operations should be capable of being initiated promptly down to the required level in the distribution chain.

6.4 An instruction should be included in the written procedures to store recalled products in a secure segregated area while their fate is decided.

6.5 All competent authorities of all countries to which a given product has been distributed should be promptly informed of any intention to recall the product because it is, or is suspected of being, defective.

6.6 The distribution records should be readily available to the authorized person, and they should contain sufficient information on wholesalers and directly supplied customers (including, for exported products, those who have received samples for clinical tests and medical samples) to permit an effective recall.

6.7 The progress of the recall process should be monitored and recorded. Records should include the disposition of the product. A final report should be issued, including a reconciliation between the delivered and recovered quantities of the products.

6.8 The effectiveness of the arrangements for recalls should be tested and evaluated from time to time.

7. Contract production and analysis

7.1 *Principle.* Contract production and analysis must be correctly defined, agreed and controlled in order to avoid misunderstandings that could result in a product or work or analysis of unsatisfactory quality.

General

7.2 All arrangements for contract manufacture and analysis, including any proposed changes in technical or other arrangements, should be in accordance with the marketing authorization for the product concerned.

7.3 The contract should permit the contract giver to audit the facilities of the contract accepter.

7.4 In the case of contract analysis, the final approval for release must be given by the authorized person.

The contract giver

7.5 The contract giver is responsible for assessing the competence of the contract accepter in successfully carrying out the work or tests required, for approval for contract activities, and for ensuring by means of the contract that the principles of GMP described in this guide are followed.

7.6 The contract giver should provide the contract accepter with all the information necessary to carry out the contracted operations correctly in accordance with the marketing authorization and any other legal requirements. The contract giver should ensure that the contract accepter is fully aware of any problems associated with the product, work or tests that might pose a hazard to premises, equipment, personnel, other materials or other products.

7.7 The contract giver should ensure that all processed products and materials delivered by the contract accepter comply with their specifications or that the product has been released by the authorized person.

The contract accepter

7.8 The contract accepter must have adequate premises, equipment, knowledge, and experience and competent personnel to carry out satisfactorily the work ordered by the contract giver. Contract manufacture may be undertaken only by a manufacturer who holds a manufacturing authorization.

7.9 The contract accepter should not pass to a third party any of the work entrusted to him or her under the contract without the contract giver's prior evaluation and approval of the arrangements. Arrangements made between the contract accepter and any third party should ensure that the manufacturing and analytical information is made available in the same way as between the original contract giver and contract accepter.

7.10 The contract accepter should refrain from any activity that may adversely affect the quality of the product manufactured and/or analysed for the contract giver.

The contract

7.11 There must be a written contract between the contract giver and the contract accepter which clearly establishes the responsibilities of each party.

7.12 The contract must clearly state the way in which the authorized person, in releasing each batch of product for sale or issuing the certificate of analysis, exercises his or her full responsibility and ensures that each batch has been manufactured in, and checked for, compliance with the requirements of the marketing authorization.

7.13 Technical aspects of the contract should be drawn up by competent persons suitably knowledgeable in pharmaceutical technology, analysis and GMP.

7.14 All arrangements for production and analysis must be in accordance with the marketing authorization and agreed by both parties.

7.15 The contract should describe clearly who is responsible for purchasing, testing and releasing materials and for undertaking production and quality controls, including in-process controls, and who has responsibility for sampling and analysis. In the case of contract analysis, the contract should state whether or not the contract accepter should take samples at the premises of the manufacturer.

7.16 Manufacturing, analytical, distribution records and reference samples should be kept by, or be available to, the contract giver. Any records relevant to assessing the quality of a product in the event of complaints or a suspected defect must be accessible and specified in the defect/recall procedures of the contract giver.

7.17 The contract should describe the handling of starting materials, intermediate and bulk products and finished products if they are rejected. It should also describe the procedure to be followed if the contract analysis shows that the tested product must be rejected.

8. Self-inspection and quality audits

8.1 *Principle.* The purpose of self-inspection is to evaluate the manufacturer's compliance with GMP in all aspects of production and quality control. The self-inspection programme should be designed to detect any shortcomings in the implementation of GMP and to recommend the necessary corrective actions. Self-inspections should be performed routinely, and may be, in addition, performed on special occasions, e.g. in the case of product recalls or repeated rejections, or when an inspection by the health authorities is announced. The team responsible for self-inspection should consist of personnel who can evaluate the implementation of GMP objectively. All recommendations for corrective action should be implemented. The procedure for self-inspection should be documented, and there should be an effective follow-up programme.

Items for self-inspection

8.2 Written instructions for self-inspection should be established to provide a minimum and uniform standard of requirements. These may include questionnaires on GMP requirements covering at least the following items:

(a) personnel;
(b) premises including personnel facilities;
(c) maintenance of buildings and equipment;
(d) storage of starting materials and finished products;
(e) equipment;
(f) production and in-process controls;
(g) quality control;
(h) documentation;
(i) sanitation and hygiene;
(j) validation and revalidation programmes;
(k) calibration of instruments or measurement systems;
(l) recall procedures;

(m) complaints management;
(n) labels control;
(o) results of previous self-inspections and any corrective steps taken.

Self-inspection team

8.3 Management should appoint a self-inspection team consisting of experts in their respective fields and familiar with GMP. The members of the team may be appointed from inside or outside the company.

Frequency of self-inspection

8.4 The frequency at which self-inspections are conducted may depend on company requirements but should preferably be at least once a year. The frequency should be stated in the procedure.

Self-inspection report

8.5 A report should be made at the completion of a self-inspection. The report should include:

(a) self-inspection results;
(b) evaluation and conclusions;
(c) recommended corrective actions.

Follow-up action

8.6 There should be an effective follow-up programme. The company management should evaluate both the self-inspection report and the corrective actions as necessary.

Quality audit

8.7 It may be useful to supplement self-inspections with a quality audit. A quality audit consists of an examination and assessment of all or part of a quality system with the specific purpose of improving it. A quality audit is usually conducted by outside or independent specialists or a team designated by the management for this purpose. Such audits may also be extended to suppliers and contractors (see section 7, "Contract production and analysis").

Suppliers' audits and approval

8.8 The person responsible for quality control should have responsibility together with other relevant departments for approving suppliers who can reliably supply starting and packaging materials that meet established specifications.

8.9 Before suppliers are approved and included in the approved suppliers' list or specifications, they should be evaluated. The evaluation should take into account a supplier's history and the nature of the materials to be supplied. If an audit is required, it should determine the supplier's ability to conform with GMP standards.

9. Personnel

9.1 *Principle.* The establishment and maintenance of a satisfactory system of quality assurance and the correct manufacture and control of pharmaceutical products and active ingredients rely upon people. For this reason there must be sufficient qualified personnel to carry out all the tasks for which the manufacturer is responsible. Individual responsibilities should be clearly defined and understood by the persons concerned and recorded as written descriptions.

General

9.2 The manufacturer should have an adequate number of personnel with the necessary qualifications and practical experience. The responsibilities placed on any one individual should not be so extensive so as to present any risk to quality.

9.3. All responsible staff should have their specific duties recorded in written descriptions and adequate authority to carry out their responsibilities. Their duties may be delegated to designated deputies of a satisfactory qualification level. There should be no gaps or unexplained overlaps in the responsibilities of personnel concerned with the application of GMP. The manufacturer should have an organization chart.

9.4 All personnel should be aware of the principles of GMP that affect them and receive initial and continuing training, including hygiene instructions, relevant to their needs. All personnel should be motivated to support the establishment and maintenance of high-quality standards.

9.5 Steps should be taken to prevent unauthorized people from entering production, storage and quality control areas. Personnel who do not work in these areas should not use them as a passageway.

Key personnel

9.6 Key personnel include the head of production, the head of quality control and the authorized person. Normally, key posts should be occupied by full-time personnel. The heads of production and quality control should be independent of each other. In large organizations, it may be necessary to delegate some of the functions; however, the responsibility cannot be delegated.

9.7 Key personnel responsible for supervising the manufacture and quality control of pharmaceutical products should possess the qualifications of a scientific education and practical experience required by national legislation. Their education should include the study of an appropriate combination of:

(a) chemistry (analytical or organic) or biochemistry;
(b) chemical engineering;
(c) microbiology;
(d) pharmaceutical sciences and technology;
(e) pharmacology and toxicology;
(f) physiology;
(g) other related sciences.

They should also have adequate practical experience in the manufacture and quality assurance of pharmaceutical products. In order to gain such experience, a preparatory period may be required, during which they should exercise their duties under professional guidance. The scientific education and practical experience of experts should be such as to enable them to exercise independent professional judgement, based on the application of scientific principles and understanding to the practical problems encountered in the manufacture and quality control of pharmaceutical products.

9.8 The heads of the production and quality control generally have some shared, or jointly exercised, responsibilities relating to quality. These may include, depending on national regulations:

(a) authorization of written procedures and other documents, including amendments;
(b) monitoring and control of the manufacturing environment;
(c) plant hygiene;
(d) process validation and calibration of analytical apparatus;
(e) training, including the application and principles of quality assurance;
(f) approval and monitoring of suppliers of materials;
(g) approval and monitoring of contract manufacturers;
(h) designation and monitoring of storage conditions for materials and products;
(i) performance and evaluation of in-process controls;
(j) retention of records;
(k) monitoring of compliance with GMP requirements;
(l) inspection, investigation and taking of samples in order to monitor factors that may affect product quality.

9.9 The head of the production generally has the following responsibilities:

(a) to ensure that products are produced and stored according to the appropriate documentation in order to obtain the required quality;
(b) to approve the instructions relating to production operations, including the in-process controls, and to ensure their strict implementation;
(c) to ensure that the production records are evaluated and signed by a designated person;
(d) to check the maintenance of the department, premises, and equipment;
(e) to ensure that the appropriate process validations and calibrations of control equipment are performed and recorded and the reports made available;
(f) to ensure that the required initial and continuing training of production personnel is carried out and adapted according to need.

9.10 The head of the quality control generally has the following responsibilities:

(a) to approve or reject starting materials, packaging materials, and intermediate, bulk and finished products in relation to their specifications;
(b) to evaluate batch records;
(c) to ensure that all necessary testing is carried out;
(d) to approve sampling instructions, specifications, test methods and other quality control procedures;
(e) to approve and monitor analyses carried out under contract;
(f) to check the maintenance of the department, premises and equipment;
(g) to ensure that the appropriate validations, including those of analytical procedures, and calibrations of control equipment are carried out;
(h) to ensure that the required initial and continuing training of quality control personnel is carried out and adapted according to need.

Other duties of the quality control are summarized in sections 17.3 and 17.4.

9.11 The authorized person is responsible for compliance with technical or regulatory requirements related to the quality of finished products and the approval of the release of the finished product for sale.

9.12 The authorized person will also be involved in other activities, including the following:

(a) implementation (and, when needed, establishment) of the quality system;
(b) participation in the development of the company's quality manual;
(c) supervision of the regular internal audits or self-inspections;
(d) oversight of the quality control department;
(e) participation in external audit (vendor audit);
(f) participation in validation programmes.

9.13 The function of the approval of the release of a finished batch or a product can be delegated to a designated person with appropriate qualifications and experience who will release the product in accordance with an approved procedure. This is normally done by quality assurance by means of batch review.

9.14 The person responsible for approving a batch for release should always ensure that the following requirements have been met:

(a) the marketing authorization and the manufacturing authorization requirements for the product have been met for the batch concerned;
(b) the principles and guidelines of GMP, as laid down in the guidelines published by WHO, have been followed;
(c) the principal manufacturing and testing processes have been validated, if different;
(d) all the necessary checks and tests have been performed and account taken of the production conditions and manufacturing records;
(e) any planned changes or deviations in manufacturing or quality control have been notified in accordance with a well defined reporting system before any product is released. Such changes may need notification to, and approval by, the drug regulatory authority;
(f) any additional sampling, inspection, tests and checks have been carried out or initiated, as appropriate, to cover planned changes and deviations;
(g) all necessary production and quality control documentation has been completed and endorsed by supervisors trained in appropriate disciplines;
(h) appropriate audits, self-inspections and spot-checks are carried out by experienced and trained staff;
(i) approval has been given by the head of quality control;
(j) all relevant factors have been considered, including any not specifically associated with the output batch directly under review (e.g. subdivision of output batches from a common input, factors associated with continuous production runs).

10. Training

10.1 The manufacturer should provide training in accordance with a written programme for all personnel whose duties take them into manufacturing areas or into control laboratories (including the technical, maintenance and cleaning personnel) and for other personnel as required.

10.2 Besides basic training on the theory and practice of GMP, newly recruited personnel should receive training appropriate to the duties assigned to them. Continuing training should also be given, and its practical effectiveness periodically assessed. Approved training programmes should be available. Training records should be kept.

10.3 Personnel working in areas where contamination is a hazard, e.g. clean areas or areas where highly active, toxic, infectious or sensitizing materials are handled, should be given specific training.

10.4 The concept of quality assurance and all the measures which aid its understanding and implementation should be fully discussed during the training sessions.

10.5 Visitors or untrained personnel should preferably not be taken into the production and quality control areas. If this is unavoidable, they should be given relevant information in advance (particularly about personal hygiene) and the prescribed protective clothing. They should be closely supervised.

10.6 Consultant and contract staff should be qualified for the services they provide. Evidence of this should be included in the training records.

11. Personal hygiene

11.1 All personnel, prior to and during employment, as appropriate, should undergo health examinations. Personnel conducting visual inspections should also undergo periodic eye examinations.

11.2 All personnel should be trained in the practices of personal hygiene. A high level of personal hygiene should be observed by all those concerned with manufacturing processes. In particular, personnel should be instructed to wash their hands before entering production areas. Signs to this effect should be posted and instructions observed.

11.3 Any person shown at any time to have an apparent illness or open lesions that may adversely affect the quality of products should not be allowed to handle starting materials, packaging materials, in-process materials or drug products until the condition is no longer judged to be a risk.

11.4 All employees should be instructed and encouraged to report to their immediate supervisor any conditions (relating to plant, equipment or personnel) that they consider may adversely affect the products.

11.5 Direct contact should be avoided between the operator's hands and starting materials, primary packaging materials and intermediate or bulk product.

11.6 To ensure protection of the product from contamination, personnel should wear clean body coverings appropriate to the duties they perform, including appropriate hair covering. Used clothes, if reusable, should be stored in separate closed containers until properly laundered and, if necessary, disinfected or sterilized.

11.7 Smoking, eating, drinking, chewing, and keeping plants, food, drink, smoking material and personal medicines should not be permitted in production, laboratory and storage areas, or in any other areas where they might adversely influence product quality.

11.8 Personal hygiene procedures including the use of protective clothing should apply to all persons entering production areas, whether they are temporary or full-time employees or non-employees, e.g. contractors' employees, visitors, senior managers, and inspectors.

12. Premises

12.1 *Principle.* Premises must be located, designed, constructed, adapted, and maintained to suit the operations to be carried out.

General

12.2 The layout and design of premises must aim to minimize the risk of errors and permit effective cleaning and maintenance in order to avoid cross-contamination, build-up of dust or dirt, and, in general, any adverse effect on the quality of products.

12.3 Where dust is generated (e.g. during sampling, weighing, mixing and processing operations, packaging of powder), measures should be taken to avoid cross-contamination and facilitate cleaning.

12.4 Premises should be situated in an environment that, when considered together with measures to protect the manufacturing process, presents minimum risk of causing any contamination of materials or products.

12.5 Premises used for the manufacture of finished products should be suitably designed and constructed to facilitate good sanitation.

12.6 Premises should be carefully maintained, and it should be ensured that repair and maintenance operations do not present any hazard to the quality of products.

12.7 Premises should be cleaned and, where applicable, disinfected according to detailed written procedures. Records should be maintained.

12.8 Electrical supply, lighting, temperature, humidity and ventilation should be appropriate and such that they do not adversely affect, directly or indirectly, either the pharmaceutical products during their manufacture and storage, or the accurate functioning of equipment.

12.9 Premises should be designed and equipped so as to afford maximum protection against the entry of insects, birds or animals. There should be a procedure for rodent and pest control.

12.10 Premises should be designed to ensure the logical flow of materials and personnel.

Ancillary areas

12.11 Rest and refreshment rooms should be separate from manufacturing and control areas.

12.12 Facilities for changing and storing clothes and for washing and toilet purposes should be easily accessible and appropriate for the number of users. Toilets should not communicate directly with production or storage areas.

12.13 Maintenance workshops should if possible be separated from production areas. Whenever parts and tools are stored in the production area, they should be kept in rooms or lockers reserved for that use.

12.14 Animal houses should be well isolated from other areas, with separate entrance (animal access) and air-handling facilities.

Storage areas

12.15 Storage areas should be of sufficient capacity to allow orderly storage of the various categories of materials and products with proper separation and segregation: starting and packaging materials, intermediates, bulk and finished products, products in quarantine, and released, rejected, returned or recalled products.

12.16 Storage areas should be designed or adapted to ensure good storage conditions. In particular, they should be clean, dry, sufficiently lit and maintained within acceptable temperature limits. Where special storage conditions are required (e.g. temperature, humidity) these should be provided, controlled, monitored and recorded where appropriate.

12.17 Receiving and dispatch bays should be separated and protect materials and products from the weather. Receiving areas should be designed and equipped to allow containers of incoming materials to be cleaned if necessary before storage.

12.18 Where quarantine status is ensured by storage in separate areas, these areas must be clearly marked and their access restricted to authorized personnel. Any system replacing the physical quarantine should give equivalent security.

12.19 Segregation should be provided for the storage of rejected, recalled, or returned materials or products.

12.20 Highly active and radioactive materials, narcotics, other dangerous drugs, and substances presenting special risks of abuse, fire or explosion should be stored in safe and secure areas.

12.21 Printed packaging materials are considered critical to the conformity of the pharmaceutical product to its labelling and special attention should be paid to sampling and the safe and secure storage of these materials.

12.22 There should normally be a separate sampling area for starting materials. (If sampling is performed in the storage area, it should be conducted in such a way as to prevent contamination or cross-contamination.)

Weighing areas

12.23 The weighing of starting materials and the estimation of yield by weighing should be carried out in separate weighing areas designed for that use, for example with provisions for dust control. Such areas may be part of either storage or production areas.

Production areas

12.24 In order to minimize the risk of a serious medical hazard due to cross-contamination, dedicated and self-contained facilities must be available for the production of particular pharmaceutical products, such as highly sensitizing materials (e.g. penicillins) or biological preparations (e.g. live microorganisms). The production of certain other highly active products, such as some antibiotics, hormones, cytotoxic substances and certain non-pharmaceutical products, should not be conducted in the same facilities. In exceptional cases, the principle of campaign working in the same facilities can be accepted provided that specific precautions are taken and the necessary validations (including cleaning validation) are made. The manufacture of technical poisons, such as pesticides and herbicides, should not be allowed in premises used for the manufacture of pharmaceutical products.

12.25 Premises should preferably be laid out in such a way as to allow the production to take place in areas connected in a logical order corresponding to the sequence of the operations and to the requisite cleanliness levels.

12.26 The adequacy of the working and in-process storage space should permit the orderly and logical positioning of equipment and materials so as to minimize the risk of confusion between different pharmaceutical products or their components, to avoid cross-contamination, and to minimize the risk of omission or wrong application of any of the manufacturing or control steps.

12.27 Where starting and primary packaging materials and intermediate or bulk products are exposed to the environment, interior surfaces (walls, floors and ceilings) should be smooth and free from cracks and open joints, should not shed particulate matter, and should permit easy and effective cleaning and, if necessary, disinfection.

12.28 Pipework, light fittings, ventilation points and other services should be designed and sited to avoid the creation of recesses that are difficult to clean. As far as possible, for maintenance purposes, they should be accessible from outside the manufacturing areas.

12.29 Drains should be of adequate size and designed and equipped to prevent back-flow. Open channels should be avoided where possible, but if they are necessary they should be shallow to facilitate cleaning and disinfection.

12.30 Production areas should be effectively ventilated, with air-control facilities (including filtration of air to a sufficient level to prevent contamination and cross-contamination, as well as control of temperature and, where necessary, humidity) appropriate to the products handled, to the operations undertaken and to the external environment. These areas should be regularly monitored during both production and non-production periods to ensure compliance with their design specifications.

12.31 Premises for the packaging of pharmaceutical products should be specifically designed and laid out so as to avoid mix-ups or cross-contamination.

12.32 Production areas should be well lit, particularly where visual on-line controls are carried out.

Quality control areas

12.33 Quality control laboratories should be separated from production areas. Areas where biological, microbiological or radioisotope test methods are employed should be separated from each other.

12.34 Quality control laboratories should be designed to suit the operations to be carried out in them. Sufficient space should be given to avoid mix-ups and cross-contamination. There should be adequate suitable storage space for samples, reference standards (if necessary, with cooling), solvents, reagents and records.

12.35 The design of the laboratories should take into account the suitability of construction materials, prevention of fumes and ventilation. There should be separate air supply to laboratories and production areas. Separate air-handling units and other provisions are needed for biological, microbiological and radioisotope laboratories.

12.36 A separate room may be needed for instruments to protect them against electrical interference, vibration, contact with excessive moisture and other external factors, or where it is necessary to isolate the instruments.

13. Equipment

13.1 Equipment must be located, designed, constructed, adapted, and maintained to suit the operations to be carried out. The layout and design of equipment must aim to minimize the risk of errors and permit effective cleaning and maintenance in order to avoid cross-contamination, build-up of dust or dirt, and, in general, any adverse effect on the quality of products.

13.2 Equipment should be installed in such a way as to minimize any risk of error or of contamination.

13.3 Fixed pipework should be clearly labelled to indicate the contents and, where applicable, the direction of flow.

13.4 All service pipings and devices should be adequately marked and special attention paid to the provision of non-interchangeable connections or adaptors for dangerous gases and liquids.

13.5 Balances and other measuring equipment of an appropriate range and precision should be available for production and control operations and should be calibrated on a scheduled basis.

13.6 Production equipment should be thoroughly cleaned on a scheduled basis.

13.7 Laboratory equipment and instruments should be suited to the testing procedures undertaken.

13.8 Washing, cleaning and drying equipment should be chosen and used so as not to be a source of contamination.

13.9 Production equipment should not present any hazard to the products. The parts of the production equipment that come into contact with the product must not be reactive, additive, or absorptive to an extent that would affect the quality of the product.

13.10 Defective equipment should be removed from production and quality control areas. If this is not possible, it should be clearly labelled as defective to prevent use.

13.11 Closed equipment should be used whenever appropriate. Where open equipment is used or equipment is opened, precautions should be taken to minimize contamination.

13.12 Non-dedicated equipment should be cleaned according to validated cleaning procedures between production of different pharmaceutical products to prevent cross-contamination.

13.13 Current drawings of critical equipment and support systems should be maintained.

14. Materials

14.1 *Principle.* The main objective of a pharmaceutical plant is to produce finished products for patients' use from a combination of materials (starting and packaging).

14.2 Materials include starting materials, packaging materials, gases, solvents, process aids, reagents and labelling materials.

General

14.3 No materials used for operations such as cleaning, lubrication of equipment and pest control, should come into direct contact with the product. Where possible, such materials should be of a suitable grade (e.g. food grade) to minimize health risks.

14.4 All incoming materials and finished products should be quarantined immediately after receipt or processing, until they are released for use or distribution.

14.5 All materials and products should be stored under the appropriate conditions established by the manufacturer and in an orderly fashion to permit batch segregation and stock rotation by a first-expire, first-out rule.

14.6 Water used in the manufacture of pharmaceutical products should be suitable for its intended use.

Starting materials

14.7 The purchase of starting materials is an important operation that should involve staff who have a particular and thorough knowledge of the products and suppliers.

14.8 Starting materials should be purchased only from approved suppliers and, where possible, directly from the producer. It is also recommended that the specifications established by the manufacturer for the starting materials be discussed with the suppliers. It is of benefit that all critical aspects of the production and control of the starting material in question, including handling, labelling and packaging requirements as well as complaints and rejection procedures, are contractually agreed between the manufacturer and the supplier.

14.9 For each consignment, the containers should be checked for at least integrity of package and seal and for correspondence between the order, the delivery note, and the supplier's labels.

14.10 All incoming materials should be checked to ensure that the consignment corresponds to the order. Containers should be cleaned where necessary and labelled, if required, with the prescribed information. Where additional labels are attached to containers, the original information should not be lost.

14.11 Damage to containers and any other problem that might adversely affect the quality of a material should be recorded and reported to the quality control department and investigated.

14.12 If one delivery of material is made up of different batches, each batch must be considered as separate for sampling, testing and release.

14.13 Starting materials in the storage area should be appropriately labelled. Labels should bear at least the following information:

(a) the designated name of the product and the internal code reference where applicable;
(b) the batch number given by the supplier and, on receipt, the control or batch number given by the manufacturer, if any, documented so as to ensure traceability;
(c) the status of the contents (e.g. on quarantine, on test, released, rejected, returned, recalled);
(d) where appropriate, an expiry date or a date beyond which retesting is necessary.

When fully validated computerized storage systems are used, not all of the above information need be in a legible form on the label.

14.14 There should be appropriate procedures or measures to ensure the identity of the contents of each container of starting material. Bulk containers from which samples have been drawn should be identified.

14.15 Only starting materials released by the quality control department and within their shelf-life should be used.

14.16 Starting materials should be dispensed only by designated persons, following a written procedure, to ensure that the correct materials are accurately weighed or measured into clean and properly labelled containers.

14.17 Each dispensed material and its weight or volume should be independently checked and the check recorded.

14.18 Materials dispensed for each batch of the final product should be kept together and conspicuously labelled as such.

Packaging materials

14.19 The purchase, handling and control of primary and printed packaging materials should be as for starting materials.

14.20 Particular attention should be paid to printed packaging materials. They should be stored in secure conditions so as to exclude the possibility of unauthorized access. Roll-feed labels should be used wherever possible. Cut labels and other loose printed materials should be stored and transported in separate closed containers so as to avoid mix-ups. Packaging materials should be issued for use only by designated personnel following an approved and documented procedure.

14.21 Each delivery or batch of printed or primary packaging material should be given a specific reference number or identification mark.

14.22 Outdated or obsolete primary packaging material or printed packaging material should be destroyed and its disposal recorded.

14.23 All products and packaging materials to be used should be checked on delivery to the packaging department for quantity, identity and conformity with the packaging instructions.

Intermediate and bulk products

14.24 Intermediate and bulk products should be kept under appropriate conditions.

14.25 Intermediate and bulk products purchased as such should be handled on receipt as though they were starting materials.

Finished products

14.26 Finished products should be held in quarantine until their final release, after which they should be stored as usable stock under conditions established by the manufacturer.

14.27 The evaluation of finished products and the documentation necessary for release of a product for sale are described in section 17, "Good practices in quality control".

Rejected, recovered, reprocessed and reworked materials

14.28 Rejected materials and products should be clearly marked as such and stored separately in restricted areas. They should either be returned to the suppliers or, where appropriate, reprocessed or destroyed in a timely manner. Whatever action is taken should be approved by authorized personnel and recorded.

14.29 The reworking or recovery of rejected products should be exceptional. It is permitted only if the quality of the final product is not affected, if the specifications are met, and if it is done in accordance with a defined and authorized procedure after evaluation of the risks involved. A record should be kept of the reworking or recovery. A reworked batch should be given a new batch number.

14.30 The introduction of all or part of earlier batches, conforming to the required quality, into a batch of the same product at a defined stage of manufacture should be authorized beforehand. This recovery should be carried out in accordance with a defined procedure after evaluation of the risks involved, including any possible effect on shelf-life. The recovery should be recorded.

14.31 The need for additional testing of any finished product that has been reprocessed, reworked or into which a recovered product has been incorporated, should be considered by the quality control department.

Recalled products

14.32 Recalled products should be identified and stored separately in a secure area until a decision is taken on their fate. The decision should be made as soon as possible.

Returned goods

14.33 Products returned from the market should be destroyed unless it is certain that their quality is satisfactory; in such cases they may be considered for resale or relabelling, or alternative action taken only after they have been critically assessed by the quality control function in accordance with a written procedure. The nature of the product, any special storage conditions it requires, its condition and history, and the time elapsed since it was issued should all be taken into account in this assessment. Where any doubt arises over the quality of the product, it should not be considered suitable for reissue or reuse. Any action taken should be appropriately recorded.

Reagents and culture media

14.34 There should be records for the receipt and preparation of reagents and culture media.

14.35 Reagents made up in the laboratory should be prepared according to written procedures and appropriately labelled. The label should indicate the concentration, standardization factor, shelf-life, the date when restandardization is due, and the storage conditions. The label should be signed and dated by the person preparing the reagent.

14.36 Both positive and negative controls should be applied to verify the suitability of culture media each time they are prepared and used. The size of the inoculum used in positive controls should be appropriate to the sensitivity required.

Reference standards

14.37 Whenever official reference standards exist, these should preferably be used.

14.38 Official reference standards should be used only for the purpose described in the appropriate monograph.

14.39 Reference standards prepared by the producer should be tested, released and stored in the same way as official standards. They should be kept under the responsibility of a designated person in a secure area.

14.40 Secondary or working standards may be established by the application of appropriate tests and checks at regular intervals to ensure standardization.

14.41 Reference standards should be properly labelled with at least the following information:

14.42 All in-house reference standards should be standardized against an official reference standard, when available, initially and at regular intervals thereafter.

14.43 All reference standards should be stored and used in a manner that will not adversely affect their quality.

(a) name of the material;
(b) batch or lot number and control number;
(c) date of preparation;
(d) shelf-life;
(e) potency;
(f) storage conditions.

Waste materials

14.44 Provision should be made for the proper and safe storage of waste materials awaiting disposal. Toxic substances and flammable materials should be stored in suitably designed, separate, enclosed cupboards, as required by national legislation.

14.45 Waste material should not be allowed to accumulate. It should be collected in suitable receptacles for removal to collection points outside the buildings and disposed of safely and in a sanitary manner at regular and frequent intervals.

Miscellaneous

14.46 Rodenticides, insecticides, fumigating agents and sanitizing materials should not be permitted to contaminate equipment, starting materials, packaging materials, in-process materials or finished products.

15. Documentation

15.1 *Principle.* Good documentation is an essential part of the quality assurance system and, as such, should exist for all aspects of GMP. Its aims are to define the specifications and procedures for all materials and methods of manufacture and control; to ensure that all personnel concerned with manufacture know what to do and when to do it; to ensure that authorized persons have all the information necessary to decide whether or not to release a batch of a drug for sale, to ensure the existence of documented evidence, traceability, and to provide records and an audit trail that will permit investigation. It ensures the availability of the data needed for validation, review and statistical analysis. The design and use of documents depend upon the manufacturer. In some cases some or all of the documents described below may be brought together, but they will usually be separate.

General

15.2 Documents should be designed, prepared, reviewed and distributed with care. They should comply with the relevant parts of the manufacturing and marketing authorizations.

15.3 Documents should be approved, signed and dated by the appropriate responsible persons. No document should be changed without authorization and approval.

15.4 Documents should have unambiguous contents: the title, nature and purpose should be clearly stated. They should be laid out in an orderly fashion and be easy to check. Reproduced documents should be clear and legible. The reproduction of working documents from master documents must not allow any error to be introduced through the reproduction process.

15.5 Documents should be regularly reviewed and kept up to date. When a document has been revised, a system should exist to prevent inadvertent use of the superseded version. Superseded documents should be retained for a specific period of time.

15.6 Where documents require the entry of data, these entries should be clear, legible and indelible. Sufficient space should be provided for such entries.

15.7 Any alteration made to a document should be signed and dated; the alteration should permit the reading of the original information. Where appropriate, the reason for the alteration should be recorded.

15.8 Records should be made or completed when any action is taken and in such a way that all significant activities concerning the manufacture of pharmaceutical products are traceable. Records should be retained for at least one year after the expiry date of the finished product.

15.9 Data (and records for storage) may be recorded by electronic data-processing systems or by photographic or other reliable means. Master formulae and detailed standard operating procedures relating to the system in use should be available and the accuracy of the records should be checked. If documentation is handled by electronic data-processing methods, only authorized persons should be able to enter or modify data in the computer, and there should be a record of changes and deletions; access should be restricted by passwords or other means and the entry of critical data should be independently checked. Batch records stored electronically should be protected by back-up transfer on magnetic tape, microfilm, paper print-outs or other means. It is particularly important that, during the period of retention, the data are readily available.

Documents required

Labels

15.10 Labels applied to containers, equipment or premises should be clear, unambiguous and in the company's agreed format. It is often helpful in addition to the wording on the labels to use colours to indicate status (e.g. quarantined, accepted, rejected, clean).

15.11 All finished drug products should be identified by labelling, as required by the national legislation, bearing at least the following information:

(a) the name of the drug product;
(b) a list of the active ingredients (if applicable, with the INNs), showing the amount of each present and a statement of the net contents (e.g. number of dosage units, weight, volume);
(c) the batch number assigned by the manufacturer;
(d) the expiry date in an uncoded form;
(e) any special storage conditions or handling precautions that may be necessary;
(f) directions for use, and warnings and precautions that may be necessary;
(g) the name and address of the manufacturer or the company or the person responsible for placing the product on the market.

15.12 For reference standards, the label and/or accompanying document should indicate potency or concentration, date of manufacture, expiry date, date the closure is first opened, storage conditions and control number, as appropriate.

Specifications and testing procedures

15.13 Testing procedures described in documents should be validated in the context of available facilities and equipment before they are adopted for routine testing.

15.14 There should be appropriately authorized and dated specifications, including tests on identity, content, purity and quality, for starting and packaging materials and for finished products; where appropriate, they should also be available for intermediate or bulk products. Specifications for water, solvents and reagents (e.g. acids and bases) used in production should be included.

15.15 Each specification should be approved, signed and dated, and maintained by quality control, quality assurance unit or documentation centre. Specifications for starting materials, intermediates, and bulk, finished products and packaging materials are referred to in sections 15.18–15.21.

15.16 Periodic revisions of the specifications may be necessary to comply with new editions of the national pharmacopoeia or other official compendia.

15.17 Pharmacopoeias, reference standards, reference spectra and other reference materials should be available in the quality control laboratory.

Specifications for starting and packaging materials

15.18 Specifications for starting, primary and printed packaging materials should provide, if applicable, a description of the materials, including:

(a) the designated name (if applicable, the INN) and internal code reference;
(b) the reference, if any, to a pharmacopoeial monograph;
(c) qualitative and quantitative requirements with acceptance limits.

Depending on the company's practice other data may be added to the specification, such as:

(a) the supplier and the original producer of the materials;
(b) a specimen of printed materials;
(c) directions for sampling and testing, or a reference to procedures;
(d) storage conditions and precautions;
(e) the maximum period of storage before re-examination.

Packaging material should conform to specifications, and should be compatible with the material and/or with the drug product it contains. The material should be examined for compliance with the specification, and for defects as well as for the correctness of identity markings.

15.19 Documents describing testing procedures should state the required frequency for re-assaying each starting material, as determined by its stability.

Specifications for intermediate and bulk products

15.20 Specifications for intermediate and bulk products should be available. The specifications should be similar to specifications for starting materials or for finished products, as appropriate.

Specifications for finished products

15.21 Specifications for finished products should include:

(a) the designated name of the product and the code reference, where applicable;
(b) the designated name(s) of the active ingredient(s) (if applicable, with the INN(s));
(c) the formula or a reference to the formula;
(d) a description of the dosage form and package details;
(e) directions for sampling and testing or a reference to procedures;
(f) the qualitative and quantitative requirements, with acceptance limits;
(g) the storage conditions and precautions, where applicable;
(h) the shelf-life.

Master formulae

15.22 A formally authorized master formula should exist for each product and batch size to be manufactured.

15.23 The master formula should include:

(a) the name of the product, with a product reference code relating to its specification;
(b) a description of the dosage form, strength of the product and batch size;
(c) a list of all starting materials to be used (if applicable, with the INNs), with the amount of each, described using the designated name and a reference that is unique to that material (mention should be made of any substance that may disappear in the course of processing);
(d) a statement of the expected final yield with the acceptable limits, and of relevant intermediate yields, where applicable;
(e) a statement of the processing location and the principal equipment to be used;
(f) the methods, or reference to the methods, to be used for preparing and operating the critical equipment, e.g. cleaning (especially after a change in product), assembling, calibrating, sterilizing, use;
(g) detailed step-wise processing instructions (e.g. checks on materials, pre-treatments, sequence for adding materials, mixing times, temperatures);
(h) the instructions for any in-process controls with their limits;
(i) where necessary, the requirements for storage of the products, including the container, the labelling, and any special storage conditions;
(j) any special precautions to be observed.

Packaging instructions

15.24 Formally authorized packaging instructions should exist for each product, pack size and type. These should normally include, or make reference to:

(a) the name of the product;
(b) a description of its pharmaceutical form, strength and, where applicable, method of application;
(c) the pack size expressed in terms of the number, weight or volume of the product in the final container;
(d) a complete list of all the packaging materials required for a standard batch size, including quantities, sizes and types, with the code or reference number relating to the specifications for each packaging material;
(e) where appropriate, an example or reproduction of the relevant printed packaging materials and specimens, indicating where the batch number and expiry date of the product have been marked;
(f) special precautions to be observed, including a careful examination of the packaging area and equipment in order to ascertain the line clearance before and after packaging operations;
(g) a description of the packaging operation, including any significant subsidiary operations, and equipment to be used;
(h) details of in-process controls with instructions for sampling and acceptance limits.

Batch processing records

15.25 A batch processing record should be kept for each batch processed. It should be based on the relevant parts of the currently approved specifications on the record. The method of preparation of such records should be designed to avoid errors. (Copying or validated computer programmes are recommended. Transcribing from approved documents should be avoided.)

15.26 Before any processing begins, a check should be made that the equipment and work station are clear of previous products, documents, or materials not required for the planned process, and that the equipment is clean and suitable for use. This check should be recorded.

15.27 During processing, the following information should be recorded at the time each action is taken, and after completion the record should be dated and signed by the person responsible for the processing operations:

(a) the name of the product;
(b) the number of the batch being manufactured;
(c) dates and times of commencement, of significant intermediate stages, and of completion of production;
(d) the name of the person responsible for each stage of production;
(e) the initials of the operator(s) of different significant steps of production and, where appropriate, of the person(s) who checked each of these operations (e.g. weighing);

(f) the batch number and/or analytical control number and the quantity of each starting material actually weighed (including the batch number and amount of any recovered or reprocessed material added);
(g) any relevant processing operation or event and the major equipment used;
(h) the in-process controls performed, the initials of the person(s) carrying them out, and the results obtained;
(i) the amount of product obtained at different and pertinent stages of manufacture (yield), together with comments or explanations for significant deviations from the expected yield;
(j) notes on special problems including details, with signed authorization for any deviation from the master formula.

Batch packaging records

15.28 A batch packaging record should be kept for each batch or part batch processed. It should be based on the relevant parts of the approved packaging instructions, and the method of preparing such records should be designed to avoid errors. (Copying or validated computer programmes are recommended. Transcribing from approved documents should be avoided.)

15.29 Before any packaging operation begins, checks should be made that the equipment and work station are clear of previous products, documents or materials not required for the planned packaging operations, and that equipment is clean and suitable for use. These checks should be recorded.

15.30 The following information should be recorded at the time each action is taken, and the date and the person responsible should be clearly identified by signature or electronic password:

(a) the name of the product, the batch number and the quantity of bulk product to be packed, as well as the batch number and the planned quantity of finished product that will be obtained, the quantity actually obtained and the reconciliation;
(b) the date(s) and time(s) of the packaging operations;
(c) the name of the responsible person carrying out the packaging operation;
(d) the initials of the operators of the different significant steps;
(e) the checks made for identity and conformity with the packaging instructions, including the results of in-process controls;
(f) details of the packaging operations carried out, including references to equipment and the packaging lines used, and, when necessary, the instructions for keeping the product unpacked or a record of returning product that has not been packaged to the storage area;
(g) whenever possible, samples of the printed packaging materials used, including specimens bearing the approval for the printing of and regular check (where appropriate) of the batch number, expiry date, and any additional overprinting;

(h) notes on any special problems, including details of any deviation from the packaging instructions, with written authorization by an appropriate person;
(i) the quantities and reference number or identification of all printed pack aging materials and bulk product issued, used, destroyed or returned to stock and the quantities of product obtained to permit an adequate reconciliation.

Standard operating procedures (SOPs) and records

15.31 Standard operating procedures and associated records of actions taken or, where appropriate, conclusions reached should be available for:

(a) equipment assembly and validation;
(b) analytical apparatus and calibration;
(c) maintenance, cleaning and sanitization;
(d) personnel matters including qualification, training, clothing and hygiene;
(e) environmental monitoring;
(f) pest control;
(g) complaints;
(h) recalls;
(i) returns.

15.32 There should be standard operating procedures and records for the receipt of each delivery of starting material and primary and printed packaging material.

15.33 The records of the receipts should include:

(a) the name of the material on the delivery note and the containers;
(b) the "in-house" name and/or code of the material if different from (a);
(c) the date of receipt;
(d) the supplier's name and, if possible, manufacturer's name;
(e) the manufacturer's batch or reference number;
(f) the total quantity, and number of containers received;
(g) the batch number assigned after receipt;
(h) any relevant comment (e.g. state of the containers).

15.34 There should be standard operating procedures for the internal labelling, quarantine and storage of starting materials, packaging materials and other materials, as appropriate.

15.35 Standard operating procedures should be available for each instrument and piece of equipment (e.g. use, calibration, cleaning, maintenance) and placed in close proximity to the equipment.

15.36 There should be standard operating procedures for sampling, which specify the person(s) authorized to take samples.

15.37 The sampling instructions should include:

(a) the method of sampling and the sampling plan;
(b) the equipment to be used;
(c) any precautions to be observed to avoid contamination of the material or any deterioration in its quality;
(d) the amount(s) of sample(s) to be taken;
(e) instructions for any required subdivision of the sample;
(f) the type of sample container(s) to be used, and whether they are for aseptic sampling or for normal sampling, and labelling;
(g) any specific precautions to be observed, especially in regard to the sampling of sterile or noxious material.

15.38 There should be a standard operating procedure describing the details of the batch (lot) numbering system, with the objective of ensuring that each batch of intermediate, bulk or finished product is identified with a specific batch number.

15.39 The standard operating procedures for batch numbering that are applied to the processing stage and to the respective packaging stage should be related to each other.

15.40 The standard operating procedure for batch numbering should ensure that the same batch numbers will not be used repeatedly; this applies also to reprocessing.

15.41 Batch-number allocation should be immediately recorded, e.g. in a logbook. The record should include at least the date of allocation, product identity and size of batch.

15.42 There should be written procedures for testing materials and products at different stages of manufacture, describing the methods and equipment to be used. The tests performed should be recorded.

15.43 Analysis records should include at least the following data:

(a) the name of the material or product and, where applicable, dosage form;
(b) the batch number and, where appropriate, the manufacturer and/or supplier;
(c) references to the relevant specifications and testing procedures;
(d) test results, including observations and calculations, and reference to any specifications (limits);
(e) date(s) and reference number(s) of testing;
(f) the initials of the persons who performed the testing;

(g) the date and initials of the persons who verified the testing and the calculations, where appropriate;
(h) a clear statement of release or rejection (or other status decision) and the dated signature of the designated responsible person.

15.44 Written release and rejection procedures should be available for materials and products, and in particular for the release for sale of the finished product by an authorized person.

15.45 Records should be maintained of the distribution of each batch of a product in order, e.g. to facilitate the recall of the batch if necessary.

15.46 Records should be kept for major and critical equipment, as appropriate, of any validations, calibrations, maintenance, cleaning, or repair operations, including dates and the identity of the people who carried these operations out.

15.47 The use of major and critical equipment and the areas where products have been processed should be appropriately recorded in chronological order.

15.48 There should be written procedures assigning responsibility for cleaning and sanitation and describing in sufficient detail the cleaning schedules, methods, equipment and materials to be used and facilities and equipment to be cleaned. Such written procedures should be followed.

16. Good practices in production

16.1 *Principle.* Production operations must follow clearly defined procedures in accordance with manufacturing and marketing authorizations, with the objective of obtaining products of the requisite quality.

General

16.2 All handling of materials and products, such as receipt and cleaning, quarantine, sampling, storage, labelling, dispensing, processing, packaging and distribution, should be done in accordance with written procedures or instructions and, where necessary, recorded.

16.3 Any deviation from instructions or procedures should be avoided as far as possible. If deviations occur, they should be done in accordance with an approved procedure. The authorization of the deviation should be approved in writing by a designated person, with the involvement of the quality control department, when appropriate.

16.4 Checks on yields and reconciliation of quantities should be carried out as necessary to ensure that there are no discrepancies outside acceptable limits.

16.5 Operations on different products should not be carried out simultaneously or consecutively in the same room or area unless there is no risk of mix-up or cross-contamination.

16.6 At all times during processing, all materials, bulk containers, major items of equipment, and where appropriate, the rooms and packaging lines being used should be labelled or otherwise identified with an indication of the product or material being processed, its strength (where applicable) and the batch number. Where applicable, this indication should also mention the stage of production. In some cases it may be useful to record also the name of the previous product that has been processed.

16.7 Access to production premises should be restricted to authorized personnel.

16.8 Normally, non-medicinal products should not be produced in areas or with equipment destined for the production of pharmaceutical products.

16.9 In-process controls are usually performed within the production area. The performance of such in-process controls should not have any negative effect on the quality of the product or another product (e.g. cross-contamination or mix-up).

Prevention of cross-contamination and bacterial contamination during production

16.10 When dry materials and products are used in production, special precautions should be taken to prevent the generation and dissemination of dust. Provision should be made for proper air control (e.g. supply and extraction of air of suitable quality).

16.11 Contamination of a starting material or of a product by another material or product must be avoided. This risk of accidental cross-contamination arises from the uncontrolled release of dust, gases, particles, vapours, sprays or organisms from materials and products in process, from residues on equipment, from intruding insects, and from operators' clothing, skin, etc. The significance of this risk varies with the type of contaminant and of the product being contaminated. Among the most hazardous contaminants are highly sensitizing materials, biological preparations such as living organisms, certain hormones, cytotoxic substances, and other highly active materials. Products in which contamination is likely to be most significant are those administered by injection or applied to open wounds and those given in large doses and/or over a long time.

16.12 Cross-contamination should be avoided by taking appropriate technical or organizational measures, for example:

(a) carrying out production in dedicated and self-contained areas (which may be required for products such as penicillins, live vaccines, live bacterial preparations and certain other biologicals);
(b) conducting campaign production (separation in time) followed by appropriate cleaning in accordance with a validated cleaning procedure;
(c) providing appropriately designed airlocks, pressure differentials, and air supply and extraction systems;
(d) minimizing the risk of contamination caused by recirculation or re-entry of untreated or insufficiently treated air;
(e) wearing protective clothing where products or materials are handled;
(f) using cleaning and decontamination procedures of known effectiveness;
(g) using a "closed system" in production;
(h) testing for residues;
(i) using cleanliness status labels on equipment.

16.13 Measures to prevent cross-contamination and their effectiveness should be checked periodically according to standard operating procedures.

16.14 Production areas where susceptible products are processed should undergo periodic environmental monitoring (e.g. for microbiological monitoring and particulate matter where appropriate).

Processing operations

16.15 Before any processing operation is started, steps should be taken to ensure that the work area and equipment are clean and free from any starting materials, products, product residues, labels or documents not required for the current operation.

16.16 Any necessary in-process controls and environmental controls should be carried out and recorded.

16.17 Means should be instituted of indicating failures of equipment or of services (e.g. water, gas) to equipment. Defective equipment should be withdrawn from use until the defect has been rectified. After use, production equipment should be cleaned without delay according to detailed written procedures and stored under clean and dry conditions in a separate area or in a manner that will prevent contamination.

16.18 Time limits for storage of equipment after cleaning and before use should be stated and based on data.

16.19 Containers for filling should be cleaned before filling. Attention should be given to avoiding and removing any contaminants such as glass fragments and metal particles.

16.20 Any significant deviation from the expected yield should be recorded and investigated.

16.21 Checks should be carried out to ensure that pipelines and other pieces of equipment used for the transportation of products from one area to another are connected in a correct manner.

16.22 Pipes used for conveying distilled or deionized water and, where appropriate, other water pipes should be sanitized and stored according to written procedures that detail the action limits for microbiological contamination and the measures to be taken.

16.23 Measuring, weighing, recording, and control equipment and instruments should be serviced and calibrated at prespecified intervals and records maintained. To ensure satisfactory functioning, instruments should be checked daily or prior to use for performing analytical tests. The date of calibration and servicing and the date when recalibration is due should be clearly indicated, preferably on a label attached to the instrument.

16.24 Repair and maintenance operations should not present any hazard to the quality of the products.

Packaging operations

16.25 When the programme for packaging operations is being set up, particular attention should be given to minimizing the risk of cross-contamination, mix-ups or substitutions. Different products should not be packaged in close proximity unless there is physical segregation or an alternative system that will provide equal assurance.

16.26 Before packaging operations are begun, steps should be taken to ensure that the work area, packaging lines, printing machines and other equipment are clean and free from any products, materials or documents used previously and which are not required for the current operation. The line clearance should be performed according to an appropriate procedure and checklist, and recorded.

16.27 The name and batch number of the product being handled should be displayed at each packaging station or line.

16.28 Normally, filling and sealing should be followed as quickly as possible by labelling. If labelling is delayed, appropriate procedures should be applied to ensure that no mix-ups or mislabelling can occur.

16.29 The correct performance of any printing (e.g. of code numbers or expiry dates) done separately or in the course of the packaging should be checked and recorded. Attention should be paid to printing by hand, which should be rechecked at regular intervals.

16.30 Special care should be taken when cut labels are used and when overprinting is carried out off-line, and in hand-packaging operations. Roll-feed labels are normally preferable to cut labels in helping to avoid mix-ups. On-line verification of all labels by automated electronic means can be helpful in preventing mix-ups, but checks should be made to ensure that any electronic code readers, label counters, or similar devices are operating correctly. When labels are attached manually, in-process control checks should be performed more frequently.

16.31 Printed and embossed information on packaging materials should be distinct and resistant to fading or erasing.

16.32 Regular on-line control of the product during packaging should include at least checks on:

(a) the general appearance of the packages;
(b) whether the packages are complete;
(c) whether the correct products and packaging materials are used;
(d) whether any overprinting is correct;
(e) the correct functioning of line monitors.

Samples taken away from the packaging line should not be returned.

16.33 Products that have been involved in an unusual event during packaging should be reintroduced into the process only after special inspection, investigation and approval by authorized personnel. A detailed record should be kept of this operation.

16.34 Any significant or unusual discrepancy observed during reconciliation of the amount of bulk product and printed packaging materials and the number of units produced should be investigated, satisfactorily accounted for, and recorded before release.

16.35 Upon completion of a packaging operation, any unused batch-coded packaging materials should be destroyed and the destruction recorded. A documented procedure requiring checks to be performed before returning unused materials should be followed if uncoded printed materials are returned to stock.

17. Good practices in quality control

17.1 Quality control is the part of GMP concerned with sampling, specifications and testing, and with the organization, documentation and release procedures which ensure that the necessary and relevant tests are actually carried out and that materials are not released for use, nor products released for sale or supply, until their quality has been judged to be satisfactory. Quality control is not confined to laboratory operations but must be involved in all decisions concerning the quality of the product.

17.2 The independence of quality control from production is considered fundamental.

17.3 Each manufacturer (the holder of a manufacturing authorization) should have a quality control function. The quality control function should be independent of other departments and under the authority of a person with appropriate qualifications and experience, who has one or several control laboratories at his or her disposal. Adequate resources must be available to ensure that all the quality control arrangements are effectively and reliably carried out. The basic requirements for quality control are as follows:

(a) adequate facilities, trained personnel and approved procedures must be available for sampling, inspecting, and testing starting materials, packaging materials, and intermediate, bulk, finished products, and where appropriate for monitoring environmental conditions for GMP purposes;
(b) samples of starting materials, packaging materials, intermediate products, bulk products and finished products must be taken by methods and personnel approved of by the quality control department;
(c) qualification and validation must be performed;
(d) records must be made (manually and/or by recording instruments) demonstrating that all the required sampling, inspecting and testing procedures have actually been carried out and that any deviations have been fully recorded and investigated;
(e) the finished products must contain ingredients complying with the qualitative and quantitative composition of the product described in the marketing authorization; the ingredients must be of the required purity, in their proper container and correctly labelled;
(f) records must be made of the results of inspecting and testing the materials and intermediate, bulk and finished products against specifications; pro- duct assessment must include a review and evaluation of the relevant production documentation and an assessment of deviations from specified procedures;
(g) no batch of product is to be released for sale or supply prior to certification by the authorized person(s) that it is in accordance with the requirements of the marketing authorization. In certain countries, by law, the batch release is a task of the authorized person from production together with the author- ized person from quality control;
(h) sufficient samples of starting materials and products must be retained to permit future examination of the product if necessary; the retained product must be kept in its final pack unless the pack is exceptionally large.

17.4 Quality control as a whole will also have other duties, such as to establish, validate and implement all quality control procedures, to evaluate, maintain, and store the reference standards for substances, to ensure the correct labelling of containers of materials and products, to ensure that the stability of the active pharmaceutical ingredients and products is monitored, to participate in the investigation of complaints related to the quality of the product, and to participate in environmental monitoring. All these operations should be carried out in accordance with written procedures and, where necessary, recorded.

17.5 Assessment of finished products should embrace all relevant factors, including the production conditions, the results of in-process testing, the manufacturing (including packaging) documentation, compliance with the specification for the finished product, and an examination of the finished pack.

17.6 Quality control personnel must have access to production areas for sampling and investigation as appropriate.

Control of starting materials and intermediate, bulk and finished products

17.7 All tests should follow the instructions given in the relevant written test procedure for each material or product. The result should be checked by the supervisor before the material or product is released or rejected.

17.8 Samples should be representative of the batches of material from which they are taken in accordance with the approved written procedure.

17.9 Sampling should be carried out so as to avoid contamination or other adverse effects on quality. The containers that have been sampled should be marked accordingly and carefully resealed after sampling.

17.10 Care should be taken during sampling to guard against contamination or mix-up of, or by, the material being sampled. All sampling equipment that comes into contact with the material should be clean. Some particularly hazardous or potent materials may require special precautions.

17.11 Sampling equipment should be cleaned and, if necessary, sterilized before and after each use and stored separately from other laboratory equipment.

17.12 Each sample container should bear a label indicating:

17.13 Out-of-specification results obtained during testing of materials or products should be investigated in accordance with an approved procedure. Records should be maintained.

(a) the name of the sampled material;
(b) the batch or lot number;
(c) the number of the container from which the sample has been taken;
(d) the number of the sample;
(e) the signature of the person who has taken the sample;
(f) the date of sampling.

Test requirements

Starting and packaging materials

17.14 Before releasing a starting or packaging material for use, the quality control manager should ensure that the materials have been tested for conformity with specifications for identity, strength, purity and other quality parameters.

17.15 An identity test should be conducted on a sample from each container of starting material (see also section 14.14).

It is permissible to sample only a proportion of the containers where a validated procedure has been established to ensure that no single container of starting material has been incorrectly labelled.

This validation should take account of at least the following aspects:

- the nature and status of the manufacturer and of the supplier and their understanding of the GMP requirements;
- the quality assurance system of the manufacturer of the starting material;
- the manufacturing conditions under which the starting material is produced and controlled; and
- the nature of the starting material and the medicinal products in which it will be used.

Under such a system it is possible that a validated procedure for exemption from the requirement for identity testing of each incoming container of starting material could be accepted for the following:

- starting materials coming from a single product manufacturer or plant; or
- starting materials coming directly from a manufacturer, or in the manufacturer's sealed container where there is a history of reliability, and regular audits of the manufacturer's quality assurance system are conducted by the purchaser (the manufacturer of the medicinal product) or by an officially accredited body.

It is improbable that such a procedure could be satisfactorily validated for either:

- starting materials supplied by intermediaries, such as brokers, where the source of manufacture is unknown or not audited; or
- starting materials for use in parenteral products.

17.16 Each batch (lot) of printed packaging materials must be examined following receipt.

17.17 In lieu of testing by the manufacturer, a certificate of analysis may be accepted from the supplier, provided that the manufacturer establishes the reliability of the supplier's analysis through appropriate periodic validation of the supplier's test results (see sections 8.8 and 8.9) and through on-site audits of the supplier's capabilities. (This does not affect section 17.15.) Certificates must be originals (not photocopies) or otherwise have their authenticity assured. Certificates must contain at least the following information (*6*):

(a) identification (name and address) of the issuing supplier;
(b) signature of the competent official, and statement of his or her qualifications;
(c) the name of the material tested;
(d) the batch number of the material tested;
(e) the specifications and methods used;
(f) the test results obtained;
(g) the date of testing.

In-process control

17.18 In-process control records should be maintained and form a part of the batch records (see section 15.25).

Finished products

17.19 For each batch of drug product, there should be an appropriate laboratory determination of satisfactory conformity to its finished product specification prior to release.

17.20 Products failing to meet the established specifications or any other relevant quality criteria should be rejected.

Batch record review

17.21 Production and quality control records should be reviewed as part of the approval process of batch release. Any divergence or failure of a batch to meet its specifications should be thoroughly investigated. The investigation should, if necessary, extend to other batches of the same product and other products that may have been associated with the specific failure or discrepancy. A written record of the investigation should be made and should include the conclusion and follow-up action.

17.22 Retention samples from each batch of finished product should be kept for at least one year after the expiry date. Finished products should usually be kept in their final packaging and stored under the recommended conditions. If exceptionally large packages are produced, smaller samples might be stored in appropriate containers. Samples of active starting materials should be retained for at least one year beyond the expiry date of the corresponding finished product. Other starting materials (other than solvents, gases, and water) should be retained for a minimum of two years if their stability allows. Retention samples of materials and products should be of a size sufficient to permit at least two full re-examinations.

Stability studies

17.23 Quality control should evaluate the quality and stability of finished pharmaceutical products and, when necessary, of starting materials and intermediate products.

17.24 Quality control should establish expiry dates and shelf-life specifications on the basis of stability tests related to storage conditions.

17.25 A written programme for ongoing stability determination should be developed and implemented to include elements such as:

(a) a complete description of the drug involved in the study;
(b) the complete set of testing parameters and methods, describing all tests for potency, purity, and physical characteristics and documented evidence that these tests indicate stability;
(c) provision for the inclusion of a sufficient number of batches;
(d) the testing schedule for each drug;
(e) provision for special storage conditions;
(f) provision for adequate sample retention;
(g) a summary of all the data generated, including the evaluation and the conclusions of the study.

17.26 Stability should be determined prior to marketing and following any significant changes in processes, equipment, packaging materials, etc.

References

1. Good Manufacturing Practices for pharmaceutical products. In: *WHO Expert Committee on Specifications for Pharmaceutical Preparations. Thirty-second report.* Geneva, World Health Organization, 1992 (WHO Technical Report Series, No. 823), Annex 1.

2. Validation of analytical procedures used in the examination of pharmaceutical materials. In: *WHO Expert Committee on Specifications for Pharmaceutical Preparations. Thirty-second report.* Geneva, World Health Organization, 1992 (WHO Technical Report Series, No. 823), Annex 5.

3. *Good manufacturing practice for medicinal products in the European Community.* Brussels, Commission of the European Communities, 1992.

4. Pharmaceutical Inspection Convention, Pharmaceutical Inspection Co-operation Scheme (PIC/S). In: *Guide to good manufacturing practice for medicinal plants*, Geneva, PIC/S Secretariat, 2000.

5. *Quality assurance of pharmaceuticals. A compendium of guidelines and related materials. Volume 2. Good manufacturing practices and inspection.* Geneva, World Health Organization, 1999.

6. Model certificate of analysis. In: *WHO Expert Committee on Specifications for Pharmaceutical Preparations. Thirty-sixth report.* Geneva, World Health Organization, 2002 (WHO Technical Report Series, No. 902), Annex 10.

7. Good Manufacturing Practices for pharmaceutical products: main principles. In: *WHO Expert Committee on Specifications for Pharmaceutical Preparations. Thirty-seventh report.* Geneva, World Health Organization, 2003 (WHO Technical Report Series, No. 908), Annex 4.

Heating, ventilation and air-conditioning systems for non-sterile pharmaceutical dosage forms[1]

1. Introduction 59
2. Scope of document 59
3. Glossary 60
4. Protection 65
   4.1 Products and personnel 65
   4.2 Air filtration 69
   4.3 Unidirectional airflow 73
   4.4 Infiltration 76
   4.5 Cross-contamination 80
   4.6 Temperature and relative humidity 85
5. Dust control 86
6. Protection of the environment 88
   6.1 Dust in exhaust air 88
   6.2 Fume removal 89
7. Systems and components 89
   7.1 General 90
   7.2 Recirculation system 91
   7.3 Full fresh air systems 93
8. Commissioning, qualification and maintenance 94
   8.1 Commissioning 94
   8.2 Qualification 95
   8.3 Maintenance 99
Bibliography 100

[1] Supplementary guidelines on good manufacturing practices for heating, ventilation and air-conditioning systems for non-sterile pharmaceutical dosage forms. In: *WHO Expert Committee on Specifications for Pharmaceutical Preparations. Fortieth report.* Geneva, World Health Organization, 2006 (WHO Technical Report Series, No. 937), Annex 2.

1. Introduction

Heating, ventilation and air-conditioning (HVAC) play an important role in ensuring the manufacture of quality pharmaceutical products. A well designed HVAC system will also provide comfortable conditions for operators. These guidelines mainly focus on recommendations for systems for manufacturers of solid dosage forms. The guidelines also refer to other systems or components which are not relevant to solid dosage form manufacturing plants, but which may assist in providing a comparison between the requirements for solid dosage-form plants and other systems.

HVAC system design influences architectural layouts with regard to items such as airlock positions, doorways and lobbies. The architectural components have an effect on room pressure differential cascades and cross-con-tamination control. The prevention of contamination and cross-contamina-tion is an essential design consideration of the HVAC system. In view of these critical aspects, the design of the HVAC system should be considered at the concept design stage of a pharmaceutical manufacturing plant.

Temperature, relative humidity and ventilation should be appropriate and should not adversely affect the quality of pharmaceutical products during their manufacture and storage, or the accurate functioning of equipment.

This document aims to give guidance to pharmaceutical manufacturers and inspectors of pharmaceutical manufacturing facilities on the design, installation, qualification and maintenance of the HVAC systems. These guidelines are intended to complement those provided in *Good manufacturing practices for pharmaceutical products* (1) and should be read in conjunction with the parent guide. The additional standards addressed by the present guidelines should therefore be considered supplementary to the general requirements set out in the parent guide.

2. Scope of document

These guidelines focus primarily on the design and good manufacturing practices (GMP) requirements for HVAC systems for facilities for the manufacture of solid dosage forms. Most of the system design principles for facilities manufacturing solid dosage forms also apply to other facilities such as those manufacturing liquids, creams and ointments. These guidelines do not cover requirements for manufacturing sites for the production of sterile pharmaceutical products.

These guidelines are intended as a basic guide for use by GMP inspectors. They are not intended to be prescriptive in specifying requirements and design parameters. There are many parameters affecting a clean area condition and it is, therefore, difficult to lay down the specific requirements for one particular parameter in isolation.

Many manufacturers have their own engineering design and qualification standards and requirements may vary from one manufacturer to the next.

Figure 1. The guidelines address the various system criteria according to the sequence set out in this diagram

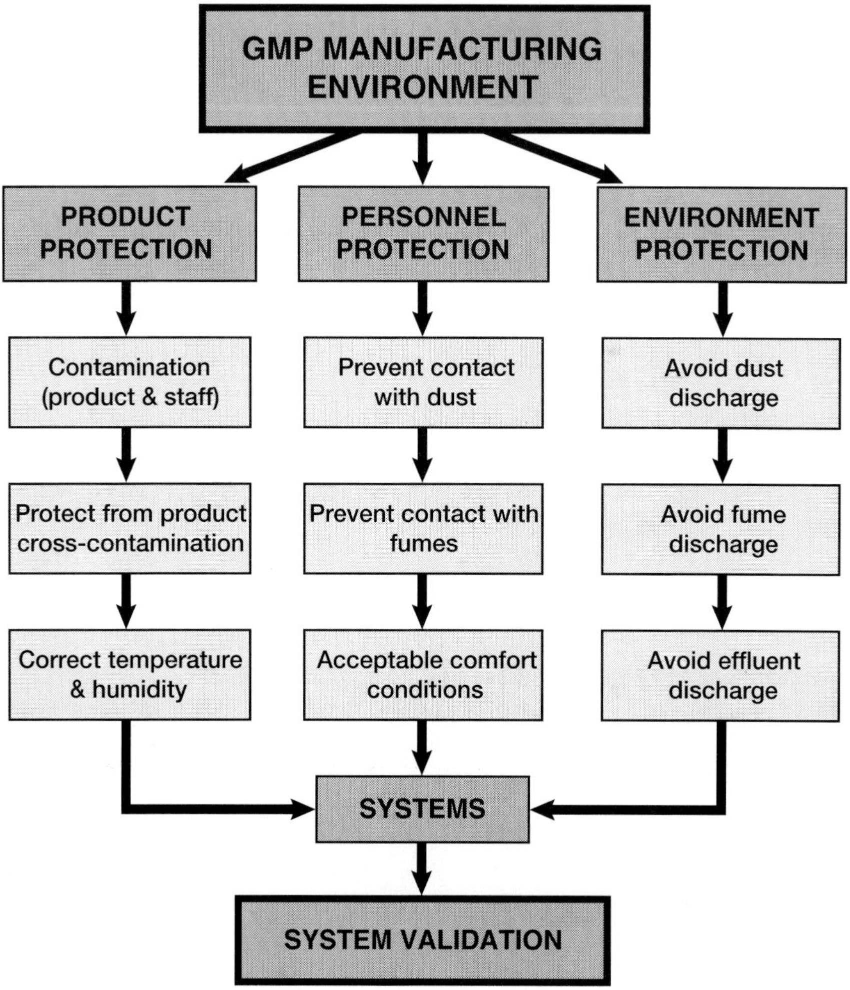

GMP, Good manufacturing practice.

Design parameters should, therefore, be set realistically for each project, with a view to creating a cost-effective design, yet still complying with all regulatory standards and ensuring that product quality and safety are not compromised.

The three primary aspects addressed in this manual are the roles that the HVAC system plays in product protection, personnel protection and environmental protection (Fig. 1).

3. Glossary

The definitions given below apply to terms used in these guidelines. They may have different meanings in other contexts.

acceptance criteria
Measurable terms under which a test result will be considered acceptable.

action limit
The action limit is reached when the acceptance criteria of a critical parameter have been exceeded. Results outside these limits will require specified action and investigation.

air-handling unit (AHU)
The air-handling unit serves to condition the air and provide the required air movement within a facility.

airlock
An enclosed space with two or more doors, which is interposed between two or more rooms, e.g. of differing classes of cleanliness, for the purpose of controlling the airflow between those rooms when they need to be entered. An airlock is designed for and used by either people or goods (PAL, personnel airlock; MAL, material airlock).

alert limit
The alert limit is reached when the normal operating range of a critical parameter has been exceeded, indicating that corrective measures may need to be taken to prevent the action limit being reached.

as-built
Condition where the installation is complete with all services connected and functioning but with no production equipment, materials or personnel present.

at-rest
Condition where the installation is complete with equipment installed and operating in a manner agreed upon by the customer and supplier, but with no personnel present.

central air-conditioning unit (see air-handling unit)

change control
A formal system by which qualified representatives of appropriate disciplines review proposed or actual changes that might affect a validated status. The intent is to determine the need for action that would ensure that the system is maintained in a validated state.

clean area (clean room)[1]

An area (or room) with defined environmental control of particulate and microbial contamination, constructed and used in such a way as to reduce the introduction, generation and retention of contaminants within the area.

commissioning

Commissioning is the documented process of verifying that the equipment and systems are installed according to specifications, placing the equipment into active service and verifying its proper action. Commissioning takes place at the conclusion of project construction but prior to validation.

containment

A process or device to contain product, dust or contaminants in one zone, preventing it from escaping to another zone.

contamination

The undesired introduction of impurities of a chemical or microbial nature, or of foreign matter, into or on to a starting material or intermediate, during production, sampling, packaging or repackaging, storage or transport.

critical parameter or component

A processing parameter (such as temperature or humidity) that affects the quality of a product, or a component that may have a direct impact on the quality of the product.

cross-contamination

Contamination of a starting material, intermediate product or finished product with another starting material or material during production.

design condition

Design condition relates to the specified range or accuracy of a controlled variable used by the designer as a basis for determining the performance requirements of an engineered system.

design qualification (DQ)

DQ is the documented check of planning documents and technical specifications for conformity of the design with the process, manufacturing, GMP and regulatory requirements.

---

[1] Note: Clean area standards, such as ISO 14644-1 provide details on how to classify air cleanliness by means of particle concentrations, whereas the GMP standards provide a grading for air cleanliness in terms of the condition (at-rest or operational), the permissible microbial concentrations, as well as other factors such as gowning requirements. GMP and clean area standards should be used in conjunction with each other to define and classify the different manufacturing environments.

direct impact system
A system that is expected to have a direct impact on product quality. These systems are designed and commissioned in line with good engineering practice (GEP) and, in addition, are subject to qualification practices.

facility
The built environment within which the clean area installation and associated controlled environments operate together with their supporting infrastructure.

good engineering practice (GEP)
Established engineering methods and standards that are applied throughout the project life-cycle to deliver appropriate, cost-effective solutions.

indirect impact system
This is a system that is not expected to have a direct impact on product quality, but typically will support a direct impact system. These systems are designed and commissioned according to GEP only.

infiltration
Infiltration is the ingress of contaminated air from an external zone into a clean area.

installation qualification (IQ)
IQ is documented verification that the premises, HVAC system, supporting utilities and equipment have been built and installed in compliance with their approved design specification.

no-impact system
This is a system that will not have any impact, either directly or indirectly, on product quality. These systems are designed and commissioned according to GEP only.

non-critical parameter or component
A processing parameter or component within a system where the operation, contact, data control, alarm or failure will have an indirect impact or no impact on the quality of the product.

normal operating range
The range that the manufacturer selects as the acceptable values for a parameter during normal operations. This range must be within the operating range.

operating limits
The minimum and/or maximum values that will ensure that product and safety requirements are met.

operating range
Operating range is the range of validated critical parameters within which acceptable products can be manufactured.

operational condition
This condition relates to carrying out room classification tests with the normal production process with equipment in operation, and the normal staff present in the room.

operational qualification (OQ)
OQ is the documentary evidence to verify that the equipment operates in accordance with its design specifications in its normal operating range and performs as intended throughout all anticipated operating ranges.

oral solid dosage (OSD)
Usually refers to an OSD plant that manufactures medicinal products such as tablets, capsules and powders to be taken orally.

performance qualification (PQ)
PQ is the documented verification that the process and/or the total process related to the system performs as intended throughout all anticipated operating ranges.

point extraction
Air extraction to remove dust with the extraction point located as close as possible to the source of the dust.

pressure cascade
A process whereby air flows from one area, which is maintained at a higher pressure, to another area at a lower pressure.

qualification
Qualification is the planning, carrying out and recording of tests on equipment and a system, which forms part of the validated process, to demonstrate that it will perform as intended.

relative humidity
The ratio of the actual water vapour pressure of the air to the saturated water vapour pressure of the air at the same temperature expressed as a percentage. More simply put, it is the ratio of the mass of moisture in the air, relative to the mass at 100% moisture saturation, at a given temperature.

standard operating procedure (SOP)
An authorized written procedure, giving instructions for performing operations, not necessarily specific to a given product or material, but of a more general nature (e.g. operation of equipment, maintenance and cleaning, validation, cleaning of premises and environmental control, sampling and inspection). Certain SOPs may be used to supplement product-specific master and batch production documentation.

turbulent flow
Turbulent flow, or non-unidirectional airflow, is air distribution that is introduced into the controlled space and then mixes with room air by means of induction.

unidirectional airflow (UDAF)
Unidirectional airflow is a rectified airflow over the entire cross-sectional area of a clean zone with a steady velocity and approximately parallel streamlines (see also turbulent flow). (Modern standards no longer refer to laminar flow, but have adopted the term unidirectional airflow.)

validation
The documented act of proving that any procedure, process, equipment, material, activity or system actually leads to the expected results.

validation master plan (VMP)
VMP is a high-level document which establishes an umbrella validation plan for the entire project, and is used as guidance by the project team for resource and technical planning (also referred to as master qualification plan).

4. Protection

4.1 Product and personnel

4.1.1 Areas for the manufacture of pharmaceuticals, where pharmaceutical starting materials and products, utensils and equipment are exposed to the environment, should be classified as "clean areas".

4.1.2 The achievement of a particular clean area classification depends on a number of criteria that should be addressed at the design and qualification stages. A suitable balance between the different criteria will be required in order to create an efficient clean area.

4.1.3 Some of the basic criteria to be considered should include:

- building finishes and structure
- air filtration
- air change rate or flushing rate

- room pressure
- location of air terminals and directional airflow
- temperature
- humidity
- material flow
- personnel flow
- equipment movement
- process being carried out
- outside air conditions
- occupancy
- type of product.

4.1.4 Air filtration and air change rates should ensure that the defined clean area classification is attained.

4.1.5 The air change rates should be determined by the manufacturer and designer, taking into account the various critical parameters. Primarily the air change rate should be set to a level that will achieve the required clean area classification.

4.1.6 Air change rates normally vary between 6 and 20 air changes per hour and are normally determined by the following considerations:

- level of protection required
- the quality and filtration of the supply air
- particulates generated by the manufacturing process
- particulates generated by the operators
- configuration of the room and air supply and extract locations
- sufficient air to achieve containment effect
- sufficient air to cope with the room heat load
- sufficient air to maintain the required room pressure.

4.1.7 In classifying the environment, the manufacturer should state whether this is achieved under "as-built" (Fig. 2), "at-rest" (Fig. 3) or "operational" (Fig. 4) conditions.

4.1.8 Room classification tests in the "as-built" condition should be carried out on the bare room, in the absence of any equipment or personnel.

4.1.9 Room classification tests in the "at-rest" condition should be carried out with the equipment operating where relevant, but without any operators. Because of the amounts of dust usually generated in a solid dosage facility most clean area classifications are rated for the "at-rest" condition.

4.1.10 Room classification tests in the "operational" condition should be carried out during the normal production process with equipment operating, and the normal number of personnel present in the room. Generally a room that is tested for an "operational" condition should be able to be cleaned up to

Figure 2. "As-built" condition

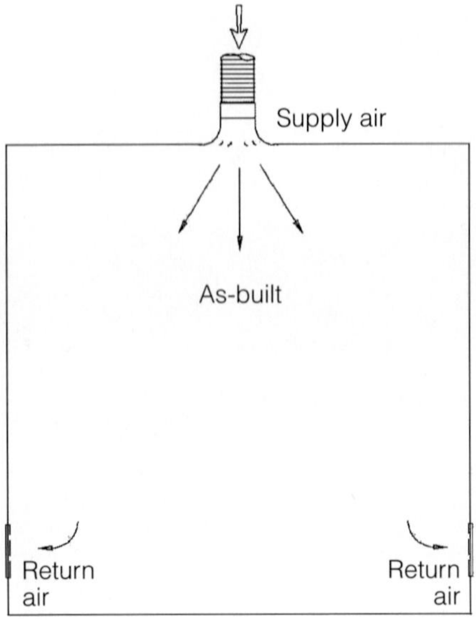

Figure 3. "At-rest" condition

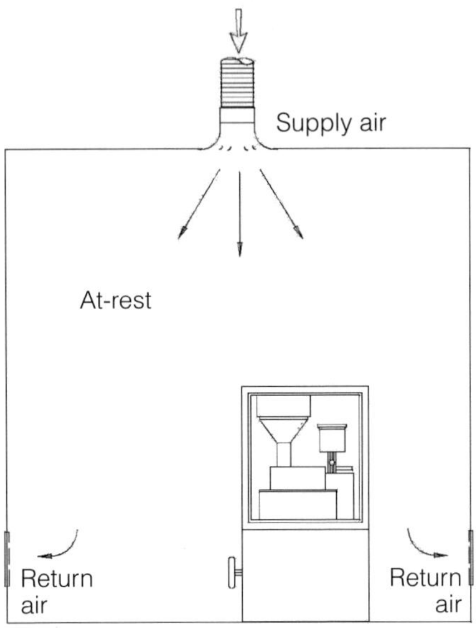

Figure 4. "Operational" Condition

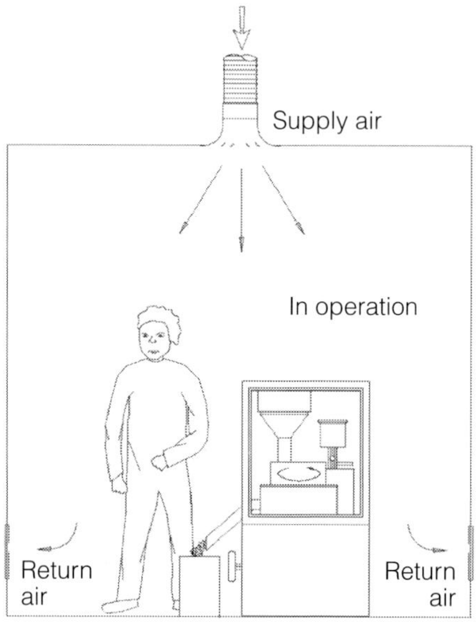

the "at-rest" clean area classification after a short clean-up time. The clean-up time should be determined through validation and is generally of the order of 20 minutes.

4.1.11 Materials and products should be protected from contamination and cross-contamination during all stages of manufacture (see also section 5.5 for cross-contamination control). *Note:* contaminants may result from inappropriate premises (e.g. poor design, layout or finishing), poor cleaning procedures, contaminants brought in by personnel, and a poor HVAC system.

4.1.12 Airborne contaminants should be controlled through effective ventilation.

4.1.13 External contaminants should be removed by effective filtration of the supply air. (See Fig. 5 for an example of a shell-like building layout to enhance containment and protection from external contaminants.)

4.1.14 Internal contaminants should be controlled by dilution and flushing of contaminants in the room, or by displacement airflow. (See Figs 6 and 7 for examples of methods for the flushing of airborne contaminants.)

4.1.15 Airborne particulates and the degree of filtration should be considered critical parameters with reference to the level of product protection required.

Figure 5. Shell-like containment control concept

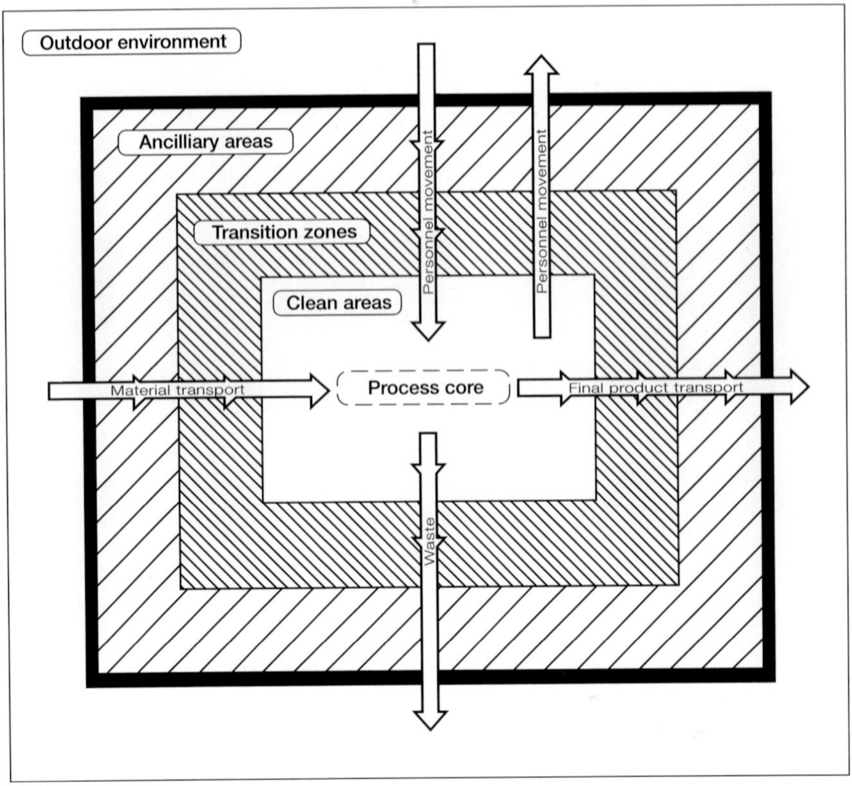

Note: The process core is regarded as the most stringently controlled clean zone which is protected by being surrounded by clean areas of a lower classification.

4.1.16 The level of protection and air cleanliness for different areas should be determined according to the product being manufactured, the process being used and the product's susceptibility to degradation (Table 1).

4.2 Air filtration

Note: The degree to which air is filtered plays an important role in the prevention of contamination and the control of cross-contamination.

4.2.1 The type of filters required for different applications depends on the quality of the ambient air and the return air (where applicable) and also on the air change rates. Table 2 gives the recommended filtration levels for different levels of protection in a pharmaceutical facility. Manufacturers should determine and prove the appropriate use of filters.

Figure 6. Turbulent dilution of dirty air

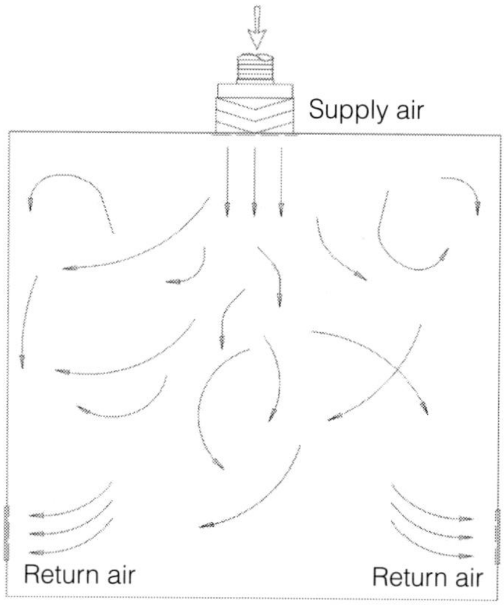

Figure 7. Unidirectional displacement of dirty air

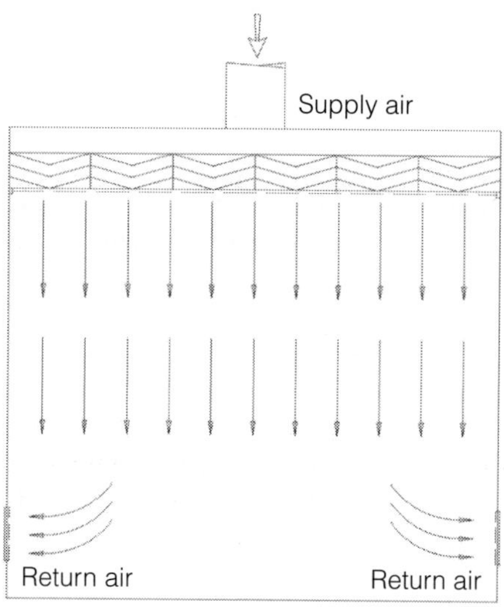

Table 1. Examples of levels of protection

Level	Condition	Example of area
Level 1	General	Area with normal housekeeping and maintenance, e.g. warehousing, secondary packing
Level 2	Protected	Area in which steps are taken to protect the exposed pharmaceutical starting material or product from contamination or degradation, e.g. manufacturing, primary packing, dispensing
Level 3	Controlled	Area in which specific environmental conditions are defined, controlled and monitored to prevent contamination or degradation of the pharmaceutical starting material or product

Table 2. Levels of protection and recommended filtration

Level of protection	Recommended filtration
Level 1	Primary filters only (e.g. EN779 G4 filters)
Level 2 and 3	Production facility operating on 100% outside air: primary plus secondary filters (e.g. EN779 G4 plus F8 filters)
Level 2 and 3	Production facility operating on recirculated plus ambient air, where potential for cross-contamination exists: Primary plus secondary plus tertiary filters (e.g. EN779 G4 plus F8 plus EN1822 H13 filters)

Note: The filter classifications referred to above relate to the EN1822 and EN779 test standards (EN 779 relates to filter classes G1 to F9 and EN 1822 relates to filter classes H10 to U16).

4.2.2 Filter classes should always be linked to the standard test method because referring to actual filter efficiencies can be very misleading (as different test methods each result in a different value for the same filter) (Fig. 8).

4.2.3 In selecting filters, the manufacturer should have considered other factors, such as particularly contaminated ambient conditions, local regulations and specific product requirements. Good prefiltration extends the life of the more expensive filters downstream.

4.2.4 Materials for components of an HVAC system should be selected with care so that they do not become the source of contamination. Any component with the potential for liberating particulate or microbial contamination into the air stream should be located upstream of the final filters.

4.2.5 Ventilation dampers, filters and other services should be designed and positioned so that they are accessible from *outside* the manufacturing areas (service voids or service corridors) for maintenance purposes.

Figure 8. Comparison of filter test standards

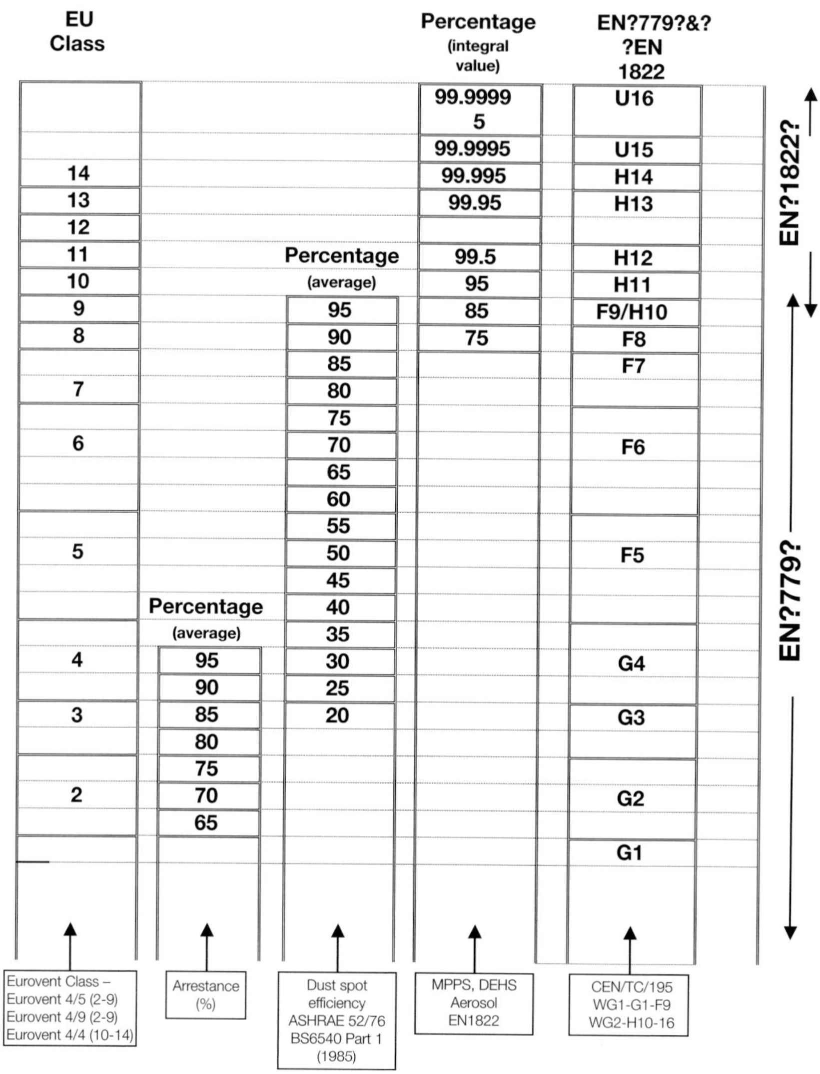

EN, European norm (Euronorm); EU, European Union.
This figure gives a rough comparison between the different filter standards (filter classes should always be connected to the standard test method).

4.2.6 Personnel should not be a source of contamination.

4.2.7 Directional airflow within production or packing areas should assist in preventing contamination. Airflows should be planned in conjunction with operator locations, so as to minimize contamination of the product by the operator and also to protect the operator from dust inhalation.

4.2.8 HVAC air distribution components should be designed, installed and located to prevent contaminants generated within the room from being spread.

4.2.9 Supply air diffusers of the high induction type (e.g. those typically used for office-type air-conditioning) should where possible not be used in clean areas where dust is liberated. Air diffusers should be of the non-induction type, introducing air with the least amount of induction so as to maximize the flushing effect. (See Figs 9–11 for illustrations of the three types of diffuser.)

4.2.10 Whenever possible, air should be exhausted from a low level in rooms to help provide a flushing effect.

4.3 Unidirectional airflow

4.3.1 Unidirectional airflow (UDAF) should be used where appropriate to provide product protection by supplying a clean air supply over the product, minimizing the ingress of contaminants from surrounding areas.

Figure 9. Induction diffuser (not recommended)

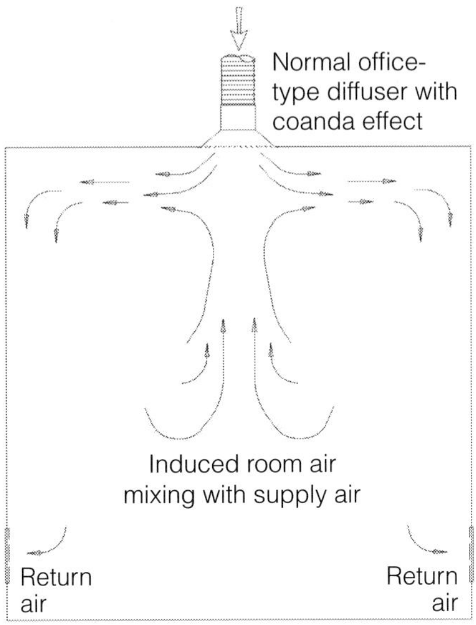

Figure 10. Perforated plate diffuser (recommended)

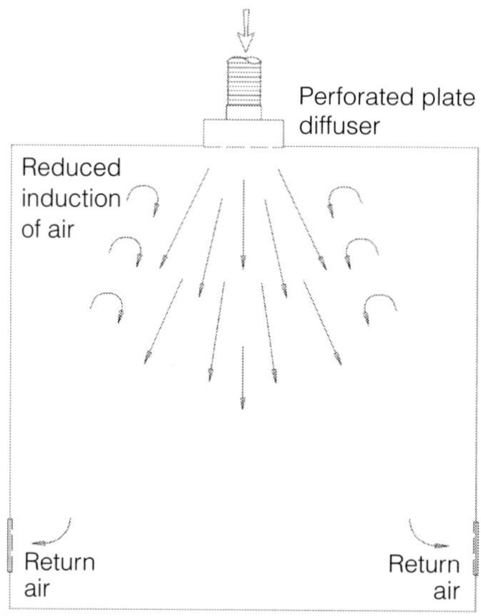

Figure 11. Swirl diffuser (recommended)

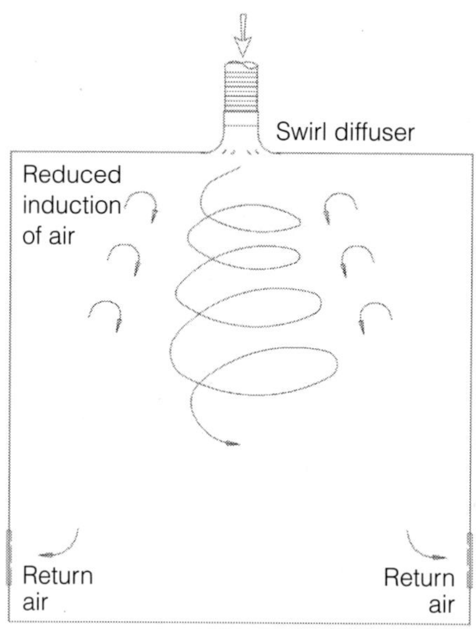

4.3.2 Where appropriate, the unidirectional airflow should also provide protection to the operator from contamination by the product.

4.3.3 Sampling of materials such as starting materials, primary packaging materials and products, should be carried out in the same environmental conditions that are required for the further processing of the product.

4.3.4 In a weighing booth situation, the aim of the design using UDAF should be to provide dust containment.

4.3.5 A dispensary or weighing booth should be provided with unidirectional airflow for protection of the product and operator.

4.3.6 The source of the dust and the position in which the operator normally stands should be determined before deciding on the direction of unidirectional flow.

Example: In Fig. 12 the dust generated at the weighing station is immediately extracted through the perforated worktop, thus protecting the operator from dust inhalation, but at the same time protecting the product from contamination by the operator by means of the vertical unidirectional airflow stream.

Figure 12. Operator protection at weighing station

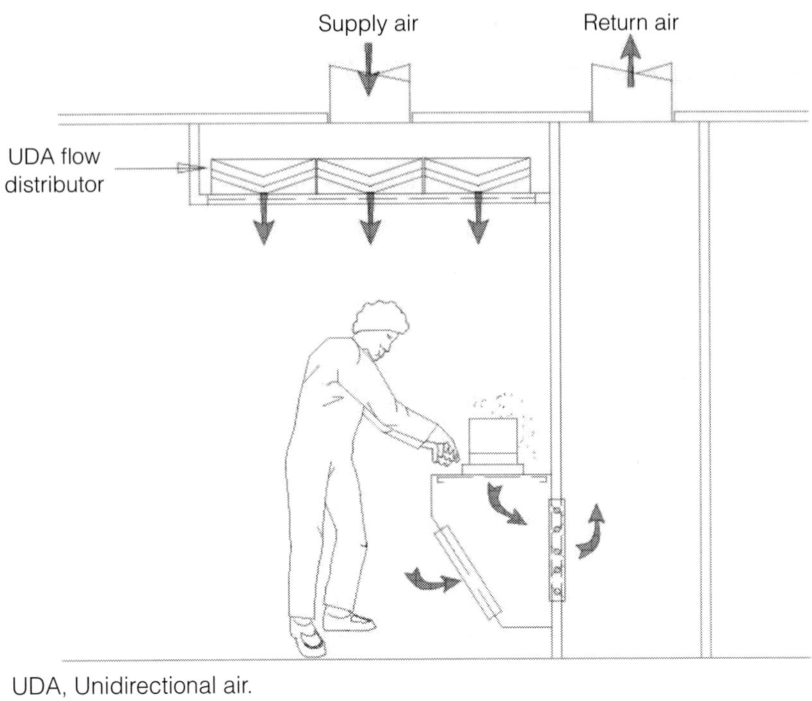

UDA, Unidirectional air.

4.3.7 The unidirectional flow velocity should be such that it does not disrupt the sensitivity of balances in weighing areas. Where necessary the velocity may be reduced to prevent inaccuracies during weighing, provided that sufficient airflow is maintained to provide containment.

4.3.8 The position in which the operator stands relative to the source of dust liberation and airflow should be determined to ensure that the operator is not in the path of an airflow that could lead to contamination of the product (Fig. 13).

4.3.9 Once the system has been designed and qualified with a specific layout for operators and processes, this should be maintained in accordance with an SOP.

4.3.10 There should be no obstructions in the path of a unidirectional flow airstream that may cause the operator to be exposed to dust.

Fig. 14 illustrates the incorrect use of a weighing scale which has a solid back. The back of the weighing scale should not block the return air path as this causes air to rise vertically, resulting in a hazardous situation for the operator.

Fig. 15 illustrates a situation where an open bin is placed below a vertical unidirectional flow distributor. The downward airflow should be prevented from entering the bin, and then being forced to rise again, as this would carry dust up towards the operator's face.

Fig. 16 shows that a solid worktop can sometimes cause deflection of the vertical unidirectional airflow resulting in a flow reversal. A possible solution would be to have a 100 mm gap between the back of the table and the wall, with the air being extracted here.

4.3.11 The manufacturer should select either vertical or horizontal unidirectional flow (Fig. 17) and an appropriate airflow pattern to provide the best protection for the particular application.

4.4 Infiltration

4.4.1 Air infiltration of unfiltered air into a pharmaceutical plant should not be the source of contamination.

4.4.2 Manufacturing facilities should be maintained at a positive pressure relative to the outside, to limit the ingress of contaminants. Where facilities are to be maintained at negative pressures relative to the ambient pressure to prevent the escape of harmful products to the outside (such as penicillin and hormones), special precautions should be taken.

4.4.3 The location of the negative pressure facility should be carefully considered with reference to the areas surrounding it, particular attention being given to ensuring that the building structure is well sealed.

Figure 13. Operator protection by horizontal airflow

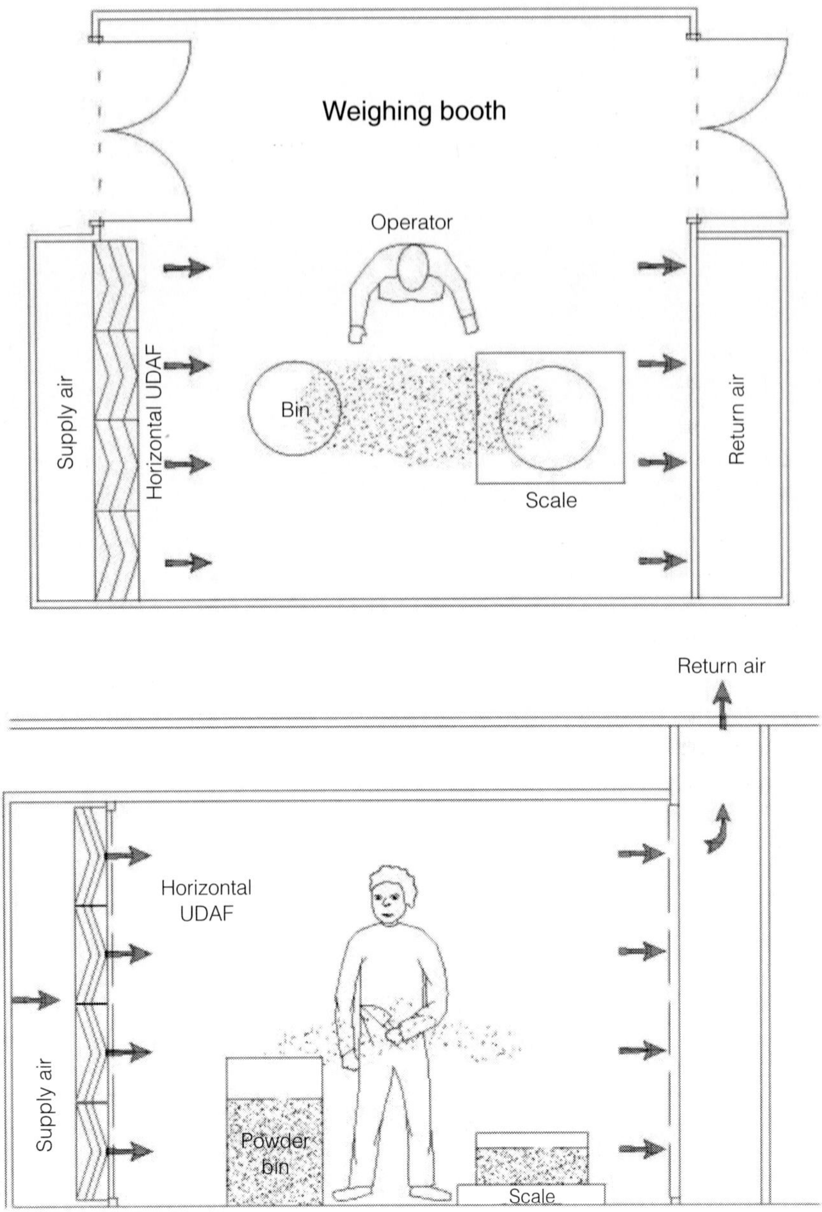

UDAF, Unidirectional airflow.

Figure 14. Operator subject to powder inhalation due to obstruction

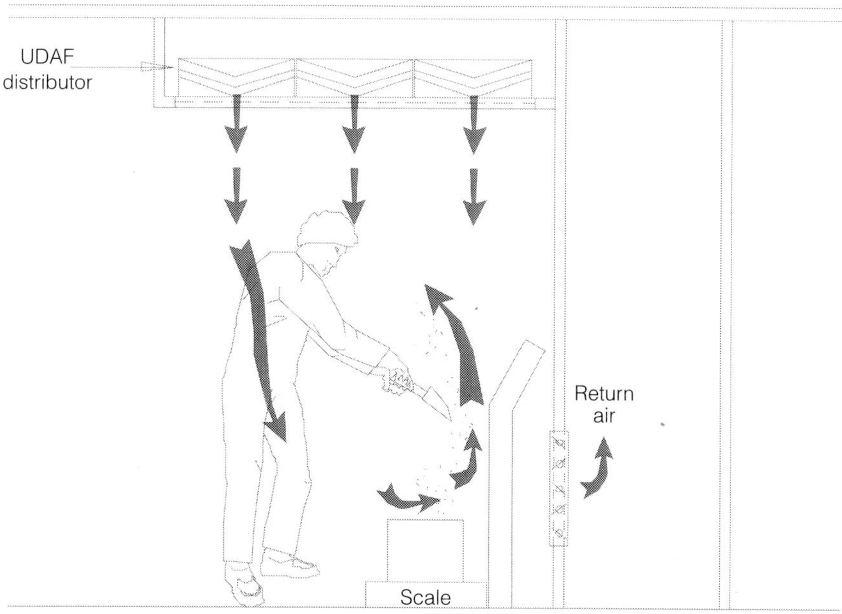

UDAF, Unidirectional airflow.

Figure 15. Operator subject to powder contamination due to airflow reversal in bin

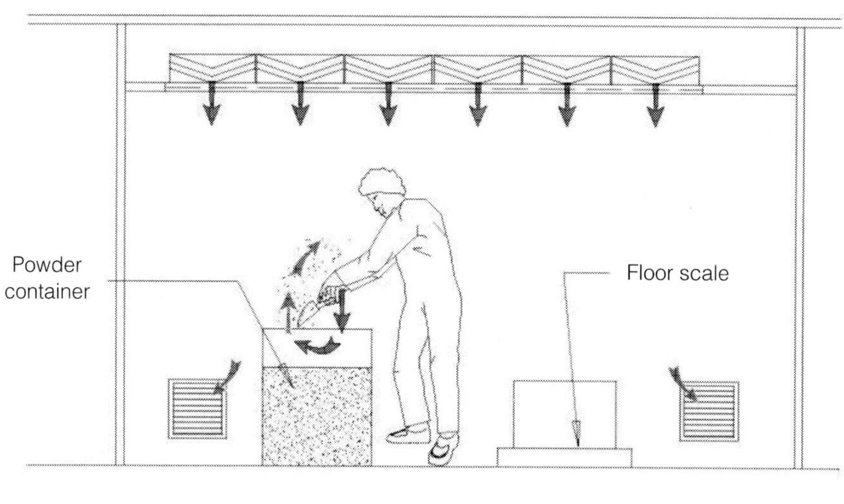

Figure 16. Operator subject to powder inhalation due to worktop obstruction

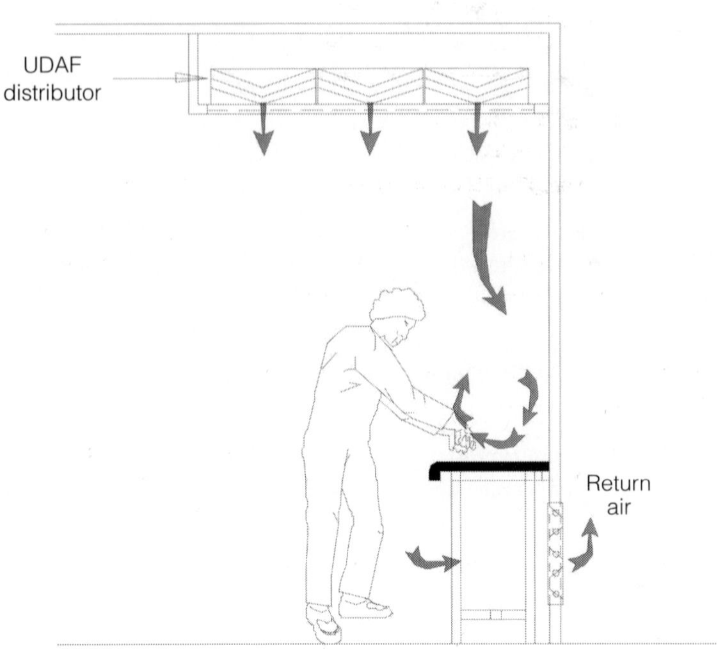

UDAF, Unidirectional airflow.

Figure 17. Diagram indicating horizontal and vertical unidirectional flow

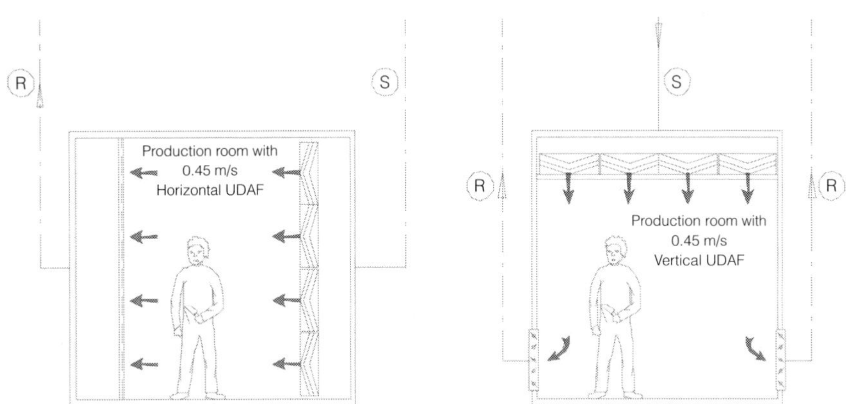

UDAF, Unidirectional airflow.

4.4.4 Negative pressure zones should, as far as possible, be encapsulated by surrounding areas with clean air supplies, so that only clean air can infiltrate into the controlled zone.

4.5 Cross-contamination

4.5.1 Where different products are manufactured at the same time, in different areas or cubicles, in a multiproduct OSD manufacturing site, measures should be taken to ensure that dust cannot move from one cubicle to another.

4.5.2 Correct directional air movement and a pressure cascade system can assist in preventing cross-contamination. The pressure cascade should be such that the direction of airflow is from the clean corridor into the cubicles, resulting in dust containment.

4.5.3 The corridor should be maintained at a higher pressure than the cubicles, and the cubicles at a higher pressure than atmospheric pressure.

4.5.4 Containment can normally be achieved by application of the displacement concept (low pressure differential, high airflow), or the pressure differential concept (high pressure differential, low airflow), or the physical barrier concept.

4.5.5 The pressure cascade regime and the direction of airflow should be appropriate to the product and processing method used.

4.5.6 Highly potent products should be manufactured under a pressure cascade regime that is negative relative to atmospheric pressure.

4.5.7 The pressure cascade for each facility should be individually assessed according to the product handled and level of protection required.

4.5.8 Building structure should be given special attention to accommodate the pressure cascade design.

4.5.9 Airtight ceilings and walls, close fitting doors and sealed light fittings should be in place.

Displacement concept (low pressure differential, high airflow)

Note: This method of containment is not the preferred method, as the measurement and monitoring of airflow velocities in doorways is difficult. This concept should ideally be applied in production processes where large amounts of dust are generated.

4.5.10 Under this concept the air should be supplied to the corridor, flow through the doorway, and be extracted from the back of the cubicle. Normally the cubicle door should be closed and the air should enter the cubicle through a door grille, although the concept can be applied to an opening without a door.

4.5.11 The velocity should be high enough to prevent turbulence within the doorway resulting in dust escaping.

4.5.12 This displacement airflow should be calculated as the product of the door area and the velocity, which generally results in fairly large air quantities.

Pressure differential concept (high pressure differential, low airflow)

Note: The pressure differential concept may normally be used in zones where little or no dust is being generated. It may be used alone or in combination with other containment control techniques and concepts, such as a double door airlock.

4.5.13 The high pressure differential between the clean and less clean zones should be generated by leakage through the gaps of the closed doors to the cubicle.

4.5.14 The pressure differential should be of sufficient magnitude to ensure containment and prevention of flow reversal, but should not be so high as to create turbulence problems.

4.5.15 In considering room pressure differentials, transient variations, such as machine extract systems, should be taken into consideration.
Note: The most widely accepted pressure differential for achieving containment between two adjacent zones is 15 Pa, but pressure differentials of between 5 Pa and 20 Pa may be acceptable. Where the design pressure differential is too low and tolerances are at opposite extremities, a flow reversal can take place. For example, where a control tolerance of ±3 Pa is specified, the implications of the upper and lower tolerances on containment should be evaluated.

4.5.16 The pressure differential between adjacent rooms could be considered a critical parameter, depending on the outcome of risk analysis. The limits for the pressure differential between adjacent areas should be such that there is no risk of overlap, e.g. 5 Pa to 15 Pa in one room and 15 Pa to 30 Pa in an adjacent room, resulting in no pressure cascade, if the first room is at the maximum tolerance and the second room is at the minimum tolerance.

4.5.17 Low pressure differentials may be acceptable when airlocks (pressure sinks or pressure bubbles) are used.

4.5.18 The effect of room pressure tolerances are illustrated in Fig. 18.

4.5.19 The pressure control and monitoring devices used should be calibrated and qualified. Compliance with specifications should be regularly verified and the results recorded. Pressure control devices should be linked to an alarm system set according to the levels determined by a risk analysis.

Figure 18. Examples of pressure cascades

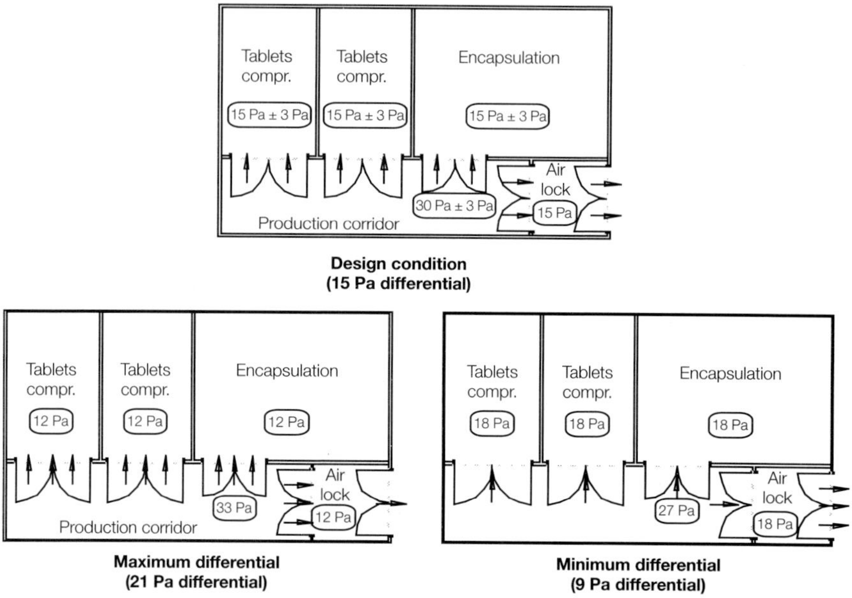

4.5.20 Manual control systems, where used, should be set up during commissioning and should not change unless other system conditions change.

4.5.21 Airlocks can be important components in setting up and maintaining pressure cascade systems.

4.5.22 Airlocks with different pressure cascade regimes include the cascade airlock, sink airlock and bubble airlock (Figs 19–21).

- Cascade airlock: high pressure on one side of the airlock and low pressure on the other.
- Sink airlock: low pressure inside the airlock and high pressure on both outer sides.
- Bubble airlock: high pressure inside the airlock and low pressure on both outer sides.

4.5.23 Doors should open to the high pressure side, and be provided with self-closers. Door closer springs, if used, should be designed to hold the door closed and prevent the pressure differential from pushing the door open. Sliding doors are not recommended.

4.5.24 Central dust extraction systems should be interlocked with the appropriate air handling systems, to ensure that they operate simultaneously.

Figure 19. Example of cascade airlock

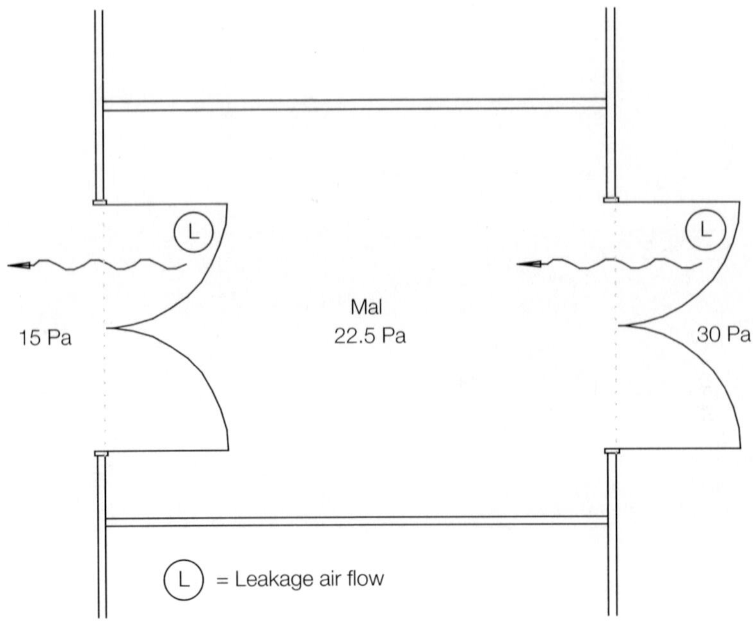

MAL, Material airlock.

Figure 20. Example of sink airlock

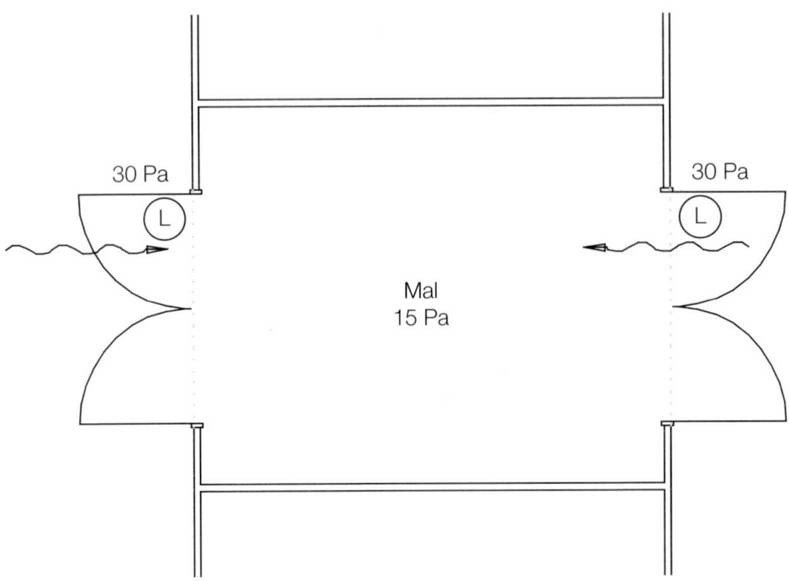

MAL, Material airlock.

Figure 21. Example of bubble airlock

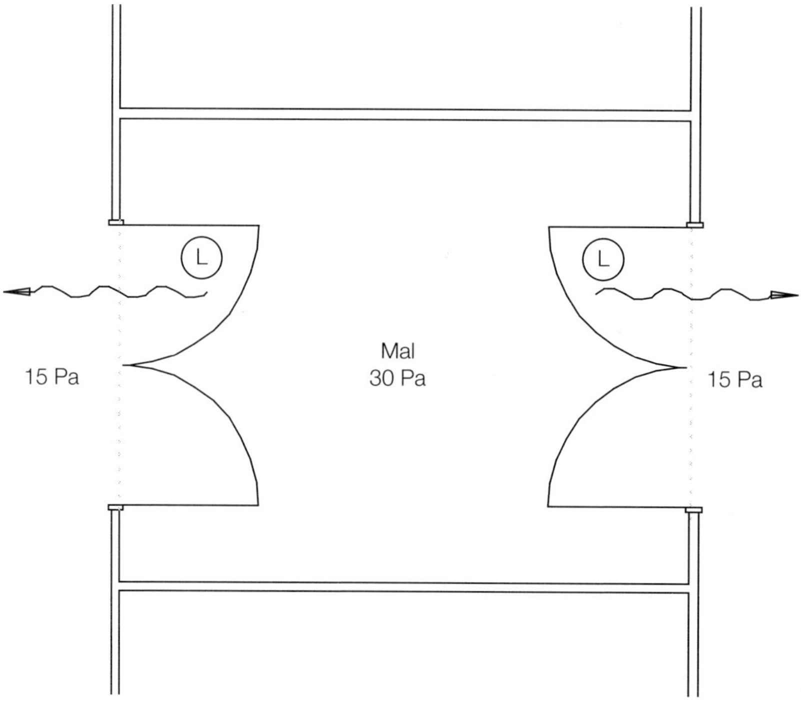

MAL, Material airlock.

4.5.25 Room pressure imbalance between adjacent cubicles which are linked by common dust extraction ducting should be prevented.

4.5.26 Air should not flow from the room with the higher pressure to the room with the lower pressure, via the dust extract ducting (this would normally occur only if the dust extraction system was inoperative).

Physical barrier concept

4.5.27 Where appropriate, an impervious barrier to prevent cross-contamination between two zones, such as barrier isolators or pumped transfer of materials, should be used.

4.5.28 Spot ventilation or capture hoods may be used as appropriate.

4.6 Temperature and relative humidity

4.6.1 Temperature and relative humidity should be controlled, monitored and recorded, where relevant, to ensure compliance with requirements pertinent to the materials and products, and to provide a comfortable environment for the operator where necessary.

4.6.2 Maximum and minimum room temperatures and relative humidity should be appropriate.

4.6.3 Temperature conditions should be adjusted to suit the needs of the operators while wearing their protective clothing.

4.6.4 The operating band, or tolerance, between the acceptable minimum and maximum temperatures should not be made too close.

4.6.5 Cubicles, or suites, in which products requiring low humidity are processed, should have well-sealed walls and ceilings and should also be separated from adjacent areas with higher humidity by means of suitable airlocks.

4.6.6 Precautions should be taken to prevent moisture migration that increases the load on the HVAC system.

4.6.7 Humidity control should be achieved by removing moisture from the air, or adding moisture to the air, as relevant.

4.6.8 Dehumidification (moisture removal) may be achieved by means of either refrigerated dehumidifiers or chemical dehumidifiers.

4.6.9 Appropriate cooling media for dehumidification such as low temperature chilled water/glycol mixture or refrigerant should be used.

4.6.10 Humidifiers should be avoided if possible as they may become a source of contamination (e.g. microbiological growth). Where humidification is required, this should be achieved by appropriate means such as the injection of steam into the air stream. A product-contamination assessment should be done to determine whether pure or clean steam is required for the purposes of humidification.

4.6.11 Where steam humidifiers are used, chemicals such as corrosion inhibitors or chelating agents, which could have a detrimental effect on the product, should not be added to the boiler system.

4.6.12 Humidification systems should be well drained. No condensate should accumulate in air-handling systems.

4.6.13 Other humidification appliances such as evaporative systems, atomizers and water mist sprays, should not be used because of the potential risk of microbial contamination.

4.6.14 Duct material in the vicinity of the humidifier should not add contaminants to air that will not be filtered downstream.

4.6.15 Air filters should not be installed immediately downstream of humidifiers.

4.6.16 Cold surfaces should be insulated to prevent condensation within the clean area or on air-handling components.

4.6.17 When specifying relative humidity, the associated temperature should also be specified.

4.6.18 Chemical driers using silica gel or lithium chloride are acceptable, provided that they do not become sources of contamination.

5. Dust control

5.1 Wherever possible, the dust or vapour contamination should be removed at source. Point-of-use extraction, i.e. as close as possible to the point where the dust is generated, should be employed.

5.2 Point-of-use extraction should be either in the form of a fixed high velocity extraction point or an articulated arm with movable hood or a fixed extraction hood.

5.3 Dust extraction ducting should be designed with sufficient transfer velocity to ensure that dust is carried away, and does not settle in the ducting.

5.4 The required transfer velocity should be determined: it is dependent on the density of the dust (the denser the dust, the higher the transfer velocity should be, e.g. 15–20 m/s).

5.5 Airflow direction should be carefully chosen, to ensure that the operator does not contaminate the product, and so that the operator is not put at risk by the product.

5.6 Dust-related hazards to which the operators may be subjected should be assessed. An analysis of the type of dust and toxicity thereof should be done and the airflow direction determined accordingly.

5.7 Point extraction alone is usually not sufficient to capture all of the contaminants, and general directional airflow should be used to assist in removing dust and vapours from the room.

5.8 Typically, in a room operating with turbulent airflow, the air should be introduced from ceiling diffusers and extracted from the room at low level to help give a flushing effect in the room.

5.9 The low-level extraction should assist in drawing air downwards and away from the operator's face. The extract grilles should be positioned strategically

Figure 22. Protective garments

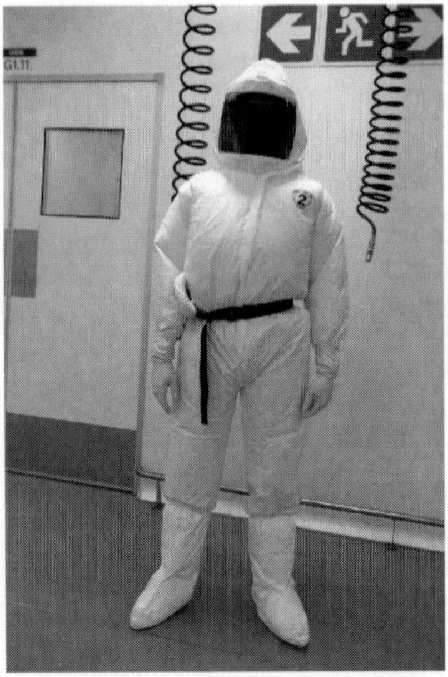

to draw air away from the operator, but at the same time to prevent the operator from contaminating the product.

5.10 When planning the system for the extraction of vapours, the density of the vapour should be taken into account. If the vapour is lighter than air, the extract grilles should be at a high level, or possibly at both high and low levels.

5.11 When dealing with particularly harmful products, additional steps, such as handling the products in glove boxes or using barrier isolator technology, should be used.

5.12 When working with exposed products such as hormones or highly potent products, operators should wear totally enclosed garments, as indicated in Fig. 22. Operators should also be equipped with an air-breathing system that provides a supply of filtered and conditioned air. The air supply to this type of breathing apparatus should normally be through an air compressor. Filtration, temperature and humidity need to be controlled to ensure operator safety and comfort.

5.13 The rates at which fresh air is supplied to the facility should comply with national, regional and/or international regulations, to provide operators with an acceptable level of comfort and safety and also to remove odours or fumes.

5.14 The rate of fresh airflow should also be determined by leakage from the building, for pressure control purposes.

6. Protection of the environment

6.1 Dust in exhaust air

6.1.1 Exhaust air discharge points on pharmaceutical equipment and facilities, such as from fluid bed driers and tablet-coating equipment, and exhaust air from dust extraction systems, carry heavy dust loads and should be provided with adequate filtration to prevent contamination of the ambient air.

6.1.2 Where the powders are not highly potent, final filters on a dust exhaust system should be fine dust filters with a filter classification of F9 according to EN779 filter standards.

6.1.3 Where harmful substances such as penicillin, hormones, toxic powders and enzymes are manufactured, the final filters on the dust exhaust system should be HEPA filters with at least an H12 classification according to EN1822 filter standards, as appropriate.

6.1.4 For exhaust systems where the discharge contaminant is considered particularly hazardous, it may be necessary to install two banks of HEPA filters in series, to provide additional protection should the first filter fail.

6.1.5 When handling hazardous compounds, safe-change filter housings, also called "bag-in-bag-out" filters, should be used.

6.1.6 All filter banks should be provided with pressure differential indication gauges to indicate the filter dust loading.

6.1.7 Filter pressure gauges should be marked with the clean filter resistance and the change-out filter resistance.

6.1.8 Exhaust filters should be monitored regularly to prevent excessive filter loading that could force dust particles through the filter media, or could cause the filters to burst, resulting in contamination of the ambient air.

6.1.9 Sophisticated computer-based data monitoring systems may be installed, with which preventive maintenance is planned by trend logging (This type of system is commonly referred to as a building management system (BMS), building automation system (BAS) or system control and data acquisition (SCADA) system.)

6.1.10 An automated monitoring system should be capable of indicating any out-of-specification condition without delay by means of an alarm or similar system.

6.1.11 Where reverse-pulse dust collectors are used for removing dust from dust extraction systems, they should usually be equipped with cartridge filters containing a compressed air lance, and be capable of continuous operation without interrupting the airflow.

6.1.12 Alternative types of dust collectors (such as those operating with a mechanical shaker, requiring that the fan be switched off when the mechanical shaker is activated) should be used in such a manner that there is no risk of cross-contamination. There should be no disruption of airflow during a production run as the loss of airflow could disrupt the pressure cascade.

6.1.13 Mechanical-shaker dust collectors should not be used for applications where continuous airflow is required.

6.1.14 When wet scrubbers are used, the dust-slurry should be removed by a suitable drainage system.

6.1.15 The quality of the exhaust air should be determined to see whether the filtration efficiency is adequate with all types of dust collectors and wet scrubbers.

6.1.16 Where necessary, additional filtration may be provided downstream of the dust collector.

6.2 Fume removal

6.2.1 The systems for fume, dust and effluent control should be designed, installed and operated in such a manner that they do not become possible sources of contamination or cross- contamination, e.g. an exhaust-air discharge point located close to the HVAC system fresh air inlet.

6.2.2 Fumes should be removed by means of wet scrubbers or dry chemical scrubbers (deep-bed scrubbers).

6.2.3 Wet scrubbers for fume removal normally require the addition of various chemicals to the water to increase the adsorption efficiency.

6.2.4 Deep-bed scrubbers should be designed with activated carbon filters or granular chemical adsorption media. The chemical media for deep-bed scrubbers should be specific to the effluent being treated.

6.2.5 The type and quantity of the vapours to be removed should be known to enable the appropriate filter media, as well as the volume of media required to be determined.

7. HVAC systems and components

Note: The required degree of air cleanliness in most OSD manufacturing facilities can normally be achieved without the use of high-efficiency particulate air (HEPA) filters, provided the air is not recirculated. Many open product zones

Figure 23. Air-handling system with chemical drying

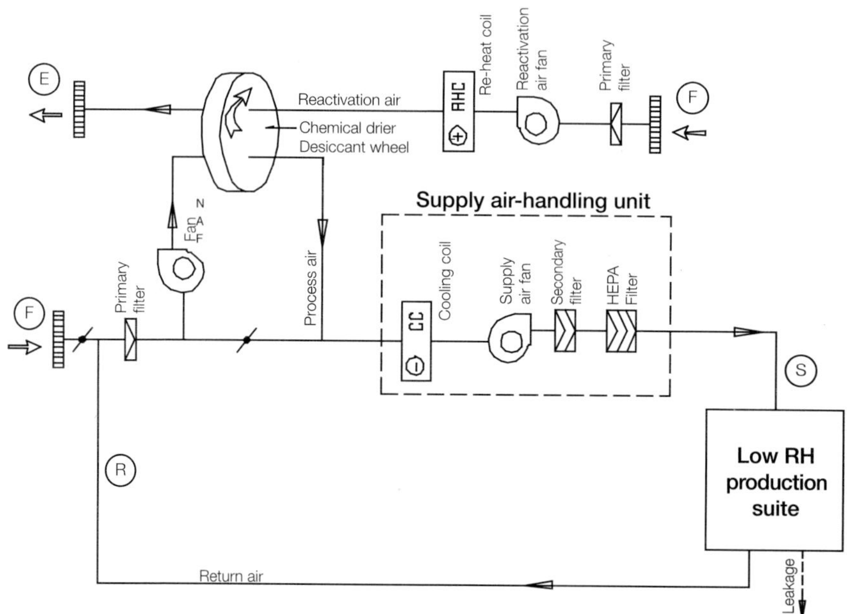

HEPA, high-efficiency particulate air; RH, relative humidity.

of OSD form facilities are capable of meeting ISO 14644-1 Class 8, "at-rest" condition, measured against particle sizes of 0.5 μm and 5 μm, but cleanliness may not be classified as such by manufacturers.

7.1 General

7.1.1 There should be no failure of a supply air fan, return air fan, exhaust air fan or dust extract system fan. Failure can cause a system imbalance, resulting in a pressure cascade malfunction with a resultant airflow reversal.

7.1.2 A schematic diagram of the airflow for a typical system serving a low humidity suite is represented in Fig. 23.

7.1.3 Air should be dried with a chemical drier (e.g. a rotating desiccant wheel which is continuously regenerated by means of passing hot air through one segment of the wheel).

7.1.4 The figure illustrates the chemical drier handling part of the fresh air/return air mixture on a by-pass flow. The location of the chemical drier should be considered in the design phase. Examples of appropriate locations include:

— full flow of fresh/return air;
— partial handling of fresh/return air (by-pass airflow);
— return air only;
— fresh air only; or
— pre-cooled air with any of the above alternatives.

7.1.5 Possible additional components that may be required should be considered depending on the climatic conditions and locations. These may include items such as:

— frost coils on fresh air inlets in very cold climates to preheat the air;
— snow eliminators to prevent snow entering air inlets and blocking airflow;
— dust eliminators on air inlets in arid and dusty locations;
— moisture eliminators in humid areas with high rainfall; and
— fresh air pre-cooling coils for very hot or humid climates.

7.1.6 Appropriate alarm systems should be in place to alert personnel if a critical fan fails.

7.1.7 Low-level return or exhaust air grilles are usually preferred. However, where this is not possible, a higher air change rate may be needed to achieve a specified clean area classification, e.g. where ceiling return air grilles are used.

7.1.8 There may be alternative locations for return air. For example, referring to Fig. 24, room D (low-level return air) and room E (ceiling return air).

The airflow schematics of the two systems (Figs 24 and 25) indicate air-handling units with return air or recirculated air, having a percentage of fresh air added. Fig. 25 is a schematic diagram of an air-handling system serving rooms with horizontal unidirectional flow, vertical unidirectional flow and turbulent flow, for rooms A, B and C, respectively.

The airflow diagram in Fig. 24 is an example of a typical system with a lower clean area classification.

Note: There are two basic concepts of air delivery to pharmaceutical production facilities: a recirculation system, and a full fresh air system (100% outside air supply).

7.2 Recirculation system

7.2.1 There should be no risk of contamination or cross-contamination (including by fumes and volatiles) due to recirculation of air.

7.2.2 Depending on the airborne contaminants in the return-air system it may be acceptable to use recirculated air, provided that HEPA filters are installed in the supply air stream to remove contaminants and thus prevent cross-contamination. The HEPA filters for this application should have an EN1822 classification of H13.

Figure 24. Air-handling system with high-efficiency particulate air filters in air-handling unit

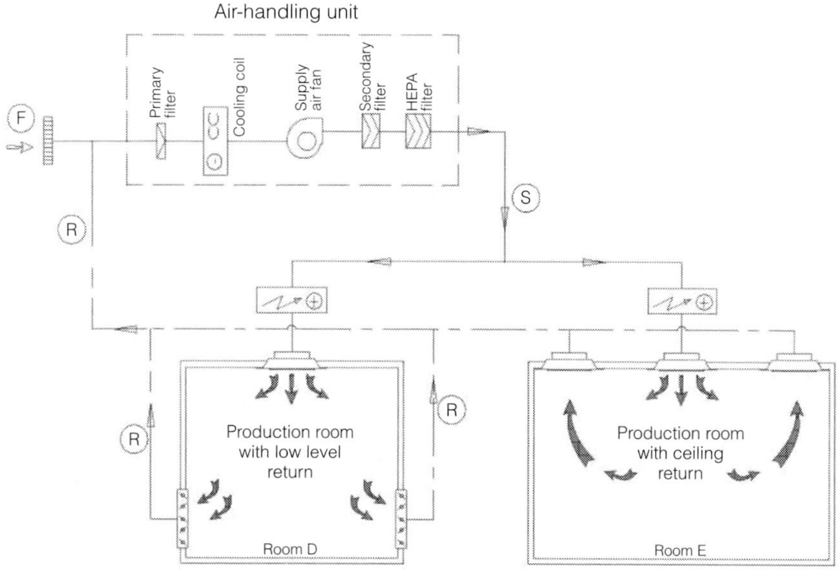

HEPA, high-efficiency particulate air

Figure 25. Horizontal unidirectional flow, vertical unidirectional flow and turbulent flow

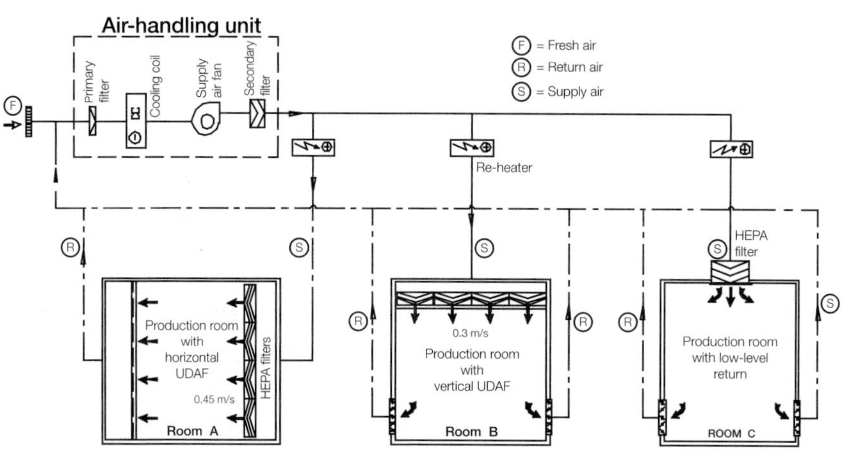

UDAF, unidirectional airflow; HEPA, high-efficiency particulate air.

Figure 26. Full fresh-air system

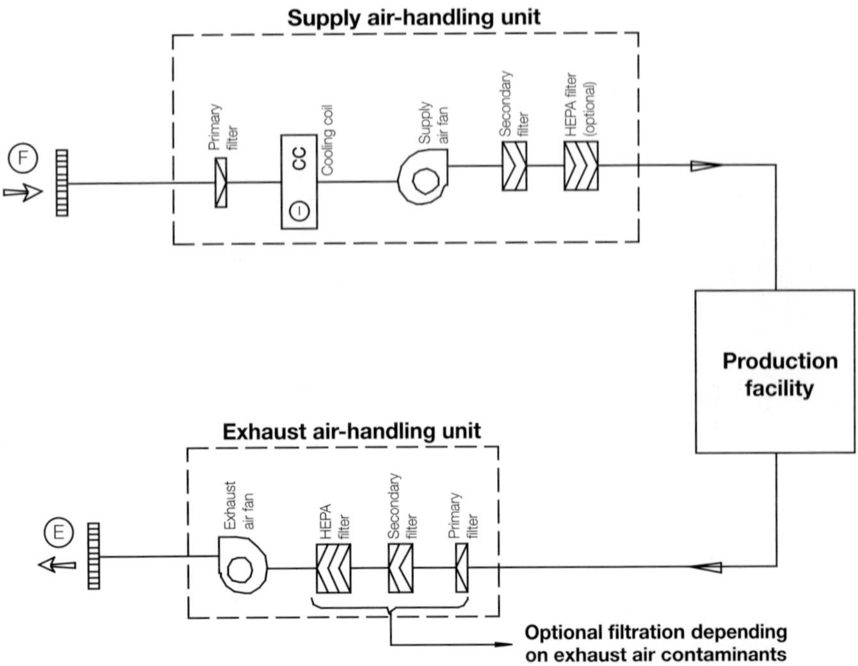

7.2.3 HEPA filters may not be required where the air-handling system is serving a single product facility and there is evidence that cross-contamination would not be possible.

7.2.4 Recirculation of air from areas where pharmaceutical dust is not generated such as secondary packing, may not require HEPA filters in the system.

7.2.5 HEPA filters may be located in the air-handling unit or placed terminally.

7.2.6 Air containing dust from highly toxic processes should never be recirculated to the HVAC system.

7.3 Full fresh-air systems

Fig. 26 indicates a system operating on 100% fresh air and would normally be used in a facility dealing with toxic products, where recirculation of air with contaminants should be avoided.

7.3.1 The required degree of filtration of the exhaust air depends on the exhaust air contaminants and local environmental regulations.

Figure 27. Full fresh-air system with energy recovery

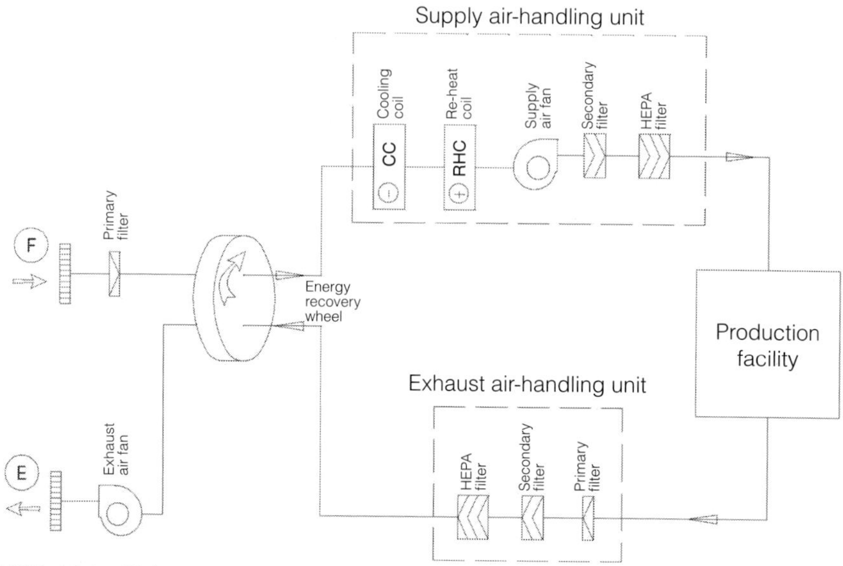

HEPA, high-efficiency particulate air.

7.3.2 Energy-recovery wheels should normally not be used in multiproduct facilities. When such wheels are used they should not become a source of possible contamination (see Fig. 27). *Note*: Alternatives to the energy-recovery wheels, such as crossover plate heat exchangers and water-coil heat exchangers, may be used in multiproduct facilities.

7.3.3 The potential for air leakage between the supply air and exhaust air as it passes through the wheel should be prevented. The relative pressures between supply and exhaust air systems should be such that the exhaust air system operates at a lower pressure than the supply system.

8. Commissioning, qualification and maintenance

8.1 Commissioning

8.1.1 Commissioning should include the setting up, balancing, adjustment and testing of the entire HVAC system, to ensure that it meets all the requirements, as specified in the user requirement specification (URS), and capacities as specified by the designer or developer.

8.1.2 The installation records of the system should provide documented evidence of all measured capacities of the system.

Figure 28. Qualification is a part of validation

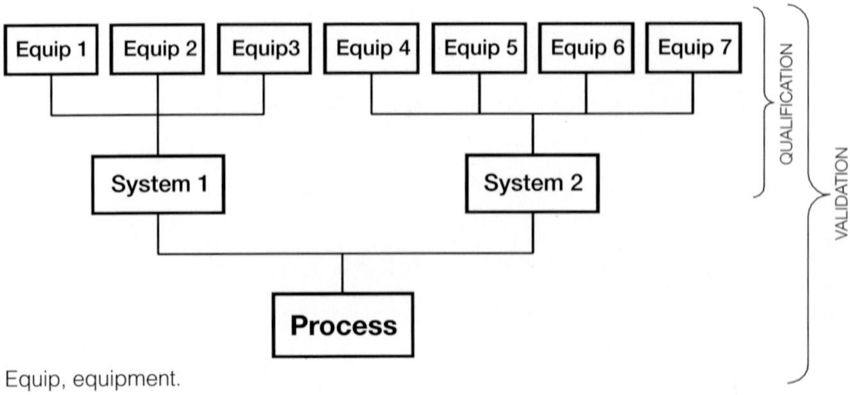

Equip, equipment.

8.1.3 The data should include items such as the design and measurement figures for airflows, water flows, system pressures and electrical amperages. These should be contained in the operating and maintenance manuals (O & M manuals).

8.1.4 Acceptable tolerances for all system parameters should be specified prior to commencing the physical installation.

8.1.5 Training should be provided to personnel after installation of the system, and should include operation and maintenance.

8.1.6 O & M manuals, schematic drawings, protocols and reports should be maintained as reference documents for any future changes and upgrades to the system.

8.1.7 Commissioning should be a precursor to system qualification and process validation.

8.2 Qualification

8.2.1 Validation is a many-faceted and extensive activity and is beyond the scope of these guidelines. Qualification and validation guidelines are included in: *Expert Committee on Specifications for Pharmaceutical Preparations. Fortieth report*. Geneva, World Health Organization, 2005 (WHO Technical Report Series, No. 937), Annex 4 (see also Fig. 28).

Manufacturers should qualify HVAC systems using a risk-based approach. The basic concepts of qualification of HVAC systems are set out below.

8.2.2 The qualification of the HVAC system should be described in a validation master plan (VMP).

8.2.3 It should define the nature and extent of testing and the test procedures and protocols to be followed.

8.2.4 Stages of the qualification of the HVAC system should include DQ, IQ, OQ and PQ.

8.2.5 Critical and non-critical parameters should be determined by means of a risk analysis for all HVAC installation components, subsystems and controls.

8.2.6 Any parameter that may affect the quality of the pharmaceutical product, or a direct impact component, should be considered a critical parameter.

8.2.7 All critical parameters should be included in the qualification process.

Note: A realistic approach to differentiating between critical and non-critical parameters is required, to avoid making the validation process unnecessarily complex.

Example:

- *The humidity of the room where the product is exposed should be considered a critical parameter when a humidity-sensitive product is being manufactured. The humidity sensors and the humidity monitoring system should, therefore, be qualified. The heat transfer system, chemical drier or steam humidifier, which is producing the humidity controlled air, is further removed from the product and may not require operational qualification.*
- *A room cleanliness classification is a critical parameter and, therefore, the room air change rates and HEPA filters should be critical parameters and require qualification. Items such as the fan generating the airflow and the primary and secondary filters are non-critical parameters, and may not require operational qualification.*

8.2.8 Non-critical systems and components should be subject to GEP and may not necessarily require qualification.

8.2.9 A change control procedure should be followed when changes are planned to the direct impact HVAC system, its components and controls that may affect critical parameters.

8.2.10 Acceptance criteria and limits should be defined during the design stage.

8.2.11 The manufacturer should define design conditions, normal operating ranges, operating ranges, and alert and action limits.

8.2.12 Design condition and normal operating ranges should be identified and set to realistically achievable parameters.

8.2.13 All parameters should fall within the design condition range during system operational qualification. Conditions may go out of the design condition

Figure 29. System operating ranges

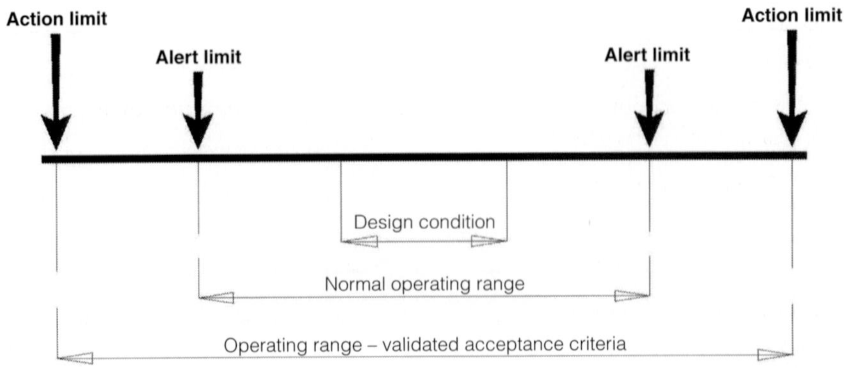

range during normal operating procedures but they should remain within the operating range.

8.2.14 Out-of-limit results (e.g. action limit deviations) should be recorded and form part of the batch manufacturing records.

8.2.15 The relationships between design conditions, operating range and qualified acceptance criteria are given in Fig. 29.

8.2.16 A narrow range of relative humidities coupled with a wide range of temperatures is unacceptable as changes in temperature will automatically give rise to variations in the relative humidity.

8.2.17 For a pharmaceutical facility, based on a risk assessment, some of the typical HVAC system parameters that should be qualified may include:

— temperature
— relative humidity
— supply air quantities for all diffusers
— return air or exhaust air quantities
— room air change rates
— room pressures (pressure differentials)
— room airflow patterns
— unidirectional flow velocities
— containment system velocities
— HEPA filter penetration tests
— room particle counts
— room clean-up rates
— microbiological air and surface counts where appropriate
— operation of de-dusting
— warning/alarm systems where applicable.

Table 3. Part A: schedule of tests to demonstrate compliance (for reference purposes only)

Schedule of tests to demonstrate continuing compliance			
Test parameter	Clean room class	Max. time interval	Test procedure
Particle count test (Verification of cleanliness)	All classes	6 months	Dust particle counts to be carried out and printouts of results produced. No. of readings and positions of tests to be in accordance with ISO 14644-1 Annex B
Air pressure difference (To verify absence of cross-contamination)	All classes	12 months	Log of pressure differential readings to be produced or critical plants should be logged daily, preferably continuously. A 15 Pa pressure differential between different zones is recommended. In accordance with ISO 14644-3 Annex B5*
Airflow volume (To verify air change rates)	All classes	12 months	Airflow readings for supply air and return air grilles to be measured and air change rates to be calculated. In accordance with ISO 14644-3 Annex B13*
Airflow velocity (To verify laminar flow or containment conditions)	All Classes	12 Months	Air velocities for containment systems and laminar flow protection systems to be measured. In accordance with ISO 14644-3 Annex B4*

8.2.18 The maximum time interval between tests should be defined by the manufacturer. The type of facility under test and the product level of protection should be considered.

Note: Table 3 gives intervals for reference purposes only. The actual test periods may be more frequent or less frequent, depending on the product and process.

8.2.19 Periodic requalification of parameters should be done at regular intervals, e.g. annually.

8.2.20 Requalification should also be done when any change, which could affect system performance, takes place.

8.2.21 Clean-up or recovery times normally relate to the time it takes to "clean up" the room from one condition to another, e.g. the relationship between "at-rest" and "operational" conditions in the clean area may be used as the criteria

Table 3. Part B: recommended optional strategic tests (ISO 14644)

Schedule of tests to demonstrate continuing compliance			
Test parameter	Clean room class	Max. time interval	Test procedure
Filter leakage tests (To verify filter integrity)	All classes	24 months	Filter penetration tests to be carried out by a recognized authority to demonstrate filter media and filter seal integrity. Only required on HEPA filters. In accordance with ISO 14644-3 Annex B6*
Containment leakage (To verify absence of cross-contamination)	All classes	24 months	Demonstrate that contaminant is maintained within a room by means of: • airflow direction smoke tests • room air pressures. In accordance with ISO 14644-3 Annex B4*
Recovery (To verify clean-up time)	All classes	24 months	Test to establish time that a clean room takes to return from a contaminated condition to the specified clean room condition. This should not take more than 15 min. In accordance with ISO 14644-3 Annex B13*
Airflow visualization (To verify required airflow patterns)	All classes	24 months	Tests to demonstrate airflows: • from clean to dirty areas • do not cause cross-contamination • uniformly from laminar flow units. Demonstrated by actual or video-taped smoke tests. In accordance with ISO 14644-3 Annex B7*

for clean-up tests. Therefore, the clean-up time can be expressed as the time taken to change from an "operational" condition to an "at rest" condition.

8.3 Maintenance

8.3.1 There should be a planned preventive maintenance programme, procedures and records for the HVAC system. Records should be kept.

8.3.2 Maintenance personnel should receive appropriate training.

8.3.3 HEPA filters should be changed either by a specialist or a trained person.

8.3.4 Any maintenance activity should be assessed critically to determine any impact on product quality including possible contamination.

8.3.5 Maintenance activities should normally be scheduled to take place outside production hours, and any system stoppage should be assessed with a view to the possible need for requalification of an area as a result of an interruption of the service.

Bibliography

ASHRAE handbook 1999. HVAC applications, SI edition. Atlanta, GA, ASHRAE, 1999.

ASHRAE handbook 2000. HVAC systems and equipment. Atlanta, GA, ASHRAE, 2000.

Daly BB. *Woods practical guide to fan engineering.* Colchester, Woods of Colchester Ltd. Third impression, June 1985. Cambridge, Cambridge University Press.

European Commission. The rules governing medicinal products in the European Community, Volume IV. *Good manufacturing practice for medicinal products.* European Commission, Brussels, 2005.

Good manufacturing practices for pharmaceutical products: main principles. *WHO Expert Committee on Specifications for Pharmaceutical Preparations. Thirty-seventh Report.* Geneva, World Health Organization, 2003 (WHO Technical Report Series, No. 908), Annex 4.

ISPE Baseline® pharmaceutical engineering guides, Volume 2. Oral solid dosage forms, 1st ed. Tampa, Fl, International Society for Pharmaceutical Engineering, 1998.

ISPE Baseline® pharmaceutical engineering guides for new and renovated facilities, Volume 5. Commissioning and qualification, 1st ed. Tampa, Fl, International Society for Pharmaceutical Engineering, 2001.

International Cleanroom Standards, ISO 14644. Geneva, International Organization for Standardization.

Luwa. Introduction to high efficiency filtration. *Bulletin* 50.10.10, Sheet 020.

Pharmaceutical Inspectorate Convention/Pharmaceutical Inspection Co-operation Scheme. *Guide to Good Manufacturing Practice for Medicinal Products.* PH 1/97 (Rev. 3), 15 January 2002.

Quality assurance of pharmaceuticals. A compendium of guidelines and related materials, Volume 1. Geneva, World Health Organization, 1997.

Quality Assurance of Pharmaceuticals. A compendium of guidelines and related materials, Volume 2, Updated edition. Good manufacturing practices and inspection. Geneva, World Health Organization, 2004.

World Health Organization. Supplements and updates available at: www.who.int/medicines.

Validation[1]

1. Introduction	101
2. Scope	102
3. Glossary	103
4. Relationship between validation and qualification	106
5. Validation	106
5.1 Approaches to validation	106
5.2 Scope of validation	106
6. Qualification	107
7. Calibration and verification	108
8. Validation master plan	108
9. Qualification and validation protocols	109
10. Qualification and validation reports	109
11. Qualification stages	110
12. Change control	112
13. Personnel	113
Appendix 1 Validation of heating, ventilation and air-conditioning systems	113
Appendix 2 Validation of water systems for pharmaceutical use	118
Appendix 3 Cleaning validation	120
Appendix 4 Analytical method validation	129
Appendix 5 Validation of computerized systems	133
Appendix 6 Qualification of systems and equipment	139
Appendix 7 Non-sterile process validation	165

1. Introduction

Validation is an essential part of good manufacturing practices (GMP). It is, therefore, an element of the quality assurance programme associated with a particular product or process. The basic principles of quality assurance have as their goal the production of products that are fit for their intended use. These principles are as follows:

---

[1] Supplementary guidelines on good manufacturing practices: validation. In: *WHO Expert Committee on Specifications for Pharmaceutical Preparations. Fortieth report.* Geneva, World Health Organization, 2006 (WHO Technical Report Series, No. 937), Annex 4.

- Quality, safety and efficacy must be designed and built into the product.
- Quality cannot be inspected or tested into the product.
- Each critical step of the manufacturing process must be validated. Other steps in the process must be under control to maximize the probability that the finished product consistently and predictably meets all quality and design specifications.

Validation of processes and systems is fundamental to achieving these goals. It is by design and validation that a manufacturer can establish confidence that the manufactured products will consistently meet their product specifications.

Documentation associated with validation includes:

— standard operating procedures (SOPs)
— specifications
— validation master plan (VMP)
— qualification protocols and reports
— validation protocols and reports.

The implementation of validation work requires considerable resources such as:

- *Time:* generally validation work is subject to rigorous time schedules.
- *Financial:* validation often requires the time of specialized personnel and expensive technology.
- *Human:* validation requires the collaboration of experts from various disciplines (e.g. a multidisciplinary team, comprising quality assurance, engineering, manufacturing and other disciplines, depending on the product and process to be validated).

These guidelines aim to give guidance to inspectors of pharmaceutical manufacturing facilities and manufacturers of pharmaceutical products on the requirements for validation. The main part covers the general principles of validation and qualification. In addition to the main part, appendices on validation and qualification (e.g. cleaning, computer and computerized systems, equipment, utilities and systems, and analytical methods) are included.

2. Scope

2.1 These guidelines focus mainly on the overall concept of validation and are intended as a basic guide for use by GMP inspectors and manufacturers. It is not the intention to be prescriptive in specific validation requirements. This document serves as general guidance only, and the principles may be considered useful in its application in the manufacture and control of active pharmaceutical ingredients (APIs) and finished pharmaceutical products. Validation of specific processes and products, for example in sterile product manufacture, requires much more consideration and a detailed approach that is beyond the scope of this document.

2.2 There are many factors affecting the different types of validation and it is, therefore, not intended to define and address all aspects related to one particular type of validation here.

2.3 Manufacturers should plan validation in a manner that will ensure regulatory compliance and ensuring that product quality, safety and consistency are not compromised.

2.4 The general text in the main part of these guidelines may be applicable to validation and qualification of premises, equipment, utilities and systems, and processes and procedures. More specific principles of qualification and validation are addressed in the appendices. Semi-automatic or fully automatic clean-in-place (CIP) systems and other special cases should be treated separately.

3. Glossary

The definitions given below apply to the terms used in these guidelines. They may have different meanings in other contexts.

calibration
The set of operations that establish, under specified conditions, the relationship between values indicated by an instrument or system for measuring (for example, weight, temperature and pH), recording, and controlling, or the values represented by a material measure, and the corresponding known values of a reference standard. Limits for acceptance of the results of measuring should be established.

cleaning validation
Documented evidence to establish that cleaning procedures are removing residues to predetermined levels of acceptability, taking into consideration factors such as batch size, dosing, toxicology and equipment size.

commissioning
The setting up, adjustment and testing of equipment or a system to ensure that it meets all the requirements, as specified in the user requirement specification, and capacities as specified by the designer or developer. Commissioning is carried out before qualification and validation.

computer validation
Documented evidence which provides a high degree of assurance that a computerized system analyses, controls and records data correctly and that data processing complies with predetermined specifications.

concurrent validation
Validation carried out during routine production of products intended for sale.

design qualification (DQ)
Documented evidence that the premises, supporting systems, utilities, equipment and processes have been designed in accordance with the requirements of GMP.

good engineering practices (GEP)
Established engineering methods and standards that are applied throughout the project life-cycle to deliver appropriate, cost-effective solutions.

installation qualification (IQ)
The performance of tests to ensure that the installations (such as machines, measuring devices, utilities and manufacturing areas) used in a manufacturing process are appropriately selected and correctly installed and operate in accordance with established specifications.

operational qualification (OQ)
Documented verification that the system or subsystem performs as intended over all anticipated operating ranges.

performance qualification (PQ)
Documented verification that the equipment or system operates consistently and gives reproducibility within defined specifications and parameters for prolonged periods. (In the context of systems, the term "process validation" may also be used.)

process validation
Documented evidence which provides a high degree of assurance that a specific process will consistently result in a product that meets its predetermined specifications and quality characteristics.

prospective validation
Validation carried out during the development stage on the basis of a risk analysis of the production process, which is broken down into individual steps; these are then evaluated on the basis of past experience to determine whether they may lead to critical situations.

qualification
Action of proving and documenting that any premises, systems and equipment are properly installed, and/or work correctly and lead to the expected results. Qualification is often a part (the initial stage) of validation, but the individual qualification steps alone do not constitute process validation.

retrospective validation
Involves the evaluation of past experience of production on the condition that composition, procedures, and equipment remain unchanged.

revalidation
Repeated validation of an approved process (or a part thereof) to ensure continued compliance with established requirements.

standard operating procedure (SOP)
An authorized written procedure giving instructions for performing operations not necessarily specific to a given product or material but of a more general nature (e.g. equipment operation, maintenance and cleaning; validation; cleaning of premises and environmental control; sampling and inspection). Certain SOPs may be used to supplement product-specific master batch production documentation.

validation
Action of proving and documenting that any process, procedure or method actually and consistently leads to the expected results.

validation master plan (VMP)
The VMP is a high-level document that establishes an umbrella validation plan for the entire project and summarizes the manufacturer's overall philosophy and approach, to be used for establishing performance adequacy. It provides information on the manufacturer's validation work programme and defines details of and timescales for the validation work to be performed, including a statement of the responsibilities of those implementing the plan.

validation protocol (or plan) (VP)
A document describing the activities to be performed in a validation, including the acceptance criteria for the approval of a manufacturing process—or a part thereof—for routine use.

validation report (VR)
A document in which the records, results and evaluation of a completed validation programme are assembled and summarized. It may also contain proposals for the improvement of processes and/or equipment.

verification
The application of methods, procedures, tests and other evaluations, in addition to monitoring, to determine compliance with the GMP principles.

worst case
A condition or set of conditions encompassing the upper and lower processing limits for operating parameters and circumstances, within SOPs, which pose the greatest chance of product or process failure when compared to ideal conditions. Such conditions do not necessarily include product or process failure.

4. Relationship between validation and qualification

Validation and qualification are essentially components of the same concept. The term qualification is normally used for equipment, utilities and systems, and validation for processes. In this sense, qualification is part of validation.

5. Validation

5.1 Approaches to validation

5.1.1 There are two basic approaches to validation—one based on evidence obtained through testing (prospective and concurrent validation), and one based on the analysis of accumulated (historical) data (retrospective validation). Whenever possible, prospective validation is preferred. Retrospective validation is no longer encouraged and is, in any case, not applicable to the manufacturing of sterile products.

5.1.2 Both prospective and concurrent validation, may include:

- extensive product testing, which may involve extensive sample testing (with the estimation of confidence limits for individual results) and the demonstration of intra- and inter-batch homogeneity;
- simulation process trials;
- challenge/worst case tests, which determine the robustness of the process; and
- control of process parameters being monitored during normal production runs to obtain additional information on the reliability of the process.

5.2 Scope of validation

5.2.1 There should be an appropriate and sufficient system including organizational structure and documentation infrastructure, sufficient personnel and financial resources to perform validation tasks in a timely manner. Management and persons responsible for quality assurance should be involved.

5.2.2 Personnel with appropriate qualifications and experience should be responsible for performing validation. They should represent different departments depending on the validation work to be performed.

5.2.3 There should be proper preparation and planning before validation is performed. There should be a specific programme for validation activities.

5.2.4 Validation should be performed in a structured way according to the documented procedures and protocols.

5.2.5 Validation should be performed:

— for new premises, equipment, utilities and systems, and processes and procedures;
— at periodic intervals; and
— when major changes have been made.

(Periodic revalidation or periodic requalification may be substituted, where appropriate, with periodic evaluation of data and information to establish whether requalification or revalidation is required.)

5.2.6 Validation should be performed in accordance with written protocols. A written report on the outcome of the validation should be produced.

5.2.7 Validation should be done over a period of time, e.g. at least three consecutive batches (full production scale) should be validated, to demonstrate consistency. Worst case situations should be considered.

5.2.8 There should be a clear distinction between in-process controls and validation. In-process tests are performed during the manufacture of each batch according to specifications and methods devised during the development phase. Their objective is to monitor the process continuously.

5.2.9 When a new manufacturing formula or method is adopted, steps should be taken to demonstrate its suitability for routine processing. The defined process, using the materials and equipment specified, should be shown to result in the consistent yield of a product of the required quality.

5.2.10 Manufacturers should identify what validation work is needed to prove that critical aspects of their operations are appropriately controlled. Significant changes to the facilities or the equipment, and processes that may affect the quality of the product should be validated. A risk assessment approach should be used to determine the scope and extent of validation required.

6. Qualification

6.1 Qualification should be completed before process validation is performed. The process of qualification should be a logical, systematic process and should start from the design phase of the premises, equipment, utilities and equipment.

6.2 Depending on the function and operation of the equipment, utility or system, only installation qualification (IQ) and operational qualification (OQ) may be required, as the correct operation of the equipment, utility or system could be considered to be a sufficient indicator of its performance (refer to Section 11 for IQ, OQ and performance qualification (PQ)). (The equipment, utility and system should then be maintained, monitored and calibrated according to a regular schedule.)

6.3 Major equipment and critical utilities and systems, however, require IQ, OQ and PQ.

7. Calibration and verification

7.1 Calibration and verification of equipment, instruments and other devices, as applicable, used in production and quality control, should be performed at regular intervals.

7.2 Personnel who carry out calibration and preventive maintenance should have appropriate qualifications and training.

7.3 A calibration programme should be available and should provide information such as calibration standards and limits, responsible persons, calibration intervals, records and actions to be taken when problems are identified.

7.4 There should be traceability to standards (e.g. national, regional or international standards) used in the calibration.

7.5 Calibrated equipment, instruments and other devices should be labelled, coded or otherwise identified to indicate the status of calibration and the date on which recalibration is due.

7.6 When the equipment, instruments and other devices have not been used for a certain period of time, their function and calibration status should be verified and shown to be satisfactory before use.

8. Validation master plan

The validation master plan (VMP) should reflect the key elements of the validation programme. It should be concise and clear and contain at least the following:

- — a validation policy
- — organizational structure of validation activities
- — summary of facilities, systems, equipment and processes validated and to be validated
- — documentation format (e.g. protocol and report format)
- — planning and scheduling
- — change control
- — references to existing documents.

9. Qualification and validation protocols

9.1 There should be qualification and validation protocols describing the qualification and validation study to be performed.

9.2 As a minimum the protocols should include the following significant background information:

— the objectives of the study
— the site of the study
— the responsible personnel
— description of SOPs to be followed
— equipment to be used; standards and criteria for the relevant products and processes
— the type of validation
— the processes and/or parameters
— sampling, testing and monitoring requirements
— predetermined acceptance criteria for drawing conclusions.

9.3 There should be a description of the way in which the results will be analysed.

9.4 The protocol should be approved prior to use. Any changes to a protocol should be approved prior to implementation of the change.

10. Qualification and validation reports

10.1 There should be written reports on the qualification and validation performed.

10.2 Reports should reflect the protocols followed and include at least the title and objective of the study; reference to the protocol; details of material, equipment, programmes and cycles used; procedures and test methods.

10.3 The results should be evaluated, analysed and compared against the predetermined acceptance criteria. The results should meet the acceptance criteria; deviations and out-of-limit results should be investigated. If these deviations are accepted, this should be justified. Where necessary further studies should be performed.

10.4 The departments responsible for the qualification and validation work should approve the completed report.

10.5 The conclusion of the report should state whether or not the outcome of the qualification and/or validation was considered successful.

10.6 The quality assurance department should approve the report after the final review. The criteria for approval should be in accordance with the company's quality assurance system.

10.7 Any deviations found during the validation process should be acted upon and documented as such. Corrective actions may be required.

11. Qualification stages

11.1 There are four stages of qualification:

— design qualification (DQ);
— installation qualification (IQ);
— operational qualification (OQ); and
— performance qualification (PQ).

11.2 All SOPs for operation, maintenance and calibration should be prepared during qualification.

11.3. Training should be provided to operators and training records should be maintained.

Design qualification

11.4 Design qualification should provide documented evidence that the design specifications were met.

Installation qualification

11.5 Installation qualification should provide documented evidence that the installation was complete and satisfactory.

11.6 The purchase specifications, drawings, manuals, spare parts lists and vendor details should be verified during installation qualification.

11.7 Control and measuring devices should be calibrated.

Operational qualification

11.8 Operational qualification should provide documented evidence that utilities, systems or equipment and all its components operate in accordance with operational specifications.

11.9 Tests should be designed to demonstrate satisfactory operation over the normal operating range as well as at the limits of its operating conditions (including worst case conditions).

11.10 Operation controls, alarms, switches, displays and other operational components should be tested.

11.11 Measurements made in accordance with a statistical approach should be fully described.

Performance qualification

11.12 Performance qualification should provide documented evidence that utilities, systems or equipment and all its components can consistently perform in accordance with the specifications under routine use.

11.13 Test results should be collected over a suitable period of time to prove consistency.

Requalification

11.14 Requalification should be done in accordance with a defined schedule. The frequency of requalification may be determined on the basis of factors such as the analysis of results relating to calibration, verification and maintenance.

11.15 There should be periodic requalification, as well as requalification after changes (such as changes to utilities, systems, equipment; maintenance work; and movement). (See also point 5.2.5 above and section 12 below.)

11.16 Requalification should be considered as part of the change control procedure.

Revalidation

11.17 Processes and procedures should be revalidated to ensure that they remain capable of achieving the intended results.

11.18 There should be periodic revalidation, as well as revalidation after changes. (See also points 5.2.5 above, point 11.21 below and section 12 below.)

11.19 Revalidation should be done in accordance with a defined schedule.

11.20 The frequency and extent of revalidation should be determined using a risk-based approach together with a review of historical data.

Periodic revalidation

11.21 Periodic revalidation should be performed to assess process changes that may occur gradually over a period of time, or because of wear of equipment.

11.22 The following should be considered when periodic revalidation is performed:

— master formulae and specifications;
— SOPs;
— records (e.g. of calibration, maintenance and cleaning); and
— analytical methods.

Revalidation after change

11.23 Revalidation should be performed following a change that could have an effect on the process, procedure, quality of the product and/or the product characteristics. Revalidation should be considered as part of the change control procedure.

11.24 The extent of revalidation will depend on the nature and significance of the change(s).

11.25 Changes should not adversely affect product quality or process characteristics.

11.26 Changes requiring revalidation should be defined in the validation plan and may include:

- changes in starting materials (including physical properties, such as density, viscosity or particle size distribution that may affect the process or product);
- change of starting material manufacturer;
- transfer of processes to a different site (including change of facilities and installations which influence the process);
- changes of primary packaging material (e.g. substituting plastic for glass);
- changes in the manufacturing process (e.g. mixing times or drying temperatures);
- changes in the equipment (e.g. addition of automatic detection systems, installation of new equipment, major revisions to machinery or apparatus and breakdowns);
- production area and support system changes (e.g. rearrangement of areas, or a new water treatment method);
- appearance of negative quality trends;
- appearance of new findings based on current knowledge, e.g. new technology;
- support system changes.

Changes of equipment which involve the replacement of equipment on a "like-for-like" basis would not normally require a revalidation. For example, installation of a new centrifugal pump to replace an older model would not necessarily require revalidation.

12. Change control

12.1 Changes should be controlled in accordance with a SOP as changes may have an impact on a qualified utility, system or piece of equipment, and a validated process and/or procedure.

12.2 The procedure should describe the actions to be taken, including the need for and extent of qualification or validation to be done.

12.3 Changes should be formally requested, documented and approved before implementation. Records should be maintained.

13. Personnel

13.1 Personnel should demonstrate that they are appropriately qualified, where relevant.

13.2 Personnel requiring qualification include, for example:

— laboratory analysts;
— personnel following critical procedures;
— personnel doing data entry in computerized systems; and
— risk assessors.

Appendix 1
Validation of heating, ventilation and air-conditioning systems

1. General	113
2. Commissioning	113
3. Qualification	114
4. Reference	118

1. General

1.1 The heating, ventilation and air-conditioning (HVAC) system plays an important role in the protection of the product, the personnel and the environment.

1.2 For all HVAC installation components, subsystems or parameters, critical parameters and non-critical parameters should be determined.

1.3 Some of the parameters of a typical HVAC system that should be qualified include:

— room temperature and humidity;
— supply air and return air quantities;
— room pressure, air change rate, flow patterns, particle count and cleanup rates; and
— unidirectional flow velocities and HEPA filter penetration tests.

2. Commissioning

2.1 Commissioning should involve the setting up, balancing, adjustment and testing of the entire HVAC system, to ensure that the system meets all the requirements, as specified in the user requirement specification, and capacities as specified by the designer or developer.

2.2 The installation records of the system should provide documented evidence of all measured capacities of the system.

2.3 The data should include items such as the design and measured figures for airflows, water flows, system pressures and electrical amperages. These should be contained in the operating and maintenance manuals (O & M manuals).

2.4 Acceptable tolerances for all system parameters should be specified prior to commencing the physical installation.

2.5 Training should be provided to personnel after installation of the system, and should include how to perform operation and maintenance.

2.6 O & M manuals, schematic drawings, protocols and reports should be maintained as reference documents for any future changes and upgrades to the system.

2.7 Commissioning should be a precursor to system qualification and validation.

3. Qualification

3.1 Manufacturers should qualify HVAC systems using a risk-based approach. The basic concepts of qualification of HVAC systems are set out in Fig. 1 below.

3.2 The qualification of the HVAC system should be described in a validation master plan (VMP).

3.3 The validation master plan should define the nature and extent of testing and the test procedures and protocols to be followed.

3.4 Stages of the qualification of the HVAC system should include design qualification (DQ), installation qualification (IQ), operational qualifi cation (OQ), and performance qualification (PQ).

3.5 Critical and non-critical parameters for all HVAC installation components, subsystems and controls should be determined by means of a risk analysis.

3.6 Any parameter that may affect the quality of the pharmaceutical product should be considered a critical parameter.

3.7 All critical parameters should be included in the qualification process.

Note: A realistic approach to differentiating between critical and noncritical parameters is required, to avoid making the validation process unnecessarily complex. Example:

Figure 1. Qualification is a part of validation

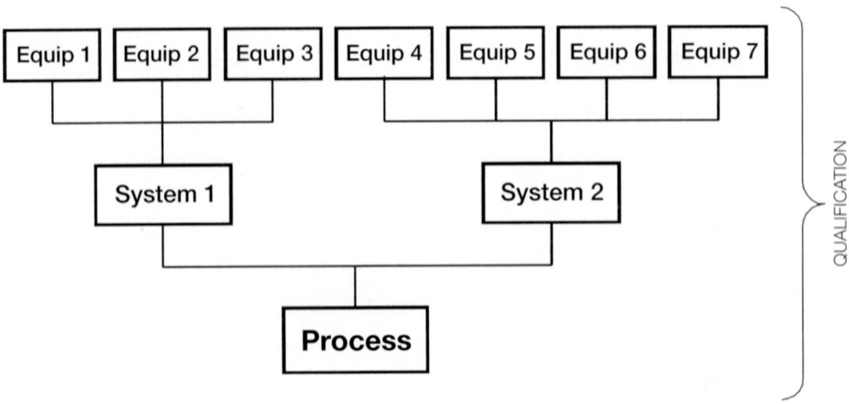

- *The humidity of the room where the product is exposed should be considered a critical parameter when a humidity-sensitive product is being manufactured. The humidity sensors and the humidity monitoring system should, therefore, be qualified. The heat transfer system, chemical drier or steam humidifier, which is producing the humidity-controlled air, is further removed from the product and may not require operational qualification.*
- *A room cleanliness classification is a critical parameter and, therefore, the room air-change rates and high-efficiency particulate air (HEPA) filters should be critical parameters and require qualification. Items such as the fan generating the airflow and the primary and secondary filters are non-critical parameters, and may not require operational qualification.*

3.8 Non-critical systems and components should be subject to good engineering practice (GEP) and may not necessarily require full qualification.

3.9 A change control procedure should be followed when changes are planned to the HVAC system, its components, and controls, that may affect critical parameters.

3.10 Acceptance criteria and limits should be defined during the design stage.

3.11 The manufacturer should define design conditions, normal operating ranges, operating ranges, and alert and action limits.

3.12 Design condition and normal operating ranges should be identified and set to realistically achievable parameters.

3.13 All parameters should fall within the design condition range during system operational qualification. Conditions may go out of the design condition range

Figure 2. System operating ranges

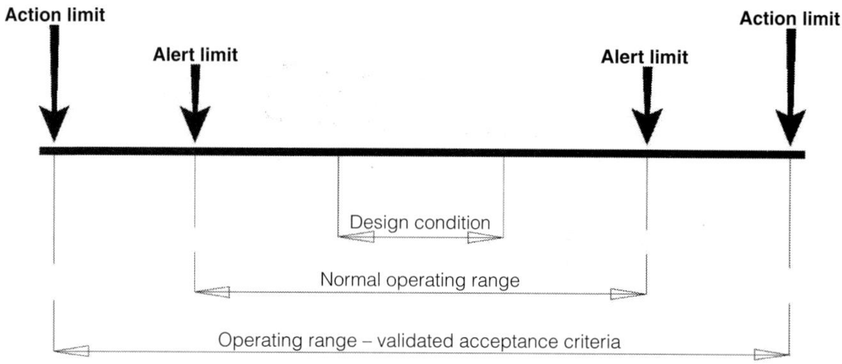

during normal operating procedures but they should remain within the operating range.

3.14 Out-of-limit results (e.g. action limit deviations) should be recorded and form part of the batch manufacturing records.

3.15 The relationships between design conditions, operating range and qualified acceptance criteria are given in Figure 2.

3.16 A narrow range of relative humidities coupled with a wide range of temperatures is unacceptable as changes in temperature will automatically give rise to variations in the relative humidity.

3.17 Some of the typical HVAC system parameters that should be qualified for a pharmaceutical facility may include:

— temperature
— relative humidity
— supply air quantities for all diffusers
— return air or exhaust air quantities
— room air-change rates
— room pressures (pressure differentials)
— room airflow patterns
— unidirectional flow velocities
— containment system velocities
— HEPA filter penetration tests
— room particle counts
— room clean-up rates
— microbiological air and surface counts where appropriate
— operation of de-dusting
— warning/alarm systems where applicable.

Table 1. Strategic tests (for reference purposes only)

Schedule of tests to demonstrate continuing compliance			
Test parameter	Clean area class	Max. time interval	Test procedure
Particle count test (verification of cleanliness)	All classes	6 months	Dust particle counts to be carried out and printouts of results produced. No. of readings and positions of tests to be in accordance with ISO 14644-1 Annex B
Air pressure difference (To verify absence of cross-contamination)	All classes	12 months	Log of pressure differential readings to be produced or critical plants should be logged daily, preferably continuously. A 15 Pa pressure differential between different zones is recommended. In accordance with ISO 14644-3 Annex B5
Airflow volume (To verify air change rates)	All classes	12 months	Airflow readings for supply air and return air grilles to be measured and air change rates to be calculated. In accordance with ISO 14644-3 Annex B13
Airflow velocity (To verify unidirectional flow or containment conditions)	All classes	12 months	Air velocities for containment systems and unidirectional flow protection systems to be measured. In accordance with ISO 14644-3 Annex B4

Source: ISO 14644 Standard, given for reference purposes only.

3.18 The maximum time interval between tests should be defined by the manufacturer. The type of facility under test and the product level of protection should be considered. *Note:* Table 1 gives intervals for reference purposes only. The actual test periods may be more or less frequent, depending on the product and process.

3.19 Periodic requalification of parameters should be done at regular intervals, e.g. annually.

3.20 Requalification should also be done when any change, which could affect system performance, takes place.

3.21 Clean-up times normally relate to the time it takes to "clean up" the room from one condition to another, e.g. the relationship between "at-rest" and "operational" conditions in the clean area may be used as the criteria for clean-up tests. Therefore, the clean-up time can be expressed as the time taken to change from an "operational" condition to an "at-rest" condition.

4. Reference

1. Supplementary guidelines on good manufacturing practices for heating, ventilation and air-conditioning systems for non-sterile pharmaceutical dosage forms. In: *WHO Expert Committee on Specifications for Pharmaceutical Preparations. Fortieth report.* Geneva, World Health Organization, 2006 (WHO Technical Report Series, No. 937), Annex 2.

Appendix 2
Validation of water systems for pharmaceutical use

1. General 118
2. Start-up and commissioning of water systems 118
3. Qualification 118
4. Reference 120

1. General

1.1 All water-treatment systems should be subject to planned maintenance, validation and monitoring.

1.2 Validation of water systems should consist of at least three phases: Phase 1: investigational phase; Phase 2: short-term control; and Phase 3: long-term control.

1.3 During the period following phase 3 (typically running for one year) the objective should be to demonstrate that the system is under control over a long period of time. Sampling may be reduced from, e.g. daily to weekly.

1.4 The validation performed and revalidation requirements should be included in the "Water quality manual".

2. Start-up and commissioning of water systems

2.1 Planned, well-defined, successful and well-documented commissioning is an essential precursor to successful validation of water systems. The commissioning work should include setting to work, system set-up, controls, loop tuning and recording of all system performance parameters. If it is intended to use or refer to commissioning data within the validation work then the quality of the commissioning work and associated data and documentation must be commensurate with the validation plan requirements.

3. Qualification

3.1 Water for pharmaceutical use (WPU), purified water (PW), highly purified water (HPW) and water for injections (WFI) systems are all considered to be direct impact, quality critical systems that should be qualified. The qualification should follow the validation convention of design review or design qualification (DQ), installation qualification (IQ), operational qualification (OQ) and performance qualification (PQ).

3.2 This guidance does not define the standard requirements for the conventional validation stages DQ, IQ and OQ, but concentrates on the particular PQ approach that should be used for WPU systems to demonstrate their consistent and reliable performance. A three-phase approach should be used to satisfy the objective of proving the reliability and robustness of the system in service over an extended period.

Phase 1. A test period of 2–4 weeks should be spent monitoring the system intensively. During this period the system should operate continuously without failure or performance deviation. The following procedures should be included in the testing approach.

- Undertake chemical and microbiological testing in accordance with a defined plan.
- Sample the incoming feed-water to verify its quality.
- Sample after each step in the purification process daily.
- Sample at each point of use and at other defined sampling points daily.
- Develop appropriate operating ranges.
- Develop and finalize operating, cleaning, sanitizing and maintenance procedures.
- Demonstrate production and delivery of product water of the required quality and quantity.
- Use and refine the standard operating procedures (SOPs) for operation, maintenance, sanitization and troubleshooting.
- Verify provisional alert and action levels.
- Develop and refine the test-failure procedure.

Phase 2. A further test period of 2–4 weeks should be spent carrying out further intensive monitoring while deploying all the refined SOPs after the satisfactory completion of phase 1. The sampling scheme should be generally the same as in phase 1. Water can be used for manufacturing purposes during this phase. The approach should also:

— demonstrate consistent operation within established ranges; and
— demonstrate consistent production and delivery of water of the required quantity and quality when the system is operated in accordance with the SOPs.

Phase 3. Phase 3 typically runs for one year after the satisfactory completion of phase 2. Water can be used for manufacturing purposes during this phase which has the following objectives and features:

- Demonstrate extended reliable performance.
- Ensure that seasonal variations are evaluated.
- The sample locations, sampling frequencies and tests should be reduced to the normal routine pattern based on established procedures proven during phases 1 and 2.

4. Reference

1. WHO good manufacturing practices: water for pharmaceutical use. In: *WHO Expert Committee on Specifications for Pharmaceutical Preparations. Thirty-ninth report.* Geneva, World Health Organization 2005 (WHO Technical Report Series, No. 929), Annex 3.

Appendix 3
Cleaning validation

1. Principle 120
2. Scope 121
3. General 121
4. Cleaning validation protocols and reports 122
   4.1 Cleaning validation protocols 122
   4.2 Cleaning validation reports 124
5. Personnel 124
6. Equipment 124
7. Detergents 124
8. Microbiology 125
9. Sampling 125
   9.1 General 125
   9.2 Direct surface sampling (direct method) 126
   9.3 Rinse samples (indirect method) 126
   9.4 Batch placebo method 126
10. Analytical methods 127
11. Establishing acceptable limits 127

1. Principle

1.1 The objectives of good manufacturing practices (GMP) include the prevention of possible contamination and cross-contamination of pharmaceutical starting materials and products.

1.2 Pharmaceutical products can be contaminated by a variety of substances such as contaminants associated with microbes, previous products (both active pharmaceutical ingredients (API) and excipient residues), residues of cleaning agents, airborne materials, such as dust and particulate matter, lubricants and ancillary material, such as disinfectants, and decomposition residues from:

— product residue breakdown occasioned by, e.g. the use of strong acids and alkalis during the cleaning process; and
— breakdown products of the detergents, acids and alkalis that may be used as part of the cleaning process.

1.3 Adequate cleaning procedures play an important role in preventing contamination and cross-contamination. Validation of cleaning methods provides documented evidence that an approved cleaning procedure will provide clean equipment, suitable for its intended use.

1.4 The objective of cleaning validation is to prove that the equipment is consistently cleaned of product, detergent and microbial residues to an acceptable level, to prevent possible contamination and cross-contamination.

1.5 Cleaning validation is not necessarily required for non-critical cleaning such as that which takes place between batches of the same product (or different lots of the same intermediate in a bulk process), or of floors, walls, the outside of vessels, and following some intermediate steps.

1.6 Cleaning validation should be considered important in multiproduct facilities and should be performed among others, for equipment, sanitization procedures and garment laundering.

2. Scope

2.1 These guidelines describe the general aspects of cleaning validation, excluding specialized cleaning or inactivation that may be required, e.g. for removal of viral or mycoplasmal contaminants in the biological manufacturing industry.

2.2 Normally cleaning validation would be applicable for critical cleaning such as cleaning between manufacturing of one product and another, of surfaces that come into contact with products, drug products and API.

3. General

3.1 There should be written SOPs detailing the cleaning process for equipment and apparatus. The cleaning procedures should be validated.

3.2 The manufacturer should have a cleaning policy and an appropriate procedure for cleaning validation, covering:

- surfaces that come into contact with the product;
- cleaning after product changeover (when one pharmaceutical formulation is being changed for another, completely different formulation);
- between batches in campaigns (when the same formula is being manufactured over a period of time, and on different days);

- bracketing products for cleaning validation. (This often arises where products contain substances with similar properties (such as solubility) or the same substance in different strengths. An acceptable strategy is to first manufacture the more dilute form (not necessarily the lowest dose) and then the most concentrated form. There are sometimes "families" of products which differ slightly as to actives or excipients.); and
- periodic evaluation and revalidation of the number of batches manufactured between cleaning validations.

3.3 At least three consecutive applications of the cleaning procedure should be performed and shown to be successful to prove that the method is validated.

4. Cleaning validation protocols and reports

4.1 Cleaning validation protocols

4.1.1 Cleaning validation should be described in cleaning validation protocols, which should be formally approved, e.g. by the quality control or quality assurance unit.

4.1.2 In preparing the cleaning validation protocol, the following should be considered:

— disassembly of system;
— precleaning;
— cleaning agent, concentration, solution volume, water quality;
— time and temperature;
— flow rate, pressure and rinsing;
— complexity and design of the equipment;
— training of operators; and
— size of the system.

4.1.3 The cleaning validation protocol should include:

- the objectives of the validation process;
- the people responsible for performing and approving the validation study;
- the description of the equipment to be used, including a list of the equipment, make, model, serial number or other unique code;
- the interval between the end of production and the commencement of the cleaning procedure (interval may be part of the validation challenge study itself)
  - — the maximum period that equipment may be left dirty before being cleaned as well as the establishment of the time that should elapse after cleaning and before use;

- the levels of microorganisms (bioburden);
- the cleaning procedures (documented in an existing SOP, including definition of any automated process) to be used for each product, each manufacturing system or each piece of equipment;
- all the equipment used for routine monitoring, e.g. conductivity meters, pH meters and total organic carbon analysers;
- the number of cleaning cycles to be performed consecutively;
- the sampling procedures to be used (direct sampling, rinse sampling, in-process monitoring and sampling locations) and the rationale for their use;
- the data on recovery studies (efficiency of the recovery of the sampling technique should be established);
- the analytical methods (specificity and sensitivity) including the limit of detection and the limit of quantification;
- the acceptance criteria (with rationale for setting the specific limits) including a margin for error and for sampling efficiency;
- the choice of the cleaning agent should be documented and approved by the quality unit and should be scientifically justified on the basis of, e.g.
  - — the solubility of the materials to be removed;
  - — the design and construction of the equipment and surface materials to be cleaned;
  - — the safety of the cleaning agent;
  - — the ease of removal and detection;
  - — the product attributes;
  - — the minimum temperature and volume of cleaning agent and rinse solution;
  - — the manufacturer's recommendations;
- revalidation requirements.

4.1.4 Cleaning procedures for products and processes which are very similar do not need to be individually validated. A validation study of the "worst case" may be considered acceptable. There should be a justified validation programme for this approach referred to as "bracketing", addressing critical issues relating to the selected product, equipment or process.

4.1.5 Where "bracketing" of products is done, consideration should be given to type of products and equipment.

4.1.6 Bracketing by product should be done only when the products concerned are similar in nature or property and will be processed using the same equipment. Identical cleaning procedures should then be used for these products.

4.1.7 When a representative product is chosen, this should be the one that is most difficult to clean.

4.1.8 Bracketing by equipment should be done only when it is similar equipment, or the same equipment in different sizes (e.g. 300-l, 500-l and 1000-l tanks). An alternative approach may be to validate the smallest and the largest sizes separately.

4.2 Cleaning validation reports

4.2.1 The relevant cleaning records (signed by the operator, checked by production and reviewed by quality assurance) and source data (original results) should be kept. The results of the cleaning validation should be presented in cleaning validation reports stating the outcome and conclusion.

5. Personnel

5.1 Personnel or operators who perform cleaning routinely should be trained and should be effectively supervised.

6. Equipment

6.1 Normally only procedures for the cleaning of surfaces of the equipment that come into contact with the product need to be validated. Consideration should be given to "non-contact" parts of the equipment into which product or any process material may migrate. Critical areas should be identified (independently from method of cleaning), particularly in large systems employing semi-automatic or fully automatic clean-in-place systems.

6.2 Dedicated equipment should be used for products which are difficult to clean, equipment which is difficult to clean, or for products with a high safety risk where it is not possible to achieve the required cleaning acceptance limits using a validated cleaning procedure.

6.3 Ideally, there should be one process for cleaning a piece of equipment or system. This will depend on the products being produced, whether the cleaning occurs between batches of the same product (as in a large campaign) or whether the cleaning occurs between batches of different products.

6.4 The design of equipment may influence the effectiveness of the cleaning process. Consideration should therefore be given to the design of the equipment when preparing the cleaning validation protocol, e.g. V-blenders, transfer pumps or filling lines.

7. Detergents

7.1 Detergents should facilitate the cleaning process and be easily removable. Detergents that have persistent residues such as cationic detergents which adhere very strongly to glass and are difficult to remove, should be avoided where possible.

7.2 The composition of the detergent should be known to the manufacturer and its removal during rinsing, demonstrated.

7.3 Acceptable limits for detergent residues after cleaning should be defined. The possibility of detergent breakdown should also be considered when validating cleaning procedures.

7.4 Detergents should be released by quality control and, where possible, should meet local food standards or regulations.

8. Microbiology

8.1 The need to include measures to prevent microbial growth and remove contamination where it has occurred should be considered.

8.2 There should be documented evidence to indicate that routine cleaning and storage of equipment does not allow microbial proliferation.

8.3 The period and conditions for storage of unclean equipment before cleaning, and the time between cleaning and equipment reuse, should form part of the validation of cleaning procedures.

8.4 Equipment should be stored in a dry condition after cleaning. Stagnant water should not be allowed to remain in equipment after cleaning.

8.5 Control of the bioburden through adequate cleaning and appropriate storage of equipment is important to ensure that subsequent sterilization or sanitization procedures achieve the necessary assurance of sterility, and the control of pyrogens in sterile processing. Equipment sterilization processes may not be adequate to achieve significant inactivation or removal of pyrogens.

9. Sampling

9.1 General

9.1.1 Equipment should normally be cleaned as soon as possible after use. This may be especially important for operations with topical products, suspensions and bulk drug or where the drying of residues will directly affect the efficiency of a cleaning procedure.

9.1.2 Two methods of sampling are considered to be acceptable. These are direct surface sampling and rinse samples. A combination of the two methods is generally thc most desirable.

9.1.3 The practice of resampling should not be used before or during cleaning and operations and is acceptable only in rare cases. Constant retesting and resampling can show that the cleaning process is not validated because these retests actually document the presence of unacceptable residue and contaminants resulting from an ineffective cleaning process.

9.2 Direct surface sampling (direct method)

Note: This method of sampling is the most commonly used and involves taking an inert material (e.g. cotton wool) on the end of a probe (referred to as a "swab") and rubbing it methodically across a surface. The type of sampling material used and its potential impact on the test data is important as the sampling material may interfere with the test. (For example, the adhesive used in swabs has been found to interfere with the analysis of samples.)

9.2.1 Factors that should be considered include the supplier of the swab, area swabbed, number of swabs used, whether they are wet or dry swabs, swab handling and swabbing technique.

9.2.2 The location from which the sample is taken should take into consideration the composition of the equipment (e.g. glass or steel) and the location (e.g. blades, tank walls or fittings). Worst case locations should be considered. The protocol should identify the sampling locations.

9.2.3 Critical areas, i.e. those hardest to clean, should be identified, particularly in large systems that employ semi-automatic or fully automatic clean-in-place systems.

9.2.4 The sampling medium and solvent used should be appropriate to the task.

9.3 Rinse samples (indirect method)

Note: This method allows sampling of a large surface, of areas that are inaccessible or that cannot be routinely disassembled and provides an overall picture. Rinse samples may give sufficient evidence of adequate cleaning where accessibility of equipment parts can preclude direct surface sampling, and may be useful for checking for residues of cleaning agents, e.g. detergents.

9.3.1 Rinse samples should be used in combination with other sampling methods such as surface sampling.

9.3.2 There should be evidence that samples are accurately recovered. For example, a recovery of $>80\%$ is considered good, $>50\%$ reasonable and $<50\%$ questionable.

9.4 Batch placebo method

Note: This method relies on the manufacture of a placebo batch which is then checked for carry-over of the previous product. It is an expensive and laborious process. It is difficult to provide assurance that the contaminants will be dislodged from the equipment surface uniformly. Additionally, if the particles of the contaminant or residue are large enough, they may not be uniformly dispersed in the placebo batch.

9.4.1 The batch placebo method should be used in conjunction with rinse and/or surface sampling method(s).

9.4.2 Samples should be taken throughout the process of manufacture. Traces of the preceding products should be sought in these samples. (Note that the sensitivity of the assay may be greatly reduced by dilution of the contaminant.)

10. Analytical methods

10.1 The analytical methods should be validated before the cleaning validation is performed.

10.2 The methods chosen should detect residuals or contaminants specific for the substance(s) being assayed at an appropriate level of cleanliness (sensitivity).

10.3 Validation of the analytical method should include as appropriate:

— precision, linearity and selectivity (the latter if specific analytes are targeted);
— limit of detection (LOD);
— limit of quantitation (LOQ);
— recovery, by spiking with the analyte; and
— reproducibility.

10.4 The detection limit for each analytical method should be sufficiently sensitive to detect the established acceptable level of the residue or contaminants.

10.5 Suitable methods that are sensitive and specific should be used where possible and may include chromatographic methods (e.g. high pressure liquid chromotography (HPLC), gas chromotography (GC), and high pressure thin-layer chromatography (HPTLC)). Other methods may include (alone or in combination) measurement of total organic carbon (TOC), pH, or conductivity; ultraviolet (UV) spectroscopy; and enzyme-linked immunosorbent assay (ELISA).

11. Establishing acceptable limits

Note: uniform distribution of contaminants is not guaranteed.

11.1 The acceptance criteria established for contaminant levels in the sample should be practical, achievable and verifiable. The rationale for the residue limits established should be logical, and based on the knowledge of the materials involved.

11.2 Each situation should be assessed individually. The manner in which limits are established should be carefully considered. In establishing residual limits it may not be adequate to focus only on the principal reactant, because other chemical variations may be more difficult to remove.

11.3 Where necessary, screening using thin-layer chromatography should be performed in addition to chemical analyses.

11.4 There should be no residue from the previous product, from reaction by-products and degradants, or from the cleaning process itself (e.g. detergents or solvents).

11.5 The limit-setting approach can:

- be product-specific;
- group products into families and choose a worst case product;
- group products into groups according to risk, e.g. very soluble products, products with similar potency, highly toxic, or difficult to detect products;
- use different safety factors for different dosage forms based on physiological response (this method is essential for potent materials).

11.6 Limits may be expressed as a concentration in a subsequent product (ppm), limit per surface area (mcg/cm^2), or in rinse water as ppm.

11.7 The sensitivity of the analytical methods should be defined to enable reasonable limits to be set.

11.8 The rationale for selecting limits for carry-over of product residues should meet defined criteria.

11.9 The three most commonly used criteria are:

- visually clean. (No residue should be visible on equipment after cleaning.) Spiking studies should determine the concentration at which most active ingredients are visible. This criterion may not be suitable for high-potency, low-dosage drugs;
- no more than 10 ppm of one product will appear in another product (basis for heavy metals in starting materials); and
- no more than 0.1% of the normal therapeutic dose of one product will appear in the maximum daily dose of a subsequent product.

11.10 The most stringent of three options should be used.

11.11 Certain allergenic ingredients (e.g. penicillins and cephalosporins) and highly potent material (e.g. anovulent steroids, potent steroids and cytotoxics) should be undetectable by the best available analytical methods. (In practice this may mean that dedicated manufacturing facilities should be used for the manufacturing and processing of such products.)

Appendix 4
Analytical method validation

1. Principle 129
2. General 129
3. Pharmacopoeial methods 130
4. Non-pharmacopoeial methods 130
5. Method validation 130
6. Characteristics of analytical procedures 131

1. Principle

1.1 This appendix presents some information on the characteristics that should be considered during validation of analytical methods. Approaches other than those specified in this appendix may be followed and may be acceptable. Manufacturers should choose the validation protocol and procedures most suitable for testing of their product.

1.2 The manufacturer should demonstrate (through validation) that the analytical procedure is suitable for its intended purpose.

1.3 Analytical methods, whether or not they indicate stability, should be validated.

1.4 The analytical method should be validated by research and development before being transferred to the quality control unit when appropriate.

2. General

2.1 There should be specifications for both, materials and products. The tests to be performed should be described in the documentation on standard test methods.

2.2 Specifications and standard test methods in pharmacopoeias ("pharmacopoeial methods"), or suitably developed specifications or test methods ("non-pharmacopoeial methods") as approved by the national drug regulatory authority may be used.

2.3 Well-characterized reference materials, with documented purity, should be used in the validation study.

2.4 The most common analytical procedures include identification tests, assay of drug substances and pharmaceutical products, quantitative tests for content of impurities and limit tests for impurities. Other analytical procedures include dissolution testing and determination of particle size.

2.5 The results of analytical procedures should be reliable, accurate and reproducible. The characteristics that should be considered during validation of analytical methods are discussed in paragraph 6.

2.6 Verification or revalidation should be performed when relevant, for example, when there are changes in the process for synthesis of the drug substance; changes in the composition of the finished product; changes in the analytical procedure; when analytical methods are transferred from one laboratory to another; or when major pieces of equipment instruments change.

2.7 The verification or degree of revalidation depend on the nature of the change(s).

2.8 There should be evidence that the analysts, who are responsible for certain tests, are appropriately qualified to perform those analyses ("analyst proficiency").

3. Pharmacopoeial methods

3.1 When pharmacopoeial methods are used, evidence should be available to prove that such methods are suitable for routine use in the laboratory (verification).

3.2 Pharmacopoeial methods used for determination of content or impurities in pharmaceutical products should also have been demonstrated to be specific with respect to the substance under consideration (no placebo interference).

4. Non-pharmacopoeial methods

4.1 Non-pharmacopoeial methods should be appropriately validated.

5. Method validation

5.1 Validation should be performed in accordance with the validation protocol. The protocol should include procedures and acceptance criteria for all characteristics. The results should be documented in the validation report.

5.2 Justification should be provided when non-pharmacopoeial methods are used if pharmacopoeial methods are available. Justification should include data such as comparisons with the pharmacopoeial or other methods.

5.3 Standard test methods should be described in detail and should provide sufficient information to allow properly trained analysts to perform the analysis in a reliable manner. As a minimum, the description should include the chromatographic conditions (in the case of chromatographic tests), reagents needed, reference standards, the formulae for the calculation of results and system suitability tests.

6. Characteristics of analytical procedures

6.1 Characteristics that should be considered during validation of analytical methods include:

— specificity
— linearity
— range
— accuracy
— precision
— detection limit
— quantitation limit
— robustness.

6.1.1 *Accuracy* is the degree of agreement of test results with the true value, or the closeness of the results obtained by the procedure to the true value. It is normally established on samples of the material to be examined that have been prepared to quantitative accuracy. Accuracy should be established across the specified range of the analytical procedure.

Note: it is acceptable to use a "spiked" placebo where a known quantity or concentration of a reference material is used.

6.1.2 *Precision* is the degree of agreement among individual results. The complete procedure should be applied repeatedly to separate, identical samples drawn from the same homogeneous batch of material. It should be measured by the scatter of individual results from the mean (good grouping) and expressed as the relative standard deviation (RSD).

6.1.2.1 *Repeatability* should be assessed using a minimum of nine determinations covering the specified range for the procedure e.g. three concentrations/three replicates each, or a minimum of six determinations at 100% of the test concentration.

6.1.2.2 *Intermediate precision* expresses within-laboratory variations (usually on different days, different analysts and different equipment). If reproducibility is assessed, a measure of intermediate precision is not required.

6.1.2.3 *Reproducibility* expresses *precision* between laboratories.

6.1.3 *Robustness* (or *ruggedness*) is the ability of the procedure to provide analytical results of acceptable accuracy and precision under a variety of conditions. The results from separate samples are influenced by changes in the operational or environmental conditions. Robustness should be considered during the development phase, and should show the reliability of an analysis when deliberate variations are made in method parameters.

6.1.3.1 Factors that can have an effect on robustness when performing chromatographic analysis include:

— stability of test and standard samples and solutions;
— reagents (e.g. different suppliers);
— different columns (e.g. different lots and/or suppliers);
— extraction time;
— variations of pH of a mobile phase;
— variations in mobile phase composition;
— temperature; and
— flow rate.

6.1.4 *Linearity* indicates the ability to produce results that are directly proportional to the concentration of the analyte in samples. A series of samples should be prepared in which the analyte concentrations span the claimed range of the procedure. If there is a linear relationship, test results should be evaluated by appropriate statistical methods. A minimum of five concentrations should be used.

6.1.5 *Range* is an expression of the lowest and highest levels of analyte that have been demonstrated to be determinable for the product. The specified range is normally derived from linearity studies.

6.1.6 *Specificity* (*selectivity*) is the ability to measure unequivocally the desired analyte in the presence of components such as excipients and impurities that may also be expected to be present. An investigation of specificity should be conducted during the validation of identification tests, the determination of impurities and assay.

6.1.7 *Detection limit* (*limit of detection*) is the smallest quantity of an analyte that can be detected, and not necessarily determined, in a quantitative fashion. Approaches may include instrumental or non-instrumental procedures and could include those based on:

— visual evaluation;
— signal to noise ratio;
— standard deviation of the response and the slope;
— standard deviation of the blank; and
— calibration curve.

6.1.8 *Quantitation limit* (*limit of quantitation*) is the lowest concentration of an analyte in a sample that may be determined with acceptable accuracy and precision. Approaches may include instrumental or non-instrumental procedures and could include those based on:

— visual evaluation;
— signal to noise ratio;
— standard deviation of the response and the slope;
— standard deviation of the blank; and
— calibration curve.

Table 1. Characteristics to consider during analytical validation

Type of analytical procedure	Identification	Testing for impurities	Testing for impurities	Assay — dissolution (measurement only) — content/potency
Characteristics		Quantitative tests	Limit tests	
Accuracy	–	+	–	+
Precision				
Repeatability	–	+	–	+
Intermediate precision[a]	–	+	–	+
Specificity	+	+	+	+
Detection limit	–	–[b]	+	–
Quantitation limit	–	+	–	–
Linearity	–	+	–	+
Range	–	+	–	+

– Characteristic is normally not evaluated;
+ Characteristic should normally be evaluated.
[a] In cases where a reproducibility study has been performed, intermediate precision is not needed.
[b] May be needed in some cases.

6.2 Characteristics (including tests) that should be considered when using different types of analytical procedures are summarized in Table 1.

6.3 System suitability testing

System suitability testing is an integral part of many analytical procedures. The tests are based on the concept that the equipment, electronics, analytical operations and samples to be analysed constitute an integral system that can be evaluated as such. System suitability test parameters that need to be established for a particular procedure depend on the type of procedure being evaluated, for instance, a resolution test for an HPLC procedure.

Appendix 5
Validation of computerized systems

1. General 134
2. System specification 134
3. Functional specification 135
4. Security 135

5. Back-ups 136
6. Validation 136
7. Validation of hardware and software 136
7.1 Hardware 136
7.2 Software 138

1. General

1.1 Computer systems should be validated at the level appropriate for their use and application. This is of importance in production as well as in quality control.

1.2 The use of a computer system includes different stages. These are planning, specification, programming, testing, commissioning, document operation, monitoring and modifying.

1.3 The purpose of validation of a computer system is to ensure an acceptable degree of evidence (documented, raw data), confidence (dependability and thorough, rigorous achievement of predetermined specifications), intended use, accuracy, consistency and reliability.

1.4 Both the system specifications and functional specifications should be validated.

1.5 Periodic (or continuous) evaluation should be performed after the initial validation.

1.6 There should be written procedures for performance monitoring, change control, programme and data security, calibration and maintenance, personnel training, emergency recovery and periodic re-evaluation.

1.7 Aspects of computerized operations that should be considered during validation include:

— networks
— manual back-ups
— input/output checks
— process documentation
— monitoring
— alarms
— shutdown recovery.

2. System specification

2.1 There should be a control document or system specification. The control document should state the objectives of a proposed computer system, the data to be entered and stored, the flow of data, how it interacts with other systems and procedures, the information to be produced, the limits of any variable and the operating programme and test programme. (Examples of each document produced by the programme should be included.)

2.2 System elements that need to be considered in computer validation include hardware (equipment), software (procedures) and people (users).

3. Functional specification

3.1 A functional or performance specification should provide instructions for testing, operating, and maintaining the system, as well as names of the person(s) responsible for its development and operation.

3.2 The following general aspects should be kept in mind when using computer systems:

— location
— power supply
— temperature, and
— magnetic disturbances.

Fluctuations in the electrical supply can influence computer systems and power supply failure can result in loss of memory.

3.3 The following general good manufacturing practice (GMP) requirements are applicable to computer systems.

- *Verification and revalidation.* After a suitable period of running a new system it should be independently reviewed and compared with the system specification and functional specification.
- *Change control.* Alterations should only be made in accordance with a defined procedure which should include provision for checking, approving and implementing the change.
- *Checks.* Data should be checked periodically to confirm that they have been accurately and reliably transferred.

4. Security

4.1 This is of importance in production as well as in quality control.

4.2 Data should be entered or amended only by persons authorized to do so. Suitable security systems should be in place to prevent unauthorized entry or manipulation of data. The activity of entering data, changing or amending incorrect entries and creating back-ups should all be done in accordance with written, approved standard operating procedures (SOPs).

4.3 The security procedures should be in writing. Security should also extend to devices used to store programmes, such as tapes, disks and magnetic strip cards. Access to these devices should be controlled.

4.4 Traceability is of particular importance and it should be able to identify the persons who made entries/changes, released material, or performed other critical steps in manufacture or control.

4.5 The entry of critical data into a computer by an authorized person (e.g. entry of a master processing formula) requires an independent verifi cation and release for use by a second authorized person.

4.6 SOPs should be validated for certain systems or processes, e.g. the procedures to be followed if the system fails or breaks down should be defined and tested. Alternative arrangements should be made by the validation team, and a disaster recovery procedure should be available for the systems that need to be operated in the event of a breakdown.

5. Back-ups

5.1 Regular back-ups of all files and data should be made and stored in a secure location to prevent intentional or accidental damage.

6. Validation

6.1 Planning, which should include the validation policy, project plan and SOPs, is one of the steps in the validation process.

6.2 The computer-related systems and vendors should be defined and the vendor and product should be evaluated. The system should be designed and constructed, taking into consideration the types, testing and quality assurance of the software.

6.3 After installation of the system it should be qualified. The extent of the qualification should depend on the complexity of the system. The system should be evaluated and performance qualification, change control, maintenance and calibration, security, contingency planning, SOPs, training, performance monitoring and periodic re-evaluation should be addressed.

7. Validation of hardware and software

Table 1 indicates aspects of computer systems that should be subjected to validation.

7.1 Hardware

7.1.1 As part of the validation process appropriate tests and challenges to the hardware should be performed.

Table 1. Summary of validation requirement for computer systems

Hardware	Software
1. Types 1.1 Input device 1.2 Output device 1.3 Signal converter 1.4 Central processing unit (CPU) 1.5 Distribution system 1.6 Peripheral devices	1. Level 1.1 Machine language 1.2 Assembly language 1.3 High-level language 1.4 Application language
2. Key aspects 2.1 Location environment distance input devices 2.2 Signal conversion 2.3 I/O operation 2.4 Command overrides 2.5 Maintenance	2. Software identification 2.1 Language 2.2 Name 2.3 Function 2.4 Input 2.5 Output 2.6 Fixed set point 2.7 Variable set point 2.8 Edits 2.9 Input manipulation 2.10 Programme overrides
3. Validation 3.1 Function 3.2 Limits 3.3 Worst case 3.4 Reproducibility/consistency 3.5 Documentation 3.6 Revalidation	3. Key aspects 3.1 Software development 3.2 Software security
	4. Validation 4.1 Function 4.2 Worst case 4.3 Repeats 4.4 Documentation 4.5 Revalidation

I/O, Input/output.

7.1.2 Static, dust, power-feed voltage fluctuations and electromagnetic interference could influence the system. The extent of validation should depend on the complexity of the system. Hardware is considered to be equipment, and the focus should be on location, maintenance and calibration of hardware, as well as on validation/qualification.

7.1.3 The validation/qualification of the hardware should prove:

- that the capacity of the hardware matches its assigned function (e.g. foreign language);

- that it operates within the operational limits (e.g. memory, connector ports, input ports);
- that it performs acceptably under worst-case conditions (e.g. long hours, temperature extremes); and
- reproducibility/consistency (e.g. by performing at least three runs under different conditions).

7.1.4 The validation should be done in accordance with written qualification protocols and the results should be recorded in the qualification reports.

7.1.5 Revalidation should be performed when significant changes are made.

7.1.6 Much of the hardware validation may be performed by the computer vendor. However, the ultimate responsibility for the suitability of equipment used remains with the company.

7.1.7 Hardware validation data and protocols should be kept by the company. When validation information is produced by an outside firm, e.g. computer vendor, the records maintained by the company need not include all of the voluminous test data; however, such records should be sufficiently complete (including general results and protocols) to allow the company to assess the adequacy of the validation. A mere certification of suitability from the vendor, for example, will be inadequate.

7.2 Software

7.2.1 Software is the term used to describe the complete set of programmes used by a computer, and which should be listed in a menu.

7.2.2 Records are considered as software; focus is placed on accuracy, security, access, retention of records, review, double checks, documentation and accuracy of reproduction.

Identification

7.2.3 The company should identify the following key computer programmes: language, name, function (purpose of the programme), input (determine inputs), output (determine outputs), fixed set point (process variable that cannot be changed by the operator), variable set point (entered by the operator), edits (reject input/output that does not conform to limits and minimize errors, e.g. four- or five-character number entry), input manipulation (and equations) and programme overrides (e.g. to stop a mixer before time).

7.2.4 The personnel who have the ability and/or are authorized to write, alter or have access to programmes should be identified.

7.2.5 Software validation should provide assurance that computer programmes (especially those that control manufacturing and processing) will consistently perform as they are supposed to, within pre-established limits.

When planning the validation, the following points should be considered.

- Function: does the programme match the assigned operational function (e.g. generate batch documentation, different batches of material used in a batch listed)?
- Worst case: perform validation under different conditions (e.g. speed, data volume, frequency).
- Repeats: sufficient number of times (replicate data entries).
- Documentation: protocols and reports.
- Revalidation: needed when significant changes are made.

Appendix 6
Qualification of systems and equipment

1. Principle 139
2. Scope 139
3. General 140
4. Design qualification 141
5. Installation qualification 141
6. Operational qualification 146
7. Performance qualification 157
8. Requalification 165
9. Qualification of “in use” systems and equipment 165

1. Principle

1.1 Systems and equipment should be appropriately designed, located, installed, operated and maintained to suit their intended purpose.

1.2 Critical systems, i.e. those whose consistent performance may have an impact on the quality of products, should be qualified. These may include, where appropriate, water purification systems, air-handling systems, compressed air systems and steam systems.

1.3 The continued suitable performance of equipment is important to ensure batch-to-batch consistency. Critical equipment should therefore be qualified.

2. Scope

2.1 These guidelines describe the general aspects of qualification for systems and equipment.

2.2 Normally qualification would be applicable to critical systems and equipment whose performance may have an impact on the quality of the product.

3. General

3.1 The manufacturer should have a qualification policy for systems and equipment.

3.2 Equipment (including instruments) used in production and quality control should be included in the qualification policy and programme.

3.3 New systems and equipment should pass through all stages of qualification including design qualification (DQ), installation qualification (IQ), operational qualification (OQ) and performance qualification (PQ) as appropriate (Fig. 1).

3.4 In some cases, not all stages of qualification may be required. See also the guidelines on the qualification of water purification systems in Appendix 2 and heating, ventilation and air-conditioning (HVAC) in Appendix 1.

3.5 Systems should be qualified before equipment.

3.6 Equipment should be qualified prior to being brought into routine use to provide documented evidence that the equipment is fit for its intended purpose.

3.7 Systems and equipment should undergo periodic requalification, as well as requalification after change.

Figure 1. Stages of qualification

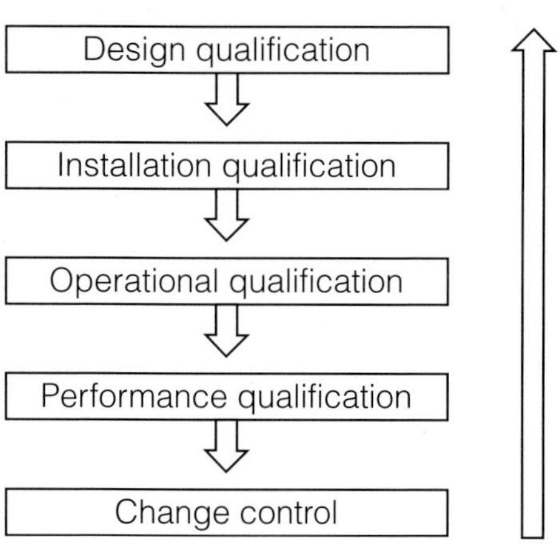

3.8 Certain stages of the equipment qualification may be done by the supplier or a third party.

3.9 The relevant documentation associated with qualification including standard operating procedures (SOPs), specifications and acceptance criteria, certificates and manuals should be maintained.

3.10 Qualification should be done in accordance with predetermined and approved qualification protocols. The results of the qualification should be recorded and reflected in qualification reports.

3.11 The extent of the qualification should be based on the criticality of a system or equipment (e.g. blenders, autoclaves or computerized systems).

4. Design qualification

Note: see also "Validation".

4.1 User requirements should be considered when deciding on the specific design of a system or equipment.

4.2 A suitable supplier should be selected for the appropriate system or equipment (approved vendor).

5. Installation qualification

Note: see also "Validation".

5.1 Systems and equipment should be correctly installed in accordance with an installation plan and installation qualification protocol.

5.2 Requirements for calibration, maintenance and cleaning should be drawn up during installation.

5.3 Installation qualification should include identification and verification of all system elements, parts, services, controls, gauges and other components.

5.4 Measuring, control and indicating devices should be calibrated against appropriate national or international standards, which are traceable.

5.5 There should be documented records for the installation (installation qualification report) to indicate the satisfactoriness of the installation, which should include the details of the supplier and manufacturer, system or equipment name, model and serial number, date of installation, spare parts, relevant procedures and certificates.

Format for an installation qualification protocol and report[a]

Validation protocol ________ Installation Qualification ________ Page _____ of _____

Title: ______________ Name and address of site: ________________________________

____

Validation Protocol # __________________________________ IQ Protocol number: ______

Title: ____

Protocol written by: __________________________________

Protocol approved by: ________________________________ Date: ____________________

QA Approval: ____ Date: ____________________

Objective

To ensure that ________________ (system/equipment) installed conforms to the purchase specifications and the manufacturer details and literature, and to document the information that ______________________ (system/equipment) meets its specifications.

Equipment inventory number: ____

Scope

To perform installation qualification as described in this IQ protocol at the time of installation, modification and relocation.

Responsibility

_________________ (post/person) overseeing the installation will perform the qualification and records results.

_________________ (post/person) will verify results and write the report.

Quality Assurance will review and approve the IQ protocol and report.

[a] This format is used for training purposes and reflects some of the possible contents for an installation qualification protocol.

Format for an installation qualification protocol and report (continued)[a]

Validation protocol ________ **Installation Qualification** ________ **Page** _____ **of** _____

Title: ______________ **Name and address of site:** ______________________________

____

System/Equipment ______________________________ **Code no.:** ________________

a. Description of the system/equipment being installed: general description of the function and the main components.

____

____

____

b. List of the main components:

1. ______________________ Code no.: ______________________
2. ______________________ Code no.: ______________________
3. ______________________ Code no.: ______________________
4. ______________________ Code no.: ______________________

c. Description of supporting utilities (e.g. piping, connections, water supply)

1. ______________________ Code no.: ______________________
2. ______________________ Code no.: ______________________
3. ______________________ Code no.: ______________________
4. ______________________ Code no.: ______________________

Procedure

1. Prepare a checklist of all components and parts, including spare parts according to the purchase order and manufacturer's specifications.
2. Record the information for each actual part, component, item of auxiliary equipment, supporting facilities, and compare with the manufacturer's specifications.
3. Record any deviations to the system/equipment.
4. Prepare a deviation report including justification of acceptance and impact on the function.
5. Prepare an IQ report.[b]
6. Submit the report to QA for review and approval.

[a] This format is used for training purposes and reflects some of the possible contents for an installation qualification protocol.

[a] As a minimum, the IQ report should include the date of initiation of the study, date completed, observations made, problems encountered, completeness of information collected, summary of deviation report, results of any tests, sample data (if appropriate), location of original data, other information relevant to the study, and the conclusion on the validity of the installation.

Format for an installation qualification protocol and report (continued)[a]

Validation protocol ________ **Installation Qualification** ________ **Page** _____ **of** _____

Title: ______________ **Name and address of site:** ________________________________

____

Checklist for component no. ______________________

Name: ____ Code no.: ____________________

Component function: ____

		Require/order	Actual	Deviations
1	Model/serial no.			
2	Specification			
3	Manual			
4	Drawing			
5	Wiring/cabling			
6	Power, fusing			
7	SOP (operation) SOP (maintenance) SOP (calibration)			
8	Input/output control			
9	Environment			
10	Test equipment or instruments			
11	Utilities and service			
12	Spare parts list, part number and supplier			
13	Other			

Performed by: _________________________________ **Date:** _______________________

Deviations: ___________________________________ **Date:** _______________________

Verified by: ___________________________________ **Date:** _______________________

[a] This format is used for training purposes and reflects some of the possible contents for an installation qualification protocol.

Format for an installation qualification protocol and report (continued)[a]

Validation protocol ________ **Installation Qualification** ________ **Page** _____ **of** _____

Title: ______________ **Name and address of site:** ________________________________

____

Deviation report

Deviations: ____

Justification for acceptance

Impact on operation:

Report written by: ______________________________ **Date:** ______________________

[a] This format is used for training purposes and reflects some of the possible contents for an installation qualification protocol.

Format for an installation qualification protocol and report (continued)[a]

Validation protocol ________ **Installation Qualification** ________ **Page** _____ **of** _____ **Title:** ______________ **Name and address of site:** ______________________________ ____
Installation qualification report Results: ____ ____ ____ ____ ____ **Conclusions:** ____ ____ ____ ____ ____ ____ ____ ____ ____
Report written by: ______________________________ **Date:** ______________________ **QA approved by:** ______________________________ **Date:** ______________________

[a] This format is used for training purposes and reflects some of the possible contents for an installation qualification protocol.

6. Operational qualification

Note: see also "Validation".

6.1 Systems and equipment should operate correctly and their operation should be verified in accordance with an operational qualification protocol.

6.2 Critical operating parameters should be identified. Studies on the critical variables should include conditions encompassing upper and lower operating limits and circumstances (also referred to as "worst case conditions").

6.3 Operational qualification should include verification of operation of all system elements, parts, services, controls, gauges and other components.

Format for an operational qualification protocol[a]

Validation protocol ________ **Operational Qualification** ________ **Page** ____ **of** ____ **Title:** ____________ **Name of Facility:** ____________________ ____	
Validation Protocol # ________________ Operational Qualification ____________ Title ____ ____ Protocol written by ____ Departmental Approval by ______________________ Date __________ QA Approval by ______________________ Date __________	
Objective To determine that the system/equipment operates according to specifications, and to record all relevant information and data to demonstrate that the system/equipment functions as expected.	
Scope To be performed after installation, modification or relocation, after the Installation Qualification has been completed.	
Responsibility Person responsible for operating the system/equipment will perform the qualification and record the information. The supervisor will supervise the study, verify the completion of the records, write the deviation report and the Operational Qualification (OQ) Report. Qualify Assurance will review and approve the OQ protocol and report.	

[a] This format is used for training purposes and reflects some of the possible contents for an operational qualification protocol.

6.4 There should be documented records for the verification of operation (operational qualification report) to indicate the satisfactory operation.

6.5 Standard operating procedures for the operation should be finalized and approved.

6.6 Training of operators for the systems and equipment should be provided, and training records maintained.

6.7 Systems and equipment should be released for routine use after completion of operational qualification, provided that all calibration, cleaning, maintenance, training and related tests and results were found to be acceptable.

Format for an operational qualification protocol (continued)[a]

Validation protocol ________ **Operational Qualification** ________ **Page** _____ **of** _____

Title: ______________ **Name of Facility:** ______________________________

____

Materials, Equipment, Documents

List of calibration equipment required (Chart 1).

Materials or supplies needed to perform the Operational Qualification

1 ______________________________ Code # ________

2 ______________________________ Code # ________

3 ______________________________ Code # ________

4 ______________________________ Code # ________

5 ______________________________ Code # ________

6 ______________________________ Code # ________

SOPs and datasheets for normal operations of the system under test (Chart 2).

Training records documenting that operators have been trained (Chart 2).

Manuals for equipment (Chart 2).

Procedure

Test and record calibration data for calibrating apparatus and instruments (Chart 1).

Test and record operative condition of control points and alarms (Chart 3).

Test and record outputs (Chart 4).

List of calibration requirements for the system under test and records of the calibration of the system (Chart 5).

Measure and record the results of specific challenge to the system in normal and worst case situation where appropriate (Chart 6).

Record any deviations to the procedures performed.

Prepare a Deviation Report including the justification of acceptance and impact on the operation.

Prepare an Operational Qualification Report. This should include date study initiated; date completed; observations made; problems encountered; completeness of information collected; summary of deviation report; results of control/alarm tests; sample data if appropriate; location of original data; other information relevant to the study; and conclusions on the validity of the equipment/system operations.

Submit QA for review and approval.

[a] This format is used for training purposes and reflects some of the possible contents for an operational qualification protocol.

Format for an operational qualification protocol (continued)[a]

Validation protocol ________ **Operational Qualification** ________ **Page** _____ **of** _____

Title: ______________ **Name of Facility:** ______________________________

____

Preparation

Chart 1: Calibrating apparatus and instruments.

Apparatus/Instrument	Calibration method	Calibration date

Performed by: ______________________________ **Date** __________

Deviations: ____

____

____

____

Verified by: ______________________________ **Date** __________

[a] This format is used for training purposes and reflects some of the possible contents for an operational qualification protocol.

Format for an operational qualification protocol (continued)[a]

Validation protocol ________ **Operational Qualification** ________ **Page** _____ **of** _____

Title: ______________ **Name of Facility:** ______________________________

____

Preparation

Chart 2: Document check

SOP Title and number	File location	QA/QC approval date
____________	____________	____________
____________	____________	____________
____________	____________	____________
____________	____________	____________
____________	____________	____________

Training Records

Course on SOP #	Staff name	Date
____________	____________	____________
____________	____________	____________
____________	____________	____________
____________	____________	____________
____________	____________	____________

Equipment Make and Model	Manual Available
______________________________	Y[ ] N[ ]
______________________________	Y[ ] N[ ]
______________________________	Y[ ] N[ ]

Performed by: ______________________________ **Date** __________

Deviations: ____

____

____

Verified by: ______________________________ **Date** __________

[a] This format is used for training purposes and reflects some of the possible contents for an operational qualification protocol.

Format for an operational qualification protocol (continued)[a]

Validation protocol ________ **Operational Qualification** _______ **Page** _____ **of** _____

Title: ______________ **Name of Facility:** ________________________________

____

Results

Chart 3: Control points and alarms.

Control point/Alarm	Results	Date

Performed by: ____ **Date** ___________

Deviations: ____

____

____

Verified by: ____ **Date** ___________

[a] This format is used for training purposes and reflects some of the possible contents for an operational qualification protocol.

Format for an operational qualification protocol (continued)[a]

Validation protocol ________ **Operational Qualification** _______ **Page** ____ **of** ____

Title: ______________ **Name of Facility:** ______________________________________

____

Results

Chart 4: Outputs

Outputs	Results	Date
____________	______________________	________
____________	______________________	________
____________	______________________	________
____________	______________________	________
____________	______________________	________
____________	______________________	________
____________	______________________	________
____________	______________________	________
____________	______________________	________
____________	______________________	________
____________	______________________	________
____________	______________________	________
____________	______________________	________
____________	______________________	________
____________	______________________	________
____________	______________________	________
____________	______________________	________

Performed by: ______________________________________ **Date** __________

Deviations: ____

____

____

Verified by: _______________________________________ **Date** __________

[a] This format is used for training purposes and reflects some of the possible contents for an operational qualification protocol.

Format for an operational qualification protocol (continued)[a]

Validation protocol ________ Operational Qualification ________ Page _____ of _____

Title: ______________ Name of Facility: ______________________________

Chart 5: Calibration of Equipment/System

Calibration SOP (short title and #)	Result	Date

Performed by: ______________________________ **Date** __________

Deviations: ______________________________

Verified by: ______________________________ **Date** __________

[a] This format is used for training purposes and reflects some of the possible contents for an operational qualification protocol.

Format for an operational qualification protocol (continued)[a]

Validation protocol ________ **Operational Qualification** _______ **Page** _____ **of** _____ **Title:** _____________ **Name of Facility:** ______________________________ ____
Chart 6: Specific challenge of the equipment or system Test in normal conditions: Test of worst case situation: (e.g. start-up after shutdown, temperature recovery time, centrifuge imbalance)
Performed by: ______________________________ **Date** __________ **Deviations:** ______________________________________ ____ ____ **Verified by:** ______________________________ **Date** __________

[a] This format is used for training purposes and reflects some of the possible contents for an operational qualification protocol.

Format for an operational qualification protocol (continued)[a]

Validation protocol ________ **Operational Qualification** _______ **Page** ____ **of** ____

Title: ______________ **Name of Facility:** ____

____

Deviation Report

Deviation(s):

Justification for acceptance:

Impact on operation:

Written by: ____ **Date** __________

[a] This format is used for training purposes and reflects some of the possible contents for an operational qualification protocol.

Format for an operational qualification protocol (continued)[a]

Validation protocol ________ **Operational Qualification** _______ **Page** ____ **of** ____

Title: ______________ **Name of Facility:** ____

____

Operational Qualification Report

Results:

Conclusions:

Written by: ____ **Date** __________

QA approved by: ____ **Date** __________

[a] This format is used for training purposes and reflects some of the possible contents for an operational qualification protocol.

7. Performance qualification

Note: see also "Validation".

7.1 Systems and equipment should consistently perform in accordance with design specifications. The performance should be verified in accordance with a performance qualification protocol.

7.2 There should be documented records for the verification of performance (performance qualification report) to indicate the satisfactory performance over a period of time. Manufacturers should justify the selected period over which performance qualification is done.

Format for a performance qualification protocol[a]

Validation protocol ________ **Performance Qualification** ________ **Page** ____ **of** ____

Title: ____________________ **Name of facility:** ____________________

____

Validation Protocol # ____________________ Performance Qualification

Title ____

____

Protocol written by ____

Departmental Approval by ______________________________ Date __________

QA Approval by ______________________________ Date __________

Objective

To determine that the systems/equipment perform as intended by repeatedly running the system on its intended schedules and recording all relevant information and data. Results must demonstrate that performance consistently meets pre-determined specifications under normal conditions, and where appropriate for worst case situations.

Scope

To be performed after the Installation and Operational Qualification have been completed and approved.

To be performed after installation, modification or relocation and for re-validation at appropriate intervals.

Each piece of equipment must be validated before it serves another piece of equipment/system during validation of the latter (e.g. water system before steam generator; steam generator before autoclave).

[a] This format is used for training purposes and reflects some of the possible contents for a performance qualification protocol.

Format for a performance qualification protocol (continued)[a]

Validation protocol ________ **Performance Qualification** ________ **Page** _____ **of** _____ **Title:** ______________________ **Name of facility:** ______________________________ ____
Responsibility Person responsible for operating the system or equipment will perform the qualification and record the information. The supervisor will supervise the study, verify the completion of the records and write the Deviation Report and the Performance Qualification Report. Qualify Assurance will review and approve the Performance Qualification Protocol and Report.
Materials, Equipment, Documents SOPs for normal operations of the equipment or system under test (including data record forms, charts, diagrams materials and equipment needed). Attach copies. SOP list: ____ ____ ____ ____ ____ ____ SOPs specific for performance tests (including data record forms, charts, diagrams, materials and equipment needed, calculations and statistical analyses to be performed, and pre-determined specifications and acceptance criteria). Attach copies. SOP list: ____ ____ ____ ____ ____ ____

[a] This format is used for training purposes and reflects some of the possible contents for a performance qualification protocol.

Format for a performance qualification protocol (continued)[a]

Validation protocol ________ **Performance Qualification** ________ **Page** _____ **of** _____

Title: ____________________ **Name of facility:** ________________________________

____

Procedure

Equipment: Run normal procedure three times for each use (configuration or load) and record all required data and any deviations to the procedure.

Systems: Run for 20 consecutive working days, recording all required data and any deviations to the procedure.

Prepare the Summary Data Record Form(Chart 1).

Evaluation

Attach all completed, signed data record forms.

Complete the Summary Data Record Form (Chart 1).

Perform all required calculations and statistical analyses (Chart 2).

Compare to acceptance criteria (Chart 3).

Prepare Deviation Report including the justification of acceptance and impact on the performance.

Prepare a Performance Qualification Report: This should include: date study initiated; date completed; observations made; problems encountered; completeness of information collected; summary of deviation report; results of any tests; do results meet acceptance criteria; location of original data; other information relevant to the study; and conclusions on the validity of the equipment/system.

Submit Performance Qualification Document to QA for review and approval.

[a] This format is used for training purposes and reflects some of the possible contents for a performance qualification protocol.

Format for a performance qualification protocol (continued)[a]

Validation protocol ________ **Performance Qualification** ________ **Page** _____ **of** _____

Title: ______________________ **Name of facility:** ____________________________________

____

Chart 1: Summary Data Record

(To be prepared for the specific procedure being tested)

Performed by: ____ **Date** ___________

Verified by: ____ **Date** ___________

[a] This format is used for training purposes and reflects some of the possible contents for a performance qualification protocol.

Format for a performance qualification protocol (continued)[a]

Validation protocol ________ **Performance Qualification** ________ **Page** _____ **of** _____ **Title:** ____________________ **Name of facility:** ________________________________ ____
Chart 2: Calculations and Statistical Analyses
Performed by: ____ **Date** ___________ **Verified by:** ____ **Date** ___________

[a] This format is used for training purposes and reflects some of the possible contents for a performance qualification protocol.

Format for a performance qualification protocol (continued)[a]

Validation protocol ________ **Performance Qualification** ________ **Page** _____ **of** _____

Title: ______________________ **Name of facility:** ______________________________________

____

Chart 3: Acceptance Criteria vs. Performance Test Results

Criteria	Results	Pass/Fail

Performed by: ____ **Date** __________

Verified by: ____ **Date** __________

[a] This format is used for training purposes and reflects some of the possible contents for a performance qualification protocol.

Format for a performance qualification protocol (continued)[a]

Validation protocol ________	**Performance Qualification** ________	**Page** _____ **of** _____
Title: ____________________	**Name of facility:** ____________________	

Deviation Report

Deviation(s):

Justification for acceptance:

Impact on operation, function or process:

Written by: ______________________________ **Date** ____________

Verified by: ______________________________ **Date** ____________

[a] This format is used for training purposes and reflects some of the possible contents for a performance qualification protocol.

Format for a performance qualification protocol (continued)[a]

Validation protocol ________ **Performance Qualification** ________ **Page** _____ **of** _____

Title: ____________________ **Name of facility:** ______________________________

____

Performance Qualification Report

Results:

Conclusions:

Written: ____ **Date** ___________

Verified by: ____ **Date** ___________

[a] This format is used for training purposes and reflects some of the possible contents for a performance qualification protocol.

8. Requalification

Note: see also "Supplementary guidelines on good manufacturing practices (GMP): validation".

8.1 Requalification of systems and equipment should be done in accordance with a defined schedule. The frequency of requalification may be determined on the basis of factors such as the analysis of results relating to calibration, verification and maintenance.

8.2 There should be periodic requalification.

8.3 There should be requalification after changes. The extent of requalification after the change should be justified based on a risk-assessment of the change. Requalification after change should be considered as part of the change control procedure.

9. Qualification of "in-use" systems and equipment

9.1 There should be data to support and verify the suitable operation and performance of systems and equipment that have been "in use" for a period of time, and which had not been subjected to installation and or operational qualification.

9.2 These should include operating parameters and limits for critical variables, calibration, maintenance and preventive maintenance, standard operating procedures (SOPs) and records.

10. Reference

A WHO guide to good manufacturing practice (GMP) requirements. Part 2: Validation. Geneva, Global Programme for Vaccines and Immunization, Vaccine Supply and Quality, Global Training Network, World Health Organization, 1997 (WHO/VSQ/97.02).

Appendix 7
Non-sterile process validation

1. Principle 166
2. Scope 166
3. General 166
4. Prospective validation 166
5. Concurrent validation 168
6. Retrospective validation 169
7. Revalidation 169
8. Change control 169

1. Principle

1.1 Process validation provides documented evidence that a process is capable of reliably and repeatedly rendering a product of the required quality.

1.2 The principles of planning, organizing and performing process validation are similar to those for qualification. It should be done in accordance with process validation protocols, data should be collected and reviewed against predetermined acceptance criteria, and reflected in process validation reports.

2. Scope

2.1 These guidelines describe the general aspects of process validation for the manufacture of non-sterile finished products.

2.2 Normally process validation should cover at least the critical steps and parameters (e.g. those that may have an impact on the quality of the product) in the process of manufacturing a pharmaceutical product.

3. General

3.1 The policy and approach to process validation should be documented, e.g. in a validation master plan, and should include the critical process steps and parameters.

3.2 Process validation should normally begin only once qualification of support systems and equipment is completed. In some cases process validation may be conducted concurrently with performance qualification.

3.3 Process validation should normally be completed prior to the manufacture of finished product that is intended for sale (*prospective validation*). Process validation during routine production may also be acceptable (*concurrent validation*).

4. Prospective validation

4.1 Critical factors or parameters that may affect the quality of the finished product should be identified during product development. To achieve this, the production process should be broken down into individual steps, and each step should be evaluated (e.g. on the basis of experience or theoretical considerations).

4.2 The criticality of these factors should be determined through a "worst-case" challenge where possible.

4.3 Prospective validation should be done in accordance with a validation protocol. The protocol should include:

— a description of the process;
— a description of the experiment;
— details of the equipment and/or facilities to be used (including measuring or recording equipment) together with its calibration status;
— the variables to be monitored;
— the samples to be taken—where, when, how, how many and how much (sample size);
— the product performance characteristics/attributes to be monitored, together with the test methods;
— the acceptable limits;
— time schedules;
— personnel responsibilities; and
— details of methods for recording and evaluating results, including statistical analysis.

4.4 All equipment, the production environment and analytical testing methods to be used should have been fully validated (e.g. during installation qualification and operational qualification).

4.5 Personnel participating in the validation work should have been appropriately trained.

4.6 Batch manufacturing documentation to be used should be prepared after these critical parameters of the process have been identified, and machine settings, component specifications and environmental conditions have been determined and specified.

4.7 A number of batches of the final product should then be produced. The number of batches produced in this validation exercise should be sufficient to allow the normal extent of variation and trends to be established and to provide sufficient data for evaluation.

4.8 Data within the finally agreed parameters, from at least three consecutive batches, giving product of the desired quality may be considered to constitute a proper validation of the process.

4.9 The batches should be of the same size, and should be the same as the batch size intended in full-scale production. Where this is not possible, the reduced batch size should be considered in the design of the protocol and when full-scale production starts, the validity of any assumptions made should be demonstrated.

4.10 Extensive testing should be performed on the product at various stages during the manufacturing process of the batches, including on the final product and its package.

4.11 The results should be documented in the validation report. As a minimum, the report should include:

- a description of the process: batch/packaging document, including details of critical steps;
- a detailed summary of the results obtained from in-process and final testing, including data from failed tests. When raw data are not included, reference should be made to the sources used and where it can be found;
- any work done in addition to that specified in the protocol, or any deviations from the protocol should be formally noted along with an explanation;
- a review and comparison of the results with those expected; and
- formal acceptance or rejection of the work by the team or persons designated as being responsible for the validation, after completion of any corrective action or repeated work.

4.12 A conclusion and recommendation should be made on the extent of monitoring and the in-process controls necessary for routine production, on the basis of the results obtained.

4.13 The conclusion and recommendation should be incorporated into the batch manufacturing and batch packaging documents and/or standard operating procedures (SOPs) for routine use. Limits and frequencies of testing and monitoring should be specified. Actions to be taken in the event of the limits being exceeded should be specified.

4.14 Batches manufactured as part of the validation exercise, and intended to be sold or supplied, should have been manufactured under conditions that comply fully with the requirements of good manufacturing practice and the marketing authorization (where applicable).

5. Concurrent validation

5.1 In certain cases, it may be appropriate to validate a process during routine production, e.g. where the product is a different strength of a previously validated product, a different tablet shape or where the process is well understood.

5.2 The decision to carry out concurrent validation should be made by appropriately authorized personnel.

5.3 It is essential that the premises and equipment to be used during concurrent validation have been previously qualified.

5.4 Prospective validation should be done in accordance with a validation protocol.

5.5 The results should be documented in the validation report.

6. Retrospective validation

6.1 Retrospective validation is based on a comprehensive review of historical data to provide the necessary documentary evidence that the process is doing what it is believed to do. This type of validation also requires the preparation of a protocol, the reporting of the results of the data review, a conclusion and a recommendation.

6.2 Retrospective validation is not the preferred method of validation and should be used in exceptional cases only. It is acceptable only for well-established processes and will be inappropriate where there have been changes in the composition of the product, operating procedures or equipment.

6.3 Sufficient data should be reviewed to provide a statistically significant conclusion.

6.4 When the results of retrospective validation are considered satisfactory, this should serve only as an indication that the process does not need to be subjected to validation in the immediate future.

7. Revalidation

Note: see main text on "Validation". The need for periodic revalidation of non-sterile processes is considered to be a lower priority than for sterile processes.

7.1 In the case of standard processes using conventional equipment, a data review similar to that which would be required for retrospective validation may provide an adequate assurance that the process continues to be under control. The following points should also be considered:

— the occurrence of any changes in the master formula, methods, starting material manufacturer, equipment and/or instruments;
— equipment calibrations and preventive maintenance carried out;
— standard operating procedures (SOPs); and
— cleaning and hygiene programme.

8. Change control

Note: see main text on "Validation".

8.1 Products manufactured by processes that have been subjected to changes should not be released for sale without full awareness and consideration of the change and its impact on the process validation.

8.2 Changes that are likely to require revalidation may include:

— changes in the manufacturing process (e.g. mixing times, drying temperatures);

— changes in the equipment (e.g. addition of automatic detection systems);
— production area and support system changes (e.g. rearrangement of areas or a new water treatment method);
— transfer of processes to another site; and
— unexpected changes (e.g. those observed during self-inspection or during routine analysis of process trend data).

Water for pharmaceutical use[1]

1. Introduction 171
   1.1 Scope of the document 171
   1.2 Background to water requirements and uses 171
   1.3 Applicable guides 172
2. General requirements for pharmaceutical water systems 172
3. Water quality specifications 173
   3.1 General 173
   3.2 Drinking-water 173
   3.3 Purified water 173
   3.4 Highly purified water 174
   3.5 Water for injections 174
   3.6 Other grades of water 174
4. Application of specific waters to processes and dosage forms 174
5. Water purification methods 175
   5.1 General considerations 175
   5.2 Production of drinking-water 176
   5.3 Production of purified water 177
   5.4 Production of highly purified water 178
   5.5 Production of water for injections 178
6. Water purification, storage and distribution systems 178
   6.1 General 178
   6.2 Materials that come into contact with systems for water for pharmaceutical use 179
   6.3 System sanitization and bioburden control 180
   6.4 Storage vessel requirements 180
   6.5 Requirements for water distribution pipework 181
7. Operational considerations 183
   7.1 Start-up and commissioning of water systems 183
   7.2 Qualification 183

[1] WHO good manufacturing practices: water for pharmaceutical use. In: *WHO Expert Committee on Specifications for Pharmaceutical Preparations. Thirty-ninth report.* Geneva, World Health Organization, 2005 (WHO Technical Report Series, No. 929), Annex 3.

7.3 Continuous system monitoring 184
7.4 Maintenance of water systems 185
7.5 System reviews 185
8. Inspection of water systems 185
Bibliography 186

1. Introduction

1.1 Scope of the document

The guidance contained in this document is intended to provide information about the available specifications for water for pharmaceutical use (WPU), guidance about which quality of water to use for specific applications, such as the manufacture of active pharmaceutical ingredients (APIs) and dosage forms, and to provide guidance on the good manufacturing practice (GMP) regarding the design, installation and operation of pharmaceutical water systems. Although the focus of this document is on water for pharmaceutical applications, the guidelines may also be relevant to other industrial or specific uses where the specifications and practices can be applied.

The GMP guidance for WPU contained in this document is intended to be supplementary to the general GMP guidelines for pharmaceutical products published by WHO (*WHO Expert Committee on Specifications for Pharmaceutical Preparations. Thirty-seventh report*. Geneva, World Health Organization, 2003 (WHO Technical Report Series, No. 908), Annex 4).

This document refers to available specifications, such as the pharmacopoeias and industry guidance for the use, production, storage and distribution of water in bulk form. In order to avoid confusion it does not attempt to duplicate such material. *Note*: This document does not cover waters for administration to patients in their formulated state or the use of small quantities of water in pharmacies to compound individually prescribed medicines.

The guidance provided in this document can be used in whole or in part as appropriate to the application under consideration.

Where subtle points of difference exist between pharmacopoeial specifications, the manufacturer will be expected to decide which option to choose in accordance with the related marketing authorization submitted to the national drug regulatory authority.

1.2 Background to water requirements and uses

Water is the most widely used substance, raw material or starting material in the production, processing and formulation of pharmaceutical products. It has unique chemical properties due to its polarity and hydrogen bonds. This means it is able to dissolve, absorb, adsorb or suspend many different compounds. These include contaminants that may represent hazards in themselves or that may be able to react with intended product substances, resulting in hazards to health.

Different grades of water quality are required depending on the route of administration of the pharmaceutical products. One source of guidance about different grades of water is the European Medicines Agency (EMEA) *Note for guidance on quality of water for pharmaceutical use* (CPMP/QWP/158/01).

Control of the quality of water throughout the production, storage and distribution processes, including microbiological and chemical quality, is a major concern. Unlike other product and process ingredients, water is usually drawn from a system on demand, and is not subject to testing and batch or lot release before use. Assurance of quality to meet the on-demand expectation is, therefore, essential. Additionally, certain microbiological tests may require periods of incubation and, therefore, the results are likely to lag behind the water use. Control of the microbiological quality of WPU is a high priority. Some types of microorganism may proliferate in water treatment components and in the storage and distribution systems. It is very important to minimize microbial contamination by routine sanitization and taking appropriate measures to prevent microbial proliferation.

1.3 Applicable guides

In addition to the specific guidance provided in this document, the Bibliography lists some relevant publications that can serve as additional background material when planning, installing and using systems intended to provide WPU.

2. General requirements for pharmaceutical water systems

Pharmaceutical water production, storage and distribution systems should be designed, installed, commissioned, validated and maintained to ensure the reliable production of water of an appropriate quality. They should not be operated beyond their designed capacity. Water should be produced, stored and distributed in a manner that prevents unacceptable microbial, chemical or physical contamination (e.g. with dust and dirt).

The use of the systems following installation, commissioning, validation and any unplanned maintenance or modification work should be approved by the quality assurance (QA) department. If approval is obtained for planned preventive maintenance tasks, they need not be approved after implementation.

Water sources and treated water should be monitored regularly for quality and for chemical, microbiological and, as appropriate, endotoxin contamination. The performance of water purification, storage and distribution systems should also be monitored. Records of the monitoring results and any actions taken should be maintained for an appropriate length of time.

Where chemical sanitization of the water systems is part of the biocontamination control programme, a validated procedure should be followed to ensure that the sanitizing agent has been effectively removed.

3. Water quality specifications

3.1 General

The following requirements concern water processed, stored and distributed in bulk form. They do not cover the specification of waters formulated for patient administration. Pharmacopoeias include specifications for both bulk and dosage-form waters.

Pharmacopoeial requirements for WPU are described in national and international pharmacopoeias and limits for various contaminants are given. Companies wishing to supply multiple markets should set specifications that meet the strictest requirements from each of the relevant pharmacopoeias.

3.2 Drinking-water

Drinking-water should be supplied under continuous positive pressure in a plumbing system free of any defects that could lead to contamination of any product.

Drinking-water is unmodified except for limited treatment of the water derived from a natural or stored source. Examples of natural sources include springs, wells, rivers, lakes and the sea. The condition of the source water will dictate the treatment required to render it safe for human consumption (drinking). Typical treatment includes softening, removal of specific ions, particle reduction and antimicrobial treatment. It is common for drinking-water to be derived from a public water supply that may be a combination of more than one of the natural sources listed above. It is also common for public water-supply organizations to conduct tests and guarantee that the drinking-water delivered is of potable quality.

Drinking-water quality is covered by the WHO drinking-water guidelines, standards from the International Organization for Standardization (ISO) and other regional and national agencies. Drinking-water should comply with the relevant regulations laid down by the competent authority.

If drinking-water is used directly in certain stages of pharmaceutical manufacture or is the feed-water for the production of higher qualities of WPU, then testing should be carried out periodically by the water user's site to confirm that the quality meets the standards required for potable water.

3.3 Purified water

Purified water (PW) should be prepared from a potable water source as a minimum-quality feed-water, should meet the pharmacopoeial specifications for chemical and microbiological purity, and should be protected from recontamination and microbial proliferation.

3.4 Highly purified water

Highly purified water (HPW) should be prepared from potable water as a minimum-quality feed-water. HPW is a unique specification for water found only in the *European Pharmacopoeia*. This grade of water must meet the same quality standard as water for injections (WFI) including the limit for endotoxins, but the water-treatment methods are not considered to be as reliable as distillation. HPW may be prepared by combinations of methods such as reverse osmosis, ultrafiltration and deionization.

3.5 Water for injections

Water for injections (WFI) should be prepared from potable water as a minimum-quality feed-water. WFI is not sterile water and is not a final dosage form. It is an intermediate bulk product. WFI is the highest quality of pharmacopoeial WPU.

Certain pharmacopoeias place constraints upon the permitted purification techniques as part of the specification of the WFI. *The International Pharmacopoeia* and the *European Pharmacopoeia*, for example, allow only distillation as the final purification step.

3.6 Other grades of water

When a specific process requires a special non-pharmacopoeial grade of water, this should be specified and should at least satisfy the pharmacopoeial requirements of the grade of WPU required for the type of dosage form or process step.

4. Application of specific waters to processes and dosage forms

Product licensing authorities define the requirement to use the specific grades of WPU for different dosage forms or for different stages in washing, preparation, synthesis, manufacturing or formulation.

The grade of water used should take into account the nature and intended use of the intermediate or finished product and the stage in the manufacturing process at which the water is used.

HPW can be used in the preparation of products when water of high quality (i.e. very low in microorganisms and endotoxins) is needed, but the process stage or product requirement does not include the constraint on the production method defined in some of the pharmacopoeial monographs for WFI.

WFI should be used in injectable product preparations, for dissolving or diluting substances or preparations for parenteral administration before use, and for sterile water for preparation of injections. WFI should also be used for the final rinse after cleaning of equipment and components that come into contact with injectable products as well as for the final rinse in a washing process in which no subsequent thermal or chemical depyrogenization process is applied.

When steam comes into contact with an injectable product in its final container, or equipment for preparing injectable products, it should conform with the specification for WFI when condensed.

5. Water purification methods

5.1 General considerations

The specifications for WPU found in compendia (e.g. pharmacopoeias) are generally not prescriptive as to permissible water purification methods other than those for WFI (refer to section 3.5).

The chosen water purification method, or sequence of purification steps, must be appropriate to the application in question. The following should be considered when selecting the water treatment method:

- the water quality specification;
- the yield or efficiency of the purification system;
- feed-water quality and the variation over time (seasonal changes);
- the reliability and robustness of the water-treatment equipment in operation;
- the availability of water-treatment equipment on the market;
- the ability to adequately support and maintain the water purification equipment; and
- the operation costs.

The specifications for water purification equipment, storage and distribution systems should take into account the following:

- the risk of contamination from leachates from contact materials;
- the adverse impact of adsorptive contact materials;
- hygienic or sanitary design, where required;
- corrosion resistance;
- freedom from leakage;
- configuration to avoid proliferation of microbiological organisms;
- tolerance to cleaning and sanitizing agents (thermal and chemical);
- the system capacity and output requirements; and
- the provision of all necessary instruments, test and sampling points to allow all the relevant critical quality parameters of the complete system to be monitored.

The design, configuration and layout of the water purification equipment, storage and distribution systems should also take into account the following physical considerations:

— the space available for the installation;
— structural loadings on buildings;
— the provision of adequate access for maintenance; and
— the ability to safely handle regeneration and sanitization chemicals.

5.2 Production of drinking-water

Drinking-water is derived from a raw water source such as a well, river or reservoir. There are no prescribed methods for the treatment of raw water to produce potable drinking-water from a specific raw water source.

Typical processes employed at a user plant or by a water supply authority include:

— filtration;
— softening;
— disinfection or sanitization (e.g. by sodium hypochlorite (chlorine) injection);
— iron (ferrous) removal;
— precipitation; and
— reduction of specific inorganic/organic materials.

The drinking-water quality should be monitored routinely. Additional testing should be considered if there is any change in the raw-water source, treatment techniques or system configuration. If the drinking-water quality changes significantly, the direct use of this water as a WPU, or as the feed-water to downstream treatment stages, should be reviewed and the result of the review documented.

Where drinking-water is derived from an "in-house" system for the treatment of raw water, the water-treatment steps used and the system configuration should be documented. Changes to the system or its operation should not be made until a review has been completed and the change approved by the QA department.

Where drinking-water is stored and distributed by the user, the storage systems must not allow degradation of the water quality before use. After any such storage, testing should be carried out routinely in accordance with a defined method. Where water is stored, its use should ensure a turnover of the stored water sufficient to prevent stagnation.

The drinking-water system is usually considered to be an "indirect impact system" and does not need to be qualified.

Drinking-water purchased in bulk and transported to the user by tanker presents special problems and risks not associated with potable water delivered by pipeline. Vendor assessment and authorized certification activities, including confirmation of the acceptability of the delivery vehicle, should be undertaken in a similar way to that used for any other starting material.

Equipment and systems used to produce drinking-water should be able to be drained and sanitized. Storage tanks should be closed with appropriately protected vents, allow for visual inspection and for being drained and sanitized. Distribution pipework should be able to be drained, or flushed, and sanitized.

Special care should be taken to control microbiological contamination of sand filters, carbon beds and water softeners. Once microorganisms have infected a system, the contamination can rapidly form biofilms and spread throughout the system. Techniques for controlling contamination such as backflushing, chemical or thermal sanitization and frequent regeneration should be considered. Additionally, all water-treatment components should be maintained with continuous water flow to inhibit microbial growth.

5.3 Production of purified water

There are no prescribed methods for the production of PW in the pharmacopoeias. Any appropriate qualified purification technique or sequence of techniques may be used to prepare PW. Typically ion exchange, ultrafiltration and/or reverse osmosis processes are used. Distillation can also be used.

The following should be considered when configuring a water purification system:

- the feed-water quality and its variation over seasons;
- the required water-quality specification;
- the sequence of purification stages required;
- the energy consumption;
- the extent of pretreatment required to protect the final purification steps;
- performance optimization, including yield and efficiency of unit treatment-process steps;
- appropriately located sampling points designed in such a way as to avoid potential contamination; and
- unit process steps should be provided with appropriate instrumentation to measure parameters such as flow, pressure, temperature, conductivity, pH and total organic carbon.

Ambient-temperature PW systems are especially susceptible to microbiological contamination, particularly when equipment is static during periods of no or low demand for water. It is essential to consider the mechanisms for microbiological control and sanitization. The following techniques should be considered:

- maintenance of flow through water-purification equipment at all times;
- control of temperature in the system by pipeline heat exchange or plant-room cooling to reduce the risk of microbial growth (guidance value <25°C);

— provision of ultraviolet disinfection;
— selection of water-treatment components that can be thermally sanitized; and/or
— application of chemical sanitization (including agents such as ozone).

5.4 Production of highly purified water

There are no prescribed methods for the production of HPW in any major pharmacopoeia, including the *European Pharmacopoeia*. Any appropriate qualified purification technique or sequence of techniques may be used to prepare HPW. Typically ion exchange, ultrafiltration and/or reverse osmosis processes are used.

The guidance provided in section 5.3 for PW is equally applicable to HPW.

5.5 Production of water for injections

The pharmacopoeias prescribe or limit the permitted final water purification stage in the production of WFI. Distillation is the preferred technique; it is considered a more robust technique based on phase change, and in some cases, high temperature operation of the process equipment.

The following should be considered when designing a water purification system:

— the feed-water quality;
— the required water quality specification;
— the optimum generator size to avoid over-frequent start/stop cycling;
— blow-down and dump functions; and
— cool-down venting to avoid contamination ingress.

6. Water purification, storage and distribution systems

This section applies to WPU systems for PW, HPW and WFI. The water storage and distribution should work in conjunction with the purification plant to ensure consistent delivery of water to the user points, and to ensure optimum operation of the water purification equipment.

6.1 General

The storage and distribution system should be considered as a key part of the whole system, and should be designed to be fully integrated with the water purification components of the system.

Once water has been purified using an appropriate method, it can either be used directly or, more frequently, it will be fed into a storage vessel for subsequent distribution to points of use. The following text describes the requirements for storage and distribution systems.

The storage and distribution system should be configured to prevent recontamination of the water after treatment and be subjected to a combination of online and offline monitoring to ensure that the appropriate water specification is maintained.

6.2 Materials that come into contact with systems for water for pharmaceutical use

This section applies to generation equipment for PW, HPW and WFI, and the associated storage and distribution systems.

The materials that come into contact with WPU, including pipework, valves and fittings, seals, diaphragms and instruments, should be selected to satisfy the following objectives.

- *Compatibility.* All materials used should be compatible with the temperature and chemicals used by or in the system.
- *Prevention of leaching.* All materials that come into contact with WPU should be non-leaching at the range of working temperatures.
- *Corrosion resistance.* PW, HPW and WFI are highly corrosive. To prevent failure of the system and contamination of the water, the materials selected must be appropriate, the method of jointing must be carefully controlled, and all fittings and components must be compatible with the pipework used. Appropriate sanitary-specification plastics and stainless steel materials are acceptable for WPU systems. When stainless steel is used it should be at least grade 316L. The system should be passivated after initial installation or after modification. When accelerated passivation is undertaken, the system should be thoroughly cleaned first, and the passivation process should be undertaken in accordance with a clearly defined documented procedure.
- *Smooth internal finish.* Once water has been purified it is susceptible to microbiological contamination, and the system is subject to the formation of biofilms when cold storage and distribution is employed. Smooth internal surfaces help to avoid roughness and crevices within the WPU system. Crevices are frequently sites where corrosion can commence. The internal finish should have an arithmetical average surface roughness of not greater than 0.8 micrometre arithmetical mean roughness (Ra). When stainlesssteel is used, mechanical and electropolishing techniques may be employed. Electropolishing improves the resistance of the stainless steel material to surface corrosion.
- *Jointing.* The selected system materials should be able to be easily jointed by welding in a controlled manner. The control of the process should include as a minimum, qualification of the operator, documentation of the welder set-up, work-session test pieces, logs of all welds and visual inspection of a defined proportions of welds.

- *Design of flanges or unions.* Where flanges or unions are used, they should be of a hygienic or sanitary design. Appropriate checks should be carried out to ensure that the correct seals are used and that they are fitted and tightened correctly.
- *Documentation.* All system components should be fully documented and be supported by original or certified copies of material certificates.
- *Materials.* Suitable materials that may be considered for sanitary elements of the system include 316L (low carbon) stainless steel, polypropylene, polyvinylidenedifluoride and perfluoroalkoxy. Other materials such as unplasticized polyvinylchloride (uPVC) may be used for treatment equipment designed for less pure water such as ion exchangers and softeners.

6.3 System sanitization and bioburden control

Water treatment equipment, storage and distribution systems used for PW, HPW and WFI should be provided with features to control the proliferation of microbiological organisms during normal use, as well as techniques for sanitizing or sterilizing the system after intervention for maintenance or modification. The techniques employed should be considered during the design of the system and their performance proven during the commissioning and qualification activities.

Systems that operate and are maintained at elevated temperatures, in the range of 70–80°C, are generally less susceptible to microbiological contamination than systems that are maintained at lower temperatures. When lower temperatures are required due to the water treatment processes employed or the temperature requirements for the water in use, then special precautions should be taken to prevent the ingress and proliferation of microbiological contaminants (see section 6.5.3 for guidance).

6.4 Storage vessel requirements

The water storage vessel used in a system serves a number of important purposes. The design and size of the vessel should take into consideration the following.

6.4.1 Capacity

The capacity of the storage vessel should be determined on the basis of the following requirements.

- It is necessary to provide a buffer capacity between the steady-state generation rate of the water-treatment equipment and the potentially variable simultaneous demand from user points.

- The water treatment equipment should be able to operate continuously for significant periods to avoid the inefficiencies and equipment stress that occur when the equipment cycles on and off too frequently.
- The capacity should be sufficient to provide short-term reserve capacity in the event of failure of the water-treatment equipment or inability to produce water due to a sanitization or regeneration cycle. When determining the size of such reserve capacity, consideration should be given to providing sufficient water to complete a process batch, work session or other logical period of demand.

6.4.2 Contamination control considerations

The following should be taken into account for the efficient control of contamination.

- The headspace in the storage vessel is an area of risk where water droplets and air can come into contact at temperatures that encourage the proliferation of microbiological organisms. The water distribution loop should be configured to ensure that the headspace of the storage vessel is effectively wetted by a flow of water. The use of spray ball or distributor devices to wet the surfaces should be considered.
- Nozzles within the storage vessels should be configured to avoid dead zones where microbiological contamination might be harboured.
- Vent filters are fitted to storage vessels to allow the internal level of liquid to fluctuate. The filters should be bacteria-retentive, hydrophobic and ideally be configured to allow in situ testing of integrity. Offline testing is also acceptable. The use of heated vent filters should be considered to prevent condensation within the filter matrix that might lead to filter blockage and to microbial grow-through that could contaminate the storage vessels.
- Where pressure-relief valves and bursting discs are provided on storage vessels to protect them from over-pressurization, these devices should be of a sanitary design. Bursting discs should be provided with external rupture indicators to prevent accidental loss of system integrity.

6.5 Requirements for water distribution pipework

The distribution of PW, HPW and WFI should be accomplished using a continuously circulating pipework loop. Proliferation of contaminants within the storage tank and distribution loop should be controlled.

Filtration should not usually be used in distribution loops or at takeoff user points to control biocontamination. Such filters are likely to conceal system contamination.

6.5.1 Temperature control and heat exchangers

Where heat exchangers are employed to heat or cool WPU within a system, precautions should be taken to prevent the heating or cooling utility from contaminating the water. The more secure types of heat exchangers of the double tube plate or double plate and frame configuration should be considered. Where these types are not used, an alternative approach whereby the utility is maintained and monitored at a lower pressure than the WPU may be considered.

Where heat exchangers are used they should be arranged in continually circulating loops or subloops of the system to avoid unacceptable static water in systems.

When the temperature is reduced for processing purposes, the reduction should occur for the minimum necessary time. The cooling cycles and their duration should be proven satisfactory during the qualification of the system.

6.5.2 Circulation pumps

Circulation pumps should be of a sanitary design with appropriate seals that prevent contamination of the system. Where stand-by pumps are provided, they should be configured or managed to avoid dead zones trapped within the system.

6.5.3 Biocontamination control techniques

The following control techniques may be used alone or more commonly in combination.

- Maintenance of continuous turbulent flow circulation within water distribution systems reduces the propensity for the formation of biofilms. The maintenance of the design velocity for a specific system should be proven during the system qualification and the maintenance of satisfactory performance should be monitored. During the operation of a distribution system, short-term fluctuations in the flow velocity are unlikely to cause contamination problems provided that cessation of flow, flow reversal or pressure loss does not occur.
- The system design should ensure the shortest possible length of pipework.
- For ambient temperature systems, pipework should be isolated from adjacent hot pipes.
- Deadlegs in the pipework installation greater than 1.5 times the branch diameter should be avoided.
- Pressure gauges should be separated from the system by membranes.
- Hygienic pattern diaphragm valves should be used.
- Pipework should be laid to falls to allow drainage.
- The growth of microorganisms can be inhibited by:

— ultraviolet radiation sources in pipework;
— maintaining the system heated (guidance temperature 70–80°C);
— sanitizing the system periodically using hot water (guidance temperature >70°C);
— sterilizing or sanitizing the system periodically using superheated hot water or clean steam; and
— routine chemical sanitization using ozone or other suitable chemical agents. When chemical sanitization is used, it is essential to prove that the agent has been removed prior to using the water. Ozone can be effectively removed by using ultraviolet radiation.

7. Operational considerations

7.1 Start-up and commissioning of water systems

Planned, well-defined, successful and well-documented commissioning is an essential precursor to successful validation of water systems. The commissioning work should include setting to work, system setup, controls loop tuning and recording of all system performance parameters. If it is intended to use or refer to commissioning data within the validation work then the quality of the commissioning work and associated data and documentation must be commensurate with the validation plan requirements.

7.2 Qualification

WPU, PW, HPW and WFI systems are all considered to be direct impact, quality critical systems that should be qualified. The qualification should follow the validation convention of design review or design qualification (DQ), installation qualification (IQ), operational qualification (OQ) and performance qualification (PQ).

This guidance does not define the standard requirements for the conventional validation stages DQ, IQ and OQ, but concentrates on the particular PQ approach that should be used for WPU systems to demonstrate their consistent and reliable performance. A three-phase approach should be used to satisfy the objective of proving the reliability and robustness of the system in service over an extended period.

Phase 1. A test period of 2–4 weeks should be spent monitoring the system intensively. During this period the system should operate continuously without failure or performance deviation. The following should be included in the testing approach.

- Undertake chemical and microbiological testing in accordance with a defined plan.
- Sample the incoming feed-water daily to verify its quality.
- Sample after each step in the purification process daily.

- Sample at each point of use and at other defined sample points daily.
- Develop appropriate operating ranges.
- Develop and finalize operating, cleaning, sanitizing and maintenance procedures.
- Demonstrate production and delivery of product water of the required quality and quantity.
- Use and refine the standard operating procedures (SOPs) for operation, maintenance, sanitization and troubleshooting.
- Verify provisional alert and action levels.
- Develop and refine test-failure procedure.

Phase 2. A further test period of 2–4 weeks should be spent carrying out further intensive monitoring while deploying all the refined SOPs after the satisfactory completion of phase 1. The sampling scheme should be generally the same as in phase 1. Water can be used for manufacturing purposes during this phase. The approach should also:

— demonstrate consistent operation within established ranges; and
— demonstrate consistent production and delivery of water of the required quantity and quality when the system is operated in accordance with the SOPs.

Phase 3. Phase 3 typically runs for 1 year after the satisfactory completion of phase 2. Water can be used for manufacturing purposes during this phase which has the following objectives and features.

- Demonstrate extended reliable performance.
- Ensure that seasonal variations are evaluated.
- The sample locations, sampling frequencies and tests should be reduced to the normal routine pattern based on established procedures proven during phases 1 and 2.

7.3 Continuous system monitoring

After completion of phase 3 of the qualification programme for the WPU system, a system review should be undertaken. Following this review, a routine monitoring plan should be established based on the results of phase 3.

Monitoring should include a combination of online instrument monitoring of parameters such as flow, pressure, temperature, conductivity and total organic carbon, and offline sample testing for physical, chemical and microbiological attributes. Offline samples should be taken from points of use and specific sample points. Samples from points of use should be taken in a similar way to that adopted when the water is being used in service.

Tests should be carried out to ensure that the selected pharmacopoeia specification has been satisfied, and should include, as appropriate, determination of conductivity, pH, heavy metals, nitrates, total organic carbon, total viable count, presence of specific pathogens and endotoxins.

Monitoring data should be subject to trend analysis.

7.4 Maintenance of water systems

WPU systems should be maintained in accordance with a controlled, documented maintenance programme that takes into account the following:

— defined frequency for system elements;
— the calibration programme;
— SOPs for specific tasks;
— control of approved spares;
— issue of clear maintenance plan and instructions;
— review and approval of systems for use upon completion of work; and
— record and review of problems and faults during maintenance.

7.5 System reviews

WPU (PW, HPW and WFI) systems should be reviewed at appropriate regular intervals. The review team should comprise representatives from engineering, QA, operations and maintenance. The review should consider matters such as:

— changes made since the last review;
— system performance;
— reliability;
— quality trends;
— failure events;
— investigations;
— out-of-specifications results from monitoring;
— changes to the installation;
— updated installation documentation;
— log books; and
— the status of the current SOP list.

8. Inspection of water systems

WPU (PW, HPW and WFI) systems are likely to be the subject of regulatory inspection from time to time. Users should consider conducting routine audit and self-inspection of established water systems. This GMP guidance can be used as the basis of inspection. The following list identifies items and a logical sequence for a WPU system inspection or audit:

— a sampling and monitoring plan with a drawing of all sample points;
— the setting of monitoring alert and action levels;

— monitoring results and evaluation of trends;
— inspection of the last annual system review;
— review of any changes made to the system since the last audit and check that the change control has been implemented;
— review of deviations recorded and their investigation;
— general inspection of system for status and condition;
— review of maintenance, failure and repair logs; and
— checking calibration and standardization of critical instruments.

For an established system that is demonstrably under control, this scope of review should prove adequate.

For new systems, or systems that display instability or unreliability, the following should also be reviewed:

— performance qualification;
— operational qualification; and
— installation qualification.

Bibliography

WHO Guidelines for drinking-water quality, 3rd edition. Geneva, World Health Organization, 2003.

Water and steam systems.International Society for Pharmaceutical Engineering, 2001. ISPE Baseline™ Pharmaceutical Engineering Guide, volume 4.

American Society of Mechanical Engineers. Bioprocessing Equipment Standard. ASME—BPE 2000

Biotechnology. Equipment. Guidance on testing procedures for cleanability. British Standards Publishing Ltd. BS EN 12296.

Harfst WH. Selecting piping materials for high-purity water systems. Ultra Pure Water, May/June 1994.

Noble PT. Transport considerations for microbial control in piping. Journal of Pharmaceutical Science and Technology, 1994, 48:76–85.

Baines PH. Passivation; understanding and performing procedures on austenitic stainless steel systems. Pharmaceutical Engineering, 1990, 10(6).

Guide to inspections of high purity water systems. Maryland, US Food and Drug Administration, 1993.

Tverberg JC, Kerber SJ. Effect of nitric acid passivation on the surface composition of mechanically polished type 316 L sanitary tube. European Journal of Parenteral Sciences1998, 3:117–124.

European Pharmacopoeia: Web site for the publishers of the European Pharmacopoeiaand supplements; http://www.pheur.org/

US Pharmacopeia: Published annually; see http://www.usp.org/

European Medicines Evaluation Agency. Note for guidance on the quality of water for pharmaceutical use. London. CPMP/QWP/158-01.

Pharmaceutical Inspection Co-operation Scheme (PIC/S). Inspection of Utilities; P1 009-1. Geneva, Pharmaceutical Inspection Co-operation Scheme, 2002.

The International Pharmacopoeia. Geneva, World Health Organization; http://www.who.int/medicines

2.
WHO good manufacturing practices: starting materials

Active pharmaceutical ingredients (bulk drug substances)[1,2]

Explanation	188
General considerations	188
1. Personnel	189
2. Premises	190
3. Equipment	190
4. Sanitation	191
5. Documentation	191
6. Production	193
7. Packaging	194

Explanation

Since there are fundamental distinctions between the production of bulk active pharmaceutical ingredients and the formulation of finished pharmaceutical products, the strict application of GMP as set forth in the main part of this guide is not always practical or necessary. The present supplementary guidelines outline procedures and practices that manufacturers should employ to ensure that the methods, facilities, and controls used for the production of active pharmaceutical ingredients are operated or managed so that such products have the quality and purity appropriate for their use in finished pharmaceutical products.

General considerations

In the manufacture of active pharmaceutical ingredients, overall control is essential to ensure high quality. Haphazard operations cannot be permitted in the manufacture of substances that may be used to save life or to restore or promote health.

---

[1] Good manufacturing practices for pharmaceutical products, Part Three, section 18. In: *WHO Expert Committee on Specifications for Pharmaceutical Preparations. Thirty-second report.* Geneva, World Health Organization, 1992: 72–79 (WHO Technical Report Series, No. 823).

[2] Introductory note, General considerations, main principles and Glossary of Good manufacturing practices for pharmaceutical products are reproduced elsewhere in this volume (see pp. 7–57).

Recommended practices for the manufacture of active pharmaceutical ingredients are set out below. Adherence to these practices, complementing the various control tests carried out from the beginning to the end of the production cycle, will contribute substantially to the production of consistently uniform batches of high-quality active pharmaceutical ingredients.

The manufacturer must assume responsibility for the quality of the active pharmaceutical ingredients produced. The manufacturer alone can avoid mistakes and prevent mishaps by exercising adequate care in both production and control procedures. Full evidence of compliance with GMP should be given from the step from which the processes or the starting materials used have a critical influence on the quality of the active pharmaceutical ingredient. This step should be determined in each individual case by agreement between the competent authority and the manufacturer.

The good practices outlined below should be considered general guides; whenever necessary, they may be adapted to meet individual needs provided the established standards of quality of the active pharmaceutical ingredients are still achieved. The good practices are intended to apply to the manufacturing processes (including packaging and labelling) used in the production of active pharmaceutical ingredients.

Sometimes several firms cooperate in the production (including packaging and labelling) of an active pharmaceutical ingredient. It may also happen that a finished, packed, and labelled active pharmaceutical ingredient is repacked and/or relabelled and given a new designation. Since such procedures constitute part of a manufacturing operation, they should be subject to the relevant guidelines set out below.

The practices outlined below are intended to apply to active pharmaceutical ingredients for both human and veterinary preparations.

1. Personnel

1.1 Each firm should employ personnel with the necessary qualifications and competence for the production and quality control of active pharmaceutical ingredients. There should be an adequate number of staff with appropriate education, technical knowledge, and practical experience related to the job they perform.

1.2 The firm should have a defined organization represented in a chart. Individual responsibilities should be laid down in written instructions, to ensure that there are no gaps or overlaps. The responsibilities placed on any one individual should not be so extensive as to incur any risk to quality.

1.3 Staff at all levels should be adequately trained for the tasks and responsibilities assigned to them.

1.4 Measures should be taken to ensure that no person affected by a disease in a communicable form or having open lesions on the exposed surface of the body is engaged in any production step involving direct contact with the active pharmaceutical ingredients.

2. Premises

2.1 Premises, including areas containing open tanks, should be of suitable construction. They should provide a suitable environment for manufacturing operations and should be adequately adapted to and of a sufficient size for their intended use. The premises should not contribute to actual or potential mix-ups or contamination of the active pharmaceutical ingredients. The arrangement should provide for a logical work flow.

2.2 For special purposes, such as the production of sterile products and of certain antibiotics, hormones, and cytostatic substances, separate specifically designed enclosed areas with completely separate air-handling systems should be provided.

2.3 To maintain hygienic working conditions, the premises should include facilities for changing clothes, washing, and toilet purposes as well as for eating, drinking, and smoking.

3. Equipment

3.1 Manufacturing equipment should be designed, constructed, located, and maintained in such a way as to:

(a) be suitable for its intended use;
(b) facilitate thorough cleaning;
(c) minimize the risk of contamination of products and containers during production; and
(d) facilitate efficient and, if applicable, validated and reliable operation.

3.2 Production and testing equipment should be cleaned, sterilized when necessary, used, and maintained in accordance with specific written instructions. Before production of another product is started, multipurpose equipment used should be thoroughly cleaned and checked for cleanliness. Appropriate records of such procedures should be maintained.

3.3 If necessary, equipment used for production and testing should have been shown to be capable of carrying out the processes for which it is intended.

3.4 Process-monitoring systems should be available where necessary. Measuring, recording, and control equipment should be calibrated and checked at suitable intervals by appropriate methods. Appropriate records of such tests should be maintained.

3.5 Defective equipment should be labelled immediately as defective and repaired or removed as soon as possible. Technical maintenance and repair should be documented.

4. Sanitation

4.1 Written sanitation programmes should be available. These should include validated cleaning procedures for premises and equipment, a quality standard for water, instructions for hygiene when manufacturing and handling goods, and instructions relating to the health, hygienic practices, and clothing of personnel and the disposal procedures for waste materials and unusable residues.

4.2 These programmes should be implemented; they should regularly be brought to the attention of the personnel involved and emphasized during continued staff training.

4.3 Protective garments and other protective items appropriate to the processes being carried out should be worn.

4.4 Eating, smoking, and unhygienic practices should not be permitted in manufacturing areas.

5. Documentation

Master formulae

5.1 Written instructions covering each stage of production, storage, and quality control should be available, and they should be updated whenever necessary.

5.2 There should be a master formula setting out in writing the starting materials and packaging materials (quality and quantity), as well as detailed production and quality control procedures for each active pharmaceutical ingredient. Wherever possible, the master formula should be prepared for standard batch sizes.

5.3 Competent persons experienced in production and quality control should be responsible for the content and distribution within the firm of instructions and master formulae. These should be duly signed and dated.

5.4 Outdated master formulae should be withdrawn but retained for reference. Copies of the master formula should be prepared in a manner that will eliminate any possibility of transcription error.

5.5 In certain circumstances, for example in the first production runs following pilot development, the master formula might need to be amended. Any amendments must be formally authorized and signed by competent person(s). The amended document should be replaced at the earliest opportunity by a newly prepared master formula.

Batch documentation

5.6 A batch manufacturing record should be completed during the production of each batch of intermediate products and of active pharmaceutical ingredients. It should contain the relevant parts of the master formula and should include the following:

(a) the name of the product (if applicable, the International Nonproprietary Name) or stage and the size and number of the batch;
(b) the dates of the different stages of production;
(c) production details, including reference to the main equipment used and yields;
(d) the batch or reference number (or analytical control number), if any, of starting materials used in the production;
(e) a record of the in-process controls followed and the results obtained;
(f) details of, and signed authorization for, any deviation from the master formula (any unplanned deviation being subject to investigation in relation to product quality);
(g) any recovered materials, and procedures applied;
(h) the initials of the operators and signature of the person responsible for the production operations and the date of signature;
(i) all analytical records relating to the batch, or a reference that will permit their retrieval;
(j) a decision for the release or rejection of the batch with the date and signature of the person responsible for the decision;
(k) the production record review (see section 17.21).

5.7 Where circumstances require the use of contract production and control facilities, this fact should be stated in the batch record.

5.8 Data may be recorded by electronic data-processing systems or by photographic or other reliable means. Master formulae and detailed standard operating procedures relating to the system in use should be available and the accuracy of the records should be checked. If documentation is handled by electronic data-processing methods, only authorized persons should be able to enter or modify data in the computer, and there should be a record of changes and deletions; access should be restricted by passwords or other means, and the entry of critical data should be independently checked. Batch records electronically stored should be protected by back-up transfer on magnetic tape, microfilm, paper print-outs, or other means. It is particularly important that, during the period of retention, the data are readily available.

Retention of records and reference samples

5.9 Records should be kept in such a way that activities concerning the production and quality control of active pharmaceutical ingredients are traceable.

5.10 Records and reference samples of the active pharmaceutical ingredients, and, where necessary, of intermediate products, should be retained at least one year beyond the expiry date of the finished product or for a specified period if there is no expiry date.

6. Production

Processing procedures

6.1 Processing should be carried out in accordance with the master formula.

6.2 Steps that are critical for the quality of the active pharmaceutical ingredient should be defined and the procedures applied should be validated.

6.3 Processing should be supervised and performed by competent persons.

6.4 During processing, vessels, containers, and significant equipment should be unambiguously labelled or identified with the name of the product and the batch number.

6.5 Information on the daily activities in each processing department should be available in addition to the batch documentation.

Starting materials

6.6 Starting materials should be received, quarantined, sampled, identified, examined for compliance with established specifications, released or rejected, stored, labelled, and dispensed in accordance with written instructions.

6.7 Some starting materials may not be tested for compliance because of the hazards involved (e.g., phosphorus pentachloride and dimethyl sulfate). This is acceptable when a batch certificate of analysis is available from the vendor and when there is a reason based on safety or other valid considerations.

Intermediate products

6.8 Intermediate products should, where necessary, be tested in accordance with the specifications and should be conspicuously labelled/identified and properly stored.

Active pharmaceutical ingredients

6.9 Each batch of finished active pharmaceutical ingredient must meet established specifications for quality, purity, identity, and potency, including, where applicable, specifications for tests and limits for residues of solvents and other reactants.

6.10 For the production of sterile active pharmaceutical ingredients, the first section of chapter 3 ("Sterile pharmaceutical products") may be applicable to the steps at which the process may have a critical influence on the quality attributes of the finished pharmaceutical product.

7. Packaging

7.1 Care should be exercised when packaging materials are selected for active pharmaceutical ingredients. The materials should have no detrimental effect on the substance, and should give adequate protection against external influences and potential contamination. Suitable written specifications should be available.

7.2 Attention should be directed at all stages to the prevention of packaging errors. Sound procedures must be employed to protect the quality of the product when it is packaged and to ensure that the correct labels are applied to the containers.

7.3 The containers should be conspicuously marked with the following information:

(a) the name of the product;
(b) its quality, if specified;
(c) the batch number;
(d) the expiry or retest date, if specified;
(e) warnings, if required;
(f) storage conditions, if specified; and
(g) the names of the manufacturer and the supplier.

Quality control

7.4 Every manufacturer should have an independent quality control unit, the head of which is directly responsible to the management of the firm. The principal duties of the quality control unit are listed below.

(a) It should approve:

  (i) specifications and testing methods for starting materials, intermediate products and, if required, packaging materials and active pharmaceutical ingredients;
  (ii) sampling procedures;
  (iii) instructions regarding sanitation and hygiene;
  (iv) reprocessing procedures for rejected batches or recovered materials;
  (v) other instructions related to the quality of the product.

(b) It should be responsible for the release or rejection of starting materials, active pharmaceutical ingredients, packaging materials, and, if required, intermediate products.

(c) It should ensure that the stability of active pharmaceutical ingredients is monitored.
(d) It should be responsible for the investigation of complaints related to the quality of active pharmaceutical ingredients.

7.5 Every manufacturer should have access to a control laboratory. The laboratory should be staffed and fully equipped for performing all quality control tests required. The tests should be performed in accordance with written and validated procedures. Instruments should be calibrated at suitable intervals and reagents should be of appropriate quality.

7.6 Where circumstances require the use of outside laboratories, this fact should be stated in the analytical records.

Stability studies

7.7 A written stability-testing programme should be established for active pharmaceutical ingredients. Stability-indicating methods should be used.

7.8 Samples should be stored in suitable containers and in simulated market containers at room temperature or the recommended temperature and under stress conditions.

7.9 Expiry dates do not usually need to be set for active pharmaceutical ingredients. If testing does not indicate a reasonable shelf-life, e.g. two years or more under anticipated storage conditions, then the product can be labelled with an appropriate arbitrary expiry date and should be retested on or before that date.

Self-inspection and quality audits

7.10 In order to maintain strict adherence to GMP and to all manufacturing procedures and prescribed controls, it is advisable for a firm to designate an expert or a team of experts to conduct regular independent inspections of its overall production and control procedures. Such experts should be as independent as possible in their inspection of production and control procedures.

7.11 Self-inspections and audits (see section 9) should be recorded.

Storage

7.12 Active pharmaceutical ingredients should be stored under conditions established by the manufacturer on the basis of stability studies.

7.13 Records should be maintained on the distribution of each batch of an active pharmaceutical ingredient in order to facilitate the recall of the batch if necessary, according to written procedures.

Complaints and defects

7.14 The manufacturer should maintain written instructions for dealing with complaints and defects concerning the quality of active pharmaceutical ingredients.

7.15 All necessary action should be taken promptly, the complaints thoroughly investigated, and all facts recorded.

7.16 The manufacturer should have a system to allow review of all products that may have been affected by a repetitive error or a failure in the procedures of the firm.

Rejected materials

7.17 The manufacturer should maintain written instructions concerning the handling of rejected materials, whether starting materials, intermediate products, packaging materials, or active pharmaceutical ingredients. Rejected materials should be conspicuously identified as such and stored in a controlled manner pending destruction, reprocessing, or return to the supplier.

Pharmaceutical excipients[1]

1. General considerations 197
2. Glossary 200
3. Self-inspection and quality audits 201
4. Equipment 202
   4.1 Use of equipment 202
   4.2 Cleaning programme 202
      4.2.1 Detailed cleaning procedure 203
      4.2.2 Sampling plan 203
      4.2.3 Analytical methods/cleaning limits 203
5. Materials 203
   5.1 General 203
   5.2 Starting materials 203
   5.3 Rejected and recovered materials 204
   5.4 Returned excipients 204
   5.5 Storage practices 205
6. Documentation 205
   6.1 General 205
   6.2 Specifications 206

[1] Good manufacturing practices: supplementary guidelines for the manufacture of pharmaceutical excipients. In: *WHO Expert Committee on Specifications for Pharmaceutical Preparations. Thirty-fifth report.* Geneva, World Health Organization, 1999 (WHO Technical Report Series, No. 885), Annex 5.

6.3 Batch production records 206
6.4 Other documents 207
7. Good practices in production and quality control 207
7.1 Change control and process validation 207
7.2 Good practices in production 208
7.2.1 Prevention of cross-contamination 208
7.2.2 In-process blending/mixing 208
7.2.3 Control of microbial contamination 209
7.2.4 Water systems/water quality 211
7.2.5 Packaging operations 211
7.2.6 Delivery 212
7.3 Good practices in quality control 212
7.3.1 General 212
7.3.2 Control of starting materials 212
7.3.3 In-process testing 212
7.3.4 Quality records and retention samples 213
7.3.5 Stability studies 213
7.3.6 Expiry/re-evaluation dating 214
7.3.7 Calibration of measuring and test equipment 214

1. General considerations

These guidelines, which focus on aspects of good manufacturing practices (GMP) specific for pharmaceutical excipients, supplement the general GMP guidelines for pharmaceutical products published by WHO.[1] They also incorporate some of the concepts for quality management systems determined by the International Organization for Standardization (ISO).

Excipients significantly affect the finished product quality, in some cases making up almost the entire formulation. Many pharmaceutical excipients are used in much greater quantities in other industries, such as the food, cosmetic or industrial chemical industry. Consistency and rigour of product specifications may not be as critical in these industries as they are for pharmaceuticals, and many of the excipients used are highly variable. Therefore, a programme must be in place which will monitor these excipients and provide the necessary assurance that they meet the quality parameters for pharmaceutical manufacturing processes. The purpose of this document is to lay out some criteria which may be used to achieve this level of assurance.

The formulator of the finished dosage form is highly dependent on the excipient manufacturer to provide bulk substances that are uniform in

[1] Good manufacturing practices for pharmaceutical products. In: *WHO Expert Committee on Specifications for Pharmaceutical Preparations, Thirty-second report.* Geneva, World Health Organization, 2003 (WHO Technical Report Series, No. 908), Annex 4. In this volume, see pp. 7–58.

chemical and physical characteristics. This is particularly important in the product approval process, where bioequivalence comparisons are made between clinical bioequivalence ("biobatch") production and commercial scale-up batches. To provide adequate assurance of drug product performance in vivo, the excipient used to manufacture commercial batches should not differ significantly from that used in biobatches. Where significant differences may be expected, additional testing by the finished dosage manufacturer may be required to establish the bioequivalence of the finished product. It remains equally important to ensure that the bioequivalence of subsequent, post-approval commercial batches of drug products is not adversely affected over time.

In general, excipients are used as purchased, with no further refinement or purification. Consequently, impurities present in the excipient will be carried over to the finished dosage form. While dosage form manufacturers may have a limited control over excipient quality (i.e. by obtaining certificates of analysis and testing representative samples), the excipient manufacturer has greater control over physical characteristics, quality, and the presence of trace-level impurities in the excipient. The excipient manufacturer should perform periodic performance trend analyses of processes, and the purchaser of the material should also maintain a trend analysis of all testing done on the excipient upon receipt.

In the manufacture of excipients, the environmental conditions, equipment and operational techniques employed reflect the chemical industry rather than the finished drug manufacturing industry. In some processes chemical and biochemical mechanisms have not been fully characterized; therefore, the methods and procedures for materials accountability will often differ from those applicable to the manufacture of finished dosage forms. Many chemical processes are performed in closed systems that tend to provide protection against contamination, even when the reaction vessels are not enclosed in buildings. However, this does not preclude the introduction of contaminants from equipment, materials used to protect equipment, corrosion, cleaning and personnel.

Some excipient manufacturing processes may require observance of GMP applicable to finished drug products or bulk active ingredients because of the excipient's intended use. However, such observance is neither feasible nor necessary in many processes, particularly during the early processing steps. The requirements increase as the process progresses. At some logical processing step, usually well before the final finishing operation, appropriate GMP should be imposed and maintained throughout the remainder of the process. To determine the processing step at which these GMP should be implemented, good judgement and a thorough knowledge of the process are required. A detailed process flow should identify the unit operations, equipment used, stages at which various substances are added, key steps in the process, critical parameters (time, temperature, pressure, etc.) and monitoring points.

An excipient manufacturer should be able to identify critical or key points in the process where selective intermediate sampling and testing is necessary in order to monitor process performance. Towards the end of the process, the records should be increasingly thorough.

Significant processing steps, required to produce an excipient that meets the established physical and chemical criteria, should be identified by the excipient manufacturer. These steps can involve a number of unit operations or unit processes. Unit operations include physical processing steps involving energy transfer where there is no chemical change of the molecule. Unit processes are those processing steps where the molecule undergoes a chemical change.

Significant processing steps include but are not limited to the following:

- Phase changes involving either the desired molecule, a solvent, inert carrier or vehicle (e.g. dissolution, crystallization, evaporation, drying, sublimation, distillation or absorption).
- Phase separation (e.g. filtration or centrifugation).
- Chemical changes involving the desired molecule (e.g. removal or addition of water of hydration, acetylation, formation of a salt).
- Adjustments of the solution containing the molecule (e.g. adjustment of pH).
- Precision measurement of added excipient components, in-process solutions, recycled materials (e.g. weighing, volumetric measuring).
- Mixing of multiple components.
- Changes that occur in surface area, particle size or batch uniformity (e.g. milling, agglomeration, blending).

Automated process controls and processing equipment are more likely to be used in an excipient plant than in a plant manufacturing finished dosage forms. Use of automated equipment is appropriate when adequate inspection, calibration, and maintenance procedures are performed. Production equipment and operations will vary depending on the type of excipient being produced, the scale of production, and the type of operation (i.e. batch versus continuous).

ISO "certification" for excipient manufacture is increasingly being required by final dosage formulators in the USA, Europe and Japan. Compliance to the International Standards of ISO 9000 series, in particular to ISO 9002, can confer greater acceptability of a supplier's excipients in world markets. There is additional value to applying the principles of ISO 9000 to excipient manufacture, since quality system measures enhance GMP. Such ISO considerations as conformance to specific customer requirements, purchase of raw materials and statistical techniques benefit both the excipient customer and the manufacturer, and strengthen the relationship between the two.

It is therefore recommended that excipient manufacturers establish and implement a formal company-wide quality policy. Management should be committed to this policy and should appoint appropriate company personnel to be responsible for coordination and implementation of the quality system. Management should participate in the development of the company's quality policy and provide the resources necessary for development, maintenance and periodic review of such a policy and quality system. Any significant changes in the processes should be validated with respect to excipient performance. It is recommended that all pharmaceutical manufacturers and also local agents should be informed of these changes. Ideally, excipient manufacturers should not subcontract any part of their process without the explicit knowledge of the pharmaceutical manufacturer.

Safe handling instructions should be provided by the excipient manufacturer to ensure that the purchaser is adequately equipped to handle the material. This should include information on the material's toxicity and the measurements to be taken upon accidental exposure. The equipment requirements for proper handling of the material should also be established.

2. Glossary

The definitions given below apply to the terms used in these guidelines. They may have different meanings in other contexts.

commingling
The blending of carry-over material from one grade of an excipient with another, usually due to a continuous process.

drug masterfile[1]
Detailed information concerning a specific facility, process or product submitted to the drug regulatory authority, intended for incorporation into the application for marketing authorization.

model product
A product which simulates a group of similar products.

mother liquor
A concentrated solution from which the product is obtained by evaporation, freezing, and/or crystallization.

pharmaceutical excipients
Substances, other than the active ingredient, which have been appropriately evaluated for safety and are included in a drug delivery system to:

— aid in the processing of the drug delivery system during its manufacture;
— protect, support or enhance stability, bioavailability, or patient acceptability;
— assist in product identification; or
— enhance any other attribute of the overall safety and effectiveness of the drug during storage or use.

---

[1] This term appears to be specific to United States regulations.

3. Self-inspection and quality audits

An inspection team consisting of appropriate personnel (e.g. auditors, engineers, laboratory analysts, purchasing agents, computer experts) should participate in inspections. The operational limitations and validation of the critical processing steps of a production process should be examined, to make sure that the manufacturer is taking adequate steps to check that the process works consistently.

The excipient's end-use should be identified and considered during inspection of excipient manufacturers. It is particularly important to know whether the excipient is a direct or indirect component of a drug dosage form; whether the excipient will be used in the preparation of a sterile dosage form; and whether the excipient is presented as pyrogen/endotoxin free. The excipient manufacturer is responsible for ensuring that excipients are pyrogen free if the manufacturer makes such a representation in specifications, labels or a drug master file.

A good starting point for an excipient plant inspection is a review of the following areas:

- Non-conformance, such as the rejection of a batch not complying with specifications, return of a product by a customer, or recall of a product. The cause of non-conformance should have been determined by the manufacturer, a report of the investigation prepared, and subsequent corrective action initiated and documented. Records and documents should be reviewed to ensure that such non-conformance is not the result of a poorly developed or inconsistent process.
- Complaint files. Customers may report some aspects of product attributes that are not entirely suitable for their use. These may be caused by impurities or inconsistencies in the excipient manufacturing process.
- Change control documentation.
- Master formula and batch production records. Frequent revisions may reveal problems in the production process.
- Specifications for the presence of unreacted intermediates and solvent residues in the finished excipient.
- Storage areas for rejected products.

In evaluating the adequacy of measures taken to preclude contamination of materials in the process, it is appropriate to consider the following factors:

- Type of system (e.g. open or closed). "Closed" systems in chemical plants are often not closed when they are being charged and/or when the final product is being removed. Also, the same reaction vessels are sometimes used for different reactions.
- Form of the material (e.g. wet or dry).
- Stage of processing and use of the equipment and/or area (e.g. multipurpose or dedicated).

Other factors that should be considered in evaluating an excipient plant are:

- Degree of exposure of the material to adverse environmental conditions.
- Relative ease and thoroughness of clean-up.
- Sterile versus non-sterile operations.

4. Equipment

4.1 Use of equipment

Many excipients are produced using multipurpose equipment. Fermentation tanks, reactors, driers, grinders, centrifuges and other pieces of equipment are readily used or adapted for a variety of products. With few exceptions such multiple usage is satisfactory provided the equipment can be adequately cleaned according to written procedures. Equipment that contains tarry or gummy residues that cannot be removed easily should be dedicated for use with these products only.

Some fermentation tanks, reaction vessels, and other equipment are not situated within a building and a considerable amount of processing occurs out of doors. Such processing is acceptable provided it occurs in a closed system.

Where temperature control is important, temperature recording devices should be used, with recording charts kept as part of the batch record.

4.2 Cleaning programme

Where multipurpose equipment is in use, it is important to be able to determine previous usage when investigating cross-contamination or the possibility of such contamination. An equipment cleaning and use log, while desirable and perhaps preferable, is not the only method of determining prior use. Any documentation system which clearly identifies the previous batch and shows that the equipment was cleaned is acceptable. For operations where multiple grades of the same chemical entity are processed, there must be documentation showing that the previous grade was removed. Validation data must exist to prove acceptability of the cleaning procedure.

Cleaning of multiple-use equipment should be confirmed. The manufacturer should determine the effectiveness of the cleaning procedure for each excipient or intermediate chemical used in that particular piece of equipment. The validation data required depend on the types of materials being made in the multiple-use equipment and the impact of trace contaminants on drug safety and performance. Validation data should verify that the cleaning process has removed residues to an acceptable level.

As an example, an equipment cleaning programme may include, but is not limited to, the following.

4.2.1 Detailed cleaning procedure

There should be a written equipment cleaning procedure that provides details of what should be done and which cleaning materials should be used. Some manufacturers list the specific solvents used for each excipient and intermediate.

4.2.2 Sampling plan

There should be some periodic testing after cleaning, to ensure that the surface has been cleaned to the required level. One common method is to analyse the final rinse water or solvent for the presence of the substance last used in that piece of equipment. In some cases, visual inspections may be appropriate. A specific analytical method to determine residual substances may not always be available, but is preferred. The need for an analytical method would be based on the potential adverse effect on product quality, performance or safety. When safety is a concern, there should be a specific analytical determination for a residual substance.

4.2.3 Analytical methods/cleaning limits

The toxicity of the residual materials should be considered when deciding on the appropriate analytical method and the residual cleaning limits. The residue limits established for each piece of apparatus should be practical, achievable and verifiable. The manufacturer should be able to show, with supporting data, that the residual level permitted is scientifically based. Another factor to consider is the possible non-uniformity of the residue. The level of residue found by random sampling, such as taking a swab from a limited area on a piece of equipment, does not necessarily represent the highest level of contamination.

5. Materials

5.1 General

In the case of labile products that may be sensitive to environmental factors such as air, light, water, heat or cold, appropriate manufacturing and storage conditions must be used to ensure product quality throughout the process.

5.2 Starting materials

The excipient manufacturer should verify that the supplier of starting materials and components can meet the agreed-upon requirements. This may require periodic audits of the vendor's plant if necessary. Purchasing agreements should contain data clearly describing the product ordered including, where applicable, the following:

- The name, type, class, style, grade, item code numbers or other precise identification as appropriate.
- Drawings, process requirements, inspection instructions and other relevant technical data, including requirements for approval or verification of product, procedures, process equipment and personnel.

Starting materials, including solvents and recovered solvents, are sometimes stored in silos or other large containers, making precise separation of batches difficult. Usage of such materials should be demonstrated, via inventory or other records, with reasonable accuracy.

When purchased and recovered solvents are commingled, the suitability of the recovered solvent must be demonstrated through either validation or actual testing. The purchased materials should comply with existing specifications.

Outdoor storage of starting materials (e.g. acids, other corrosive substances, explosive materials) is acceptable if the containers give suitable protection to their contents, identifying labels remain legible and containers are adequately cleaned prior to opening and use.

5.3 Rejected and recovered materials

Any starting material or intermediate or finished excipient not complying with specifications must be clearly identified and segregated to prevent inadvertent use or release for sale. A record of non-compliance should be maintained. All cases of non-compliance should be investigated to identify the root cause.

These materials may be:

— reprocessed/reworked to meet the specified requirements;
— regraded for alternative applications; or
— rejected or scrapped.

Occasional reprocessing/reworking of an excipient may be acceptable. However, relying on the final testing only of the reprocessed excipient to demonstrate compliance to specification is not acceptable. The quality of the reprocessed material must be evaluated and documented showing adequate investigation and demonstrating that the reprocessed excipient is at least equivalent to other acceptable excipients. When reprocessing has to be done frequently, it may be an indication that the process, work instruction or training is inadequate and needs to be adjusted or reinforced.

5.4 Returned excipients

Returned excipients should be identified as such and kept. If the conditions under which the products have been stored and shipped or if the condition of the container itself casts doubt on the safety, quality or purity of the excipient, the product should be destroyed, unless thorough examination, testing, or other investigation shows that the product meets the appropriate predefined standards. If returned excipient containers are reused, all previous labelling should be removed or defaced. If the containers are used repeatedly solely for the same excipient, all previous batch numbers, or the entire label, should be removed or completely obliterated.

5.5 Storage practices

Pharmaceutical excipients should be stored under conditions established by the manufacturer on the basis of stability data. Records should be kept of the distribution of each batch of pharmaceutical excipient, to facilitate the recall of the batch if necessary, according to written procedures.

6. Documentation

6.1 General

The excipient manufacturer should have a system to cover all documents and data that relate to the requirements of the quality system. Documents, and subsequent changes to the documents, should be reviewed and approved by designated personnel before being issued to the appropriate areas identified in the documents. A record should be kept of where the documents are located.

The following minimal requirements for documentation should be applied:

- To assign a unique batch number to the excipient to be released and/or certified.
- To prepare a batch record.
- To demonstrate that the batch has been prepared under GMP conditions from the processing point at which excipient GMP have been applied.
- To demonstrate that the batch is homogeneous within the manufacturer's specifications.

This does not require a final blending of continuous process material, if process controls can demonstrate compliance with specifications throughout the batch.

- To demonstrate that the batch has not been commingled with material from other batches for the purpose of either hiding or diluting an adulterated substance.
- To demonstrate that the batch has been sampled in accordance with a sampling plan that ensures a representative sample of the batch is taken.
- To demonstrate that the batch has been analysed using scientifically established tests and methods designed to ensure that the product meets accepted standards and specifications for quality, identity and purity.
- To demonstrate that the batch has stability data to support the intended period of use; these data can be obtained from actual studies on the specific excipient or from applicable "model product" stability studies that can reasonably be expected to simulate the performance of the excipient.

6.2 Specifications

Starting material specifications should be organized to separate those tests that are routine from those that are performed infrequently or only for new suppliers. Relevant pharmacopoeial monographs, when available, provide a basis for the development of internal manufacturer's specifications.

A positive identification test uniquely applicable to the excipients should be established through analytical technology, such as infrared spectrophotometry and chromatography.

It is important that manufacturers identify and set appropriate limits for impurities. These limits should be based upon appropriate toxicological data, or limits described in national compendial requirements. Manufacturing processes should be adequately controlled so that the impurities do not exceed such established specifications.

Many excipients are extracted from or purified by the use of organic solvents. These solvents are normally removed by drying the moist excipient. In view of the varying and sometimes unknown toxicity of solvents, it is important that excipient specifications include tests and limits for residues of solvents and other reactants.

Container specifications should be established for all excipients to assure consistency in protecting the product during transport from the excipient manufacturer to the pharmaceutical producer. The specifications should not only provide for containers that maintain the stability of the product, but should also meet requirements for protection during shipping, against insect infestation, during handling, etc.

6.3 Batch production records

Computer systems are increasingly used to initiate, monitor, adjust and otherwise control manufacturing processes. These operations may be accompanied by recording charts that show key parameters (e.g. temperature) at suitable intervals, or even continuously, throughout the process. In other cases, key measurements (e.g. pH) may be displayed temporarily on a monitor screen, but are not available in hard copy.

Records showing addition of ingredients, actual performance of operations by identifiable individuals, and other information usually seen in conventional records, may be missing. When computers and other sophisticated equipment are employed, the emphasis must change from conventional, hand-written records to:

— systems and procedures that show that the equipment and software is in fact performing as intended;
— checking and calibration of the equipment at appropriate intervals;
— retention of suitable back-up systems such as copies of the programme and files, duplicate tapes or microfilm;

— assurance that changes in the programme are made only by authorized personnel and that they are clearly documented and validated.

6.4 Other documents

Shipping and storage requirements should be established to ensure that the product reaches the manufacturer with proper quality attributes. This should be mutually agreed upon between the vendor and the purchaser and established prior to transportation of the product.

Written procedures should be established and followed for maintenance of the equipment. All maintenance activities performed must be recorded; this may be in the form of a log, computer database or other appropriate documentation, as long as the system can identify who was responsible for performing each function.

7. Good practices in production and quality control

7.1 Change control and process validation

Process changes may lead to changes in inherent product characteristics. Manufacturers should have a formal process change system in place, with written standard operating procedures covering such changes. Management of the change system should be assigned to an independent quality unit having responsibility and authority for final approval of process changes.

Manufacturers of excipients often produce laboratory or pilot batches. Scale-up to commercial production may involve several stages and data should be reviewed to demonstrate the adequacy of the scale-up process. Scale-up may introduce significant problems of consistency between batches. Pilot batches should serve as the basis for establishing in-process and finished product purity specifications.

Typically, manufacturers will generate reports that discuss the development and limitation of the manufacturing process. Summaries of such reports should be reviewed to determine if the plant is capable of producing the excipient. The reports serve as the basis for the validation of the manufacturing and control procedures, as well as the basic documentation to demonstrate that the process works consistently.

A document comprising scale-up data and describing the process reactions, operating parameters, purifications, impurities and key tests needed for process control should be written. A retrospective analysis of historical data (through statistical data and process capability data analysis) as well as the previous documentation will provide a good basis for validation.

7.2 Good practices in production

7.2.1 Prevention of cross-contamination

The potential for cross-contamination should be considered in the design of the manufacturing process and facility. The degree to which cross-contamination should be minimized depends on the safety and intended use of the excipient.

The precautions taken to minimize cross-contamination should be appropriate to the conditions of the manufacturing facility and will take account of the range of materials manufactured. When the excipient product is initially recovered, it should be in a clean environment and not exposed to airborne contaminants, such as dust from other excipient or industrial chemicals. Typically, the damp product will be unloaded into clean, covered containers and transported for drying and other manipulations. These subsequent operations should be performed in separate areas or under controlled conditions because once dry, the excipient is more likely to contaminate its environment, including any surrounding products. The primary consideration is that the building and facilities should not contribute to an actual or potential contamination of the excipient.

The air-handling systems at the site of manufacture should be designed to prevent cross-contamination. In dedicated areas processing the same excipient, it is permissible to recycle a portion of the exhaust air back into the same area. The adequacy of such a system of operation for multi-use areas, especially if several products are processed simultaneously, should be carefully analysed. In multi-use areas where several products are completely confined in closed vessels and piping systems, filtration of the supply air (combined fresh make-up air and recycled air) is acceptable if the conditions are consistent with other existing regulations (e.g. environmental, safety).

In those areas where the excipient is in a damp or moistened form, such as filter or centrifuge cake, and may be exposed to room air, filter efficiencies in the supply air system as low as 85% may be adequate. In those areas where one or more of the products is being processed in a dry form, such filtration may not be enough to prevent cross-contamination. In all cases, manufacturers should be able to demonstrate the adequacy of their air-handling systems.

Excipient manufacturers should have a documented programme identifying all insecticides, pesticides, rodenticides and herbicides used at the site of manufacture. Adequate measures should be taken to prevent these agents from contaminating the excipients.

7.2.2 In-process blending/mixing

Some processes require blending or mixing. Such in-process blending is acceptable provided it is adequately documented in batch production records. Examples include:

- Collection of multiple batches or continuous accumulation of batches with defined endpoint in a single holding tank (with a new batch number).
- Recycling material from one batch for further use in a subsequent batch.
- Repeated crystallizations of the same mother liquor for better yield of crystals.
- Collecting several centrifuge loads in a single drier/blender.

Incidental carry-over is another type of in-process mixing that frequently occurs. Examples include:

- Residue adhering to the wall of a micronizer used for milling the finished excipient.
- Residual layer of damp crystals remaining in a centrifuge bowl after discharge of the bulk of the crystals from a prior batch.
- Incomplete discharge of fluids, crystals or particles from a processing vessel upon transfer of the material to the next step in the process.

These residues are usually acceptable since clean-up between successive batches of the same excipient is not normally required during production. However, in the case of non-dedicated production units, complete cleaning procedures designed to prevent contamination that would alter the quality of the substance must be employed when changing from one excipient to another. Checking the effectiveness of these cleaning procedures may require the use of analytical testing for the substances involved.

In contrast to in-process blending and incidental carry-over discussed above, other blending operations should be directed towards achieving homogeneity of the finished excipient batch. Three areas in the processing of finished batches of an excipient which should be examined carefully and critically are:

— the final blending operation to produce the finished batch;
— the point in the process at which the batch number is assigned;
— the sampling procedure used to obtain the sample that is intended to be representative of the batch.

Blending of excipient batches to salvage adulterated material is not an acceptable practice.

Mother liquors containing recoverable amounts of excipients are frequently reused. Secondary recovery procedures for such excipients are acceptable, if the recovered excipient meets its specifications and if recovery procedures are indicated in batch production records. Secondary recovery procedures for reactants and intermediates are acceptable provided that the recovered materials meet suitable specifications.

7.2.3 Control of microbial contamination

The manufacture of sterile excipients for use in aseptic/sterile processing presents technical challenges. It is essential that adequately qualified and trained personnel be used to supervise and perform procedures associated with the manufacture of sterile excipients. The environment in which procedures are conducted, and the operators themselves, are significant potential sources of contamination in aseptic operations. Processes should be designed to minimize contact between excipient and the environment and operators. Those aseptic excipient operations which require considerable operator involvement must have adequate controls. Major potential problem areas include aseptic removal of the excipient from centrifuges, manual transfer to drying trays and mills, and the inability to sterilize the drier. Not all equipment currently in use can be sterilized.

The excipient manufacturer must document the cleaning of critical processing equipment such as centrifuges and driers. Any manipulation of sterile excipients after sterilization must be performed as a validated aseptic process. This is particularly important for those excipients which are not further sterilized prior to packaging into final containers. In some instances, the compendial monographs may specify that an excipient which does not meet parenteral grade standards must be labelled as not suitable for use in the preparation of injectable products.

Some manufacturers of non-sterile excipients use heat, gamma radiation and other methods to reduce the microbial burden. These methods are acceptable provided the manufacturer has shown that the product meets microbial requirements and that the process is under control within the manufacturer's specifications. Any procedure should be validated in accordance with recognized international standards to demonstrate that the process will produce the intended result. Post-production treatment of excipients should not be used as a substitute for attention to microbiological control during production.

A protected environment may be necessary to avoid microbial contamination or degradation caused by exposure to heat, air or light. The degree of protection required may vary depending on the stage of the process. Often, direct operator contact is involved in the unloading of centrifuge bags, transfer hoses (particularly those used to transfer powders), drying equipment and pumps, and equipment should be designed to minimize the possibility of contamination. The sanitary design of transfer and processing equipment should be evaluated. Those with moving parts should be assessed for the integrity of seals and other packing materials to avoid product contamination.

Special environments required by some processes must be monitored at all times to ensure product quality (e.g. inert atmosphere, protection from light). If interruptions in the special environment occur, adequate evidence must be provided that they have not compromised the quality of the excipient. Such environmental concerns become increasingly important after purification of the excipient has been completed.

The environment to which the excipient may be exposed should be similar to that used in the manufacture of the final dosage form. This is especially true in the case of excipients intended for parenteral dosage forms. For example, controlled areas may need to be established along with appropriate air quality classifications. Such areas should be serviced by suitable air-handling systems and there should be adequate environmental monitoring programmes. Any manipulation of sterile excipient after sterilization must be performed as an aseptic process, using Class 100 air[1] and other aseptic controls.

7.2.4 Water systems/water quality

While drinking-water is used for many excipient processes, purified water is also widely used. Because of the well-known potential for microbial growth in deionizers and ultrafiltration or reverse-osmosis systems used to produce purified water, such systems must be properly validated and checked. Proper control methods include the establishment of water quality specifications and corresponding action levels, remedial action when microbial levels are exceeded, and adequate maintenance procedures such as regeneration and sanitation/sterilization.

Appropriate specifications for chemical and microbial quality should be established and periodic testing conducted. Such specifications will vary depending on the process and the point in the process when the water is used. For example, in some cases, if the water is used in later processing steps such as for a final wash of the filter cake, or if the excipient is crystallized from an aqueous system, the water quality standards may need to be higher than normally specified for purified water. This is particularly important where the excipient's intended use is in parenteral dosage forms. The frequency of microbial and chemical testing of purified water depends on a variety of factors, including the test results and the point in the process (e.g. final wash in centrifuge) at which such water is used.

Most purified water and water for injection systems, including reverse-osmosis and ultrafiltration systems, have the potential for endotoxin contamination. If the final excipient is supposed to be pyrogen free or sterile, or will be used in preparing parenteral products, validation of the system to control endotoxins should be conducted and routine testing of the process water for endotoxins should be performed (preferably by the LAL (*Limulus* amoebocyte lysate) method).

7.2.5 Packaging operations

When the programme for packaging operations is being set up, particular attention should be given to minimizing the risk of cross-contamination, mix-ups, or

---

[1] Good manufacturing practices for pharmaceutical products. In: *WHO Expert Committee on Specifications for Pharmaceutical Preparations. Thirty-second report.* Geneva, World Health Organization, 1992 (WHO Technical Report Series, No. 823), Annex 1, Section 17.3. In this volume, see p. 88.

substitutions. Different products should not be packaged in close proximity unless there is physical segregation or the use of electronic surveillance.

7.2.6 Delivery

The manufacturer should arrange for the protection of the product after final inspection and testing. Where contractually agreed, this protection should include delivery to destination. Distribution records should be kept.

7.3 Good practices in quality control

7.3.1 General

The quality control unit, in addition to having the responsibility and authority to approve or reject all components, in-process materials, packaging materials and finished excipients, and to review production records, etc., should also be responsible for approving or rejecting excipients manufactured, processed, packaged, or held under contract by another company, as well as for approving or rejecting all procedures, specifications and process changes having an effect on the quality of the excipient.

7.3.2 Control of starting materials

All starting materials must be tested or otherwise verified prior to use. Verification should include a certificate of analysis from the supplier and, wherever feasible, an identification test. There should be clear guidance or standard operating procedures established for the approval of each starting material.

Starting materials are usually subjected to an identity test and additional testing to confirm that they meet appropriate specifications. Some starting materials may not be acceptance tested by the manufacturer because of the hazards involved or other valid considerations. In such cases, quality certification for each batch from the vendor should be on file. There should always be some evidence of an attempt by the excipient manufacturer to establish identity, even if it is only a visual examination of containers, examination of labels, or recording of batch numbers from the labels.

7.3.3 In-process testing

In-process inspection and testing should be performed by monitoring the process or by actual sample analysis at defined locations and times. The results should conform to established process parameters or acceptable tolerances. Work instructions should delineate the procedure to follow and how to use the inspection and test data to control the process.

7.3.4 Quality records and retention samples

The manufacturer should establish and maintain procedures for identification, collection, indexing, filing, storage, maintenance and availability of quality records. Quality records should be maintained to demonstrate achievement of the required quality and the effective operation of the quality system. These data should include pertinent subcontractor quality records.

All quality records should be legible and identifiable with the product involved. Quality records should be stored and maintained in such a way that they are readily retrievable, in facilities that provide a suitable environment to minimize deterioration or damage and to prevent loss. Retention times of quality records should be established and recorded. Where agreed contractually, quality records should be made available for evaluation by the purchaser or the purchaser's representative for an agreed period.

All appropriate records relating to inspection and testing must be available for review. Where the process is continuously monitored, acknowledgement must be made of this and the results of the monitoring should be available.

Reserve samples of the released excipient should be retained for one year after the expiry or re-evaluation date, or for one year after distribution is complete. Sample size should be twice the amount required to perform release specification testing.

7.3.5 Stability studies

Many excipient products are very stable and may not require extensive testing to check stability. The stability of some excipients may be affected by undetected changes in starting material specifications, or subtle changes in manufacturing procedures. Excipients may also be shipped in a large variety of different packaging types that can affect their stability (e.g. metal and plastic drums, bags, plastic and glass bottles, bulk tankers).

Some excipients may be similar in chemical structure to other excipients, and some may be mixtures or blends of other excipients. These excipients may be very similar to others within a product group. Minor quantitative differences of some of the components may be the only significant variation from one product to another. For these excipients, a "model product" approach to assess the stability may be appropriate. Stability studies of this type should involve selection of several "model products" that would be expected to simulate the stability of the product group being assessed. This selection must be scientifically based. Data from stability studies of these "model products" can be used to determine the theoretical stability of similar products.

The full stability testing programme, when needed, usually contains the following features and takes into account historical data:

- The programme should be formalized in writing and ongoing studies should be reviewed at least annually.
- The programme should periodically include a sample from at least one commercial size batch.
- Stability samples should be stored in containers that approximate the primary market container. Simulations of all types of containers are not required, unless there are theoretical reasons to indicate that stability may be affected by container type.
- The samples should be stored under conditions similar to those recommended for the marketed excipient product.
- Additional samples may be stored under stress conditions (e.g. elevated temperature, light, humidity or freezing) if such conditions might reasonably be encountered during distribution and storage.
- Stability-indicating test methods should be used.
- Where stability of the excipient appears to be a significant issue in its use in pharmaceutical manufacturing, additional periodic testing of either the specific material or "model products" may have to be performed to ensure that the expected stability does not significantly change with future batches. The frequency of testing should be determined by the impact that the excipient's stability may have on its usage.

7.3.6 Expiry/re-evaluation dating

Conducting a stability testing programme does not necessarily mean that expiry dates must be used. Where stability testing indicates a limited shelf-life, the label should declare an expiry date or indicate the need for re-evaluation testing at an appropriate interval to assure quality at time of use.

If the need for special storage conditions exists (e.g. protection from light, heat), such restrictions should be placed on the label.

7.3.7 Calibration of measuring and test equipment

All measuring and test equipment identified as being part of the quality system should be properly calibrated and maintained. This includes all in-process instruments identified as critical quality instruments, as well as test equipment used in the laboratory. The control programme should include the standardization or calibration of reagents, instruments, apparatus, gauges and recording devices at suitable intervals, in accordance with an established written programme containing specific directions, schedules, limits for accuracy and precision, and provisions for remedial action in the event that accuracy and/or precision limits are not met. Reagents, instruments, apparatus, gauges and recording devices not meeting established specifications should not be used. Computer systems used to verify that the product conforms to specifications must be audited to ensure satisfactory performance in the laboratory.

3. WHO good manufacturing practices: specific pharmaceutical products

Sterile pharmaceutical products[1]

Introductory note	215
1. General considerations	215
2. Quality control	216
3. Sanitation	216
4. Manufacture of sterile preparations	217
5. Sterilization	222
6. Terminal sterilization	223
7. Aseptic processing and sterilization by filtration	226
8. Personnel	227
9. Premises	229
10. Equipment	230
11. Finishing of sterile products	231
References	231

Introductory note

This document is a revision of section 17 of Part Three of "Good manufacturing practices for pharmaceutical products" (*1*), which emphasizes specific points for the manufacture of sterile preparations to minimize the risks of microbiological, particulate and pyrogen contamination. It is not exhaustive in character, and some technical requirements may change in line with developments in the field of good manufacturing practices (GMP) or advances in engineering design.

1. General considerations

1.1 The production of sterile preparations should be carried out in clean areas, entry to which should be through airlocks for personnel and/or for equipment and materials. Clean areas should be maintained to an appropriate standard of

[1] Good manufacturing practices for sterile pharmaceutical products. In: *WHO Expert Committee on Specifications for Pharmaceutical Preparations. Thirty-sixth report.* Geneva, World Health Organization, 2002 (WHO Technical Report Series, No. 902), Annex 6.

cleanliness and supplied with air that has passed through filters of the required efficiency.

1.2 The various operations of component preparation (such as those involving containers and closures), product preparation, filling and sterilization should be carried out in separate areas within a clean area. These areas are classified into four grades (see section 4.1).

1.3 Manufacturing operations are divided here into two categories: first, those where the product is terminally sterilized, and second, those which are conducted aseptically at some or all stages.

2. Quality control

2.1 Samples taken for sterility testing should be representative of the whole of the batch, but should, in particular, include samples taken from parts of the batch considered to be most at risk of contamination, for example:

(a) for products that have been filled aseptically, samples should include containers filled at the beginning and end of the batch and after any significant interruption of work;
(b) for products that have been heat sterilized in their final containers, consideration should be given to taking samples from that part of the load that is potentially the coolest.

2.2 The sterility of the finished product is ensured by validation of the sterilization cycle in the case of terminally sterilized products, and by "media-fills" runs for aseptically processed products. Batch processing records and, in the case of aseptic processing, environmental quality records, should be examined in conjunction with the results of the sterility tests. The sterility test procedure should be validated for a given product. Pharmacopoeial methods must be used for the validation and performance of the sterility test.

2.3 For injectable products, the water for injection and the intermediate and finished products should be monitored for endotoxins, using an established pharmacopoeial method that has been validated for each type of product. For large-volume infusion solutions, such monitoring of water or intermediates should always be done, in addition to any tests required by an approved monograph for the finished product. When a sample fails a test, the cause of such failure should be investigated and remedial action taken where necessary.

3. Sanitation

3.1 The sanitation of clean areas is particularly important. They should be cleaned frequently and thoroughly in accordance with an approved written programme. Monitoring should be regularly undertaken in order to detect the

Table 1. Limits for microbiological contamination[a]

Grade[b]	Air sample (CFU/m^3)	Settle plates (diameter 90 mm) (CFU/4 hours)[c]	Contact plates (diameter 55 mm) (CFU/plate)	Glove print (5 fingers) (CFU/glove)
A	<1	<1	<1	<1
B	10	5	5	5
C	100	50	25	—
D	200	100	50	—

[a] These are average values. The grades are defined in section 4.1.
[b] The airborne particulate classification for the four grades is given in Table 2.
[c] Individual settle plates may be exposed for less than 4 hours.

emergence of resistant strains of microorganisms. In view of its limited effectiveness, ultraviolet light should not be used as a substitute for chemical disinfection.

3.2 Disinfectants and detergents should be monitored for microbiological contamination; dilutions should be kept in previously cleaned containers and should only be stored for defined periods unless sterilized. Disinfectants and detergents used in grade A and B areas (see section 4.1) should be sterilized before use.

3.3 In order to control the microbiological cleanliness of the various grades in operation, the clean areas should be monitored. Where aseptic operations are performed, monitoring should be frequent and methods such as settle plates, and volumetric air and surface sampling (e.g. swabs and contact plates) should be used. The zones should not be contaminated through the sampling methods used in the operations. The results of monitoring should be considered when batch documentation for release of the finished product is reviewed. Both surfaces and personnel should be monitored after critical operations.

3.4 Levels (limits) of detection of microbiological contamination should be established for alert and action purposes, and for monitoring the trends in air quality in the facility. Limits expressed in colony-forming units (CFU) for the microbiological monitoring of clean areas in operation are given in Table 1. The sampling methods and numerical values included in the table are not intended to represent specifications, but are for information only.

4. Manufacture of sterile preparations

4.1 Clean areas for the manufacture of sterile products are classified according to the required characteristics of the environment. Each manufacturing operation requires an appropriate environmental cleanliness level in the operational state in order to minimize the risks of particulate or microbiological contamination of the product or materials being handled.

In order to meet "in operation" conditions, these areas should be designed to reach certain specified air-cleanliness levels in the "at rest" occupancy state. This latter state is the condition where the installation is complete, and production equipment has been installed and is operating, but no operating personnel are present. The "in operation" state is the condition where the installation is functioning in the defined operating mode and the specified number of personnel are present.

For the manufacture of sterile pharmaceutical preparations, four grades are distinguished here, as follows:

- *Grade A*: The local zone for high-risk operations, e.g. filling and making aseptic connections. Normally such conditions are provided by a laminar-airflow workstation. Laminar-airflow systems should provide a homogeneous air speed of approximately 0.45 m/s ± 20% (guidance value) at the working position.
- *Grade B*: In aseptic preparation and filling, the background environment for the grade A zone.
- *Grades C and D*: Clean areas for carrying out less critical stages in the manufacture of sterile products.

The airborne particulate classification for the four grades is given in Table 2. To obtain air of the required characteristics, methods specified by national authorities should be used. It should be noted that:

- In order to reach the B, C and D air grades, the number of air changes should be appropriate for the size of the room and the equipment and personnel present in it. At least 20 air changes per hour are usually required for a room with a good airflow pattern and appropriate high-efficiency particulate air (HEPA) filters.

Table 2. Airborne particulate classification for manufacture of sterile pharmaceutical preparations

	At rest		In operation	
	Maximum number of particles permitted/m³		Maximum number of particles permitted/m³	
Grade	**0.5–5.0 μm**	**>5.0 μm**	**0.5–5.0 μm**	**>5.0 μm**
A	3 500	0	3 500	0
B	3 500	0	350 000	2 000
C	350 000	2 000	3 500 000	20 000
D	3 500 000	20 000	Not defined	Not defined

- Detailed information on methods for determining the microbiological and particulate cleanliness of air, surfaces, etc. is not given here. Reference should be made to other guidelines published in compendia such as the European, Japanese or United States pharmacopoeias, or in documents issued by the European Committee for Standardization and the International Organization for Standardization (ISO).

The different airborne particulate classification systems for clean areas are shown in Table 3.

4.2 The particulate conditions given in Table 2 for the "at rest" state should be achieved in the absence of the operating personnel after a short "clean-up" period of about 15–20 minutes (guidance value), after completion of the operations. The particulate conditions given in Table 2 for grade A "in operation" should be maintained in the zone immediately surrounding the product whenever the product or open container is exposed to the environment. It is accepted that it may not always be possible to demonstrate conformity with particulate standards at the point of fill when filling is in progress, owing to the generation of particles or droplets from the product itself.

4.3 In order to control the particulate cleanliness of the various clean areas during operation, they should be monitored.

4.4 Appropriate alert and action limits should be set for the results of particulate and microbiological monitoring. If these limits are exceeded, the appropriate corrective actions should be taken, as prescribed in the operating procedures.

4.5 The area grades as specified in sections 4.6–4.14 must be selected by the manufacturer on the basis of the nature of the process operations being performed and validation runs (e.g. sterile media fills). The determination of an appropriate process area environment and a time limit should be based on the microbiological contamination (bioburden) found.

Table 3. Comparison of different airborne particulate classification systems for clean areas[a]

WHO (GMP)	United States (209E)	United States (customary)	ISO/TC (209)	EEC (GMP)
Grade A	M 3.5	Class 100	ISO 5	Grade A
Grade B	M 3.5	Class 100	ISO 5	Grade B
Grade C	M 5.5	Class 10 000	ISO 7	Grade C
Grade D	M 6.5	Class 100 000	ISO 8	Grade D

EEC: European Commission; ISO/TC: International Organization for Standardization Technical Committee.
[a] *Source*: references 1–4.

Terminally sterilized products

4.6 Components and most products should be prepared in at least a grade D environment in order to give low microbial and particulate counts, suitable for filtration and sterilization. Where the product is at unusual risk of microbial contamination (e.g. because it actively supports microbial growth, must be held for a long period before sterilization, or is necessarily not processed mainly in closed vessels), the preparation should generally be done in a grade C environment.

4.7 The filling of products for terminal sterilization should generally be done in at least a grade C environment.

4.8 Where the product is at unusual risk of contamination from the environment (e.g. because the filling operation is slow or the containers are wide-necked or are necessarily exposed for more than a few seconds before sealing), the filling should be done in a grade A zone with at least a grade C background.

4.9 The preparation and filling of ointments, creams, suspensions and emulsions should generally be done in a grade C environment before terminal sterilization.

Aseptic preparation

4.10 Components after washing should be handled in at least a grade D environment. The handling of sterile starting materials and components, unless subjected to sterilization or filtration through a microorganism-retaining filter later in the process, should be done in a grade A environment with a grade B background.

4.11 The preparation of solutions which are to be sterile filtered during the process should be done in a grade C environment; if not sterile filtered, the preparation of materials and products should be done in a grade A environment with a grade B background.

4.12 The handling and filling of aseptically prepared products, as well as the handling of exposed sterile equipment, should be done in a grade A environment with a grade B background.

4.13 The transfer of partially closed containers, as used in freeze-drying, should, before stoppering is completed, be done either in a grade A environment with a grade B background or in sealed transfer trays in a grade B environment.

4.14 The preparation and filling of sterile ointments, creams, suspensions and emulsions should be done in a grade A environment with a grade B background when the product is exposed and is subsequently filtered.

Processing

4.15 Precautions to minimize contamination should be taken during all processing stages, including the stages before sterilization.

4.16 Preparations containing live microorganisms should not be made or containers filled in areas used for the processing of other pharmaceutical products; however, vaccines consisting of dead organisms or of bacterial extracts may be dispensed into containers, after validated inactivation and validated cleaning procedures, in the same premises as other sterile pharmaceutical products.

4.17 The validation of aseptic processing should include simulating the process using a nutrient medium. The form of the nutrient medium used should generally be equivalent to the dosage form of the product. The process-simulation test should imitate as closely as possible the routine aseptic manufacturing process and include all the critical subsequent manufacturing steps. Consideration should be given to simulation of the worst expected condition. The process-simulation test should be repeated at defined intervals and after any significant modification to the equipment and process. The number of containers used for a medium fill should be sufficient to ensure a valid evaluation. For small batches, the number of containers for the medium fill should be at least equal to the size of the product batch.

4.18 Care should be taken to ensure that any validation does not compromise the processes.

4.19 Water sources, water-treatment equipment and treated water should be monitored regularly for chemicals, biological contamination and contamination with endotoxins to ensure that the water complies with the specifications appropriate to its use. Records should be maintained of the results of the monitoring and of any action taken.

4.20 Activities in clean areas, especially when aseptic operations are in progress, should be kept to a minimum, and the movement of personnel should be controlled and methodical, so as to avoid excessive shedding of particles and organisms due to over-vigorous activity. The ambient temperature and humidity should not be uncomfortably high because of the nature of the garments worn.

4.21 The presence of containers and materials liable to generate fibres should be minimized in clean areas and avoided completely when aseptic work is in progress.

4.22 Components, bulk-product containers and equipment should be handled after the final cleaning process in such a way that they are not recontaminated. The stage of processing of components, bulk-product containers and equipment should be properly identified.

4.23 The interval between the washing and drying and the sterilization of components, bulk-product containers and equipment, as well as between sterilization and use, should be as short as possible and subject to a time-limit appropriate to the validated storage conditions.

4.24 The time between the start of the preparation of a solution and its sterilization or filtration through a bacteria-retaining filter should be as short as possible. A maximum permissible time should be set for each product that takes into account its composition and the prescribed method of storage.

4.25 Any gas that is used to purge a solution or blanket a product should be passed through a sterilizing filter.

4.26 The bioburden of products should be monitored before sterilization. There should be a working limit on the contamination of products immediately before sterilization that is related to the efficiency of the method to be used and the risk of pyrogens. All solutions, in particular large-volume parenterals, should be passed through a microorganism-retaining filter, if possible immediately before the filling process. Where aqueous solutions are held in sealed vessels, any pressure-release outlets should be protected, e.g. by hydrophobic microbiological air filters.

4.27 Components, bulk-product containers, equipment and any other articles required in a clean area where aseptic work is in progress should be sterilized and, wherever possible, passed into the area through double-ended sterilizers sealed into the wall. Other procedures that prevent the introduction of contamination (e.g. triple wrapping) may be acceptable in some circumstances.

4.28 The efficacy of any new processing procedure should be validated, and the validation should be repeated at regular intervals thereafter or when any significant change is made in the process or equipment.

5. Sterilization

5.1 Whenever possible, products intended to be sterile should preferably be terminally sterilized by heat in their final container. Where it is not possible to carry out terminal sterilization by heating due to the instability of a formulation, a decision should be taken to use an alternative method of terminal sterilization following filtration and/or aseptic processing.

5.2 Sterilization can be achieved by the use of moist or dry heat, by irradiation with ionizing radiation (but not with ultraviolet radiation unless the process is thoroughly validated), by ethylene oxide (or other suitable gaseous sterilizing agents) or by filtration with subsequent aseptic filling of sterile final containers. Each method has its particular advantages and disadvantages. Where possible and practicable, heat sterilization is the method of choice.

5.3 The microbiological contamination of starting materials should be minimal, and their bioburden should be monitored before sterilization. Specifications should include requirements for microbiological quality when the need for this has been indicated by monitoring.

5.4 All sterilization processes must be validated. Particular attention should be given when the adopted sterilization method is not in accordance with pharmacopoeial or other national standards or when it is used for a preparation that is not a simple aqueous or oily solution.

5.5 Before any sterilization process is adopted, its suitability for the product and its efficacy in achieving the desired sterilizing conditions in all parts of each type of load to be processed should be demonstrated by physical measurements and by biological indicators, where appropriate. The validity of the process should be verified at scheduled intervals, at least annually, and whenever significant modifications have been made to the equipment. Records should be kept of the results.

5.6 For effective sterilization, the whole of the material should be subjected to the required treatment and the process should be designed to ensure that this is achieved.

5.7 Biological indicators should be considered only as an additional method of monitoring the sterilization process. They should be stored and used according to the manufacturer's instructions, and their quality checked by positive controls. If they are used, strict precautions should be taken to avoid any transfer of microbiological contamination from them.

5.8 There should be a clear means of differentiating products that have not been sterilized from those that have. Each basket, tray, or other carrier of products or components should be clearly labelled with the name of the material, its batch number, and an indication of whether or not it has been sterilized. Indicators such as autoclave tape may be used, where appropriate, to indicate whether or not a batch (or sub-batch) has passed through a sterilization process, but they do not give a reliable indication that the batch is, in fact, sterile.

5.9 Sterilization records should be available for each sterilization run. They should be approved as part of the batch-release procedure.

6. Terminal sterilization

Sterilization by heat

6.1 Each heat-sterilization cycle should be recorded by means of appropriate equipment of suitable accuracy and precision, e.g. on a time/temperature chart with a suitably large scale. The temperature should be recorded by a probe at the coolest part of the load or loaded chamber, this point having been determined during the validation; the temperature should preferably be checked against a second independent temperature probe located at the same position. The chart, or a photocopy of it, should form part of the batch record. Chemical or biological indicators may also be used but should not take the place of physical controls.

6.2 Sufficient time must be allowed for the whole of the load to reach the required temperature before measurement of the sterilizing time is started. This time must be determined for each type of load to be processed.

6.3 After the high-temperature phase of a heat sterilization cycle, precautions should be taken against contamination of a sterilized load during cooling. Any cooling fluid or gas in contact with the product should be sterilized.

Sterilization by moist heat

6.4 Sterilization by moist heat (heating in an autoclave) is suitable only for water-wettable materials and aqueous formulations. Both temperature and pressure should be used to monitor the process. The temperature recorder should normally be independent of the controller, and there should be an independent temperature indicator, the reading from which should be routinely checked against the chart recorder during the sterilization period. For sterilizers fitted with a drain at the bottom of the chamber, it may also be necessary to record the temperature at this position throughout the sterilization period. There should be regular leak tests on the chamber when a vacuum phase is part of the cycle.

6.5 The items to be sterilized, other than products in sealed containers, should be wrapped in a material that allows the removal of air and the penetration of steam but prevents recontamination after sterilization. All parts of the load should be in contact with water or saturated steam at the required temperature for the required time.

6.6 Care should be taken to ensure that the steam used for sterilization is of suitable quality and does not contain additives at a level that could cause contamination of the product or equipment.

Sterilization by dry heat

6.7 Sterilization by dry heat may be suitable for non-aqueous liquids or dry powder products. The process used should include air circulation within the chamber and the maintenance of a positive pressure to prevent the entry of non-sterile air. If air is supplied, it should be passed through a microorganism-retaining filter (e.g. an HEPA filter). Where sterilization by dry heat is also intended to remove pyrogens, challenge tests using endotoxins will be required as part of the validation.

Sterilization by radiation

6.8 Sterilization by radiation is used mainly for the sterilization of heat-sensitive materials and products. Many pharmaceutical products and some packaging materials are radiation-sensitive, so this method is permissible only when the absence of deleterious effects on the product has been confirmed experimentally. Ultraviolet irradiation is not an acceptable method for terminal sterilization.

6.9 If sterilization by radiation is carried out by an outside contractor, the manufacturer is responsible for ensuring that the requirements of section 6.8 are met, and that the sterilization process is validated. The responsibilities of the radiation plant operator (e.g. for using the correct dose) should also be specified.

6.10 During the sterilization procedure, the radiation dose should be measured. For this purpose, the dosimeters used must be independent of the dose rate and must provide a quantitative measurement of the dose received by the product itself. Dosimeters should be inserted in the load in sufficient number, and close enough together to ensure that there is always a dosimeter in the chamber. Where plastic dosimeters are employed, they should be used within the time-limit of their calibration. Dosimeter absorbances should be read shortly after exposure to radiation. Biological indicators may be used only as an additional control. Radiation-sensitive colour discs may be used to differentiate between packages that have been subjected to irradiation and those that have not; they are not indicators of successful sterilization. The information obtained should constitute part of the batch record.

6.11 Validation procedures should ensure that consideration is given to the effects of variations in the density of the packages.

6.12 Handling procedures should prevent any misidentification of irradiated and non-irradiated materials. Each package should carry a radiation-sensitive indicator to show whether or not it has been subjected to radiation treatment.

6.13 The total radiation dose should be administered within a predetermined period of time.

Sterilization by gases and fumigants

6.14 This method of sterilization should only be used for products where there is no suitable alternative.

6.15 Various gases and fumigants may be used for sterilization (e.g. ethylene oxide, hydrogen peroxide vapour). Ethylene oxide should be used only when no other method is practicable. During process validation it should be shown that the gas has no damaging effect on the product and that the conditions and time allowed for degassing are such as to reduce any residual gas and reaction products to defined acceptable limits for the type of product or material concerned. These limits should be incorporated in the specifications.

6.16 Direct contact between gas and microorganisms is essential; precautions should therefore be taken to avoid the presence of organisms likely to be enclosed in materials such as crystals or dried protein. The nature and quantity of packaging materials can significantly affect the process.

6.17 Before exposure to the gas, materials should be brought into equilibrium with the humidity and temperature required by the process. This requirement should be balanced against the need to minimize the waiting time before sterilization.

6.18 Each sterilization cycle should be monitored with suitable biological indicators, using the appropriate number of test pieces distributed throughout the load. The information so obtained should form part of the batch record.

6.19 Biological indicators should be stored and used according to the manufacturer's instructions, and their performance checked by positive controls.

6.20 For each sterilization cycle, records should be made of the time taken to complete the cycle, of the pressure, temperature and humidity within the chamber during the process, and of the gas concentration. The pressure and temperature should be recorded on a chart throughout the cycle. The records should form part of the batch record.

6.21 After sterilization, the load should be stored in a controlled manner under ventilated conditions to allow concentrations of residual gas and reaction products to fall to their prescribed levels. This process should be validated.

7. Aseptic processing and sterilization by filtration

7.1 The objective of aseptic processing is to maintain the sterility of a product that is assembled from components, each of which has been sterilized by one of the above methods (see sections 5 and 6).

7.2 The operating conditions should be such as to prevent microbial contamination.

7.3 In order to maintain the sterility of the components and the product during aseptic processing, careful attention needs to be given to: (a) the environment; (b) the personnel; (c) the critical surfaces; (d) the container/closure sterilization and transfer procedures; (e) the maximum holding period of the product before filling into the final container; and (f) the sterilizing filter.

7.4 Certain solutions and liquids that cannot be sterilized in the final container can be filtered through a sterile filter of nominal pore size 0.22 mm (or less), or with at least equivalent microorganism-retaining properties, into a previously sterilized container. Such filters can remove bacteria and moulds, but not all viruses or mycoplasmas. Consideration should be given to complementing the filtration process with some degree of heat treatment.

7.5 Owing to the potential additional risks of the filtration method as compared with other sterilization processes, a double filter layer or second filtration via a further sterilized microorganism-retaining filter immediately prior to filling may be advisable. The final sterile filtration should be carried out as close as possible to the filling point.

7.6 The fibre-shedding characteristics of filters should be minimal (virtually zero). Asbestos-containing filters must not be used under any circumstances.

7.7 The integrity of the filter should be checked by an appropriate method such as a bubble-point, diffusive-flow or pressure-hold test, immediately after use (it may also be useful to test the filter in this way before use). The time taken to filter a known volume of bulk solution and the pressure difference to be used across the filter should be determined during validation, and any significant differences from these values should be noted and investigated. The results of these checks should be recorded in the batch record. The integrity of critical gas and air vent filters should be confirmed after use. The integrity of other filters should be confirmed at appropriate intervals. Consideration should be given to increased monitoring of filter integrity in processes that involve harsh conditions, e.g. the circulation of high-temperature air.

7.8 The same filter should not be used for more than one working day unless such use has been validated.

7.9 The filter should not affect the product either by removing ingredients from it or by releasing substances into it.

8. Personnel

8.1 Only the minimum number of personnel required should be present in clean areas; this is particularly important during aseptic processes. Inspections and controls should be conducted from outside such areas as far as possible.

8.2 All personnel (including those concerned with cleaning and maintenance) employed in such areas should receive initial and regular training in disciplines relevant to the correct manufacture of sterile products, including hygiene and the basic elements of microbiology. When outside staff who have not received such training (e.g. building or maintenance contractors) need to be brought in, particular care should be taken over their instruction and supervision.

8.3 Staff who have been engaged in the processing of animal-tissue materials or of cultures of microorganisms other than those used in the current manufacturing process should not enter sterile-product areas unless rigorous and clearly defined decontamination procedures have been followed.

8.4 High standards of personal hygiene and cleanliness are essential, and personnel involved in the manufacture of sterile preparations should be instructed to report any conditions that may cause the shedding of abnormal numbers or types of contaminants; periodic health checks for such conditions are desirable. The action to be taken in respect of personnel who might be introducing undue microbiological hazards should be decided by a designated competent person.

8.5 Outdoor clothing should not be brought into clean areas, and personnel entering changing rooms should already be clad in standard factory protective garments. Changing and washing should follow a written procedure designed to minimize the contamination of clean area clothing or the carry-through of contaminants to clean areas.

8.6 Wrist-watches and jewellery should not be worn in clean areas, and cosmetics that can shed particles should not be used.

8.7 The clothing worn and its quality should be appropriate for the process and the grade of the working area (workplace). It should be worn in such a way as to protect the product from contamination. The clothing required for each grade is as follows:

- *Grade D*. The hair and, where relevant, beard and moustache should be covered. Protective clothing and appropriate shoes or overshoes should be worn. Appropriate measures should be taken to avoid any contamination from outside the clean area.
- *Grade C*. The hair and, where relevant, beard and moustache should be covered. A single or two-piece trouser suit, gathered at the wrists and with a high neck, and appropriate shoes or overshoes should be worn. The clothing should shed virtually no fibres or particulate matter.
- *Grades A/B*. Headgear should totally enclose the hair and, where relevant, beard and moustache. A single or two-piece trouser suit, gathered at the wrists and with a high neck, should be worn. The headgear should be tucked into the neck of the suit. A face mask should be worn to prevent the shedding of droplets. Appropriate, sterilized, non-powdered rubber or plastic gloves and sterilized or disinfected footwear should be worn. Trouser-bottoms should be tucked inside the footwear and garment sleeves into the gloves. The protective clothing should shed virtually no fibres or particulate matter and should retain particles shed by the body.

8.8 Outdoor clothing should not be brought into changing rooms leading to grade B and C rooms. For every worker in a grade A/B room, clean, sterilized or adequately sanitized protective garments should be provided at each work session, or at least once a day if monitoring results justify this. Gloves should be regularly disinfected during operations. Masks and gloves should be changed at least at every working session. The use of disposable clothing may be necessary.

8.9 Clothing used in clean areas should be laundered or cleaned in such a way that it does not gather additional particulate contaminants that can later be shed. Separate laundry facilities for such clothing are desirable. If fibres are damaged by inappropriate cleaning or sterilization, there may be an increased risk of shedding particles. Washing and sterilization operations should follow standard operating procedures.

9. Premises

9.1 All premises should, as far as possible, be designed to avoid the unnecessary entry of supervisory or control personnel. Grade B areas should be designed so that all operations can be observed from outside.

9.2 In clean areas, all exposed surfaces should be smooth, impervious and unbroken in order to minimize the shedding or accumulation of particles or microorganisms and to permit the repeated application of cleaning agents and disinfectants, where used.

9.3 To reduce the accumulation of dust and to facilitate cleaning, there should be no uncleanable recesses and a minimum of projecting ledges, shelves, cupboards and equipment. Doors should be carefully designed to avoid uncleanable recesses; sliding doors are undesirable for this reason.

9.4 False ceilings should be sealed to prevent contamination from the space above them.

9.5 Pipes and ducts and other utilities should be installed so that they do not create recesses, unsealed openings and surfaces that are difficult to clean.

9.6 Sinks and drains should be avoided wherever possible and should be excluded from grade A/B areas where aseptic operations are carried out. Where installed, they should be designed, located and maintained so as to minimize the risks of microbiological contamination; they should be fitted with effective, easily cleanable traps and with air breaks to prevent backflow. Any floor channels should be open and easily cleanable and be connected to drains outside the area in a manner that prevents the ingress of microbiological contaminants.

9.7 Changing rooms should be designed as airlocks and used to separate the different stages of changing, thus minimizing particulate and microbiological contamination of protective clothing. They should be effectively flushed with filtered air. The use of separate changing rooms for entering and leaving clean areas is sometimes necessary. Hand-washing facilities should be provided only in the changing rooms, not in areas where aseptic work is done.

9.8 Airlock doors should not be opened simultaneously. An interlocking system and a visual and/or audible warning system can be installed to prevent the opening of more than one door at a time.

9.9 A filtered air supply should be used to maintain a positive pressure and an airflow relative to surrounding areas of a lower grade under all operational conditions; it should flush the area effectively. Adjacent rooms of different grades should have a pressure differential of approximately 10–15 pascals (guidance value). Particular attention should be paid to the protection of the zone of greatest risk, i.e. the immediate environment to which the product and the cleaned components in contact with it are exposed. The various recommendations regarding air supplies and pressure differentials may need to be modified where it becomes necessary to contain certain materials, e.g. pathogenic, highly toxic, radioactive or live viral or bacterial materials or products. The decontamination of the facilities and the treatment of air leaving a clean area may be necessary for some operations.

9.10 It should be demonstrated that airflow patterns do not present a contamination risk; for example, care should be taken to ensure that particles from a particle-generating person, operation or machine are not conveyed to a zone of higher product risk.

9.11 A warning system should be included to indicate failure in the air supply. An indicator of pressure difference should be fitted between areas where this difference is important, and the pressure difference should be regularly recorded.

9.12 Consideration should be given to restricting unnecessary access to critical filling areas, e.g. grade A filling zones, by means of a physical barrier.

10. Equipment

10.1 A conveyor belt should not pass through a partition between a grade A or B clean area and a processing area of lower air cleanliness, unless the belt itself is continuously sterilized (e.g. in a sterilizing tunnel).

10.2 Whenever possible, equipment used for processing sterile products should be chosen so that it can be effectively sterilized by steam or dry heat or other methods.

10.3 As far as possible, equipment fittings and services should be designed and installed so that operations, maintenance and repairs can be carried out outside the clean area. Equipment that has to be taken apart for maintenance should be resterilized after complete reassembly, wherever possible.

10.4 When equipment maintenance is carried out within a clean area, clean instruments and tools should be used, and the area should be cleaned and disinfected again, where appropriate, before processing recommences if the required standards of cleanliness and/or asepsis have not been maintained during the maintenance work.

10.5 All equipment, including sterilizers, air-filtration systems, and water-treatment systems, including stills, should be subject to planned maintenance, validation and monitoring; its approved use following maintenance work should be documented.

10.6 Water-treatment plants and distribution systems should be designed, constructed and maintained so as to ensure a reliable source of water of an appropriate quality. They should not be operated beyond their designed capacity. Consideration should be given to including a testing programme in the maintenance of a water system. Water for injection should be produced, stored and distributed in a manner which prevents the growth of microorganisms, e.g. by constant circulation at a temperature above 70°C or not more than 4°C.

11. Finishing of sterile products

11.1 Containers should be closed by appropriately validated methods. Samples should be checked for integrity according to appropriate procedures.

11.2 Containers sealed under vacuum should be sampled and the samples tested, after an appropriate predetermined period, to ensure that the vacuum has been maintained.

11.3 Filled containers of parenteral products should be inspected individually. When inspection is done visually, it should be done under suitable and controlled conditions of illumination and background. Operators doing the inspection should pass regular eyesight checks, with spectacles if worn, and be allowed frequent breaks from inspection. Where other methods of inspection are used, the process should be validated and the performance of the equipment checked at intervals. The results should be recorded.

References

1. Good manufacturing practices for pharmaceutical products. In: *WHO Expert Committee on Specifications for Pharmaceutical Preparations. Thirty-second report.* Geneva, World Health Organization, 1992 (WHO Technical Report Series, No. 823), Annex 1.

2. *Airborne particulate cleanliness classes in clean rooms and clean zones. Federal Standard 209E.* Mount Prospect, IL, Institute of Environmental Sciences, 1992.

3. *Clean rooms and associated controlled environments. Part 1: Classification of airborne particulates.* Geneva, International Organization for Standardization, 1999.

4. *The rules governing medicinal products in the European Union. Vol. 4. Good manufacturing practices: medicinal products for human and veterinary use.* Brussels, European Commission, 1998.

Biological products[1]

1. Scope of these guidelines 232
2. Principles 233
3. Personnel 233
4. Premises and equipment 235
5. Animal quarters and care 237
6. Production 238
7. Labelling 238
8. Lot processing records (protocols) and distribution records 239
9. Quality assurance and quality control 240
Authors 241
Acknowledgements 241
References 242

1. Scope of these guidelines

These guidelines are intended to complement those provided in "Good manufacturing practices for pharmaceutical products" (*1*).

The regulatory procedures necessary to control biological products are in large part determined by the sources of products and methods of manufacture. Manufacturing procedures within the scope of these guidelines include:

— growth of strains of microorganisms and eukaryotic cells,
— extraction of substances from biological tissues, including human, animal and plant tissues (allergens),
— recombinant DNA (rDNA) techniques,
— hybridoma techniques,
— propagation of microorganisms in embryos or animals.

Biological products manufactured by these methods include allergens, antigens, vaccines, hormones, cytokines, enzymes, human whole blood and plasma derivatives, immune sera, immunoglobulins (including monoclonal antibodies), products of fermentation (including products derived from rDNA) and diagnostic agents for *in vitro* use.

[1] Good manufacturing practices for biological products. In: *WHO Expert Committee on Biological Standardization. Forty-second report.* Geneva, World Health Organization, 1992 (WHO Technical Report Series, No. 822), Annex 1; and *WHO Expert Committee on Specifications for Pharmaceutical Preparations. Thirty-second report.* Geneva, World Health Organization, 1993 (WHO Technical Report Series, No. 834), Annex 3.

2. Principles

The manufacture of biological products shall be undertaken in accordance with the basic principles of good manufacturing practices (GMP). The points covered by these guidelines should therefore be considered supplementary to the general requirements set out in "Good manufacturing practices for pharmaceutical products" (*1*), and relate specifically to the production and control of biological products. In drawing up these guidelines, due consideration was given to the draft "Guidelines for national authorities on quality assurance for biological products", the final version of which appears as Annex 2 to the forty-second report of the WHO Expert Committee on Biological Standardization (*2*).

The way in which biological products are produced, controlled and administered makes some particular precautions necessary. Unlike conventional pharmaceutical products, which are normally produced and controlled using reproducible chemical and physical techniques, biological products are manufactured by methods involving biological processes and materials, such as cultivation of cells or extraction of material from living organisms. These processes display inherent variability, so that the range and nature of by-products are variable. For this reason, in the manufacture of biological products full adherence to GMP is necessary for all production steps, beginning with those from which the active ingredients are produced.

Control of biological products nearly always involves biological techniques that have a greater variability than physicochemical determinations. In-process controls take on a great importance in the manufacture of biological products because certain deficiencies may not be revealed by testing the finished product.

The present guidelines do not lay down detailed requirements for specific classes of biological products, and attention is therefore directed to other guidance issued by WHO, and in particular to the Requirements for Biological Substances, which include requirements for vaccines (*2*, Annex 7).

3. Personnel

3.1 The manufacturing establishment and its personnel shall be under the authority of a person who has been trained in the techniques used in manufacturing biological substances and who possesses the scientific knowledge upon which the manufacture of these products is based. The personnel shall include specialists with training appropriate to the products made in the establishment.

3.2 Personnel required to work in clean and aseptic areas should be selected with care, to ensure that they may be relied upon to observe the appropriate codes of practice and are not subject to any disease or condition that could compromise the integrity of the product microbiologically or otherwise. High standards of personal hygiene and cleanliness are essential. Staff should be instructed to report any conditions (e.g. diarrhoea, coughs, colds, infected skin or hair, wounds, fever of unknown origin) that may cause the shedding of abnormal numbers or types of organisms into the working environment. Health checks on personnel for such conditions should be required before employment and periodically thereafter. Any changes in health status that could adversely affect the quality of the product shall preclude the person concerned from working in the production area.

3.3 Only the minimum number of personnel required should be present in clean and aseptic areas when work is in progress. Inspection and control procedures should be conducted from outside these areas as far as possible.

3.4 During the working day, personnel shall not pass from areas where live microorganisms or animals are handled to premises where other products or organisms are handled unless clearly defined decontamination measures, including a change of clothing and shoes, are followed. Persons not concerned with the production process should not enter the production area except for essential purposes, and in that case they shall be supplied with sterile protective clothing.

3.5 The staff engaged in the manufacturing process should be separate from the staff responsible for animal care.

3.6 The names and qualifications of those responsible for approving lot processing records (protocols) should be registered with the national control authority.

3.7 To ensure the manufacture of high-quality products, personnel should be trained in good manufacturing and laboratory practices in appropriate fields such as bacteriology, virology, biometry, chemistry, medicine, immunology and veterinary medicine.

3.8 Training records should be maintained and periodic assessments of the effectiveness of training programmes should be made.

3.9 All personnel engaged in production, maintenance, testing and animal care (and inspectors) should be vaccinated with appropriate vaccines and, where appropriate, be submitted to regular testing for evidence of active tuberculosis. Apart from the obvious problem of exposure of staff to infectious agents, potent toxins or allergens, it is necessary to avoid the risk of contamination of a production batch with these agents.

3.10 Where BCG vaccines are being manufactured, access to production areas shall be restricted to staff who are carefully monitored by regular health checks. In the case of manufacture of products derived from human blood or plasma, vaccination of workers against hepatitis B is recommended.

4. Premises and equipment

4.1 As a general principle, buildings must be located, designed, constructed, adapted and maintained to suit the operations to be carried out within them. Laboratories, operating rooms and all other rooms and buildings (including those for animals) that are used for the manufacture of biological products shall be designed and constructed of materials of the highest standard so that cleanliness, especially freedom from dust, insects and vermin, can be maintained.

4.2 Interior surfaces (walls, floors and ceilings) shall be smooth and free from cracks; they shall not shed matter and shall permit easy cleaning and disinfection. Drains should be avoided wherever possible and, unless essential, should be excluded from aseptic areas. Where installed they should be fitted with effective, easily cleanable traps and with breaks to prevent back-flow. The traps may contain electrically operated heating devices or other means for disinfection. Any floor channels should be open, shallow and easily cleanable and be connected to drains outside the area in a manner that prevents ingress of microbial contaminants.

4.3 Sinks shall be excluded from aseptic areas. Any sink installed in other clean areas shall be of suitable material such as stainless steel, without an overflow, and be supplied with water of potable quality. Adequate precautions shall be taken to avoid contamination of the drainage system with dangerous effluents. Airborne dissemination of pathogenic microorganisms and viruses used for production and the possibility of contamination by other types of viruses or substances during the production process, including those from personnel, shall be avoided.

4.4 Lighting, heating, ventilation and, if necessary, air-conditioning should be designed to maintain a satisfactory temperature and relative humidity, to minimize contamination and to take account of the comfort of personnel working in protective clothing. Buildings shall be in a good state of repair. The condition of the buildings should be reviewed regularly and repairs carried out when and where necessary. Special care should be exercised to ensure that building repair or maintenance operations do not compromise products. Premises should provide sufficient space to suit the operations to be carried out, allowing an efficient flow of work and effective communication and supervision. All buildings and rooms shall be clean and sanitary at all times. If rooms intended for the manufacture of biological substances are used for other purposes, they shall be cleaned thoroughly and, if necessary, sanitized before the manufacture of biological substances is resumed. Areas used for processing animal tissue materials and microorganisms not required for the current manufacturing process and for performing tests involving animals or microorganisms must be separated from premises used for manufacturing sterile biological products and have completely separate ventilation systems and separate staff.

4.5 If certain products are to be produced on a campaign basis, the layout and design of the premises and equipment shall permit effective decontamination by fumigation, where necessary, as well as cleaning and sanitizing after the production campaign.

4.6 Seed lots and cell banks used for the production of biological products should be stored separately from other material. Access should be restricted to authorized personnel.

4.7 Live organisms shall be handled in equipment that ensures that cultures are maintained in a pure state and are not contaminated during processing.

4.8 Products such as killed vaccines, including those made by rDNA techniques, toxoids and bacterial extracts may after inactivation be dispensed into containers on the same premises as other sterile biological products, providing that adequate decontamination measures are taken after filling, including, if appropriate, sterilization and washing.

4.9 Spore-forming organisms shall be handled in facilities dedicated to this group of products until the inactivation process is accomplished. For *Bacillus anthracis*, *Clostridium botulinum* and *Clostridium tetani*, strictly dedicated facilities should be utilized for each individual product. Where campaign manufacture of spore-forming organisms occurs in a facility or suite of facilities, only one product should be processed at any one time.

4.10 Dedicated facilities and equipment shall be used for the manufacture of medicinal products derived from human blood or plasma.

4.11 All containers of biological substances, regardless of the stage of manufacture, shall be identified by securely attached labels. Cross-contamination should be prevented by adoption of some or all of the following measures:

- processing and filling in segregated areas;
- avoiding manufacture of different products at the same time, unless they are effectively segregated;
- containing material transfer by means of airlocks, air extraction, clothing change and careful washing and decontamination of equipment;
- protecting against the risks of contamination caused by recirculation of untreated air, or by accidental re-entry of extracted air;
- using "closed systems" of manufacture;
- taking care to prevent aerosol formation (especially by centrifugation and blending);
- excluding pathological specimens sent in for diagnosis from areas used for manufacturing biological substances;
- using containers that are sterilized or are of documented low "bioburden".

4.12 Positive-pressure areas should be used to process sterile products, but negative pressure is acceptable in specific areas where pathogens are processed. In general, any organisms considered to be pathogenic should be handled within specifically designed areas under negative pressures, in accordance with containment requirements for the product concerned.

4.13 Air-handling units should be dedicated to the processing area concerned. Air from operations involving pathogens shall not be recirculated and, in the cases of organisms in a group above Risk Group 2 (*3*), shall be exhausted through sterilizing filters that are regularly checked for performance.

4.14 Specific decontamination systems should be considered for effluent when infectious and potentially infectious materials are used for production.

4.15 Pipework, valves and vent filters shall be properly designed to facilitate cleaning and sterilization. Valves on fermentation vessels shall be completely steam-sterilizable. Air-vent filters shall be hydrophobic and shall be validated for their designated use.

4.16 Small stocks of substances that have to be measured or weighed during the production process (e.g. buffers) may be kept in the production area, provided that they are not returned to the general stocks. Otherwise, dry materials used to formulate buffers, culture media, etc. should be weighed and put into solution in a contained area outside the purification and aseptic areas in order to minimize particulate contamination of the product.

5. Animal quarters and care[1]

5.1 Animals are used for the manufacture and control of a number of biological products. Animals shall be accommodated in separate buildings with self-contained ventilation systems. The buildings' design and construction materials shall permit maintenance in a clean and sanitary condition free from insects and vermin. Facilities for animal care shall include isolation units for quarantine of incoming animals and provision for vermin-free food storage. Provision shall also be made for animal inoculation rooms, which shall be separate from the postmortem rooms. There shall be facilities for the disinfection of cages, if possible by steam, and an incinerator for disposing of waste and of dead animals.

5.2 The health status of animals from which starting materials are derived and of those used for quality control and safety testing should be monitored and recorded. Staff employed in animal quarters must be provided with special clothing, changing facilities and showers. Where monkeys are used for the production or quality control of biological products, special consideration is required, as laid down in the revised Requirements for Biological Substances No. 7 (Requirements for Poliomyelitis Vaccine (Oral)) (*5*).

---

[1] General requirements for animal quarters, care and quarantine are given in reference 4.

6. Production

6.1 Standard operating procedures shall be available and maintained up to date for all manufacturing operations.

6.2 Specifications for starting materials should include details of their source, origin and method of manufacture and of the controls applied, in particular microbiological controls, to ensure their suitability for use. Release of a finished product is conditional on satisfactory results being obtained in the tests on starting materials.

6.3 Media and cultures shall be added to fermenters and other vessels under carefully controlled conditions to avoid contamination. Care shall be taken to ensure that vessels are correctly connected when cultures are added.

6.4 If possible, media should be sterilized in situ. In-line sterilizing filters for routine addition of gases, media, acids, alkalis, defoaming agents, etc. to fermenters should be used where possible.

6.5 Careful consideration should be given to the validation of sterilization methods.

6.6 When an inactivation process is performed during manufacture, measures should be taken to avoid the risk of cross-contamination between treated and untreated products.

6.7 A wide variety of equipment is used for chromatography; in general such equipment should be dedicated to the purification of one product and should be sterilized or sanitized between batches. Problems of decontamination and purification may arise through repeated use of the same equipment at the same or different stages of processing. The life span of columns and the sterilization method shall be defined. Particular care should be given to monitoring microbial loads and endotoxins.

7. Labelling

7.1 All products shall be clearly identified by labels. The labels used must remain permanently attached to the containers under all storage conditions and an area of the container should be left uncovered to allow inspection of the contents. If the final container is not suitable for labelling (for example a capillary tube), it should be in a labelled package.

7.2 The information given on the label on the container and the label on the package shall be approved by the national control authority.

7.3 The label on the container shall show:

— the name of the drug product;
— a list of the active ingredients and the amount of each present, with a statement of the net contents, e.g. number of dosage units, weight or volume;
— the batch or final lot number assigned by the manufacturer;
— the expiry date;
— recommended storage conditions or handling precautions that may be necessary;
— directions for use, and warnings and precautions that may be necessary;
— the nature and amount of any substance used in the preparation of the biological product that is likely to give rise to an adverse reaction in some recipients;
— the name and address of the manufacturer or the company and/or the person responsible for placing the drug on the market.

7.4 The label on the package shall, in addition to the information shown on the label on the container, show at least the nature and amount of any preservative or additive in the product.

7.5 The leaflet in the package should provide instructions for the use of the product, and mention any contraindications or potential adverse reactions.

8. Lot processing records (protocols) and distribution records

8.1 Processing records of regular production lots must provide a complete account of the manufacturing history of each lot of a biological preparation, showing that it has been manufactured, tested, dispensed into containers and distributed in accordance with the licensed procedures.

8.2 A separate processing record should be prepared for each lot of biological product, and should include the following information:

— the name and dosage of the product;
— the date of manufacture;
— the lot identification number;
— the complete formulation of the lot, including identification of seed or starting materials;
— the batch number of each component used in the formulation;
— the yield obtained at different stages of manufacture of the lot;
— a duly signed record of each step followed, precautions taken and special observations made throughout the manufacture of the lot;
— a record of all in-process control tests and of the results obtained;
— a specimen of the label;
— identification of packaging materials, containers and closures used;
— a dated signature of the expert responsible for approving the manufacturing operations;

— an analytical report, dated and signed by the responsible expert, showing whether the lot complies with the specifications described in the standard operating procedure registered with the national control authority;
— a record of the decision regarding the release or rejection of the lot by the quality control department and, if the lot is rejected, a record of its disposal or use.

8.3 The records shall be of a type approved by the national control authority. They shall be retained for at least two years after the expiry date of a lot or batch of a biological product and be available at all times for inspection by the national control authority.

8.4 Records must make it possible to trace all steps in the manufacture and testing of a lot, and should include records of sterilization of all apparatus and materials used in its manufacture. Distribution records must be kept in a manner that permits rapid recall of any particular lot, if necessary.

9. Quality assurance and quality control

9.1 The quality assurance and/or quality control department should have the following principal duties:

— to prepare detailed instructions for each test and analysis;
— to ensure adequate identification and segregation of test samples to avoid mix-up and cross-contamination;
— to ensure that environmental monitoring and equipment validation are conducted as appropriate for evaluating the adequacy of the manufacturing conditions;
— to release or reject raw materials and intermediate products, if necessary;
— to release or reject packaging and labelling materials and the final containers in which drugs are to be placed;
— to release or reject each lot of finished preparation;
— to evaluate the adequacy of the conditions under which raw materials, intermediate products, and finished biological preparations are stored;
— to evaluate the quality and stability of finished products and, when necessary, of raw materials and intermediate products;
— to establish expiry dates on the basis of the validity period related to specified storage conditions;
— to establish and, when necessary, revise control procedures and specifications; and
— to be responsible for the examination of returned preparations to determine whether such preparations should be released, reprocessed or destroyed; adequate records of the distribution of such preparations should be maintained.

9.2 A manufacturer's quality control laboratory shall be separated from the production area and ideally should be in a separate building. The control laboratory should be designed and equipped and of such a size as to be a self-contained entity, with adequate provision for the storage of documents and samples, preparation of records and performance of the necessary tests.

9.3 In-process controls play a specially important role in ensuring the consistent quality of biological products. Tests that are crucial for quality control but that cannot be carried out on the finished product shall be performed at an appropriate stage of production.

9.4 Performance of all qualitative and quantitative tests mentioned in the specifications for starting materials may be replaced by a system of certificates issued by the producer of the starting material, provided that:

- there is a history of reliable production,
- the producer is regularly audited, and
- at least one specific identity test is conducted by the manufacturer of the final product.

9.5 Samples of intermediate and final products shall be retained in sufficient amount and under appropriate storage conditions to allow the repetition or confirmation of a batch control. However, reference samples of certain starting materials, e.g. components of culture media, need not necessarily be retained.

9.6 Certain operations require the continuous monitoring of data during a production process, for example monitoring and recording of physical parameters during fermentation.

9.7 Special consideration needs to be given to the quality control requirements arising from production of biological products by continuous culture.

Authors

The first draft of "Good manufacturing practices for biological products" was prepared in January 1991 by Dr V.P. Grachev, Scientist and Dr D.I. Magrath, former Chief, Biologicals, World Health Organization, Geneva, Switzerland.

Acknowledgements

Acknowledgements are due to the following experts for their comments and advice on the draft of "Good manufacturing practices for biological products": Professor I. Addae-Mensah, Chemistry Department, University of Ghana, Accra, Ghana; Professor H. Blume, Bad Homburg, Germany; Dr A. Fenyves, Paul Ehrlich Institute, Langen, Germany; Dr C. Guthrie, General Manager, Blood Products Division, CSL Ltd, Parkville, Australia; Dr U. Ihrig, German Pharmacists' Central Laboratory, Eschborn, Germany; Mr K. Kawamura, Takeda Chemical Industries Ltd, Nihonbashi, Chuo-ku, Tokyo, Japan; Mr L.G. Kinnander, Chief Pharmaceutical Inspector, Medical Products

Agency, Uppsala, Sweden; Mrs S.F. Langlois, Director, Regulatory Affairs, Connaught Laboratories Ltd, Willowdale, Ontario, Canada; Mr P. Lemoine, Institute of Hygiene and Epidemiology, Brussels, Belgium; Mr J. Lyng, State Serum Institute, Copenhagen, Denmark; Professor N.V. Medunitsin, Director, Tarasevich State Institute for the Standardization and Control of Medical Biological Preparations, Moscow, Russian Federation; Dr R. Netter, Paris, France; Professor A.A. Olaniyi, Pharmaceutical and Chemistry Department, Faculty of Pharmacy, University of Ibadan, Ibadan, Nigeria.

References

1. Good manufacturing practices for pharmaceutical products. In: *WHO Expert Committee on Specifications for Pharmaceutical Preparations. Thirty-second report.* Geneva, World Health Organization, 1992 (WHO Technical Report Series, No. 823), Annex 1.

2. *WHO Expert Committee on Biological Standardization. Forty-second report.* Geneva, World Health Organization, 1992 (WHO Technical Report Series, No. 822).

3. *Laboratory biosafety manual*, 2nd ed. Geneva, World Health Organization, 1993.

4. *Quality management for chemical safety testing.* Geneva, World Health Organization, 1992 (Environmental Health Criteria, No. 141).

5. *WHO Expert Committee on Biological Standardization. Fortieth report.* Geneva, World Health Organization, 1990 (WHO Technical Report Series, No. 800), Annex 1.

Investigational pharmaceutical products for clinical trials in humans[1]

1. Introductory note

The legal status of investigational pharmaceutical products for human use varies from country to country; in some of them (e.g. Germany, the United States and others), these products are manufactured and inspected like "normal" licensed pharmaceutical products. In most other countries, however, they are not covered by legal and regulatory provisions in the areas of good manufacturing practice (GMP) inspection, etc.

However, the EC guide on GMP (*1*) recommends that the principles of GMP should be applied, as appropriate, to the preparation of these products,

[1] Good manufacturing practices: supplementary guidelines for the manufacture of investigational pharmaceutical products for clinical trials in humans. In: *WHO Expert Committee on Specifications for Pharmaceutical Preparations. Thirty-fourth report.* Geneva, World Health Organization, 1996 (WHO Technical Report Series, No. 863), Annex 7.

and the WHO guide on GMP, according to the statement in the general considerations, is applicable to "the preparation of clinical trials supplies" (*2*, page 18).

2. General considerations

The present guidelines supplement both the WHO guide on GMP and the guidelines on good clinical practice (GCP) for trials on pharmaceutical products (*3*). The application of the principles of GMP to the preparation of investigational products is necessary for several reasons:

- To assure consistency between and within batches of the investigational product and thus assure the reliability of clinical trials.
- To assure consistency between the investigational product and the future commercial product and therefore the relevance of the clinical trial to the efficacy and safety of the marketed product.
- To protect subjects of clinical trials from poor-quality products resulting from manufacturing errors (omission of critical steps such as sterilization, contamination and cross-contamination, mix-ups, wrong labelling, etc.), or from starting materials and components of inadequate quality.
- To document all changes in the manufacturing process.

In this context, the selection of an appropriate dosage for clinical trials is important. While it is accepted that in early trials the dosage form may be very different from the anticipated final formulation (e.g. a capsule instead of a tablet), in the pivotal Phase III studies it should be similar to the projected commercial presentation; otherwise these trials will not necessarily prove that the marketed product is both efficacious and safe.

If there are significant differences between the clinical and commercial dosage forms, data should be submitted to the registration authorities to demonstrate that the final dosage form is equivalent, in terms of bioavailability and stability, to that used in the clinical trials. Final manufacturing methods must be revalidated following changes in processes, scaling-up, transfer to other manufacturing sites, etc.

This section specifically addresses those practices that may be different for investigational products, which are usually not manufactured in accordance with a set routine, and which may possibly be incompletely characterized during the initial stages of clinical development.

3. Glossary

The definitions given below apply to the terms used in these guidelines. They may have different meanings in other contexts.

clinical trial

Any systematic study on pharmaceutical products in human subjects, whether in patients or other volunteers, in order to discover or verify the effects of, and/or identify any adverse reaction to, investigational products, and/or to study the absorption, distribution, metabolism and excretion of the products with the object of ascertaining their efficacy and safety.

Clinical trials are generally divided into Phases I–IV. It is not possible to draw clear distinctions between these phases, and different opinions about details and methodology do exist. However, the individual phases, based on their purposes as related to the clinical development of pharmaceutical products, can be briefly defined as follows:

Phase I. These are the first trials of a new active ingredient or new formulations in humans, often carried out in healthy volunteers. Their purpose is to make a preliminary evaluation of safety, and an initial pharmacokinetic/ pharmacodynamic profile of the active ingredient.

Phase II. The purpose of these therapeutic pilot studies is to determine activity and to assess the short-term safety of the active ingredient in patients suffering from a disease or condition for which it is intended. The trials are performed in a limited number of subjects and are often, at a later stage, of a comparative (e.g. placebo-controlled) design. This phase is also concerned with the determination of appropriate dose ranges/regimens and (if possible) the clarification of dose-response relationships in order to provide an optimal background for the design of extensive therapeutic trials.

Phase III. This phase involves trials in large (and possibly varied) patient groups for the purpose of determining the short- and long-term safety-efficacy balance of formulation(s) of the active ingredient, and assessing its overall and relative therapeutic value. The pattern and profile of any frequent adverse reactions must be investigated, and special features of the product must be explored (e.g. clinically relevant drug interactions, factors leading to differences in effect, such as age). The trials should preferably be randomized double-blind, but other designs may be acceptable, e.g. long-term safety studies. In general, the conditions under which the trials are conducted should be as close as possible to the normal conditions of use.

Phase IV. In this phase studies are performed after the pharmaceutical product has been marketed. They are based on the product characteristics on which the marketing authorization was granted and normally take the form of post-marketing surveillance, and assessment of therapeutic value or treatment strategies. Although methods may differ, the same scientific and ethical standards should apply to Phase IV studies as are applied in premarketing studies. After a product has been placed on the market, clinical trials designed to explore new indications, new methods of administration or new combinations, etc., are normally regarded as trials of new pharmaceutical products.

investigational product
Any pharmaceutical product (new product or reference product) or placebo being tested or used as a reference in a clinical trial.

investigator
The person responsible for the trial and for protecting the rights, health and welfare of the subjects in the trial. The investigator must be an appropriately qualified person legally allowed to practise medicine/dentistry.

monitor
A person appointed by, and responsible to, the sponsor for monitoring and reporting the progress of the trial and for the verification of data.

order
An instruction to process, package and/or ship a certain number of units of an investigational product.

pharmaceutical product
For the purpose of this Annex, this term is defined in the same way as in the WHO guidelines on GCP (*3*), i.e. as any substance or combination of substances which has a therapeutic, prophylactic or diagnostic purpose, or is intended to modify physiological functions, and is presented in a dosage form suitable for administration to humans.

product specification file(s)
Reference file(s) containing all the information necessary to draft the detailed written instructions on processing, packaging, labelling, quality control testing, batch release, storage conditions and shipping.

protocol
A document which gives the background, rationale and objectives of the trial and describes its design, methodology and organization, including statistical considerations, and the conditions under which it is to be performed and managed. It should be dated and signed by the investigator/institution involved and the sponsor, and can, in addition, function as a contract.

shipping/dispatch
The assembly, packing for shipment, and sending of ordered medicinal products for clinical trials.

sponsor
An individual, company, institution or organization which takes responsibility for the initiation, management and/or financing of a clinical trial. When an

investigator independently initiates and takes full responsibility for a trial, the investigator then also assumes the role of the sponsor.

4. Quality assurance

Quality assurance of pharmaceutical products has been defined and discussed in detail in the guide on GMP (*2*, pages 25–26).

The quality of dosage forms in Phase III clinical studies should be characterized and assured at the same level as for routinely manufactured products. The quality assurance system, designed, established and verified by the manufacturer, should be described in writing, taking into account the GMP principles to the extent that they are applicable to the operations in question. This system should also cover the interface between the manufacture and the trial site (e.g. shipment, storage, occasional additional labelling).

5. Validation[1]

Some of the production processes for investigational products that have not received marketing authorization may not be validated to the extent necessary for a routine production operation. The product specifications and manufacturing instructions may vary during development. This increased complexity in the manufacturing operations requires a highly effective quality assurance system.

For sterile products, there should be no reduction in the degree of validation of sterilizing equipment required. Validation of aseptic processes presents special problems when the batch size is small, since the number of units filled may not be adequate for a validation exercise. Filling and sealing, which is often done by hand, can compromise the maintenance of sterility. Greater attention should therefore be given to environmental monitoring.

6. Complaints

The conclusions of any investigation carried out in response to a complaint should be discussed between the manufacturer and the sponsor (if different) or between the persons responsible for manufacture and those responsible for the relevant clinical trial in order to assess any potential impact on the trial and on the product development, to determine the cause, and to take any necessary corrective action.

---

[1] For additional advice on validation, see Validation of manufacturing processes, pp. 53–71.

7. Recalls

Recall procedures should be understood by the sponsor, investigator and monitor in addition to the person(s) responsible for recalls, as described in the guide on GMP (2, pages 28–29).

8. Personnel

Although it is likely that the number of staff involved will be small, people should be separately designated as responsible for production and quality control. All production operations should be carried out under the control of a clearly identified responsible person. Personnel concerned with development, involved in production and quality control, need to be instructed in the principles of GMP.

9. Premises and equipment

During the manufacture of investigational products, different products may be handled in the same premises and at the same time, and this reinforces the need to eliminate all risks of contamination, including cross-contamination. Special attention should be paid to line clearance in order to avoid mix-ups. Validated cleaning procedures should be followed to prevent cross-contamination.

For the production of the particular products referred to in section 11.20 of the guide on GMP (2, page 38), campaign working may be acceptable in place of dedicated and self-contained facilities. Because the toxicity of the materials may not be fully known, cleaning is of particular importance; account should be taken of the solubility of the product and excipients in various cleaning agents.

10. Materials

Starting materials

The consistency of production may be influenced by the quality of the starting materials. Their physical, chemical and, when appropriate, microbiological properties should therefore be defined, documented in their specifications, and controlled. Existing compendial standards, when available, should be taken into consideration. Specifications for active ingredients should be as comprehensive as possible, given the current state of knowledge. Specifications for both active and non-active ingredients should be periodically reassessed.

Detailed information on the quality of active and non-active ingredients, as well as of packaging materials, should be available so as to make it possible to recognize and, as necessary, allow for any variation in production.

Chemical and biological reference standards for analytical purposes

Reference standards from reputable sources (WHO or national standards) should be used, if available; otherwise the reference substance(s) for the active ingredient(s) should be prepared, tested and released as reference material(s) by the producer of the investigational pharmaceutical product, or by the producer of the active ingredient(s) used in the manufacture of that product.

Principles applicable to reference products for clinical trials

In studies in which an investigational product is compared with a marketed product, steps should be taken to ensure the integrity and quality of the reference products (final dosage form, packaging materials, storage conditions, etc.). If significant changes are to be made in the product, data should be available (e.g. on stability, comparative dissolution) that demonstrate that these changes do not influence the original quality characteristics of the product.

11. Documentation

Specifications (for starting materials, primary packaging materials, intermediate and bulk products and finished products), master formulae, and processing and packaging instructions may be changed frequently as a result of new experience in the development of an investigational product. Each new version should take into account the latest data and include a reference to the previous version so that traceability is ensured. Rationales for changes should be stated and recorded.

Batch processing and packaging records should be retained for at least 2 years after the termination or discontinuance of the clinical trial, or after the approval of the investigational product.

Order

The order may request the processing and/or packaging of a certain number of units and/or their shipping. It may only be given by the sponsor to the manufacturer of an investigational product. It should be in writing (though it may be transmitted by electronic means), precise enough to avoid any ambiguity and formally authorized, and refer to the approved product specification file (see below).

Product specification file(s)

A product specification file (or files) should contain the information necessary to draft the detailed written instructions on processing, packaging, quality control testing, batch release, storage conditions and/or shipping. It should indicate who has been designated or trained as the authorized person responsible for the release of batches (see reference *2*, page 18). It should be continuously updated while at the same time ensuring appropriate traceability to the previous versions.

Specifications

In developing specifications, special attention should be paid to characteristics which affect the efficacy and safety of pharmaceutical products, namely:

- The accuracy of the therapeutic or unitary dose: homogeneity, content uniformity.
- The release of active ingredients from the dosage form: dissolution time, etc.
- The estimated stability, if necessary, under accelerated conditions, the preliminary storage conditions and the shelf-life of the product.[1]

In addition, the package size should be suitable for the requirements of the trial.

Specifications may be subject to change as the development of the product progresses. Changes should, however, be made in accordance with a written procedure authorized by a responsible person and clearly recorded. Specifications should be based on all available scientific data, current state-of-the-art technology, and the regulatory and pharmacopoeial requirements.

Master formulae and processing instructions

These may be changed in the light of experience, but allowance must be made for any possible repercussions on stability and, above all, on bioequivalence between batches of finished products. Changes should be made in accordance with a written procedure, authorized by a responsible person and clearly recorded.

It may sometimes not be necessary to produce master formulae and processing instructions, but for every manufacturing operation or supply there should be clear and adequate written instructions and written records. Records are particularly important for the preparation of the final version of the documents to be used in routine manufacture.

Packaging instructions

The number of units to be packaged should be specified before the start of the packaging operations. Account should be taken of the number of units

[1] See *Quality assurance of pharmaceuticals: a compendium of guidelines and related materials. Vol. 1.* Geneva, World Health Organization, 1997:46–61.

necessary for carrying out quality controls and of the number of samples from each batch used in the clinical trial to be kept as a reference for further rechecking and control. A reconciliation should be carried out at the end of the packaging and labelling process.

Labelling instructions

The information presented on labels should include:

- The name of the sponsor.
- A statement: "for clinical research use only".
- A trial reference number.
- A batch number.
- The patient identification number.[1]
- The storage conditions.
- The expiry date (month/year) or a retest date.

Additional information may be displayed in accordance with the order (e.g. dosing instructions, treatment period, standard warnings). When necessary for blinding purposes, the batch number may be provided separately (see also "Blinding operations" on p. 123). A copy of each type of label should be kept in the batch packaging record.

Processing and packaging batch records

Processing and packaging batch records should be kept in sufficient detail for the sequence of operations to be accurately traced. They should contain any relevant remarks which increase existing knowledge of the product, allow improvements in the manufacturing operations, and justify the procedures used.

Coding (or randomization) systems

Procedures should be established for the generation, distribution, handling and retention of any randomization code used in packaging investigational products.

A coding system should be introduced to permit the proper identification of "blinded" products. The code, together with the randomization list, must permit proper identification of the product, including any necessary traceability to the codes and batch number of the product before the blinding operation. The coding system must permit determination without delay in an emergency situation of the identity of the actual treatment product received by individual subjects.

[1] This is not necessarily inserted at the manufacturing facility but may be added at a later stage.

12. Production

Products intended for use in clinical trials (late Phase II and Phase III studies) should as far as possible be manufactured at a licensed facility, e.g.:

- A pilot plant, primarily designed and used for process development.
- A small-scale facility (sometimes called a "pharmacy")[1] separate both from the company's pilot plant and from routine production.
- A larger-scale production line assembled to manufacture materials in larger batches, e.g. for late Phase III trials and first commercial batches.
- The normal production line used for licensed commercial batches, and sometimes for the production of investigational pharmaceutical products if the number, e.g. of ordered ampoules, tablets or other dosage forms, is large enough.

The relation between the batch size for investigational pharmaceutical products manufactured in a pilot plant or small-scale facility and the planned full-size batches may vary widely depending on the pilot plant or "pharmacy" batch size demanded and the capacity available in full-size production.

The present guidelines are applicable to licensed facilities of the first and second types. It is easier to assure compliance with GMP in facilities of the second type, since processes are kept constant in the course of production and are not normally changed for the purpose of process development. Facilities of the remaining types should be subject to all GMP rules for pharmaceutical products.

Administratively, the manufacturer has yet another possibility, namely to contract out the preparation of investigational products. Technically, however, the licensed facility will be of one of the above-mentioned types. The contract must then clearly state, inter alia, the use of the pharmaceutical product(s) in clinical trials. Close cooperation between the contracting parties is essential.

Manufacturing operations

Validated procedures may not always be available during the development phase, which makes it difficult to know in advance what are the critical parameters and what in-process controls would help to control these parameters. Provisional production parameters and in-process controls may then usually be deduced from experience with analogous products. Careful consideration by key personnel is called for in order to formulate the necessary instructions and to adapt them continuously to the experience gained in production.

For sterile investigational products, assurance of sterility should be no less than for licensed products. Cleaning procedures should be appropriately

[1] Some manufacturers use the term "pharmacy" to designate other types of premises, e.g. areas where starting materials are dispensed and batches compounded.

validated and designed in the light of the incomplete knowledge of the toxicity of the investigational product. Where processes such as mixing have not been validated, additional quality control testing may be necessary.

Packaging and labelling

The packaging and labelling of investigational products are likely to be more complex and more liable to errors (which are also harder to detect) when "blinded" labels are used than for licensed products. Supervisory procedures such as label reconciliation, line clearance, etc., and the independent checks by quality control staff should accordingly be intensified.

The packaging must ensure that the investigational product remains in good condition during transport and storage at intermediate destinations. Any opening of, or tampering with, the outer packaging during transport should be readily discernible.

Blinding operations

In the preparation of "blinded" products, in-process control should include a check on the similarity in appearance and any other required characteristics of the different products being compared.

13. Quality control

As processes may not be standardized or fully validated, end-product testing is more important in ensuring that each batch meets its specification.

Product release is often carried out in two stages, before and after final packaging:[1]

1. Bulk product assessment: this should cover all relevant factors, including production conditions, the results of in-process testing, a review of manufacturing documentation and compliance with the product specification file and the order.
2. Finished product assessment: this should cover, in addition to the bulk product assessment, all relevant factors, including packaging conditions, the results of in-process testing, a review of packaging documentation and compliance with the product specification file and the order.

When necessary, quality control should also be used to verify the similarity in appearance and other physical characteristics, odour, and taste of "blinded" investigational products.

---

[1] This practice also exists at certain large companies with regard to licensed products.

Samples of each batch of product should be retained in the primary container used for the study or in a suitable bulk container for at least 2 years after the termination or completion of the relevant clinical trial. If the sample is not stored in the pack used for the study, stability data should be available to justify the shelf-life in the pack used.

14. Shipping, returns, and destruction

The shipping, return and destruction of unused products should be carried out in accordance with the written procedures laid down in the protocol. All unused products sent outside the manufacturing plant should, as far as possible, either be returned to the manufacturer or destroyed in accordance with clearly defined instructions.

Shipping

Investigational products should be shipped in accordance with the orders given by the sponsor.

A shipment is sent to an investigator only after the following two-step release procedure: (i) the release of the product after quality control ("technical green light"); and (ii) the authorization to use the product, given by the sponsor ("regulatory green light"). Both releases should be recorded.

The sponsor should ensure that the shipment will be received and acknowledged by the correct addressee as stated in the protocol.

A detailed inventory of the shipments made by the manufacturer should be maintained, and should make particular mention of the addressee's identification.

Returns

Investigational products should be returned under agreed conditions defined by the sponsor, specified in written procedures, and approved by authorized staff members.

Returned investigational products should be clearly identified and stored in a dedicated area. Inventory records of returned medicinal products should be kept. The responsibilities of the investigator and the sponsor are dealt with in greater detail in the WHO guidelines on GCP (*3*).

Destruction

The sponsor is responsible for the destruction of unused investigational products, which should therefore not be destroyed by the manufacturer without prior authorization by the sponsor. Destruction operations should be carried out in accordance with environmental safety requirements.

Destruction operations should be recorded in such a manner that all operations are documented. The records should be kept by the sponsor.

If requested to destroy products, the manufacturer should deliver a certificate of destruction or a receipt for destruction to the sponsor. These documents should permit the batches involved to be clearly identified.

References

1. *Good manufacturing practice for medicinal products in the European Community.* Brussels, Commission of the European Communities, 1992.

2. Good manufacturing practices for pharmaceutical products. In: *WHO Expert Committee on Specifications for Pharmaceutical Preparations. Thirty-second report.* Geneva, World Health Organization, 1992:14–79 (WHO Technical Report Series, No. 823).

3. Guidelines for good clinical practice (GCP) for trials on pharmaceutical products. In: *The use of essential drugs. Model List of Essential Drugs (Eighth List). Sixth report of the WHO Expert Committee.* Geneva, World Health Organization, 1995:97–137 (WHO Technical Report Series, No. 850).

The manufacture of herbal medicines[1]

Introduction 255
General 256
Glossary 256
1. Quality assurance in the manufacture of herbal medicines 258
2. Good manufacturing practice for herbal medicines 258
3. Sanitation and hygiene 258
4. Qualification and validation 259
5. Complaints 259
6. Product recalls 260
7. Contract production and analysis 260
8. Self-inspection 260
9. Personnel 261
10. Training 261
11. Personal hygiene 261
12. Premises 261
13. Equipment 263
14. Materials 263

[1] Supplementary guidelines on good manufacturing practices for the manufacture of herbal medicines. In: *WHO Expert Committee on Specifications for Pharmaceutical Preparations. Fortieth report.* Geneva, World Health Organization, 2006 (WHO Technical Report Series, No. 937), Annex 3.

15. Documentation	264
16. Good practices in production	267
17. Good practices in quality control	270
17.1 General	270
17.2 Sampling	270
17.3 Testing	270
17.4 Stability studies	271
17.5 Packaging materials and labeling	272
References	275

Introduction

Following the publication of the last revised WHO guidelines on *Good manufacturing practices for pharmaceutical products: main principles* (*1*), supporting and supplementary guidelines were developed to address specific issues connected with the manufacture of certain types of pharmaceutical product. As part of this series, the WHO *Supplementary guidelines for the manufacture of herbal medicinal products* (*2*) were issued in 1996. The guidelines were also reproduced in the second volume of the WHO compendium on *Quality assurance of pharmaceuticals* (*3*). Related WHO documents such as *Guidelines for the assessment of herbal medicines* (*4*), *General Guidelines for methodologies on research and evaluation of traditional medicine* (*5*), *Quality control methods for medicinal plant materials* (*6*), *Guidelines on good agricultural and collection practices for medicinal plants* (*7*) were also issued.

WHO's *Good manufacturing practices: main principles for pharmaceutical products* were updated in 2003 (*1, 8*). Around the turn of the millenium, various product-specific good manufacturing practice (GMP) guidelines covering herbal medicines were developed by several WHO Member States, and by the European Union. They covered several issues relevant to the production and quality control of herbal medicines in more detail. For this reason, within the framework of the *WHO Traditional Medicine Strategy: 2000–2005*, revision of the present supplementary guidelines was considered desirable; this was also endorsed by the WHO Expert Committee on Pharmaceutical Specifications at its meetings in 2002, 2003 and 2004.

These guidelines are intended to complement those provided in *Good manufacturing practices for pharmaceutical products* (*1*) and should be read in conjunction with the parent guide. The additional standards addressed by the present guidelines should therefore be considered supplementary to the general requirements set out in (*1*). They relate specifically to the production and control of herbal medicines, insofar as they mainly focus on identifying the critical steps needed to ensure good quality. Therefore the structure of these supplementary guidelines follows that of WHO's GMP main principles.

The supplementary guidelines are intended to provide WHO Member States with general and minimum technical requirements for quality assurance and control in the manufacture of herbal medicines. Each Member State should develop its own national GMP for manufacturing herbal medicines that are appropriate to the country's actual situation. These supplementary guidelines deal exclusively with herbal medicines. Combination of herbal materials with animal materials, mineral materials, chemicals and other substances is not covered in these guidelines.

General

Unlike conventional pharmaceutical products, which are usually produced from synthetic materials by means of reproducible manufacturing techniques and procedures, herbal medicines are prepared from materials of herbal origin, which are often obtained from varied geographical and/or commercial sources. As a result it may not always be possible to ascertain the conditions to which they may have been subjected. In addition, they may vary in composition and properties. Furthermore, the procedures and techniques used in the manufacture and quality control of herbal medicines are often substantially different from those employed for conventional pharmaceutical products.

Because of the inherent complexity of naturally grown medicinal plants and the often variable nature of cultivated ones, the examples of contamination with toxic medicinal plants and/or plant parts and the number and small quantity of defined active ingredients, the production and primary processing has a direct influence on the quality of herbal medicines. For this reason, application of GMPs in the manufacture of herbal medicines is an essential tool to assure their quality.

Glossary

Established terms such as batch, bulk, intermediate product, qualification, starting material and validation are used as defined in the *WHO Good manufacturing practices for pharmaceutical products* (*1*).

The definitions given below apply to the terms as used in these guidelines. These terms and their definitions have been selected and adopted from other WHO documents and guidelines that are widely used by the WHO Member States (*1*, *2*, *5*, *7*, *8*). However, they may have different meanings in other contexts.

It should be noted that, as a consequence of the various types of "herbal medicines", the same type of material may be classified, depending on the case, in different ways (e.g. powdered plant material may be both *herbal material* and *herbal preparation* or, in a packed form, *herbal medicinal product*).

active ingredients (5)

The herbal material(s) or the herbal preparation(s) will be considered to be active ingredient(s) of a herbal medicine(s). However, if constituents with known therapeutic activities are known, the active ingredients should be standardized to contain a defined amount of this/these constituent(s).

blending
Blending is the process of combining materials or different batches to produce a homogeneous intermediate or finished product.

constituents with known therapeutic activity (5)
Constituents with known therapeutic activity are substances or groups of substances which are chemically defined and known to contribute to the therapeutic activity of a herbal material or of a preparation.

herbal medicines (5)
Herbal medicines include *herbs, herbal materials, herbal preparations* and *finished herbal products.*

> *Herbs* include crude materials which could be derived from lichen, algae, fungi or higher plants, such as leaves, flowers, fruit, fruiting bodies, seeds, stems, wood, bark, roots, rhizomes or other parts, which may be entire, fragmented or powdered.
>
> *Herbal materials* include, in addition to herbs, fresh juices, gums, fixed oils, essential oils, resins and dry powders of herbs. In some countries, these materials may be processed by various local procedures, such as steaming, roasting or stir-baking with honey, alcoholic beverages or other materials (*5*).
>
> *Herbal preparations* are the basis for finished herbal products and may include comminuted or cut herbal materials, or extracts, tinctures and fatty oils of herbal materials. They are produced by extraction, fractionation, purification, concentration, or other physical or biological processes. They also include preparations made by steeping or heating herbal materials in alcoholic beverages and/or honey, or in other materials.
>
> *Finished herbal products* consist of herbal preparations made from one or more herbs. If more than one herb is used, the term "mixture herbal product" can also be used. Finished herbal products and mixture herbal products may contain excipients in addition to the active ingredients. However, finished herbal products or mixture herbal products to which chemically defined active substances have been added, including synthetic compounds and/or isolated constituents from herbal materials, are not considered to be herbal (*5*).

markers
Markers are chemically defined constituents of a herbal material utilized for control purposes. They may or may not contribute to the clinical efficacy. When

they contribute to the clinical efficacy, however, evidence that they are solely responsible for the clinical efficacy may or may not be available. Markers are generally employed when constituents of known therapeutic activity are not known or are not clearly identified, and may be used to identify the herbal material or preparation or calculate their quantity in the finished product.

medicinal plant (2)
Medicinal plants are plants (wild or cultivated) used for medicinal purposes.

medicinal plant materials see herbal materials (2)

therapeutic activity (5)
Therapeutic activity refers to the successful prevention, diagnosis and treatment of physical and mental illnesses, improvement of symptoms of illnesses, as well as beneficial alteration or regulation of the physical and mental status of the body and development of a sense of general well-being.

1. Quality assurance in the manufacture of herbal medicines

In addition to the use of modern analytical techniques (especially high-performance thin-layer chromatography (HPTLC), gas chromatography (GC), high-performance liquid chromatography (HPLC), capillary electrophoresis (CE), mass spectrometry (MS) and atomic absorption (AA) to characterize herbal medicines, quality assurance also requires the control of starting materials, storage and processing. For this reason, an appropriate quality assurance system should be applied in the manufacture of herbal medicines.

Note: The methods of choice may depend on the country's infrastructure.

2. Good manufacturing practice for herbal medicines

2.1 The general principles of GMP are set out in the parent guidelines (*1*). Cultivation and collection of medicinal plants, as the starting materials for herbal medicines, are covered by other guidelines (7). The first critical step of their production where the application of GMP starts should be clearly designated (see subsection 16.1). This is of particular importance for those products which consist solely of comminuted or powdered herbal materials.

3. Sanitation and hygiene

3.1 Because of their origin, herbal materials may contain microbiological contaminants. Furthermore, during the course of harvesting and processing, herbal products that may be especially prone to microbiological contamination are produced. To avoid alterations and to reduce contamination in general, a high level of sanitation and hygiene during manufacture is necessary (for guidelines on personal hygiene see section 11, and for those on sanitation see section 12).

3.2 Water supply to the manufacturing unit should be monitored, and, if necessary treated appropriately to ensure consistency of quality.

3.3 Waste from the manufacturing unit should be disposed of regularly so as to maintain a high standard of hygiene in the manufacturing area. Clearly marked waste-bins should be available, emptied and cleaned as needed, but at least daily.

4. Qualification and validation

4.1 Qualification of critical equipment, process validation and change control are particularly important in the production of herbal medicines with unknown therapeutically active constituents. In this case, the reproducibility of the production process is the main means for ensuring consistency of quality, efficacy and safety between batches.

4.2 The written procedure should specify critical process steps and factors (such as extraction time, temperature and solvent purity) and acceptance criteria, as well as the type of validation to be conducted (e.g. retrospective, prospective or concurrent) and the number of process runs.

4.3 A formal change control system should be established to evaluate the potential effects of any changes on the quality of the herbal medicines, particularly content of the active ingredients. Scientific judgement should be used to determine which additional testing and validation studies are appropriate to justify a change in a validated process.

5. Complaints

5.1 The person responsible for handling complaints and deciding on the measures to be taken to deal with them should have appropriate training and/or experience in the specific features of the quality control of herbal medicines.

5.2 There are basically two types of complaint, product quality complaints and adverse reactions/events.

5.3 The first type of complaint may be caused by problems such as faulty manufacture, product defects or deterioration as well as, particular to herbal medicines, adulteration of the herbal material. These complaints should be recorded in detail and the causes thoroughly investigated (e.g. by comparison with the reference samples kept from the same batch). There should also be written procedures to describe the action to be taken.

5.4 To address the second type of complaint, reports of any adverse reaction/event should be entered in a separate register in accordance with national and international requirements. An investigation should be conducted to find out whether the adverse reaction/event is due to a quality problem and whether such reactions/events have already been reported in the literature or whether it is a new observation. In either case, complaint records should be reviewed regularly to detect any specific or recurring problems requiring special attention and possible recall of marketed products. The *WHO guidelines on safety monitoring of herbal medicines in pharmacovigilance systems* deal with specific issues relating to adverse reactions and adverse events following treatment with herbal medicines (*9*).

5.5 The licensing authority should be kept informed of any complaints leading to a recall or restriction on supply and the records should be available for inspection.

6. Product recalls

6.1 The product recall procedure depends very much on the national regulations. There should be a standard operating procedure (SOP) for storage of recalled herbal medicines in a secure segregated area, complying with the requirements specified under subsection 12.1 (Storage areas), while their fate is decided.

7. Contract production and analysis

7.1 The contract partner should have adequate premises and equipment for the production of herbal medicines according to GMP. Validated methods should be applied for cleaning the equipment and premises carefully before using them to produce different herbal medicinal, food or cosmetic products. In the case of raw materials used for producing food, it is realistic to require manufacturing departments to be separated from those where the plant raw material will be cut or powdered for use in the preparation of medicines.

7.2 Technical aspects of the contract should be drawn up by competent persons suitably knowledgeable on the specific characteristics of herbal medicines, including their production and quality control testing.

8. Self-inspection

8.1 At least one member of the self-inspection team should possess a thorough knowledge of herbal medicines.

9. Personnel

9.1 General guidance in relation to personnel involved in the manufacture of medicinal products is given in the parent guide (*1*).

9.2 The release of herbal medicines should be authorized by a person who has been trained in the specific features of the processing and quality control of herbal materials, herbal preparations and finished herbal products.

9.3 Personnel dealing with the production and quality control of herbal medicines should have adequate training in the specific issues relevant to herbal medicines.

10. Training

10.1 The personnel should have adequate training in appropriate fields such as pharmaceutical technology, taxonomic botany, phytochemistry, pharmacognosy, hygiene, microbiology and related subjects (such as traditional use of herbal medicines).

10.2 Training records should be maintained and periodic assessments of the effectiveness of training programmes should be made.

11. Personal hygiene

11.1 Personnel entrusted with the handling of herbal materials, herbal preparations and finished herbal products should be required to have a high degree of personal hygiene and to have received adequate training in maintaining appropriate standards of hygiene. The personnel should not work if they have infectious diseases or skin diseases. Written procedures listing the basic hygiene requirements should be made available.

11.2 Personnel must be protected from contact with toxic irritants and potentially allergenic plant materials by means of adequate protective clothing. They should wear suitable gloves, caps, masks, work suits and shoes throughout the whole procedure from plant processing to product manufacture.

12. Premises

12.1 As a general principle, premises should be designed, located, constructed, adapted and maintained to suit the operations to be carried out according to GMP (*1*).

12.2 Because of their potential for degradation and infestation with certain pests as well as their sensitivity to microbiological contamination, production, and particularly storage, of herbal materials and herbal preparations assume special importance.

Storage areas

12.3 Storage areas should be well organized and tidy. Special attention should be paid to cleanliness and good maintenance. Any accidental spillage should be cleaned up immediately using methods that minimize the risk of cross-contamination of other materials, and should be reported.

12.4 The set-up of storage areas depends on the type of materials stored. The areas should be well labelled and materials stored in a such a way as to avoid any risk of cross-contamination. An area should be identified for the quarantine of all incoming herbal materials.

12.5 Storage areas should be laid out to permit effective and orderly segregation of the various categories of materials stored, and to allow rotation of stock. Different herbal materials should be stored in separate areas.

12.6 To protect the stored material, and reduce the risk of pest attacks, the duration of storage of any herbal material in unpacked form should be kept to a minimum.

12.7 Incoming fresh herbal materials should be processed, unless specified otherwise, as soon as possible. If appropriate, they should be stored between 2 °C and 8 °C, whereas frozen materials should be stored below −18 °C.

12.8 Where materials are stored in bulk, to reduce the risk of mould formation or fermentation it is advisable to store them in aerated rooms or containers using natural or mechanical aeration and ventilation. These areas should also be equipped in such a way as to protect against the entry of insects or animals, especially rodents. Effective measures should be taken to limit the spread of animals and microorganisms brought in with the plant material and to prevent cross-contamination.

12.9 Herbal materials, even when stored in fibre drums, bags or boxes, should be stored off the floor and suitably spaced to permit cleaning and inspection.

12.10 The storage of plants, extracts, tinctures and other preparations may require special conditions of humidity and temperature or protection from light; appropriate steps should be taken to ensure that these conditions are provided, maintained, monitored and recorded.

12.11 Herbal materials, including raw herbal materials, should be kept in a dry area protected from moisture and processed following the principle of "first in, first out" (FIFO).

Production areas

12.12 Production areas should comply with the general requirements of GMP (*1*). As a rule, campaign work in their processing is necessary. However, if feasible, the use of dedicated premises is encouraged. Moreover, the special nature of the production of herbal medicines requires that particular attention be given to processing products that generate dust. When heating or boiling of the materials is necessary, a suitable air exhaust mechanism should be employed to prevent accumulation of fumes and vapours.

12.13 To facilitate cleaning and to avoid cross-contamination, adequate precautions should be taken during the sampling, weighing, mixing and processing of medicinal plants, e.g. by use of dust extraction and air-handling systems to achieve the desired differential pressure and net airflow.

13. Equipment

13.1 Processing of herbal materials may generate dust or material which is susceptible to pest-infestation or microbiological contamination and cross-contamination. Effective cleaning of the equipment is therefore particularly important.

13.2 Vacuum or wet-cleaning methods are preferred. If wet-cleaning is done, the equipment should be dried immediately after cleaning to prevent the growth of microorganisms. Cleaning with compressed air and brushes should be used with care and avoided if possible, as these methods increase the risk of product contamination.

13.3 Non-wooden equipment should be used unless tradition demands wooden material. Where it is necessary to use traditional equipment (such as wooden implements, clay pots, pallets, hoppers, etc.), this should be dedicated, unless otherwise justified. When such equipment is used, it is advisable that it does not come into direct contact with chemicals or contaminated material. If the use of wooden equipment is unavoidable, special consideration must be given to its cleaning as wooden materials may retain odours, be easily discoloured and are easily contaminated.

14. Materials

14.1 All incoming herbal materials should be quarantined and stored under appropriate conditions that take into account the degradability of herbal materials and herbal preparations.

14.2 Only permitted substances should be used for fumigation, and allowable limits for their residues together with specifications for the apparatus used should be set according to the national regulations.

Reference samples and standards

14.3 The reference standard for a herbal medicine may be a botanical sample of the herbal material; a sample of the herbal preparation, e.g. extract; or a chemically defined substance, e.g. a known active constituent, a marker substance or a known impurity. The reference standard should be of a quality appropriate to its purpose. If the herbal medicine is not described in a recognized pharmacopoeia, a herbarium sample of the flowering or fruiting top of the whole medicinal plant or part of the medicinal plant (e.g. if the whole medicinal plant is a tree) should be available. All reference standards should be stored under appropriate conditions to prevent degradation. Their expiry and/or revalidation date should be determined and indicated.

15. Documentation

15.1 The general principles for documentation are set out in the parent guidelines (*1*).

Specifications

15.2 The specifications for herbal starting materials, for herbal preparations and finished herbal products are primarily intended to define the quality rather than to establish full characterization, and should focus on those characteristics found to be useful in ensuring safety and efficacy. Consistent quality for herbal medicines (finished herbal products) can only be assured if the starting herbal materials are defined in a rigorous and detailed manner. In some cases more detailed information may be needed on aspects of collection or agricultural production. For instance, the selection of seeds, conditions of cultivation and harvesting are important aspects in producing a reproducible quality of herbal medicines (*7*). Their characterization (which also includes a detailed evaluation of the botanical and phytochemical aspects of the medicinal plant, manufacture of the herbal preparation and the finished herbal product) is therefore essential to allow the establishment of specifications which are both comprehensive and relevant.

15.3 For this reason, in addition to the data called for in (*1*), the specifications for herbal materials should as far as possible include, as a minimum, the following information:

15.4 *Herbal materials*

- The family and botanical name of the plant used according to the binomial system (genus, species, variety and the authority, i.e. the reference to the originator of the classification, e.g. Linnaeus). It may also be appropriate to add the vernacular name and the therapeutic use in the country or region of origin of the plant.
- Details of the source of the plant, such as country and/or region (also state and province, if applicable) of origin, whether it was cultivated or collected from the wild and, where applicable, method of cultivation, dates and

conditions of harvesting (e.g. whether there was extreme weather), collection procedures, collection area, and brand, quantity and date of pesticide application, as required by the *WHO Guideline on good agricultural and collection practices* (*7*).

- Whether the whole plant or only a part is used. In the latter case, which part of the plant is used and its state, e.g. whole or reduced. For dried plant material, the drying system should be specified, if applicable.
- A description of the plant material based on visual (macroscopic) and/or microscopic examination.
- Suitable identity tests including, where appropriate, identification tests (such as TLC or other chromatographic fingerprint) for known active ingredients or markers. A reference sample should be available for identification purposes.
- Details of the assay, where appropriate, of active constituents or markers.
- Limit tests such as dry residue of liquids, ash value (total ash, and ash insoluble in hydrochloric acid), water-soluble extractives, moisture/water content and loss on drying (taking into account the presence of essential oils if any).
- Suitable methods for the determination of possible pesticide contamination and the acceptable limits for such contamination in herbal materials or herbal preparations used in the manufacture of herbal medicines.
- Tests for toxic metals and for likely contaminants, foreign materials and adulterants.
- Tests for fungal and/or microbiological contamination, fumigant residues (if applicable), mycotoxins, pest-infestations, radioactivity and their acceptable limits.
- Other appropriate tests (e.g. particle size, swelling index and residual solvents in herbal preparations and biological fingerprints such as induced fluorescent markers).

15.5 Specifications for starting materials (and also of primary or printed packaging materials) should include, if applicable, reference to a pharmacopoeial monograph.

15.6 If the herbal material for processing does not comply with its quality specifications, the rules that apply for its rejection, and to storage and disposal of the rejected herbal material should be included.

15.7 Starting materials derived from or comprising genetically modified organisms should comply with existing national or international regulations and the label should include this information. Chemical protection of herbal materials should be in accordance with national and/or international regulations (*7*).

15.8 Qualitative and quantitative information on the active ingredients or constituents with known therapeutic activity in herbal materials and herbal preparations should be given as described in subsection 17.5 (labelling).

15.9 *Finished herbal products*

- Tests for microbiological contamination and tests for other toxicants.
- Uniformity of weight (e.g. for tablets, single-dose powders, suppositories, capsules and herbal tea in sachets), disintegration time (for tablets, capsules, suppositories and pills), hardness and friability (for example, uncoated tablets), viscosity (for internal and external fluids), consistency (semisolid preparations), and dissolution (tablets or capsules), if applicable.
- Physical appearance such as colour, odour, form, shape, size and texture.
- Loss on drying, or water content.
- Identity tests, qualitative determination of relevant substances of the plants (e.g. fingerprint chromatograms).
- Quantification of relevant active ingredients, if they have been identified, and the analytical methods that are available.
- Limit tests for residual solvents.

15.10 The control tests and specifications for the finished herbal product should be such as to allow the qualitative and quantitative determination of the main active constituents. If the therapeutic activity of constituents is known, these constituents should be indicated in the documentation. If such substances are not known (e.g. because they are part of a complex mixture), the constituents useful for assessing the quality should be identified as markers. In both cases, the assay (i.e. quantitative determination) specifications should be defined. When the therapeutic activity of the constituents cannot be determined quantitatively, specifications should be based on the determination of markers.

15.11 If either the final product or the herbal preparation contains several herbal materials and a quantitative determination of each active ingredient is not feasible, the mixture of several active ingredients may be determined. The need for such a procedure should be justified.

15.12 The concept of different acceptance criteria for release versus shelf-life specifications applies to finished herbal medicines only and not to herbal materials and herbal preparations. Adequate retest periods should be established for the latter. Examples where this may be applicable include assay and impurity (degradation product) levels.

15.13 *Herbal preparations*

The specifications of herbal preparations consist, depending on the preparation in question, of the relevant items of the specifications for herbal materials or for finished herbal products as outlined above.

Processing instructions

15.14 The processing instructions should describe the different operations to be performed on the plant material, such as drying, crushing, milling and sifting.

They should also include the time and, if applicable, temperatures required in the drying process, and the methods to be used to control fragment or particle size. Instructions on removing foreign matters and other unwanted materials should also be given.

15.15 The drying conditions chosen should be appropriate to the type of plant material processed. These depend on both the character of the active ingredients (e.g. essential oils) and the type of plant part collected (e.g. root, leaf or flower). Drying by direct exposure to sunlight, if not specifically contraindicated, is possible, but drying on the ground should be avoided. If the plant should be processed fresh, without drying, the reasons and criteria determining the use of fresh material should be stated.

15.16 For the production of processed extracts, the instructions should specify details of any vehicle or solvent that may be used, the durations and temperatures needed for extraction, and any concentration stages and methods that may be required.

15.17 The permissible environmental conditions e.g. temperature, humidity and standard of cleanliness, should be stated.

15.18 Any treatment, such as fumigation, used to reduce fungal or microbiological contamination or other infestation, together with methods of determining the extent of such contamination and potential residues, should be documented. Instructions on the conduct of such procedures should be available and should include details of the process, tests and allowable limits for residues together with specifications for apparatus used.

15.19 Steps in the processes of blending and adjustment to reach defined contents of pharmacologically active constituents should be clearly documented.

15.20 The rules that apply to the disposal of spent herbal material after processing should also be elaborated.

16. Good practices in production

16.1 To ensure not only the quality, but also the safety and efficacy of complex products of biological origin such as herbal medicines, it is essential that the steps in their production are clearly defined.

Selection of the first production step covered by these guidelines

16.2 For medicinal plants–-which are either cultivated or collected from the wild, and which may be used in crude form or subjected to simple processing techniques (such as cutting or comminuting)–-the first critical step of their production, i.e. where the application of these guidelines starts, should be clearly designated. The rationale for this designation should be stated and documented.

Guidance is provided below. However, for processes such as extraction, fermentation and purification, this rationale should be established on a case-by-case basis.

- Collection/cultivation and/or harvesting of medicinal plants should follow other relevant guidance such as the *WHO Guideline on good agriculture and collection practices (GACP) for medicinal plants* (*7*) or a national guideline.
- Generally, postharvest processing including primary cutting is (or should be) covered by GACP. If further comminuting is carried out in the manufacturing processing, it should be covered by GMP, or by these supplementary guidelines. If cutting and comminuting considerably reduce the probability of detection of adulteration or mix-up of herbal materials, application of these supplementary guidelines may be extended to encompass these steps.
- When the active ingredient, as defined in the Glossary, consists exclusively of comminuted or powdered herbs, application of these guidelines starts at the physical processing following primary cutting and comminuting, and includes packaging.
- When herbal extracts are used, the principles of these guidelines should apply to any production step following postharvest processing.
- In the case of finished herbal products manufactured by fermentation, application of GMP should cover any production step following primary cutting and comminuting. Particular attention should be given to the introduction of cells from a cell bank into the fermentation process.

General considerations

16.3 Materials should be handled in a fashion that is not detrimental to the product. On arrival at the processing facility, the herbal material should be promptly unloaded and unpacked. During this operation, the herbal material should not come into direct contact with the soil. Moreover, it should not be exposed directly to the sun (except in cases where this is a specific requirement, e.g. sun-drying) and it should be protected from rain and microbiological contamination.

16.4 Attention should be paid to "classification" of clean area requirements taking into account the possible high degree of initial microbial contamination of herbal materials. Classification of premises as applied to sites for the production of other pharmaceutical substances may not be applicable to processing of herbal materials. Specific and detailed requirements should be developed to cover microbial contamination of equipment, air, surfaces and personnel, and also for rest rooms, utilities, ancillary and supporting systems (e.g. water and compressed air).

16.5 Care should be taken to choose cleaning methods appropriate to the characteristics of the herbal materials being processed. Washing dried herbal materials with water is generally inappropriate. When it is necessary to clean them, an air duster or air shower should be employed. In cases when immersion of herbal materials in water or other appropriate agents (such as disinfectants) for cleaning is unavoidable (e.g. to eliminate suspected coliform bacteria), it should be kept to a minimum.

16.6 The presence of plant materials from different species and varieties, or different plant parts should be controlled during the entire production process to avoid contamination, unless it is assured that these materials are equivalent.

16.7 If time limits are specified in the master production instructions, these limits should not be exceeded, to ensure the quality of intermediates and finished products. The less is known about the constituents responsible for the therapeutic activity, the more strictly this rule should be obeyed. Such time limits, however, may be inappropriate when processing to achieve a target value (e.g. drying to a predetermined specification) because completion of processing steps is determined by in-process sampling and testing.

Mixing of batches and blending

16.8 Herbal medicines with constituents of known therapeutic activity are often standardized (i.e. adjusted to a defined content of such constituents). The methods used to achieve such standardization should be documented. If another substance is added for these purposes, it is necessary to specify, as a range, the quantity that may be added. Blending different batches of a specific herbal material (e.g. before extraction) or by mixing different lots of similar herbal preparations may also be acceptable. Records should be maintained to ensure traceability. The blending process should be adequately controlled and documented and the blended batch should be tested for conformity with established specifications where appropriate.

16.9 Batches should be mixed only if it can be guaranteed that the mixture will be homogeneous. Such processes should be well documented.

16.10 Out-of-specification batches of herbal medicines should not be blended with other batches for the purpose of meeting specifications, except for standardization of the content of constituents with known pharmaceutical therapeutic effect. Every batch incorporated into the blend should have been manufactured using an established process and should have been individually tested and found to meet appropriate specifications prior to blending.

16.11 Where particular physical attributes of the material are critical, blending operations should be validated to show uniformity of the combined batch. Validation should include testing of critical attributes (e.g. particle size distribution, bulk density and tap density) that may be affected by the blending process.

16.12 The expiry date of the blended batch should be chosen according to the date of manufacture of the oldest batch in the blend.

17. Good practices in quality control

17.1 General

17.1.1 The personnel of quality control units should have the necessary expertise in herbal medicines to enable them to carry out identification tests and recognize adulteration, the presence of fungal growth or infestations and lack of uniformity in a consignment of herbal materials.

17.1.2 The quality control of the herbal material, herbal preparations and finished herbal products should establish their quality but does not imply the control of every single constituent.

17.2 Sampling

17.2.1 Because herbal materials are an aggregate of individual plants and/ or different parts of the same plant and thus have an element of heterogeneity, sampling should be carried out with special care by personnel with the necessary expertise.

17.2.2 Further advice on sampling and visual inspection is given in the WHO document *Quality control methods for medicinal plant materials* (6).

17.3 Testing

17.3.1 The identity and quality of herbal material, herbal preparations and of finished herbal products should be tested as described in the *Quality control methods for medicinal plant materials* (6). The minimum requirement for the technical equipment is for instruments to perform the tests described in (6). Moreover, each country should develop this basic requirement for technical equipment further, according to the country's needs.

17.3.2 Herbal material, herbal preparations (including extracts) and finished herbal products can be categorized as follows:

(a) the active constituents are identified, and may be quantified as such;
(b) the main group of components which contribute to the activity (i.e. the constituents with known therapeutic activity) are known and can be quantified as a total (e.g. essential oils) or calculated using a representative substance belonging to the group (e.g. fl avonoids);
(c) the former are not identified and/or not quantifiable, but marker substances are;
(d) others, where quantification (i.e. specification for a certain quantity of a constituent) is not applicable or feasible.

17.3.3 Identification methods may be based on:

- physical and, if applicable, macroscopic (organoleptic) and microscopic tests;
- chromatographic procedures (TLC, HPLC, HPTLC or gas-liquid chromatography (GLC)), spectrometric techniques (ultraviolet-visible (UV-VIS), IR, nuclear magnetic resonance (NMR), MS); and/or
- chemical reactions.

17.3.4 The identification test methods should be specific for the herbal material, herbal preparation or finished herbal product and ideally should be capable of discriminating between the required herbal material and potential substitutes or adulterants that are likely to occur. The identification methods used for groups a and b should be capable of detecting the said active ingredients and at least the main ingredients should be stated on the label. For group c, the analytical procedure should be based on characteristic constituents, if any.

17.3.5 Reference samples of herbal materials should be made available for use in comparative tests, e.g. visual and microscopic examination and chromatography.

17.3.6 Quantitative determination of known active components for members of groups a and b and of markers for members of group c is necessary.

17.3.7 The development and execution of quality control methods for herbal materials, herbal preparations and the finished herbal products should be in line with subsection 15.1 (Specifications). Tests and quality requirements that are characteristic of the given analyte should be selected.

17.3.8 Particularly for herbal materials in group d and for finished herbal products containing such materials, characteristic chromatograms (and/or fingerprint chromatograms) may be applicable. Using these methods may ensure that the main constituents can be easily followed throughout the production process. Caution is necessary, however, for every delivery of herbal materials and every batch of herbal preparations (including extracts) will have slightly different chromatograms/fingerprints resulting from differences in chemical compositions caused by intrinsic or extrinsic factors.

17.4 Stability studies

17.4.1 If the expiry date for a herbal material or herbal preparation is given, some stability data to support the proposed shelf-life under the specified storage conditions should be available. Stability data are always required to support the shelf-life proposed for the finished herbal products.

17.4.2 Finished herbal products may contain several herbal materials or herbal preparations, and it is often not feasible to determine the stability of each active ingredient. Moreover, because the herbal material, in its entirety, is regarded as the active ingredient, a mere determination of the stability of the constituents with known therapeutic activity will not usually be sufficient. Chromatography allows tracing of changes which may occur during storage of a complex mixture of biologically active substances contained in herbal materials. It should be shown, as far as possible, e.g. by comparisons of appropriate characteristic/fingerprint chromatograms, that the identified active ingredient (if any) and other substances present in the herbal material or finished herbal product are likewise stable and that their content as a proportion of the whole remains within the defined limits.

17.4.3 The fingerprint methods used for the stability studies should be as similar as possible to those used for quality control purposes.

17.4.4 For identified active ingredients, constituents with known therapeutic activity and markers, widely used general methods of assay, and physical and sensory or other appropriate tests may be applied.

17.4.5 To determine the shelf-life of finished herbal products, strong emphasis should also be placed on other tests in subsection 15.1 (Specifications), such as moisture content, microbial contamination and general dosage form control tests.

17.4.6 The stability of preservatives and stabilizers should be monitored. When these are not used, alternative tests should be done to ensure that the product is self-preserving over its shelf-life.

17.4.7 Samples used for stability studies should be stored in the containers intended for marketing.

17.4.8 Normally the first three commercial production batches should be included in the stability-monitoring programme to confirm the expiry date. However, where data from previous studies, including pilot batches, show that the product is expected to remain stable for at least two years, fewer than three batches can be used. The testing frequency depends on the characteristics of the herbal medicinal products and should be determined on a case-by-case basis.

17.4.9 The protocol for ongoing stability studies should be documented. This would normally involve one batch per year being included in a stability-monitoring programme.

17.5 Packaging materials and labelling

17.5.1 All packaging materials, such as bottles and other materials, should be stored properly. Controls on the issue and use of these packaging materials should be adequate to ensure that incorrect labels and cartons are not used.

17.5.2 All containers and closures should be thoroughly cleaned and dried before being used to pack the products.

17.5.3 There should be adequate information on the label (or the package insert) to inform the users of the composition of the product (in addition to the brand name, if any), indications or actions, directions for use, cautions and adverse reactions if any, and the expiry date.

17.5.4 Finished herbal products may contain several herbal materials and/ or herbal preparations. Unless otherwise fully justified, the full quantitative composition of the herbal ingredients should be stated on the product label. If this is not possible, at least the main ingredients should be stated on the label while the full qualitative composition could appear on the package insert.

17.5.5 The qualitative and quantitative particulars of the active ingredients in herbal materials and herbal preparations should be expressed in the following ways:

- For herbal materials and herbal preparations consisting of comminuted or powdered herbal materials:
  - (a) the quantity of the herbal material must be stated or, if constituents with known therapeutic activity are unidentified, the quantity of the herbal material/herbal preparation should be stated; or
  - (b) the quantity of the herbal material/herbal preparation should be given as a range, corresponding to a defined quantity of constituents with known therapeutic activity (see examples).

Examples:

(a)

Name of the active ingredient or active plant materials	*Quantity of constituent*
Valerianae radix	900 mg

(b)

Name of the active ingredient or active herbal materials	*Quantity of constituent*
Sennae folium	415–500 mg, corresponding to 12.5 mg of hydroxyanthracene glycosides, calculated as sennoside B

- For herbal preparations produced by steps, which exceed comminution, the nature and concentration of the solvent and the physical state of the extract should be given. Furthermore, the following should be indicated:
  (a) the equivalent quantity or the ratio of a herbal material to herbal preparation must be stated if therapeutic activity of the constituents is unknown (this does not apply to fatty or essential oils); or
  (b) if the therapeutic activity of the constituents is known, the quantity of the herbal preparation may be given as a range, corresponding to a defined quantity of the constituents with known therapeutic activity (see examples).

Examples:

(a)

Name of the active substance or active herbal materials	*Quantity of constituent*
Valerianae radix	25 mg dry ethanolic (96% v/v) extract (8:1) or 125 mg ethanolic (96% v/v) extract, equivalent to 1000 mg of *Valerianae radix*
other ingredient	
Dextrin	20–50 mg

(b)

Name of the active substance or active herbal materials	*Quantity of constituent*
Sennae folium	100–130 mg dry ethanolic (96% v/v) extract (8:1), corresponding to 25 mg of hydroxyanthracene glycosides, calculated as sennoside B
other ingredient	
Dextrin	20–50 mg

17.5.6 The composition of any solvent or solvent mixture used and the physical state of the extract should be identified.

17.5.7 If any other substance is added during the manufacture of the herbal preparation to adjust the level of constituents of known therapeutic activity, or for any other purpose, the added substance(s) should be described as such or as "other ingredients" and the genuine extract as the "active ingredient". However, where different batches of the same extract are used to adjust constituents with known therapeutic activity to a defined content or for any other purpose, the final mixture should be regarded as the genuine extract and listed as the "active ingredient" in the unit formula.

References

1. Good Manufacturing Practices for pharmaceutical products: main principles. In: *WHO Expert Committee on Specifications for Pharmaceutical Preparations. Thirty-seventh report.* Geneva, World Health Organization, 2003 (WHO Technical Report Series, No. 908), Annex 4.

2. Good Manufacturing Practices: supplementary guidelines for the manufacture of herbal medicinal products. In: *WHO Expert Committee on Specifications for Pharmaceutical Preparations. Thirty-fourth report.* Geneva, World Health Organization, 1996 (WHO Technical Report Series, No. 863), Annex 8.

3. *Quality assurance of pharmaceuticals. A compendium of guidelines and related materials.* Volume 2. Geneva, World Health Organization, 1999 (Volume 2, Updated edition, 2004).

4. Guidelines for the assessment of herbal medicines. In: *WHO Expert Committee on Specifications for Pharmaceutical Preparations. Thirty-fourth report.* Geneva, World Health Organization, 1996 (WHO Technical Report Series, No. 863), Annex 11. These guidelines were reproduced in *Quality assurance of pharmaceuticals. A compendium of guidelines and related materials. Volume 1.* Geneva, World Health Organization, 1997.

5. *General guidelines for methodologies on research and evaluation of traditional medicine.* Geneva, World Health Organization, 2000.

6. *Quality control methods for medicinal plant materials.* Geneva, World Health Organization, 1998.

7. *WHO Guideline on good agricultural and collection practices (GACP) for medicinal plants.* Geneva, World Health Organization, 2003.

8. *Quality assurance of pharmaceuticals. A compendium of guidelines and related materials.* Volume 2, Updated edition. Geneva, World Health Organization, 2004.

9. *WHO guidelines on safety monitoring of herbal medicines in pharmacovigilance systems.* Geneva, World Health Organization, 2004.

Radiopharmaceutical products[1]

1. Scope of these guidelines 276
2. Principles 277
3. Personnel 277
4. Premises and equipment 278
5. Production 280
6. Labelling 280
7. Production and distribution records 282
8. Quality assurance and quality control 282
Acknowledgements 284
References 284

1. Scope of these guidelines

These guidelines are intended to complement those already available for pharmaceutical products (*1, 2*) as well as those for sterile pharmaceutical products (*3*).

The regulatory procedures necessary to control radiopharmaceutical products are in large part determined by the sources of these products and the methods of manufacture. Manufacturing procedures within the scope of these guidelines include:

- The preparation of radiopharmaceuticals in hospital radiopharmacies.
- The preparation of radiopharmaceuticals in centralized radiopharmacies.
- The production of radiopharmaceuticals in nuclear centres and institutes or by industrial manufacturers.
- The preparation and production of radiopharmaceuticals in positron emission tomography (PET) centres.

Radiopharmaceuticals can be classified into four categories:

1. Ready-for-use radioactive products.
2. Radionuclide generators.
3. Non-radioactive components ("kits") for the preparation of labelled compounds with a radioactive component (usually the eluate from a radionuclide generator).
4. Precursors used for radiolabelling other substances before administration (e.g. samples from patients).

Radiopharmaceutical products include inorganic compounds, organic compounds, peptides, proteins, monoclonal antibodies and fragments, and

[1] Guidelines on good manufacturing practices for pharmaceutical products. In: *WHO Expert Committee on Specifications for Pharmaceutical Preparations. Thirty-seventh report.* Geneva, World Health Organization, 2003 (WHO Technical Report Series, No. 908), Annex 3.

oligonucleotides labelled with radionuclides with half-lives from a few seconds to several days.

2. Principles

Radiopharmaceuticals must be manufactured in accordance with the basic principles of good manufacturing practices (GMP). The matters covered by these guidelines should therefore be considered as supplementary to the general requirements for GMP previously published (*1, 2*) and relate specifically to the production and control of radiopharmaceuticals. In the preparation of these guidelines, due consideration was given to national or international radiation safety guidelines (*4*).

Because of their short half-lives, many radiopharmaceuticals are released and administered to patients shortly after their production, so that quality control may sometimes be retrospective. Strict adherence to GMP is therefore mandatory.

3. Personnel

3.1 The manufacturing establishment, whether a hospital radiopharmacy, centralized radiopharmacy, nuclear centre or institution, industrial manufacturer or PET centre, and its personnel should be under the control of a person who has a proven record of academic achievement together with a demonstrated level of practical expertise and experience in radiopharmacy and radiation hygiene. Supporting academic and technical personnel should have the necessary postgraduate or technical training and experience appropriate to their function.

3.2 Personnel required to work in radioactive, clean and aseptic areas should be selected with care, to ensure that they can be relied on to observe the appropriate codes of practice and are not subject to any disease or condition that could compromise the integrity of the product. Health checks on personnel should be requested before employment and periodically thereafter. Any changes in personal health status (e.g. in haematology) may require the temporary exclusion of the person from further radiation exposure.

3.3 Only the minimum number of personnel required should be present in clean and aseptic areas when work is in progress. Access to these areas should be restricted during the preparation of radiopharmaceuticals, kits or sterile setups. Inspection and control procedures should be conducted from outside these areas as far as possible.

3.4 During the working day, personnel may pass between radioactive and non-radioactive areas only if the safety rules of radiation control (health physics control) are respected.

3.5 The release of a batch may be approved only by a pharmacist or a person with academic qualifications officially registered as a suitably qualified person, and with appropriate experience in the manufacture of radiopharmaceuticals.

3.6 To ensure the safe manufacture of radiopharmaceuticals, personnel should be trained in GMP, the safe handling of radioactive materials and radiation safety procedures. They should also be required to take periodic courses and receive training to keep abreast of the latest developments in their fields.

3.7 Training records should be maintained and periodic assessments of the effectiveness of training programmes should be made.

3.8 All personnel engaged in production, maintenance and testing should follow the relevant guidelines for handling radioactive products and be monitored for possible contamination and/or irradiation exposure.

4. Premises and equipment

4.1 As a general principle, buildings must be located, designed, constructed, adapted and maintained to suit the operations to be carried out within them. Laboratories for the handling of radioactive materials must be specially designed to take into consideration aspects of radiation protection in addition to cleanliness and sterility. Interior surfaces (walls, floors and ceilings) should be smooth, impervious and free from cracks; they should not shed matter and should permit easy cleaning and decontamination. Drains should be avoided wherever possible and, unless essential, should be excluded from aseptic areas.

4.2 Specific disposal systems should be mandatory for radioactive effluents. These systems should be effectively and carefully maintained to prevent contamination and exposure of personnel to the radioactive waste both within and outside the facility.

4.3 Sinks should be excluded from aseptic areas. Any sink installed in other clean areas should be of suitable material and be regularly sanitized. Adequate precautions should be taken to avoid contamination of the drainage system with radioactive effluents.

4.4 Lighting, heating, ventilation and, if necessary, air-conditioning should be designed to maintain a satisfactory temperature and relative humidity to ensure the comfort of personnel working in protective clothing. Buildings should be in a good state of repair. The condition of the buildings should be reviewed regularly and repairs carried out when and where necessary. Special care should be exercised to ensure that building repair or maintenance operations do not compromise products. Premises should provide sufficient space for the operations to be carried out, allowing an efficient flow of work and effective communication and supervision. All buildings and rooms should be clean, sanitary and free from radioactive contamination.

4.5 Ventilation of radiopharmaceutical production facilities should meet the requirement to prevent the contamination of products and the exposure of working personnel to radioactivity. Suitable pressure and airflow patterns should be maintained by appropriate isolation/enveloping methods. Air-handling systems for both radioactive and non-radioactive areas should be fitted with alarms so that the working personnel in the laboratory are warned of any failure of these systems.

4.6 Dedicated facilities and equipment should be used for the manufacture of any radiopharmaceutical product derived from human blood or plasma. Autoclaves used in production areas for radiopharmaceuticals may be placed behind a lead shield to minimize the radiation exposure of the operators. Such autoclaves should be checked for contamination immediately after use to minimize the possibility of cross-contamination by radioactivity of the products in the next autoclave cycles.

4.7 All containers of radiopharmaceutical substances, regardless of the stage of manufacture, should be identified by securely attached labels. Cross-contamination should be prevented by the adoption of some or all of the following measures:

— processing and filling in segregated areas;
— avoiding the manufacture of different products at the same time, unless they are effectively segregated;
— containing material transfer by means of airlocks, air extraction, changing clothes and careful washing and decontamination of equipment;
— protecting against the risks of contamination caused by recirculation of untreated air, or by accidental re-entry of extracted air;
— using "closed systems" of manufacture;
— taking care to prevent aerosol formation;
— using sterilized containers.

4.8 Positive pressure areas should be used to process sterile products. In general, any radioactivity should be handled within specifically designed areas maintained under negative pressures. The production of sterile radioactive products should therefore be carried out under negative pressure surrounded by a positive pressure zone ensuring that appropriate air quality requirements are met.

4.9 Separate air-handling units should be used for radioactive and nonradioactive areas. Air from operations involving radioactivity should be exhausted through appropriate filters that are regularly checked for performance.

4.10 Pipework, valves and vent filters should be properly designed to facilitate validated cleaning and decontamination.

5. Production

5.1 Standard operating procedures (SOPs) must be available for all operating procedures and should be regularly reviewed and kept up to date for all manufacturing operations. All entries on batch records should be initiated by the operator and independently checked by another operator or supervisor.

5.2 Specifications for starting materials should include details of their source, origin and (where applicable) method of manufacture and of the controls used to ensure their suitability for use. Release of a finished product should be conditional on satisfactory results being obtained in the tests on starting materials.

5.3 Careful consideration should be given to the validation of sterilization methods.

5.4 A wide variety of equipment is used in the preparation of radiopharmaceuticals. Equipment for chromatography should, in general, be dedicated to the preparation and purification of one or several products labelled with the same radionuclide to avoid radioactive cross-contamination. The life span of columns should be defined. Great care should be taken in cleaning, sterilizing and operating freeze-drying equipment used for the preparation of kits.

5.5 A list of critical equipment should be drawn up, including any equipment such as a balance, pyrogen oven, dose calibrator, sterilizing filter, etc., where an error in the reading or function could potentially cause harm to the patient being given the final product. These devices should be calibrated or tested at regular intervals and should be checked daily or before production is started. The results of these tests should be included in the daily production records.

5.6 Specific equipment for radioactive measurements may be required as well as radioactive reference standards. For the measurement of very short half-lives, national central laboratories should be contacted to calibrate the apparatus. Where this is not possible, alternative approaches, such as documented procedures, may be used.

5.7 In the case of labelling kits, freeze drying should be carried out as an aseptic procedure. If an inert gas such as nitrogen is used to fill vials, it must be filtered to remove possible microbial contamination.

5.8 The dispensing, packaging and transportation of radiopharmaceuticals should comply with the relevant national regulations and international guidelines (*5*).

6. Labelling

6.1 All products should be clearly identified by labels, which must remain permanently attached to the containers under all storage conditions. An area of the container should be left uncovered to allow inspection of the contents. If the final container is not suitable for labelling, the label should appear on its package. Information on batch coding must be provided to the national and/or regional authorities.

6.2 The labels of radiopharmaceuticals must comply with the relevant national regulations and international agreements. For registered radiopharmaceuticals, the national control authority should approve the labels.

6.3 The label on the container should show:

(a) the name of the drug product and/or the product identification code;
(b) the name of the radionuclide;
(c) the name of the manufacturer or the company and/or the person responsible for placing the drug on the market;
(d) the radioactivity per unit dose:

- — for liquid preparations, the total radioactivity in the container, or the radioactive concentration per millilitre, at a stated date and, if necessary, hour, and the volume of liquid in the container;
- — for solid preparations, such as freeze-dried preparations, the total radioactivity at a stated date and, if necessary, hour;
- — for capsules, the radioactivity of each capsule at a stated date and, if necessary, hour, and the number of capsules in the container;
- — where relevant, the international symbol for radioactivity.

6.4 The label on the package should state:

(a) the qualitative and quantitative composition;
(b) the radioactive isotopes and the amount of radioactivity at the time of dispatch;
(c) the route of administration;
(d) the expiry date;
(e) any special storage conditions;
(f) mandatory information related to transport regulations for radioactive materials.

6.5 The leaflet in the package should contain the specific product information and indications for use. This information is especially important for preparation kits (cold kits), and should include:

(a) the name of the product and a description of its use;
(b) the contents of the kit;
(c) the identification and quality requirements concerning the radiolabelling materials that can be used to prepare the radiopharmaceutical, namely:

- — the directions for preparing the radiopharmaceutical, including the range of activity and the volume, together with a statement of the storage requirements for the prepared radiopharmaceutical;

- a statement of the shelf-life of the prepared radiopharmaceutical;
- the indications and contraindications (pregnancy, children, drug reactions, etc.) in respect of the prepared radiopharmaceutical;
- warnings and precautions in respect of the components and the prepared radiopharmaceutical, including radiation safety aspects;
- where applicable, the pharmacology and toxicology of the prepared radiopharmaceutical, including the route of elimination and the effective half-life;
- the radiation dose that a patient will receive from the prepared radiopharmaceutical;
- the precautions to be taken by users and patients during the preparation and administration of the product and the special precautions for the disposal of the container and any unconsumed portions;
- a statement of the recommended use of the prepared radiopharmaceutical and the recommended dosage;
- a statement of the route of administration of the prepared radiopharmaceutical;
- if appropriate for particular kits (i.e. those subject to variability beyond the recommended limits), the methods and specifications needed to check radiochemical purity.

7. Production and distribution records

7.1 The processing records of regular production batches must provide a complete account of the manufacturing history of each batch of a radiopharmaceutical, showing that it has been manufactured, tested, dispensed into containers and distributed in accordance with the written procedures.

7.2 Separate records for the receipt, storage, use and disposal of radioactive materials should be maintained in accordance with radiation protection regulations.

7.3 Distribution records should be kept. Since the return of radioactive products is not practical, the purpose of recall procedures for such products is to prevent their use rather than an actual return. If necessary, the return of radioactive products should be carried out in accordance with international and national transport regulations.

8. Quality assurance and quality control

8.1 Radiopharmaceuticals are nearly always used before all quality control testing (e.g. tests for sterility, endotoxin, radionuclidic purity, etc.) has been completed. The implementation of and compliance with the quality assurance programme are therefore essential.

8.2 Quality assurance and/or quality control should have the following principal responsibilities:

(a) the preparation of detailed instructions for each test and analysis;
(b) ensuring the adequate identification and segregation of test samples to avoid mix-ups and cross-contamination;
(c) ensuring that environmental monitoring and equipment and process validation are conducted as appropriate for evaluating the adequacy of the manufacturing conditions;
(d) the release or rejection of starting materials and intermediate products;
(e) the release or rejection of packaging and labelling materials;
(f) the release or rejection of each batch of finished preparation;
(g) the evaluation of the adequacy of the conditions under which the starting materials, intermediate products and finished radiopharmaceutical preparations are stored;
(h) the evaluation of the quality and stability of the finished products and, when necessary, of the starting materials and intermediate products;
(i) the establishment of expiry dates on the basis of the validity period related to specified storage conditions;
(j) the establishment and revision of the control procedures and specifications;
(k) assuming the responsibility for retaining samples of radiopharmaceutical products;
(l) assuming the responsibility for keeping adequate records of the distribution of the radiopharmaceutical products.

8.3 Whenever the size of the establishment permits, quality assurance and quality control duties should be organized in separate groups. Quality assurance should also include the monitoring and validation of the production process.

8.4 A manufacturer's quality control laboratory should be separated from the production area. The control laboratory should be designed, equipped and of such a size as to be a self-contained entity, with adequate provision for the storage of documents and samples, the preparation of records and the performance of the necessary tests.

8.5 The performance of all qualitative and quantitative tests mentioned in the specifications for the starting materials may be replaced by a system of certificates issued by the supplier of these materials, provided that:

(a) there is a history of reliable production;
(b) the producer or supplier is regularly audited;
(c) at least one specific identity test is conducted by the manufacturer of the finished radiopharmaceutical.

8.6 Samples of the intermediate and final products should be retained in sufficient amounts and under appropriate storage conditions to allow repeated testing or verification of a batch control. These samples should be kept for an appropriate period in accordance with the shelf-lives of the radioactive components concerned. However, this may sometimes not be applicable, e.g. for radiopharmaceuticals with a short half-life.

8.7 Sampling procedures may be adapted to the purpose of the sampling, the type of controls being applied, and the nature of the material being sampled (e.g. a small batch size and/or its radioactive content). The procedure should be described in a written protocol.

Acknowledgements

These guidelines were prepared by the following experts: Mr P.O. Bremer (Norway), Mr C. Fallais (Belgium), Mr K.B. Park (Republic of Korea), Ms S. Vasanavathana (Thailand), Mr P.V. Kulkarni (India), Dr S. Kopp (World Health Organization), and Mr D.V.S. Narasimhan (International Atomic Energy Agency) and Mr H. Vera Ruiz (International Atomic Energy Agency).

References

1. Good manufacturing practices for pharmaceutical products. In: *WHO Expert Committee on Specifications for Pharmaceutical Preparations. Thirty-second report.* Geneva, World Health Organization, 1992 (WHO Technical Report Series, No. 823), Annex 1.

2. *Quality assurance of pharmaceuticals. A compendium of guidelines and related materials. Volume 2. Good manufacturing practices and inspection.* Geneva, World Health Organization, 1999.

3. Good manufacturing practices for sterile pharmaceutical products. In: *WHO Expert Committee on Specifications for Pharmaceutical Preparations. Thirty-sixth report.* Geneva, World Health Organization, 2002 (WHO Technical Report Series, No. 902), Annex 6.

4. *International basic safety standards for protection against ionizing radiation and for the safety of radiation sources: a safety standard.* Vienna, International Atomic Energy Authority, 1996 (Safety Series, No. 115).

5. *Regulations for the safe transport of radioactive material.* Vienna, International Atomic Energy Authority, 1996 (IAEA Safety Requirements Safety Standards Series, No. TS-R-1, Revised).

4.
Inspection

Pre-approval inspections[1]

1. General 285
2. Glossary 285
3. Objectives 286
4. Priorities 287
5. Preparation for the inspection 287
6. Carrying out the inspection 288
7. Sample collection and testing 289
8. Follow-up regulatory/administrative decisions 290
References 291

1. General

The advice provided here extends that given in the "Provisional guidelines on the inspection of pharmaceutical manufacturers" (*1*). The objectives of an inspection, as given in the introduction to the guidelines, are:

— to control and enforce compliance with general good manufacturing practices (GMP) (*2*); and
— to authorize the manufacture of specific pharmaceutical products, normally in response to a licensing application.

These guidelines are applicable mainly to inspections of the first type, whether performed as a condition for the issue of a manufacturing licence/authorization, or on a periodic, routine basis. They are essentially concerned with inspections of manufacturing and quality control facilities conducted before a marketing authorization (product licence or registration) for a pharmaceutical product is granted.

2. Glossary

The definitions given below apply to the terms used in this guide. They may have different meanings in other contexts.

[1] Guidelines on pre-approval inspections. In: *WHO Expert Committee on Specifications for Pharmaceutical Preparations. Thirty-sixth report.* Geneva, World Health Organization, 2002 (WHO Technical Report Series, No. 902), Annex 7.

application
A marketing authorization for a new drug application.

manufacture
All operations concerned with the purchase of materials and products, production (including packaging), quality control, release, storage, the distribution of pharmaceutical products, and the related controls (*2*).

manufacturer
A company that carries out at least one step of manufacture (*2*).

method validation/verification
Method validation is conducted where non-compendial analytical methods are included in the application to confirm that the applicants' proposed analytical methods are suitable for regulatory purposes. A side-by-side comparison with a compendial method, if available, should be included. Method verification is conducted where the methods are compendial, to confirm whether the product as compounded can be analysed satisfactorily by the official method.

pre-approval batches
Pilot or laboratory-scale batches, upon which the application is based, e.g. batches used for pivotal clinical trials and/or those used for bioavailability, bioequivalence and stability studies, and scale-up batches.

3. Objectives

Before any application is approved, it is necessary to determine whether all establishments participating in the manufacture of the finished dosage form are in compliance with GMP and the application commitments. Pre-approval inspections have the following specific objectives:

- Evaluation of the establishment's compliance with GMP requirements, particularly regarding proper environment, quality management, personnel, facilities and equipment.
- Evaluation of the procedures and controls implemented in the manufacture of the product (pre-approval batches), to determine whether they are in conformity with the application commitments.
- Audit of the completeness and accuracy of the manufacturing and testing information submitted with the application, and of the conformity of pre-approval batches with planned commercial batches (process validation protocol).
- The collection of samples for the validation or verification of the analytical methods included in the application.

4. Priorities

Pre-approval inspections are considered to be an important part of the application review and approval process. However, since this represents a considerable workload, inspections are not normally carried out routinely, but rather only in specific cases where non-compliance is possible. Thus inspections may be required for:

- new chemical entities;
- drugs of narrow therapeutic range, and drugs for serious conditions requiring an assured therapeutic response;
- products previously associated with serious adverse effects, complaints, recalls, etc.;
- products that are difficult to manufacture or test, or that are of doubtful stability (and therefore associated with the risk of defects);
- new applicants or manufacturers; and
- applications from manufacturers who have previously failed to comply with GMP or official quality specifications.

For other applications, the drug regulatory authority will rely on the results of recent inspections of the applicant's or manufacturer's facilities for the production of dosage forms similar to that of the proposed product.

5. Preparation for the inspection

An inspection team should, where possible, include analysts and other specialists, e.g. in pharmaceutical technology, or if available, persons with expertise in these fields, when needed. Team members may be assigned to inspect new operations or manufacturing sites associated with product failures. When possible, the analyst involved in the laboratory evaluation of the product under review should participate in the inspection. Pre-approval inspection is often carried out by a single inspector.

It is necessary to verify that the applicant holds an appropriate manufacturing authorization and that manufacturing is carried out in conformity with that authorization (licence).

An essential step in the review of applications is determining whether the commitments made by the manufacturer are reflected in actual practice. A review of the application information is also important in preparing for inspections of firms or processes with which the inspector is unfamiliar. The drug regulatory authority should provide inspectors with relevant information on the application. (Some countries request an additional copy of this information from applicants which is forwarded to the inspection team.) The information provided should include a copy of the manufacturing and controls section of the application, together with information relating to pre-approval batches.

Reasonable efforts should be made to conduct pre-approval inspections at the earliest possible opportunity, since unnecessary delays will prevent the timely review of applications. However, in some facilities the development or the manufacturing processes may not have been completed. In addition, changes may have occurred in the status of the application, e.g. major deficiencies in the application or the closure of an ancillary facility may affect the need for an inspection. In any case, the timing of the inspection should be coordinated between the inspectorate and the applicant.

For the inspection of major new facilities involving many applications, special coordination efforts are often beneficial.

When desirable, pre-approval inspections should be coordinated with the laboratory scheduled for method validation so as to enable it to participate in the inspection and in the collection of samples.

6. Carrying out the inspection

Emphasis should be placed on the evaluation of the manufacturing process, including data verification and the assessment of compliance with GMP. The production and control procedures described in the application must be compared with those used for the manufacture of pre-approval batches. If warranted by records of past label mix-ups, packaging and labelling control procedures should be evaluated. A programme of ongoing stability testing needs to be addressed.

The inspection team will determine whether the application provides the scientific data justifying full-scale production procedures and controls. The validation of pertinent manufacturing procedures, including equipment qualification, will also be evaluated.[1] However, inspectors should not recommend withholding approval of applications based on a lack of complete full-scale, multiple-batch validation of sterile and non-sterile processes, unless the data submitted in the application are found to be of questionable validity or completeness. It should be understood that full-scale validation may be completed after approval of the application, but before shipment of the first commercial batches. Nevertheless, certain data must be included in the application to demonstrate that the sterilization or aseptic fill process has been qualified. The inspection team is expected to audit the data to determine their authenticity, accuracy and completeness.

Investigational products are often produced in facilities other than those used for full-scale production (*4*). These facilities and the associated manufacturing and control procedures are not routinely inspected unless validation of the transfer of the methods from the "investigational" facilities to the full-scale facilities is lacking or questionable. The facilities may be periodically inspected when this is required by national legislation/regulation.

---

[1] For details of recommended validation programmes, see reference 3.

All suppliers and manufacturers of starting materials used in the formulation of pre-approval batches should be identified. The physical characteristics and specifications of the drug substance should be reviewed. This is particularly important for solid oral dosage forms where the physical characteristics of the drug substance often affect uniformity, dissolution and absorption of the dose.

When a pharmaceutical manufacturer replaces the supplier or manufacturer of the drug substance used for the manufacture of the pre-approval batches by another supplier or manufacturer, the application should include data demonstrating that the dosage forms formulated with the drug substance from the two different sources are equivalent in terms of conformity with established specifications, including those given in the application. Specifications should also cover the physical characteristics of the drug substances.

The addition of any new drug substance and/or dosage form to a production environment must be carefully evaluated in terms of its impact on other products already under production. Any changes that may be necessary in the building and facility must be assessed for their effect on overall compliance with GMP requirements. For example, a new toxic, potent or highly sensitizing product may require additional measures against cross-contamination, and facilities already operating at full capacity may not have adequate space for additional products. The evaluation should also include an assessment of whether any change in the manufacturing authorization is necessary.

Laboratory equipment and procedures must be qualified and validated. Every pre-approval inspection should include an evaluation of laboratory controls and procedures, and a review of some of the raw data used to generate results. The authenticity and accuracy of the data used in the development of a test method should be reviewed.

The inspection team should pay special attention to any newly established facilities, newly installed equipment and/or new raw material suppliers. If unapproved facilities are in use, this should be reported immediately. Inspections of these facilities are not normally required.

7. Sample collection and testing

The pre-approval inspection may include the collection of samples for validation of the analytical methods. Normally the sample size should be sufficient for three full analyses. Unless otherwise indicated by the laboratory, samples of the following sizes may be taken, depending on the dosage form of the product:

- — tablets and capsules: 300 units of production;
- — injections (single component): 100 units of production;
- — injections (combination): 100 units of production plus 10 samples of each component;
- — oral powders for reconstitution: 10 units of production;
- — oral liquids: 1 litre.

It is important to collect, with the samples, the relevant manufacturer's analytical documentation, namely a copy of the analytical methods used by the inspected laboratory and the report of the analyses performed by the applicant on the batch sampled. A method validation report may be of some use in better understanding and reproducing the analytical methods. Problems encountered in the performance of the analyses may be resolved by an exchange of information between the applicant and the government laboratory.

Samples are tested in accordance with methods described in the application. If there are problems with the methods that require additional information from the applicant, the laboratory director must review the situation and decide whether the applicant should be contacted. The written request should be included in the documentation submitted to the review analyst.

Each method validation/verification report should contain the following:

- The identification of the test samples received, a description of the product tested, and confirmation of conformity with the product described in the application.
- The original analytical worksheets with calculations, the results of all tests performed, comments by the analyst(s), associated spectra, chromatograms, etc., and a comparison of the results obtained with the applicant's data and with the applicable specifications.
- An evaluation of each test performed by the applicant and the laboratory.
- A recommendation as to whether the methods are acceptable, acceptable only after specified changes have been made, or unacceptable.

If samples have not been collected in the course of a pre-approval inspection, the results of the analytical examination of the samples submitted by the applicant may nevertheless be used as supporting information.

The reserve samples, associated documentation and copies of laboratory reports should be stored in an orderly and retrievable way for a time period specified by national regulations. It is usually recommended that all material should be kept for a minimum of 3 years or for 1 year after the expiry date of the finished product.

8. Follow-up regulatory/administrative decisions

The inspectorate (inspection group of the drug regulatory authority) should recommend withholding approval when significant deviations from GMP requirements and other application commitments have occurred having an adverse effect on the product covered by the application. Examples of significant problems are:

- Misrepresentation of data or conditions relating to pre-approval batches.
- Pre-approval batches not manufactured in accordance with GMP.
- Inconsistencies and/or discrepancies raising significant questions concerning the validity of the records.

If applications are refused because of significant non-compliance with GMP, action must be taken to ensure that the necessary corrective measures are taken.

The drug regulatory authority is expected to advise the applicant that the inspectorate has recommended withholding approval of the application and give the reasons for this recommendation.

References

1. Provisional guidelines on the inspection of pharmaceutical manufacturers. In: *WHO Expert Committee on Specifications for Pharmaceutical Preparations. Thirty-second report.* Geneva, World Health Organization, 1992 (WHO Technical Report Series, No. 823), Annex 2.

2. *Quality assurance of pharmaceuticals. A compendium of guidelines and related materials. Volume 2. Good manufacturing practices and inspection.* Geneva, World Health Organization, 1999.

3. Good manufacturing practices: guidelines on the validation of manufacturing processes. In: *WHO Expert Committee on Specifications for Pharmaceutical Preparations. Thirty-fourth report.* Geneva, World Health Organization, 1996 (WHO Technical Report Series, No. 863), Annex 6.

4. Good manufacturing practices: supplementary guidelines for the manufacture of investigational pharmaceutical products for clinical trials in humans. In: *WHO Expert Committee on Specifications for Pharmaceutical Preparations. Thirty-fourth report.* Geneva, World Health Organization, 1996 (WHO Technical Report Series, No. 863), Annex 7.

Inspection of pharmaceutical manufacturers[1]

These guidelines are intended to promote harmonization of pharmaceutical inspection practices among WHO Member States. They are directed to government inspectors—particularly those operating within small national regulatory authorities (*1*)—to assist them in assessing manufacturers' compliance with good manufacturing practices (GMP) (*2*). They will also be of value to manufacturers themselves when engaged in self-inspection or audit.

They cover inspection of the production and control of final dosage forms of pharmaceutical products destined for human and veterinary use and of drug substances (active pharmaceutical ingredients or bulk drug substances) employed in their manufacture. Within the national context their scope may need to be extended since similar regulations are often enforced to control

[1] Provisional guidelines on the inspection of pharmaceutical manufacturers. In: *WHO Expert Committee on Specifications for Pharmaceutical Preparations. Thirty-second report.* Geneva, World Health Organization, 1992 (WHO Technical Report Series, No. 823), Annex 2.

pharmaceutical and biological products, medical devices, diagnostic products, foods, and food additives. In all cases the same fundamental principles apply.

Inspection and licensing of pharmaceutical manufacturing facilities on the basis of compliance with GMP are a vital element of drug control. They are also pivotal to the operation of the WHO Certification Scheme on the Quality of Pharmaceutical Products Moving in International Commerce (*3*), which requires an attestation by the competent regulatory authority in the exporting country that a given product is manufactured in premises and using operating practices that conform with GMP.

The guidelines also have relevance in various other contexts, including:

- self-inspection or internal audit of a factory or a part of it carried out by personnel of the company;
- Inspection by an independent person or group of persons as a review of the quality system of a company in compliance with the standards issued by the International Organization for Standardization (ISO 9000–9004 (*4*)) or the British Standards Institution (BS 5750 (*5*)) or with other equivalent national standards;
- audit of a manufacturer or supplier by authorized agents of the customer.

The government inspectorate represents the enforcement arm of the national drug regulatory authority. Its function is to ensure adherence by manufacturers to all licensing provisions and specifically to GMP. The objectives are to control and enforce general standards of production and to provide authorization for the manufacture of specific pharmaceutical products. The first objective involves a sequential examination of production and control activities on the basis of the GMP guidelines issued by WHO or of nationally determined requirements. The second requires verification that production and quality control procedures employed in the manufacture of specific products are performed correctly and that they accord with data supplied in the relevant licensing applications.

Inspection will, of course, depend on national legislation and regulations and/or the resources available.

The role of the inspector

Inspectors should have previous training and practical experience in the manufacture and/or quality control of pharmaceutical products. Graduate pharmacists, chemists, or scientists with an industrial background in pharmaceutical production would qualify for consideration.

In-post training should include an element of apprenticeship gained by accompanying experienced inspectors on site visits as well as participation in courses and seminars on relevant subjects including modern pharmaceutical technology, microbiology, and the statistical aspects of quality control.

The primary responsibility of an inspector is to present a detailed factual report on standards of manufacture and control applied to specific products. However, inspection should not be limited to compilation of an inventory of faults, irregularities, and discrepancies. Provided it is in keeping with national policy and does not breach understandings regarding confidentiality of information having commercial value, advice may be offered on how production and control procedures can be usefully upgraded. An inspector should always be expected, for example, to offer advice on how to improve an in-process test procedure or to offer other assistance which, in his or her opinion, serves the public interest. An inspection should be regarded as an opportunity to assist and motivate a manufacturer to comply with GMP and to correct any specific deficiencies.

The inspection process

The planning, organization, method of work, and format of the resultant report should always be determined by the precise objective of the inspection. Inspections vary in nature according to the objective:

Routine inspection

This is a full inspection of all applicable components of GMP and licensing provisions. It may be indicated when the manufacturer:

- is newly established;
- requests renewal of a licence to operate;
- has introduced new product lines or new products, or has made significant modifications to manufacturing methods or processes, or has made changes in key personnel, premises, equipment, etc.;
- has a history of non-compliance with GMP;
- has not been inspected during the last 3–5 years.

Concise inspection

Manufacturers with a consistent record of compliance with GMP through previous routine inspections are eligible for concise inspection. The focus of a concise inspection is on a limited number of GMP requirements selected as indicators of overall GMP performance, plus the identification of any significant changes that could have been introduced since the last inspection. Collectively, the information obtained will indicate the overall attitude of the firm towards GMP. Evidence of unsatisfactory GMP performance observed during a concise inspection should trigger a more comprehensive inspection.

Follow-up inspection (reassessment or reinspection)

Follow-up visits are made to monitor the result of corrective actions. They are normally carried out from 6 weeks to 6 months after the initial inspection, depending on the nature of the defects and the work to be undertaken. They are limited to specific GMP requirements that have not been observed or that have been inadequately implemented.

Special inspection

Special visits may be necessary to undertake spot checks following complaints or recalls related to suspected quality defects in products. Reports of adverse drug reactions may also indicate that all is not well. Such inspections may be focused on one product, a group of related products, or specific operations such as mixing, sterilization, or labelling.

Special visits may also be made to establish how a specific product is manufactured as a prerequisite for marketing approval or issuance of an export certificate.

A further reason for special visits is to gather specific information on—or to investigate—specific operations and to advise the manufacturer of regulatory requirements.

Quality systems review

A quality systems review is a relatively new concept. Its purpose is to describe a quality assurance system that has been shown to operate satisfactorily. It entails a description of the quality system and the standards to be observed, normally in a manual containing a statement of the manufacturer's policy on quality assurance. It should also define the management structure needed to implement the policy, along with the procedures in each management area needed to ensure that adequate quality standards are set for the product, manufacturing processes are correctly defined, records are kept, and quality control and other quality assurance activities are carried out.

Frequency and duration of inspections

The frequency and duration of visits should be determined by the type of inspection required as well as by the workload and number of inspectors. New manufacturing establishments must be inspected before they are licensed, and new facilities must be inspected before production is started.

For all companies, inspections should be carried out on a regular schedule, ideally annually.

For large companies marketing a wide range of products, the inspection of the site may be split up into several visits over a longer period, e.g. 5 years where this is the period of validity of the manufacturing licence or the GMP certificates.

The length of a given inspection is determined by the size of the company and the purpose of the visit. It can extend from a few days to 2 weeks or more. The time taken also depends on the number of inspectors assigned to the visit. In many countries, visits are made by one (or more) inspectors, sometimes accompanied by a specialist when production of biologicals, sterile production areas, or other special facilities are to be examined.

Preparing for the inspection

Drug inspection begins at the desk of the inspector. A review should be made of the documents relating to the company to be visited, available from the drug regulatory authority. These may include the manufacturing licence, the marketing authorization dossiers for leading products, reports of adverse drug reactions, complaints and recall records, the results of regulatory (surveillance) testing, and the previous inspection reports.

Company documents, including the annual report for the shareholders, the complaints file, and self-inspection/internal audit reports, are valuable sources of information. The last of these, depending on national legislation, may be withheld from the inspector. In some countries, a compromise is reached, the company presenting the internal audit reports to the inspector for general information after the latter's own report has been finalized. In any case, it should be possible to verify the frequency of self-inspections, and to which parts of the plant they have been applied.

Conduct

Announced inspections cover regular visits to evaluate new plants and new production lines and to decide on the renewal of a licence.

Unannounced inspections are necessary for concise, follow-up, and special visits.

In certain countries regular inspections are unannounced as a matter of policy.

The visit usually begins with a meeting between the inspector(s), representatives of the company or plant management, and those responsible for the products or areas to be inspected. Credentials should be presented, letters of authority inspected, and an explanation given of why the inspection is being carried out.

It is advantageous for the company to appoint at least one "escort" who is directly involved in the preparation of the products that are the object of the inspection. Escorts should be chosen who are generally familiar with the quality systems of the company and who are involved in the self-inspection programme.

The meeting may be followed by a perusal of the company's documents by the inspector or by a walk-through visit, or both. This will permit the inspector to finalize the plan for the inspection. It is recommended that the inspector both develops and follows this plan independently, rather than accepting guidance from company management. Some basic rules for conducting the inspection are as follows:

- Inspection should follow the original plan as far as possible; items that are specific to certain areas of the facility, such as in-process testing and working documents, may need to be checked at the point of operation. Care should be taken to cover activities such as water production, sample storage, and validation.
- It is advisable to follow production flow from reception of the starting materials to the shipment of the finished products. The frequency of recalls and return of goods should be carefully noted.
- Documents such as master formulae, test specifications, standard operating procedures, and batch records (including protocols of analyses, etc. and documents relating to the control of printed materials and labelling operations) require close verification.

Without prejudice to the need to verify documentation, it is essential that the inspection be based largely on observation and cover the total working hours of the manufacturer. It is recommended that the inspector start the plant tour as soon as possible after arrival.

Inspectors can profitably use a short checklist to ensure that all areas of operations have been investigated. A very detailed checklist developed from GMP guidelines is of use specifically for the training of inspectors. Experience has shown that rigid adherence to a too-detailed checklist can lead to possible overlooking of vulnerable areas of a quality assurance system specific to the company/plant under investigation. For an experienced inspector, knowledge of the manufacturer's weak points allied with intuition may serve better than a checklist. Different checklists may be found in the recommended publications and documents listed in Appendix 1.

Stability testing programme. The inspector should be satisfied that there exists a documented ongoing programme specifying the regular withdrawal of samples of all products from the production line for stability testing. The testing schedule for stored samples should employ appropriate conditions of temperature and light stress, and suitable stability-indicating analytical methods that yield conclusions consistent with claimed shelf-life. The systems should permit reevaluation of product stability following any changes in the manufacturing process or formula.

Significant changes in facilities, equipment, products, and senior personnel since the last inspection should be noted. The principle here is that changes represent possible areas of weakness or causes of non-compliance with GMP. For example, new equipment may require changes to be made in procedures; new product lines may require new product master files; and departures of senior personnel such as the quality control manager may result in behavioural or procedural changes.

Occasionally, an inspector may require access to other premises, documents, or information on the company. Ideally, the inspector's authority should be determined by legislation, but in the absence of clear legal or regulatory provisions, it is suggested that the GMP code is used as a guide and the inspector should have the right to verify compliance with every requirement listed in the code.

The inspector should not be concerned about information not covered by GMP—e.g. finance and personnel—where this does not infringe on the company's responsibilities or staff education and training.

Photographs or videos taken during the visit may be excellent illustrative material for the report. National legislation should stipulate that the inspector has the right to take visual records during the inspection to document the production premises or laboratories.

In many cases, an aerial photograph of the manufacturing site, possibly with surrounding grounds, may be obtained from the company together with other relevant materials for inclusion in the report.

Collecting samples. It is normal practice during the visit for the inspector to take samples for testing by the official quality control laboratory. Samples are usually taken from released products (e.g. from the finished-goods warehouse) but may also be taken from stocks of raw materials or in-process material. In order to protect sample integrity, any protocol meant for enforcement or legal purposes should set out the procedures for sample collection, analysis, and documentation. The following should be stated:

— name(s) of the sampled product(s), batch number(s), date, source, number of samples, and remarks on type of packaging and storage conditions;
— circumstances of sampling, e.g., suspected quality defects, routine surveillance, verification of compliance with GMP;
— instructions for the placing of seals on containers of sample materials;
— written confirmation of the receipt of the samples by the inspector (possibly together with the manufacturer's certificates of analysis and any other supporting documents).

The manufacturer, represented by the company escort, should be encouraged to take duplicate samples from the same batch(es), for "in-house" testing if a problem is later identified.

Before the inspector leaves the premises after the inspection, a final discussion with company management is recommended. If possible, the inspector should list any unsatisfactory findings and outline any irregularities or other observations to which management may wish to respond.

Report

It is recommended that reports be divided into four parts: general information on the company or manufacturing facility, description of the inspection, observations, and conclusions. Annexes may contain supporting information (a list of products manufactured, an organization chart, the annual company report, photographs, etc.). The third and fourth parts may be combined. Appendix 2, which is an extract from a document prepared for the Pharmaceutical Inspection Convention, provides an example of the form and content of the inspector's report.

In order to save the inspector's time, the first part of the report containing basic data may be supplied by the company beforehand, provided that this fact is clearly stated in the report and the information supplied is verified by the inspector during the visit. An example of items that should be considered for inclusion is given in Appendix 2, section C, "Site master file".

The second part should describe the complete progress of the inspection step by step, documenting which parts of the factory, warehouses, laboratories, records, documents, etc. were inspected.

The third part is devoted to observations. Changes, improvements, and examples of deterioration since the previous inspection should be noted by the inspector.

Positive observations should take the form of a description of the processes that the firm is carrying out particularly well and that may be considered examples of particularly good manufacturing practice.

Negative observations (non-compliance with GMP requirements) should distinguish between whether the defect lies in the system itself or in a failure to comply with the system. For instance, when cleaning is found to be suboptimal, it is important to know whether the standard operating procedures are inadequate or lacking, or whether adequate written procedures exist but are not being followed by personnel.

In the final part of the report, the inspector should summarize deficiencies, unsatisfactory practices, etc. (listed in decreasing order of importance), suggest corrective actions, and make recommendations. This part, together with the third part, should be discussed with the company management and responsible authorized persons at the end of the inspection.

A copy of the complete written report, after supervisory approval, should be provided to the company management with a covering letter. The corrective actions to be taken, together with a time limit for their execution, should also be presented to the management of the company.

Inspection reports may be treated as confidential documents depending on national legislation. Under certain international agreements, reports may be exchanged between drug regulatory authorities.

Regulatory actions

Depending on national legislation, regulatory authorities may take action to correct unsatisfactory practices and prevent the distribution of products with suspected quality defects or manufactured under conditions that do not comply with GMP requirements. In extreme cases, the closing down of operations may be required. In practice, these measures are used only in exceptional cases constituting a hazard to health.

In many countries, the drug regulatory authority has the legal power to suspend or revoke the marketing authorization for a product when the manufacturer does not comply with GMP. In addition, manufacturing or marketing authorizations (licences), the reregistration of products, and the issue of a variation licence or a GMP certificate may be delayed until appropriate measures have been taken by the company, and possibly have been confirmed by reinspection. As a rule, the manufacturer concerned has the right to appeal.

References

1. Guiding principles for small national drug regulatory authorities. In: *WHO Expert Committee on Specifications for Pharmaceutical Preparations. Thirty-first report.* Geneva, World Health Organization, 1990: 64–79 (WHO Technical Report Series, No. 790).

2. Good manufacturing practices for pharmaceutical products. In: *WHO Expert Committee on Specifications for Pharmaceutical Preparations. Thirty-second report.* Geneva, World Health Organization, 1992: 14–79 (WHO Technical Report Series, No. 823).

3. WHO Certification Scheme on the Quality of Pharmaceutical Products Moving in International Commerce. In: *WHO Expert Committee on Specifications for Pharmaceutical Preparations. Thirty-first report.* Geneva, World Health Organization, 1990: 57–63 (WHO Technical Report Series, No. 790).

4. *International Standards: Quality management and quality assurance standards—Guidelines for selection and use (ISO 9000), Quality systems—Model for quality assurance in design/ development, production, installation and servicing (ISO 9001); Quality systems—Model for quality assurance in production and installation (ISO 9002); Quality systems—Model for quality assurance in final inspection and test (ISO 9003); Quality management and quality system elements—Guidelines (ISO 9004).* Geneva, International Organization for Standardization, 1987 (rev. 1990).

5. *Quality systems. Part 2. Specification for manufacture and installation (BS 5750: Part 2).* London, British Standards Institution, 1979.

Appendix 1. Recommended publications and documents

ASEAN manual for inspection of GMP. Association of South East Asian Nations, 1988.

Drug manufacturer's self-inspection manual as to conformity with GMP requirements. In: *GMP regulations of Japan*, 3rd ed. Tokyo, Ministry of Health and Welfare, 1988: 101–195.

Good drug manufacturing practices (GMP), audit check-list. Government of Brazil, Ministry of Health, 1983.

Grundregeln für die Herstellung von Wirkstoffen und die Sicherung ihrer Qualität; Fragebogen zu den Grundregeln für die Herstellung von Wirkstoffen und die Sicherung ihrer Qualität [Basic rules for the production of active ingredients and their quality assurance; audit checklist to the basic rules for the production of active ingredients and their quality assurance]. *Pharmazeutische Industrie*, 1981, 43: 537– 542 (republished in: Oeser W, Sander A. *Pharma-Betriebsverordnung, Kommentar [GMP comments]*. Stuttgart, Wissenschaftliche Verlagsgesellschaft, 1988).

Guide to inspection of bulk pharmaceutical chemical manufacturing. Food and Drug Administration, US Department of Health and Human Services, Public Health Service, 1987.

Steinborn L. *Quality assurance manual for the pharmaceutical and medical device industries*. Buffalo Grove, IL, Interpharm Press, 1986.

Appendix 2. Form and content of the inspector's report[1]

A. Inspector's information

1. Date of inspection(s) on which the information is based and name(s) of inspector(s).
2. Brief report of inspection activities undertaken.
3. Samples taken and results obtained.
4. Assessment of the site master file (see section C).
5. GMP-related recalls from the market of any product in the last two years.

B. Summary and conclusions

1. The inspector's general impression of the firm and his or her assessment of the acceptability of its GMP status for the range of products concerned.
2. Failures to comply with the PIC Guide to Good Manufacturing Practice (in order of importance) and with the time limits set for them to be corrected by the manufacturer.

[1] Extracted (with permission and minor changes) from an unpublished document (PH 6/91) prepared for the Pharmaceutical Inspection Convention (PIC), November 1991.

C. Site master file

A site master file is a document prepared by the manufacturer containing specific and factual GMP information about the production and/or control of pharmaceutical manufacturing operations carried out at the named site and any closely integrated operations at adjacent and nearby buildings. If only part of a pharmaceutical operation is carried out on the site, the site master file need describe only those operations, e.g. analysis, packaging.

A site master file should be succinct and, as far as possible, should not exceed 25 A4 pages.

1. General information

1.1 Brief information on the firm (including name and address), relation to other sites, and, in particular, any information relevant to understanding the manufacturing operations.

1.2 Pharmaceutical manufacturing activities as licensed by the national authority.

1.3 Any other manufacturing activities carried out on the site.

1.4 Name and exact address of the site, including telephone, fax, and 24-hour telephone numbers.

1.5 Type of products manufactured on the site, and information about any specifically toxic or hazardous substances handled, mentioning the way they are manufactured (in dedicated facilities or on a campaign basis).

1.6 Short description of the site (size, location, and immediate environment and other manufacturing activities on the site).

1.7 Number of employees engaged in production, quality control, storage, and distribution.

1.8 Use of outside scientific, analytical, or other technical assistance in relation to manufacture and analysis.

1.9 Short description of the quality management system of the firm responsible for manufacture.

2. Personnel

2.1 Organization chart showing the arrangements for quality assurance, including production and quality control.

2.2 Qualifications, experience, and responsibilities of key personnel.

2.3 Outline of arrangements for basic and in-service training and how records are maintained.

2.4 Health requirements for personnel engaged in production.

2.5 Personnel hygiene requirements, including clothing.

3. Premises and equipment

Premises

3.1 Simple plan or description of manufacturing areas with indication of scale (architectural or engineering drawings not required).

3.2 Nature of construction and finishes.

3.3 Brief description of ventilation systems. More details should be given for critical areas with potential risks of airborne contamination (schematic drawings of the systems are desirable). Classification of the rooms used for the manufacture of sterile products should be mentioned.

3.4 Special areas for the handling of highly toxic, hazardous, and sensitizing materials.

3.5 Brief description of water systems (schematic drawings of the systems are desirable), including sanitation.

3.6 Description of planned preventive maintenance programmes for premises and of the recording system.

Equipment

3.7 Brief description of major equipment used in production and control laboratories (a list of equipment is not required).

3.8 Description of planned preventive maintenance programmes for equipment and of the recording system.

3.9 Qualification and calibration, including the recording system. Arrangements for computerized systems validation.

Sanitation

3.10 Availability of written specifications and procedures for cleaning manufacturing areas and equipment.

4. Documentation

4.1 Arrangements for the preparation, revision, and distribution of necessary documentation for manufacture.

4.2 Any other documentation related to product quality that is not mentioned elsewhere (e.g. microbiological controls on air and water).

5. Production

5.1 Brief description of production operations using, wherever possible, flow sheets and charts specifying important parameters.

5.2 Arrangements for the handling of starting materials, packaging materials, and bulk and finished products, including sampling, quarantine, release, and storage.

5.3 Arrangements for the handling of rejected materials and products.

5.4 Brief description of general policy for process validation.

6. Quality control

6.1 Description of the quality control system and of the activities of the quality control department. Procedures for the release of finished products.

7. Contract manufacture and analysis

7.1 Description of the way in which the GMP compliance of the contract accepter is assessed.

8. Distribution, complaints, and product recall

8.1 Arrangements and recording system for distribution.

8.2 Arrangements for the handling of complaints and product recalls.

9. Self-inspections

9.1 Short description of the self-inspection system.

Inspection of drug distribution channels[1]

Introductory note 304
General considerations 305
Glossary 306
1. Drug inspectors 309
   1.1 Qualifications 309
   1.2 Organizational aspects 310

[1] Guidelines for inspection of drug distribution channels. In: *WHO Expert Committee on Specifications for Pharmaceutical Preparations. Thirty-fifth report.* Geneva, World Health Organization, 1999 (WHO Technical Report Series, No. 885), Annex 6.

1.3 Methods of inspection 311
1.4 Reference/information sources 312
2. Inspection of establishments in the drug distribution chain 313
2.1 Broad objectives 313
2.2 Establishments 313
2.3 Inspections 313
2.4 Special categories of drugs 313
References 314
Selected further reading 314
Appendix 1
Checklist for inspection and the preparation of a report 315
Appendix 2
Guidance on sampling 319
Appendix 3
Guidance for inspection when pharmaceutical products are suspected to be counterfeit, spurious or substandard 320
Appendix 4
Sample receipt form 321

Introductory note

The quality assurance of drugs at the level of the manufacturer is outlined in the guidelines on good manufacturing practices for pharmaceutical products (GMP) published by WHO (*1*). Compliance with these guidelines will ensure that products released for distribution are of the appropriate quality. However, if this is to be realized in practice, it is essential that an established drug regulatory authority exists in a Member State, which complies at least with the "Guiding principles for small national drug regulatory authorities" (*2*).

In addition, the holder of a marketing authorization for a pharmaceutical product, or alternatively the (legal) person responsible for the initial marketing of a product, who ideally should be a pharmacist or a pharmaceutical company authorized to practise in the Member State, should ensure that the product is only released for distribution after it has been established that it conforms with the product specification lodged with the drug regulatory authority.

This level of quality should be maintained throughout the pharmaceutical supply system or distribution network. Basic principles of GMP are applicable to wholesale operations and (to some extent) to retail outlets. These principles may be summarized as follows:

— only authorized products are distributed;
— a quality system is in place which includes quality policy, quality management, appropriate analytical controls, self-inspection;
— personnel are quality-conscious, adequately trained and motivated;

— premises and equipment are suitable for their intended use, and kept in a good sanitary condition;
— all products are received, stored and handled appropriately (protected against contamination, cross-contamination, mix-ups, environmental factors such as heat, severe cold, moisture, light);
— all drug-related operations are performed in accordance with written procedures, are properly supervised and adequately documented; documentation ensures complete traceability of receipt of all materials, quality testing processes (if any) and shipping;
— adequate provisions exist to handle complaints, recalls, and returned goods.

At the same time, many provisions of the GMP guidelines published by WHO are clearly not addressed to wholesalers and retail pharmacies where specific rules and requirements apply. These rules are determined partly by pharmaceutical science and common sense, and partly by national (regional) regulations and standards. In this context reference is made particularly to the guidelines entitled "Good pharmacy practice in community and hospital pharmacy settings" (*3*). It follows then that the "Provisional guidelines on the inspection of pharmaceutical manufacturers" (*4*), which are directed to government GMP inspectors, are not adequate to cover inspection in the distribution system. The present document addresses this specific issue.

These guidelines are intended for use by pharmaceutical inspectors in national drug regulatory authorities. They are therefore presented in a format that will allow for easy reference in the field. They should, however, be adapted by national drug regulatory authorities to suit their national legal requirements and available resources.

This document discusses the "simplified" situation when there is a single authority, the drug regulatory authority, where all kinds of drug inspections are located, ranging from those of drug manufacture to the inspections of pharmacies. In reality, these tasks, requiring different inspection skills, are usually distributed among different (national and local) authorities.

General considerations

A comprehensive system to assure the safety, efficacy and quality of pharmaceutical products at a national level has the following elements:

- Legal: drug legislation
- Administrative:
  — drug regulatory authority with functions of product registration, licensing of manufacturers, importers and distributors (wholesale, retail and for institutional supply), inspection and independent testing of samples;
  — enforcement.

- Technical:
  - — regulations
  - — standards and norms
  - — guidelines
  - — independent quality control laboratory(ies).

This document focuses on one element—inspection—and in particular on inspection in the pharmaceutical supply system.

The usefulness of drugs in the treatment of ailments, diseases and disorders is well recognized and appreciated. It is also recognized that the inappropriate use of drugs can produce severe toxic effects, some of which may be fatal. National drug laws have therefore been introduced to reduce risks associated with the use, misuse and abuse of pharmaceutical preparations.

Drugs differ in the severity of their side-effects and toxicity and these differences are taken into consideration in the classification of drugs in national drug laws. Drugs may be classified into four types as follows: over-the-counter drugs, pharmacy-only drugs, prescription-only drugs and prohibited drugs.

The distribution, supply, import, export, sale, storage, advertisement and dispensing of drugs are normally regulated by national drug laws, which provide for a system of licences to be issued by a drug regulatory authority for such drug-related activities. The drug laws may identify a ministry/department/agency that would function as the drug regulatory authority as well as provide for the enforcement of the drug laws, using a system of inspections organized through an inspectorate(s).

The inspectorate advises on whether applicants and premises should be issued licences to engage in drug-related activities. The inspectorate ensures that counterfeit, spurious and substandard pharmaceutical products are not found in the national pharmaceutical supply system or outside it, and that licensed premises and authorized persons adhere to existing laws and regulations. To do this, the inspectorate gathers information on the working of the drug laws by liaising with other law enforcement agencies and health institutions, including health-care professional associations.

Glossary

The definitions given below apply to the terms used in these guidelines. They may have different meanings in other contexts.

batch

A defined quantity of any drug product processed in a single process or series of processes such that it can reasonably be expected to be uniform in character and quality.

batch number[1]
A distinctive combination of numbers and/or letters which specifically identifies a batch on the labels, the batch records, the certificate of analysis, etc.

controlled drugs
Narcotic drugs and psychotropic substances regulated by provisions of national drug laws.

counterfeit pharmaceutical product
A pharmaceutical product which is deliberately and fraudulently mislabelled with respect to identity and/or source. Counterfeiting can apply to both branded and generic products and counterfeit products may include products with the correct ingredients, with the wrong ingredients, without active ingredients, with an insufficient quantity of active ingredient or with fake packaging.

drug (pharmaceutical product)
Any substance or mixture of substances that is manufactured for sale or distribution, sold, supplied, offered for sale or presented for use in:

(i) the treatment, mitigation, cure, prevention or diagnosis of disease, an abnormal physical state or the symptoms thereof and abnormal physiological conditions in human or animal; or
(ii) the restoration, correction or modification of organic functions in human or animal.

finished pharmaceutical product
A pharmaceutical product that has undergone all stages of production and quality control, including being packaged in its final container and labelled.

good manufacturing practice[1]
Good manufacturing practice is that part of quality assurance which ensures that products are consistently produced and controlled to the quality standards appropriate to their intended use and as required by the marketing authorization.

good pharmacy practice
The practice of pharmacy aimed at providing and promoting the best use of drugs and other health care services and products, by patients and members of the public. It requires that the welfare of the patient is the pharmacist's prime concern at all times.

[1] As defined in "Good manufacturing practices for pharmaceutical products" (*1*).

over-the-counter drugs

These are drugs that can be sold from licensed dealers without professional supervision and without prescriptions. These drugs are suitable for self-medication for minor diseases and symptoms.

pharmacist

A pharmacist is a holder of a degree or diploma in pharmacy from a recognized higher institution of learning and is registered or licensed to practise pharmacy.

pharmacy-only drugs

These are drugs authorized to be sold only in licensed pharmacies under the supervision of licensed and registered pharmacists; they may be sold without a prescription.

poison

A preparation or substance defined by a national drug law as a poison.

prescription-only drugs

These are drugs supplied only in licensed pharmacies on the presentation of signed prescriptions issued by a licensed and registered medical practitioner, licensed and/or registered dentist (for dental treatment only), and/or licensed and/or registered veterinarian (for animal treatment only), and the supply and dispensing of these drugs must be carried out by a pharmacist or under the supervision of a pharmacist. Prescription drugs are further subdivided into controlled drugs (narcotic drugs and psychotropic substances) and non-controlled drugs.

product recall

Product recall is a process for withdrawing or removing a pharmaceutical product from the pharmaceutical distribution chain because of defects in the product or complaints of serious adverse reactions to the product. The recall might be initiated by the manufacturer/importer/distributor or a responsible agency.

prohibited drugs

These are drugs with toxicity or side-effects that outweigh their therapeutic usefulness, so that public health and welfare are protected by prohibiting their production, manufacture, export, import, trade, distribution, supply, possession or use, except in amounts required for medical and scientific research. Prohibited drugs are normally determined by the national or supranational registration/licensing authority.

quality assurance[1]
Quality assurance is a wide-ranging concept covering all matters that individually or collectively influence the quality of a product. It is the totality of the arrangements made with the object of ensuring that pharmaceutical products are of the quality required for their intended use.

quality control
Quality control covers all measures taken, including the setting of specifications, sampling, testing and analytical clearance, to ensure that raw materials, intermediates, packaging materials and finished pharmaceutical products conform with established specifications for identity, strength, purity and other characteristics.

unauthorized market (in some countries called parallel market)
The unauthorized market consists of wholesale establishments and retail outlets distributing or selling drugs without authorization from a competent authority.

1. Drug inspectors

1.1 Qualifications

Inspectors should normally be pharmacists who have working experience in community and/or hospital pharmacy. Where persons other than pharmacists are employed as drug inspectors, they should be adequately experienced in drug control affairs and suitably trained in inspectorate functions. The possibility of having part-time inspectors with specialist knowledge as part of inspection teams should also be considered.

The inspector should possess the following attributes:

— good knowledge of pharmacy, drugs, and poisons
— good knowledge of the laws and regulations to be enforced
— good command of technical terms and excellent communication skills
— awareness of the probable methods of using forged or false documents for transactions in pharmaceutical preparations and skill in determining the genuineness of documents presented for examination
— maturity, honesty and integrity
— responsible conduct which commands respect
— willingness to accept challenges
— ability to organize their own work with minimum supervision
— ability to assess facts quickly and take rational and sound decisions without delay
— ability to assess character and honesty of persons being interviewed

[1] As defined in "Good manufacturing practices for pharmaceutical products" (*1*).

— good public relations image with key personnel/pharmacists in charge of premises while remaining firm, fair and resolute
— ability to hold discussions with company management at the completion of inspection
— ability to motivate others
— commitment to hard work and long hours
— ethical approach to any potential conflict of interest.

1.2 Organizational aspects

Inspectors should be embedded in an organization, usually called an inspectorate, which ensures the following aspects:

- A job description which describes the duties of the inspector.
- Proper reporting: inspectors should report either to the drug regulatory authority or to the pharmaceutical department (chief pharmacist) of the ministry of health.
- Uniformity of approach:
  (a) Regular meetings of inspectors, in which experiences on the job are exchanged, will help promote a uniform approach to inspection as well as enhance the performance of the inspectors.
  (b) Inspectors should work according to a work plan and to standard operating procedures (SOPs).
  (c) Inspection reports should preferably be in three or four parts:
    (i) date of inspection and general information on the establishment inspected,
    (ii) description of the inspection activities undertaken, including analytical data of samples taken,
    (iii) observations and recommendations,
    (iv) conclusions.
  (d) Inspectors should be encouraged to submit weekly reports of work to headquarters.
- Total coverage of the country. This can be achieved by:
  (a) dividing the country into defined areas for the purpose of inspection and placing an inspector in charge of a defined area for the purpose of inspecting wholesale, community and hospital pharmacies, and clinics,
  (b) inspection of ports and border posts in a defined area.
- Total coverage of the field. The inspector will be expected to inspect establishments such as:
  (a) pharmaceutical manufacturers in respect of drug distribution,
  (b) pharmaceutical importers/exporters,
  (c) pharmaceutical wholesalers and retailers,
  (d) hospital pharmacies/clinics,
  (e) ports and international border posts,

(f) drug warehouses, stores and unauthorized markets. (*Note*: The existence of unauthorized markets for the distribution of drugs poses considerable health hazards. The inspectors should, with the assistance of task forces if necessary, investigate the extent of the unauthorized market, the types of drugs distributed and supplied, and the sources of the drugs. Where possible, unauthorized markets for drugs should be prohibited through effective inspectorate activities. Inspectors should also investigate the sources of supply of suspect counterfeit or substandard pharmaceutical products.)

- Cooperation with other agencies. The inspector will be expected to interact and cooperate with other interested parties such as:
  (a) industrial, community and hospital pharmacists,
  (b) management and supervisory staff of pharmaceutical establishments and hospitals,
  (c) medical practitioners, dentists, veterinarians, nurses and midwives and other health workers,
  (d) public analysts,
  (e) ministry of justice officials and court officials,
  (f) drug law enforcement officers including the police and customs,
  (g) officers of port authorities, clearing agents at the ports, importers and exporters,
  (h) members of the public,
  (i) staff of faculties of medicine/pharmacy,
  (j) foreign drug regulatory authorities.
- Independence. Inspectors should, for example, have the use of official vehicles.
- Adherence to a code of inspection.

1.3 Methods of inspection

The inspector uses different methods to check compliance with the national, supranational or international drug laws and regulations. Among these methods are:

- *Comprehensive/routine inspection*. This form of inspection is generally reserved for a new pharmaceutical establishment, when an establishment is applying for permit to extend its scope of operations beyond that for which it was originally licensed, has made important changes in key personnel or is changing premises, has not been inspected for a long time (3–5 years), or when there is information (even of an informal nature) of serious lapses. Where the inspection is for a new establishment or for extension of scope of operation or because of changes in key personnel, the inspection should be announced.

- *Concise inspection.* This is reserved for establishments that have previously been inspected with a view to assessing standards of good pharmacy practice. The outcome of the inspection will help in the proper assessment of the establishment. The inspection may be unannounced.
- *Follow-up inspection.* This is normally carried out to ensure that corrective measures have been undertaken following advice and notice given during a previous inspection. Where a time limit was given for applying the corrective measures, the inspection may be unannounced.
- *Special inspection.* This is undertaken to deal with specific complaints received about lapses or non-compliance with standards of professional practice. The inspection should preferably be unannounced.
- *Investigative inspection.* This type of inspection is used to assess the performance of a new establishment whose scope of operation was previously unknown.

Any of these methods may be applied with or without prior announcement. Normally inspections should be announced but it serves a useful purpose to undertake some unannounced inspections. Follow-up, special and investigative inspections should preferably be unannounced.

Inspections should be held regularly. Premises should be inspected at least once every 12–18 months. Where contravention is often noticed, the inspection should be more frequent (e.g. every six months). For premises with a good record, less frequent inspections may be needed.

1.4 Reference/information sources

The reference/information sources of an inspector should include:

- Existing national and international drug laws and regulations, covering such aspects as:
  - — licensing
  - — GMP
  - — good distribution practice
  - — good pharmacy practice
  - — promotion of pharmaceutical products
  - — controlled drugs
  - — counterfeit, spurious or substandard pharmaceutical products.
- Codes of inspection (national and regional), where in existence.
- Codes of professional ethics.
- Health consequences of drug abuse and misuse.
- Available data on imports/exports/prohibited drugs.

2. Inspection of establishments in the drug distribution chain

2.1 Broad objectives

The welfare of patients and other members of the public is of prime concern in the distribution chain of drugs, either manufactured within the country or imported. Inspections of establishments are therefore undertaken to ensure:

- Protection of patients and members of the public from malpractice by distributors and suppliers of drugs.
- Adherence to the drug laws and regulations governing compounding, distribution, importation, export and storage of drugs.
- High ethical and professional standards of pharmaceutical practice.

2.2 Establishments

In the drug distribution chain several kinds of establishments can be distinguished:

— production sites
— storage or warehouse facilities
— establishments for the supply, sale, dispensing and distribution of drugs, such as pharmacies, hospitals, clinics, ports and stores.

2.3 Inspections

When inspecting these establishments the inspector uses the appropriate references. The method of inspection should be laid down in a SOP which also contains the requirements for a specific type of establishment. The inspection SOP may be in the format of a checklist (see Appendix 1 for an example applicable to most drug distribution establishments). When sampling is part of the inspection procedure, the SOP should contain detailed guidance for the inspector; an example of this guidance is to be found in Appendix 2.

2.4 Special categories of drugs

When special categories of drugs are present the inspector may require a modified SOP. This situation is likely to occur with controlled drugs, pharmaceutical products moving in international commerce, or with counterfeit, spurious or substandard pharmaceutical products. For this last category, an example of extra guidance is given in Appendix 3.

References

1. Good manufacturing practices for pharmaceutical products. In: *WHO Expert Committee on Specifications for Pharmaceutical Preparations. Thirty-second report.* Geneva, World Health Organization, 1992 (WHO Technical Report Series, No. 823), Annex 1.

2. Guiding principles for small national drug regulatory authorities. In: *WHO Expert Committee on Specifications for Pharmaceutical Preparations. Thirty-first report.* Geneva, World Health Organization, 1990 (WHO Technical Report Series, No. 790), Annex 6.

3. Good pharmacy practice in community and hospital pharmacy settings. In: *WHO Expert Committee on Specifications for Pharmaceutical Preparations. Thirty-fifth report.* Geneva, World Health Organization, 1998 (WHO Technical Report Series, No. 885), Annex 7.

4. Provisional guidelines on the inspection of pharmaceutical manufacturers. In: *WHO Expert Committee on Specifications for Pharmaceutical Preparations. Thirty-second report.* Geneva, World Health Organization, 1992 (WHO Technical Report Series, No. 823), Annex 2.

Selected further reading

ASEAN good manufacturing practices guidelines, 2nd ed. Jakarta, Technical Cooperation on Pharmaceuticals, 1988.

Basic tests for pharmaceutical substances. Geneva, World Health Organization, 1986.

Basic tests for pharmaceutical dosage forms. Geneva, World Health Organization, 1991.

Bulk pharmaceutical chemicals. London, Institute of Quality Assurance, 1992 (Pharmaceutical Quality Group Monograph).

Code of ethics. *Pharmaceutical journal*, 1992, 248:545–556.

Convention on Psychotropic Substances, 1971. New York, United Nations, 1977.

Ethical criteria for medicinal drug promotion. Geneva, World Health Organization, 1988.

Hayes P, Kayne S, Martin T, McMurdo A. Use of professional self audit in pharmacy practice. *Pharmaceutical journal*, 1992, 249:650–652.

International nonproprietary names (INN) for pharmaceutical substances: Lists 1–73 of proposed INN and lists 1–35 of recommended INN; cumulative list no. 9. Geneva, World Health Organization, 1996.

Sampling procedures for industrially manufactured pharmaceuticals. In: *WHO Expert Committee on Specifications for Pharmaceutical Preparations. Thirty-first report.* Geneva, World Health Organization, 1990 (WHO Technical Report Series, No. 790), Annex 2.

Single Convention on Narcotic Drugs, 1961, as amended by the 1972 Protocol. New York, United Nations, 1977.

Statutory Committee: professional conduct. *Pharmaceutical Journal*, 1969, 203:472.

Statutory Committee: three names to be removed from register. *Pharmaceutical Journal*, 1973, 210:212.

Turner JL. The implementation of European Community directives concerning GMP. *Drug Information Journal*, 1991, 25:537–544.

United Nations Convention against Illicit Traffic in Narcotic Drugs and Psychotropic Substances, 1988. New York, United Nations, 1991.

Wingfield J. Misconduct and the pharmacist. *Pharmaceutical Journal*, 1990, 245:531–533.

Appendix 1
Checklist for inspection and the preparation of a report

Inspection applicable to all drug distribution establishments

1. General information

(a) name of establishment inspected
(b) date of inspection
(c) name(s) of the inspector(s)
(d) date of last inspection.

2. Type of inspection

Comprehensive, concise, follow-up, special, investigative, announced, unannounced.

3. Licensing

(a) licensing of premises
(b) person with supervisory role in establishments handling prescriptions and pharmacy sale-only drugs (is normally a registered pharmacist or a person so prescribed by national legislation)
(c) personnel authorized to sell only over-the-counter drugs (licensed, where such licensing is required)
(d) adherence to licensing provisions.

4. Activities undertaken on premises

Manufacturing, wholesale, importation, export, retail, hospital pharmacy, clinic, nursing and maternity homes.

5. Adequacy and suitability of premises

(a) premises clean, tidy and in good state of repair
(b) premises secure
(c) floor durable and easily cleaned
(d) premises constructed to prevent infestation by vermin and pests
(e) clean shelves in retail pharmacy and premises for sale of over-the-counter drugs
(f) changing rooms and toilet available
(g) adequacy of lighting and ventilation
(h) appropriate layout of premises.

6. Warehouse/store

(a) adequacy and suitability of warehouse/store
(b) warehouse/store clean and uncluttered
(c) warehouse/store inaccessible to unauthorized persons
(d) temperature and humidity control
(e) enforcement of stock rotation
(f) adequacy of shelving
(g) existence of areas for returned drugs, recalled drugs, expired drugs, and drugs in quarantine
(h) warehouse/store free from vermin and insects.

7. Special storage

(a) availability of cold room storage or refrigerator for vaccines and biological products
(b) suitability of the cold storage facilities
(c) standard written procedure prepared by an appropriate national regulatory agency for the maintenance of cold chain
(d) special storage area for controlled drugs and other prescription drugs
(e) suitable and secure storage facility for controlled drugs and poisons.

8. Record-keeping

(a) name and address of supplier of each drug product with date
(b) name and address of purchaser of each drug product with date
(c) supplier or purchaser licensed

(d) retention of order forms, copy of delivery notes, stores receipt, and issue vouchers, and book of records (controlled drugs book/prescription drugs book) on the premises as provided for in the drug laws
(e) accuracy of records kept.

9. Conditions for sale and supply

(a) sale and supply of prescription and pharmacy sale-only drugs under the control of a registered pharmacist
(b) sale and supply of prescription and pharmacy sale-only drugs effected from registered/licensed premises
(c) sale of prescription drugs on the basis of valid prescription
(d) sale and supply of over-the-counter drugs undertaken in registered premises under the supervision of a pharmacist or premises licensed for the purpose of sale and supply of over-the-counter drugs only, where such registration or licence is required by law.

10. Diversion of controlled drugs

Diversion of controlled drugs prevented by examining the records and by physical examination of stock.

11. Returned and expired drugs

Procedures in place for handling returned and time-expired drugs.

12. Product recall

Procedures in place for recall of drugs and handling recalled drugs.

13. Product complaints

Procedures in place for dealing with complaints about drugs.

14. Promotional activities

Assess promotional materials for compliance with drug laws.

15. Personnel

(a) person responsible for supervising sale in a wholesale/retail pharmacy is a registered/licensed pharmacist
(b) name of the pharmacist in continuous personal control noted
(c) personnel wear clean protective clothing.

16. Labelling of drug products and package inserts

Check adequacy of labelling of drug and information on package inserts.

17. Physical examination and sampling of drugs

Conduct physical examination of drugs in stock and take samples of drugs for quality assessment.

18. Reference books

Check existence of reference books on premises, where they are required.

Specific inspection applicable to individual establishments

19. Importer

(a) all drugs accompanied by import documents such as bill of lading, export authorization, product licence and batch certificate
(b) controlled drugs also accompanied by export authorization certificate or export declaration, whichever is applicable
(c) imported drugs are in original packs, except for drugs imported in bulk for repackaging and/or manufacturing drug formulations.

20. Retail and hospital pharmacy

(a) compounding of drugs carried out by or under the supervision of a pharmacist
(b) quality of raw materials used in compounding complies with pharmacopoeial specifications
(c) dispensing of prescription drugs carried out by or under the supervision of a pharmacist
(d) entries of dispensed prescription drugs made in prescription book and for controlled drugs in controlled drugs book
(e) prescriptions for prescription drugs retained on premises for periods provided in the drug laws
(f) dispensed drugs labelled appropriately with name of drug, name of patient, name and address of pharmacy, clinic or hospital, instructions for using the drugs and, where appropriate, warning labels
(g) counselling of patients on use of dispensed drugs
(h) adequacy of containers for dispensed drugs
(i) personnel observe high standard of personal hygiene and wear clean protective clothing
(j) dispensing area clean, adequate and has necessary equipment
(k) walls in dispensing area easily cleaned

(l) quality of extemporaneous preparations
(m) sources of drugs sold and supplied from the pharmacy
(n) suitable cabinets for storage of controlled drugs and poisons.

21. Clinics, nursing and maternity homes

(a) sources of drugs used, supplied and administered
(b) records of controlled drugs used, supplied and administered
(c) storage facilities and security for controlled drugs.

22. Unauthorized markets

(a) investigate sources of drugs in the unauthorized market
(b) sample drugs for quality assessment
(c) seize drugs in the unauthorized market.

Appendix 2
Guidance on sampling

This guidance is applicable to collecting samples of drugs to be tested by the official quality control laboratory. The collection may be aimed either at assessing the quality of products on the market, in which case adequate sampling plans should apply (see, for example, "Sampling procedures for industrially manufactured pharmaceuticals" (*1*, *2*)), or at detecting substandard, spurious and counterfeit pharmaceutical products. In this case sampling shall be based on information and may involve confiscation of entire stocks to prevent further distribution. Compliance with legal procedures for sample collection, analysis and documentation is obligatory.

(a) Check that the sample is properly labelled with the following:
    (i) name of sampled pharmaceutical preparation
    (ii) batch number
    (iii) date and source of sample; the original manufacturer's label may be helpful.
(b) Check that the records contain the following:
    (i) number of samples
    (ii) types of packaging and storage conditions
    (iii) circumstances of sampling that may include suspected quality defects.
(c) Place seals on containers of the samples.
(d) Hand over one-third of the samples to the representative of the inspected establishment.
(e) Confirm in writing that samples were taken from the premises and have the confirmation countersigned by an appropriate official of the inspected establishment (see, for example, the sample receipt form in Appendix 4).

References

1. *WHO Expert Committee on Specifications for Pharmaceutical Preparations. Thirty-first report.* Geneva, World Health Organization, 1990 (WHO Technical Report Series, No. 790), Annex 2.

2. *Quality assurance of pharmaceuticals. A compendium of guidelines and related materials. Volume 1.* Geneva, World Health Organization, 1997.

Appendix 3
Guidance for inspection when pharmaceutical products are suspected to be counterfeit, spurious or substandard

This section addresses specifically the situation in which the inspector suspects counterfeit, spurious or substandard pharmaceutical products to be present during an inspection. This may be during either a regular inspection or an investigation aimed at detecting such products.

1. Broad objective

The presence of counterfeit, substandard and spurious pharmaceutical products in the drug distribution channels may present a danger to public health, and it is imperative that suspect products are effectively and rapidly taken out of the distribution channels and quarantined. In order to facilitate the work of the inspector, the help of capable and experienced persons involved in the distribution of products should be obtained on a proactive basis to help identify such products.

2. Standard operating procedures

(a) A written SOP for inspectors should be drawn up and made available to them. This SOP should include at least the following information:
   - (i) how the suspect product should be isolated to prevent its further distribution
   - (ii) the size of the samples required for testing purposes
   - (iii) the manner in which the samples should be taken
   - (iv) the record-keeping procedure to be followed in recording the details of the action taken
   - (v) the details which should be recorded on the receipt issued for the embargoed product and/or samples taken
   - (vi) the type of materials which should be used for sealing samples or for embargoing or confiscating suspect products
   - (vii) the names, addresses and telephone numbers of persons who should be contacted to report on the action taken

(viii) special precautions to be noted by the person initiating the sampling or seizure procedure, with particular reference to correct legal procedures to be followed

(ix) where appropriate, the manner in which the suspect product should be destroyed.

(b) Where other persons are involved in the detection of counterfeit pharmaceutical products they shall operate on the basis of a suitable SOP. In any case of suspicion of counterfeit pharmaceutical products an inspector shall be notified immediately.

3. Counterfeit products

The following applies specifically to counterfeit products:

(a) When examining a possible counterfeit pharmaceutical product the inspector shall first screen the product by looking, smelling, touching and listening to the sound of the packing and its contents. The inspector shall look for anything, in particular its labelling and packing, that makes the product look different from an original reference sample. A SOP may assist in examining the product in this way.

(b) When the organoleptic examination does not give conclusive evidence the inspector shall have a sample tested using appropriate simple screening methods, such as the basic tests recommended by WHO or a suitable thin-layer chromatography method.

(c) In addition to any full analytical testing, the drug regulatory authority of the country of origin stated on the label of the product may be asked to establish whether the product is counterfeit.

(d) Proven cases of counterfeit pharmaceutical products shall be fully documented and communicated to all other inspectors, to increase their level of expertise. Information on counterfeit products shall also immediately be made available to drug regulatory authorities of other countries concerned and to WHO.

Appendix 4
Sample receipt form

Institution/company (under inspection) . . . .

Address . . . .

. . . .

Date of inspection . . . .

Name of representative of the inspected establishment . . . .

Name of inspector . . . .

Name of the drug and description of sample ....
....

Dosage form ....

Batch no ....

Place sampled (warehouse, production line, packaging section, etc.)
....

No. of samples taken (tins, packets, etc.) ....
....

Signature	Signature
Inspector	Representative of the inspected establishment

Quality systems requirements for national good manufacturing practice inspectorates[1]

Background 323
1. Introduction 323
2. Glossary 323
3. Administrative structure 324
4. Terms of reference 325
5. Organizational structure 326
6. Inspection personnel 327
7. Documentation 328
8. Records 329
9. Inspection procedures 330
10. Inspection facilities required 332
11. Quality manual 333
12. Confidentiality 334
13. Publications 335
14. Appeals 335
15. Internal audit and periodic review 336
16. Complaints 337
17. Recalls 337
References 338

[1] Quality systems requirements for national good manufacturing practice inspectorates. In: *WHO Expert Committee on Specifications for Pharmaceutical Preparations. Thirty-sixth report.* Geneva, World Health Organization, 2002 (WHO Technical Report Series, No. 902), Annex 8.

Background

Following the provisional guidelines on the inspection of pharmaceutical manufacturers (*1*), the WHO Expert Committee on Specifications for Pharmaceutical Preparations acknowledged that additional guidelines concerning national inspectorates would be of value in strengthening the implementation of good manufacturing practices (GMP) (*2*) and enhancing mutual recognition among inspectorates.

A trend has recently become apparent in WHO Member States for non-commercial institutions, such as certification bodies, testing laboratories, etc., to introduce quality systems principles in their internal operations. The same principles are also being applied by governmental pharmaceutical inspectorates and drug control laboratories.

The Pharmaceutical Inspection Convention (PIC) published a document (*3*), with the objective of adapting the standards of the International Organization for Standardization (ISO) of the 9000 series and related norms (*4–8*) to the activities of the GMP inspectorates of Member States. It is based on European Standard EN 45012, *General criteria for certification bodies operating quality systems certification* (*9*), but was modified for this particular purpose.

1. Introduction

These requirements are applicable to quality systems for the operation of inspection services within competent authorities concerned with GMP inspections. It is intended that each inspection service should use these requirements as the basis for developing its own quality system.

The establishment and operation of a quality system is an essential element in the mutual recognition of national GMP inspections. The willingness to accept national inspections is significantly enhanced when it is known that the GMP inspectorate of the competent authority follows uniform procedures incorporating quality system principles. The quality system should include all the activities involved in the inspection.

2. Glossary

authorized person
A person (among key personnel of a manufacturing establishment) responsible for the release of batches of finished products for sale (*10*).

quality audit
An examination and assessment of all or part of a quality system with the specific purpose of improving it. A quality audit is usually conducted by outside or independent specialists or a team designated by the management for this purpose. Such audits may also be extended to suppliers and contractors (*2*).

quality manual
A handbook that describes the various elements of the system for assuring the quality of the test results generated by a laboratory (see section 11).

quality system
An appropriate infrastructure, encompassing the organizational structure, procedures, processes and resources necessary to ensure adequate confidence that a product (or service) will satisfy given requirements for quality (*2*).

standard operating procedure (SOP)
An authorized written procedure giving instructions for performing operations not necessarily specific to a given product or material but of a more general nature (e.g. equipment operation, maintenance and cleaning; validation; cleaning of premises and environmental control; sampling and inspection). Certain SOPs may be used to supplement product-specific master and batch production documentation (*2*).

3. Administrative structure

3.1 The structure, membership and operation of the GMP inspectorate should be such that impartiality is safeguarded.

3.2 The national inspection services are responsible for ensuring that the requirements of the relevant national legislation are satisfied.

3.3 All personnel employed or used by the GMP inspectorate, including outside inspectors or subcontracted personnel, should not be subject to any commercial, financial or other pressures which might affect their judgement. They should not be under the control of pharmaceutical manufacturers, and must be assessed and licensed.

3.4 The system for obtaining fees should not improperly influence the inspection procedure.

Recommended procedure

The administrative structure, membership, operation and legal status of the GMP inspectorate should be described in the quality manual (see section 11).

The quality manual should show how all personnel working for the GMP inspectorate, including subcontracted staff or advisers, and persons serving on committees providing advice, can maintain their impartiality. The GMP inspectorate should ensure that such persons:

(a) are not subject to any commercial, financial or other pressures which might influence their judgement;

(b) are not improperly influenced in their inspection of pharmaceutical manufacturers or persons assessed;
(c) have not been involved in the design or maintenance of inspected facilities by way of any consultancy service or commercial arrangement.

The remuneration of GMP inspectorate personnel engaged in inspection activities should not depend on the result of such activities or on the granting of a marketing authorization.

Only in exceptional cases may GMP inspectorates provide advisory or consultancy services. Where the GMP inspectorate does provide such services, it should develop a code of conduct or defined policy which clearly distinguishes between the process of inspection and that of providing an advisory or consultancy service to clients. This service should be of benefit to all of industry, and not solely to individual manufacturers.

4. Terms of reference

4.1 The functions of the GMP inspectorate should be clearly defined and should cover:

(a) legal responsibilities;
(b) the formulation of policies;
(c) an overview of the implementation of its policies;
(d) an overview of its finances;
(e) as required, the setting up of committees to which defined activities are delegated.

Recommended procedure

The terms of reference, legal responsibilities and functions of the GMP inspectorate and the way in which policy guidelines are established should be documented in the quality manual.

For any committee established to advise the GMP inspectorate or the chief inspector, the following details should be included:

(a) its role and function;
(b) the procedure for selecting and appointing the members (the names of the chairperson, secretary and members, their current appointments and the interests, if any, which they represent on the committee, should be available);
(c) the rules of procedure.

5. Organizational structure

5.1 The GMP inspectorate should have an organization that enables it to maintain the capability to perform its technical functions satisfactorily.

5.2 The GMP inspectorate should have:

(a) documentation clearly identifying its legal status;
(b) an organizational chart showing clearly the responsibility and reporting structure of the inspectorate and, in particular, the relationship between its inspection and authorization (licensing) functions;
(c) a description of the means by which the inspectorate obtains financial support;
(d) a description of the relationship between the GMP inspectorate and other departments within the drug regulatory authority and other government agencies, where they operate as separate bodies.

5.3 The GMP inspectorate should have and make available a formal statement explaining how the results of inspections are taken into account in granting and maintaining authorizations (licences).

5.4 The senior management of the GMP inspectorate should make a formal commitment to the recommended principles by ensuring that the quality policy of the inspectorate is documented, relevant to the objectives, and implemented.

5.5 The responsibility, authority and reporting structure of the GMP inspectorate should be clearly defined and documented (see above) and should be supported by written job descriptions for each member of staff.

5.6 An appropriately experienced, responsible and qualified person (*2*) should be nominated to carry out the quality assurance function, including implementing and maintaining the quality system. This person should have direct access to senior management. If necessary, this task may be assigned to more than one person.

5.7 The GMP inspectorate should have sufficient resources at all levels to enable it to attain its objectives effectively and efficiently. Senior management should ensure that all personnel are competent to carry out their assigned duties. They should receive appropriate training that should be documented and its effectiveness assessed.

5.8 Periodic management reviews of the quality system should be conducted and documented; records of these reviews should be retained for a specified period of time.

Recommended procedure

The above-mentioned recommendations are intended to ensure a reasonable level of transparency, both nationally and internationally.

The organizational chart, source(s) of finance, legal status of the GMP inspectorate and its relationship with the drug regulatory authority and other government agencies should be documented in the quality manual, together with a description of the quality system.

6. Inspection personnel

6.1 The personnel of the GMP inspectorate should be competent to perform the functions that they undertake.

6.2 The GMP inspectorate should maintain information on the relevant qualifications, training and experience of each inspector. Records of training and experience should be kept up to date.

6.3 Personnel should have clear, documented instructions specifying their duties and responsibilities. These instructions should be kept up to date.

6.4 When work is subcontracted to an external body or use is made of experts, the inspectorate should ensure that the personnel employed meet the relevant requirements of the quality system. The liability of third party inspectors should be clearly defined in the contract or agreement.

6.5 The GMP inspectorate should possess the required personnel, expertise and other resources to perform inspections of manufacturers and wholesale distributors to determine whether they comply with the principles and guidelines of current good practices and with the relevant legislation.

6.6 The staff responsible for inspections should have appropriate qualifications, training, experience and knowledge of the inspection process. They should have the ability to make professional judgements as to the conformity of the inspected party with the requirements of good practices and the relevant legislation and be able to make an appropriate risk assessment. Knowledge of current technology is essential, including computerized systems and information technology.

6.7 The GMP inspectorate should establish a documented system for recruiting and training its personnel. The training received and the training needs of each member of staff should be regularly reviewed, and individual training records should be maintained.

Recommended procedure

The credibility of the GMP inspection process will depend to a large degree on the technical competence and integrity of the inspectors. The quality manual should provide up-to-date details of the names, qualifications, experience and terms of reference (job description and duties to be performed) of each member of staff engaged in the GMP inspection process (see also section 10).

Formal arrangements should exist for personnel training, and details of these arrangements should be documented. Training undertaken by each member of staff engaged in GMP inspections should be documented (see also "Recommended procedure" in section 10).

A documented procedure for selecting the members of an inspection team and deciding on its size should be available. The inspection team may include a person or persons with specialist knowledge and/or experience of a particular area of technology.

If an inspection is carried out on behalf of the GMP inspectorate by an external body or person, the GMP inspectorate should ensure that the external personnel satisfy the relevant requirements contained in these recommendations.

GMP inspectors working with or advising the GMP inspectorate should:

(a) be academically qualified in a recognized scientific/technological discipline related to pharmaceuticals (normally pharmacy, chemistry or microbiology); direct personal experience of pharmaceutical manufacture or control is not a requirement but would be considered as a valuable asset for an inspector;
(b) have satisfactorily completed a recognized training course on auditing quality management systems;
(c) undergo at least 10 days of training per year (e.g. courses, symposia, conferences, etc.);
(d) have a competent working knowledge of the WHO guidelines on GMP for pharmaceutical products (*2*) and/or the GMP inspection procedures of the relevant national regulatory authority;
(e) have undergone appropriate training in the current procedures and techniques of GMP inspections before conducting an inspection alone;
(f) have the necessary personal qualities of integrity, tact and character to perform the duties of a GMP inspector.

7. Documentation

7.1 The GMP inspectorate should maintain a system for the control of all documentation relating to GMP inspections of manufacturers and recommendations relating to authorization holders, and should ensure that:

(a) the current versions of the appropriate documentation are available at all relevant locations;
(b) all revised documents or amendments to documents are correctly authorized and processed in a manner which ensures that they are introduced without delay;
(c) superseded documents are removed from use throughout the GMP inspectorate and elsewhere in the organization and its agencies, but are retained for a defined period of time.

7.2 The GMP inspectorate should ensure that all of its activities are described in SOPs that clearly describe the responsibilities, policy and actions. These should include, but not be limited to, training (introduction, GMP and task-related), inspections, reporting after inspections, handling of complaints, licensing (issue, suspension, revocation), certification, documentation control, planning and handling of appeals.

7.3 Proper and accessible records should be maintained of the activities carried out, including training, as well as the assessment of inspectors after training, the preparation of inspection reports, the handling of complaints, and the drawing up of authorized checklists (where in use) and other related documents.

7.4 Reports should be prepared on all inspections performed. They should be prepared in the approved format, and signed and dated by the relevant inspector.

7.5 The documentation system should ensure that any changes to documents are made in a controlled manner and are properly authorized. There should be a means of identifying changes in individual documents.

Recommended procedure

The following information should be included or referred to in the quality manual:

(a) a list of all the documents used;
(b) for each document, the name(s) or position(s) of the person(s) responsible for authorizing its issue and any subsequent amendments or changes;
(c) a description of the system whereby relevant documents and subsequent amendments are made available at the appropriate location from the point of view of the functioning of the inspection process;
(d) the method by which amendments and changes are made, so that documents are speedily updated, changes recorded and superseded documents promptly withdrawn and archived.

8. Records

8.1 The GMP inspectorate should maintain a system of records to suit its particular method of operation and circumstances. It must comply with the relevant obligations under national legislation and demonstrate that the quality system is operating satisfactorily.

8.2 Records should be available which demonstrate that all the relevant procedures have been followed in the performance of each GMP inspection, including the initial inspection, the recommendation for issue of a marketing authorization, routine inspections and corrective action.

8.3 All records should be safely stored for an adequate period, and held under conditions that guarantee their security and confidentiality, unless otherwise required by the national legislation.

Recommended procedure

The quality manual should describe or refer to separate SOPs which describe the system adopted by the GMP inspectorate for maintaining its records. The manual should include blank specimen copies of the various checklists, certificates and reports used during the inspection process and describe the way in which these are processed, stored and archived, and/or disposed of.

The procedures for recommending to the authorization holder the issue, suspension or revocation of marketing authorizations should be described.

Documented staff instructions on security and on the use and handling of inspection reports should be identified and described in accordance with the confidentiality requirements specified in national legislation. Information as to who should have access to confidential information should be given and such access should be controlled.

Records associated with inspection activities should be retained for a minimum period of three full inspection cycles or for 6 years, whichever is the longer.

9. Inspection procedures

9.1 The GMP inspectorate should have the required resources (financial, human, facilities and others) and documented procedures to enable the inspection of manufacturing operations to be carried out in accordance with the requirements of the WHO guidelines on GMP (*2*) and/or the national GMP guidelines.

9.2 The GMP inspectorate should require the manufacturer to have documented procedures in accordance with a quality management system, and complying with the WHO guidelines on GMP (*2*) and/or the national GMP guidelines.

9.3 The GMP inspectorate should perform regular inspections of the manufacturing premises, procedures and quality systems of authorization holders at least once every 2 years in accordance with a written inspection programme. Written inspection reports should be prepared and sent to the national regulatory authority to keep it informed of the outcome of such inspections.

9.4 The planning of inspections of manufacturers and the assessment of compliance with the planning regarding the performance of the different types of inspections should be documented. The types of inspections should include as a minimum routine inspections, specific inspections, follow-up inspections and concise inspections.

9.5 The activity of the GMP inspectorate should be described, indicating how it relates to the system(s) for granting manufacturers' and product authorizations.

9.6 The activities relating to post-marketing surveillance and product testing should be described. The description should also cover the process of handling non-conforming products (e.g. substandard or counterfeit products).

9.7 The procedure for operations in support of a surveillance sampling programme should be documented.

9.8 The GMP inspectorate should have the documented procedures and resources to enable the inspection of manufacturing and wholesale distribution operations to be carried out in accordance with the official guidelines and national legislation. A formal inspection plan should be followed. All instructions, standards or written procedures, worksheets, checklists and reference data relevant to the work of the GMP inspectorate should be kept up to date and be readily available to staff.

9.9 A chief inspector should be appointed to coordinate inspection activities if more than one inspector is involved in an inspection. The lead inspector, who should be selected by all the participating inspectors, should normally prepare the inspection report.

9.10 Observations and/or data obtained in the course of inspections should be recorded in a timely manner to prevent loss of relevant information.

9.11 Completed inspections should be reviewed to ensure that the requirements have been met.

Recommended procedure

The procedures covering initial inspections of new applicants for marketing authorizations and ongoing inspections of authorization holders should be documented.

Manufacturers should be inspected at least every one or 2 years, although new authorization holders should be inspected more frequently until inspectors are confident that the manufacturers are complying with the WHO guidelines on GMP and/or the national GMP guidelines. The frequency of inspection should not normally fall below once every 2 years as lack of continuity may give rise to a reduced awareness of current GMP or allow significant deficiencies to develop.

The time available for undertaking inspections should be adequate to enable sufficient investigations and enquiries to be made to give confidence in the findings of the inspection.

The report to the authorization holders following GMP inspections should include as a minimum:

(a) the name and location of the manufacturing site(s);
(b) the date(s) of the inspection(s);
(c) the reason for the inspection and the product categories and manufacturing areas inspected;
(d) the suitability of key personnel, including the authorized person;
(e) observations, failures to comply with the WHO guidelines on GMP and/or the national GMP guidelines, and the recommended frequency of reinspection;
(f) a recommendation on the issue/continuation, suspension or revocation of the marketing authorization.

The GMP inspectorate should have the power, under the national or regional legislation or other arrangements, to require reinspection of a manufacturer's premises if there are changes in personnel, facilities, internal organization or scope of activity, or if analysis of a complaint or any other information indicates that the manufacturer is failing to comply with the requirements of the WHO guidelines on GMP and/or the national GMP guidelines, or with the conditions imposed by the marketing authorization.

10. Inspection facilities required

10.1 The inspection service should have the required facilities in terms of staff, expertise, equipment and other resources to perform inspections of manufacturers to determine compliance with the requirements of the WHO guidelines on GMP and/or the national GMP guidelines. This does not preclude the use of external resources, when necessary, provided that the requirements as described for "subcontracting" are met (see section 3.3).

10.2 If inspections are carried out on behalf of the GMP inspectorate by an external body or person, the GMP inspectorate should ensure that this body or person satisfies the requirements specified in section 3.3. A properly documented agreement covering these arrangements, including confidentiality aspects and the declaration of any conflict of interests, should be drawn up.

Recommended procedure

A sufficient number of competent personnel should support the GMP inspectorate, whether employed or contracted for the functions that they undertake.

The quality manual should describe the procedures for the management of the GMP inspectors and of the necessary records. A record should be kept for each individual employed to carry out GMP inspections (whether an employee or under contract), which should include the following information:

(a) the name;
(b) the designated area of responsibility within the declared scope of the GMP inspectorate;
(c) the educational qualifications;
(d) the professional qualifications, where relevant to the activities of the GMP inspectorate;
(e) the work experience;
(f) details of the GMP inspector training received, supported by documentary evidence of course attendance and assessment results.

Where an external body or person carries out a GMP inspection, the quality manual should describe the process adopted by the GMP inspectorate to comply with the above-mentioned requirements.

Whenever an external body or person is used to carry out any function on behalf of a GMP inspectorate, the GMP inspectorate should have documented evidence to demonstrate that the external body or person concerned is competent to do so.

Staff members authorized to carry out audits of external bodies or persons should be identified.

Documented agreements with all external bodies or persons should be available for scrutiny.

A register of all external bodies or persons employed by the GMP inspectorate should be maintained. The register should include:

(a) the name of the external body or person;
(b) the legal status of the external body and details of any relationship with a parent company, group of companies or any other organization of which the external body or person is part, with specific reference to possible conflicts of interest;
(c) the names and qualifications of all personnel engaged in GMP inspection work for the GMP inspectorate.

11. Quality manual

11.1 The GMP inspectorate should define and document its policy and objectives for, and commitment to, quality in a quality manual. It should ensure that this policy is understood, implemented and maintained at all levels in the organization.

11.2 The information contained in the quality manual and procedures should include at least:

(a) a quality policy statement;
(b) a brief description of the legal status of the GMP inspectorate (see section 4.1(a));

(c) a code of ethics and conduct relating to GMP inspection activities;
(d) a description of the organization of the GMP inspectorate, including details of any governing board, its constitution, terms of reference and rules of procedure (see section 5.2(b));
(e) the names, qualifications, experience and terms of reference of the senior staff and other GMP inspection personnel, both internal and external (see sections 6 and 10);
(f) details of training arrangements for inspection personnel (see sections 6 and 10);
(g) an organizational chart showing the responsibility and reporting structure of the inspectorate and the allocation of functions stemming from the person in charge of the GMP inspectorate (see section 5.2(b));
(h) details of the documented procedures for inspecting manufacturers under the WHO guidelines on GMP and/or the national GMP guidelines (see section 8);
(i) details of the documented procedures for recommendations to the authorization holder for the issue, suspension or revocation of marketing authorizations (see sections 7.2 and 8.1);
(j) a list of any subcontractors used for GMP inspections and details of the documented procedures for assessing and monitoring their competence (see section 6);
(k) details of appeals procedures (see section 14);
(l) a procedure for ensuring that complaints made to the GMP inspectorate are investigated so that any shortcomings of the authorization holders are revealed (see section 16);
(m) a list of those staff members responsible for investigating complaints and those with the authority to take remedial action (see section 16);
(n) details of internal quality audits (see section 15);
(o) details of testing of samples (see sections 9.6–9.8);
(p) the control of non-conforming products (see section 9.6).

Recommended procedure

In order to keep the quality manual brief, reference may be made to other documents and/or procedures contained in other manuals.

12. Confidentiality

12.1 The GMP inspectorate should have adequate arrangements to ensure confidentiality of the information obtained in the course of its inspection activities at all levels of its organization, including committees.

12.2 The exchange of inspection reports between countries should be described. The format and content of reports should be specified.

Recommended procedure

The quality manual should describe how the GMP inspectorate discharges its responsibility for ensuring that all communications between itself and the companies inspected are kept confidential. The following are necessary:

(a) instructions to personnel on confidentiality;
(b) a written undertaking by all personnel not to divulge to third parties any information gained about any business affairs of clients;
(c) the inclusion of provisions in all subcontracts to maintain confidentiality;
(d) provisions to ensure the physical security of all documents and records relating to inspection activities.

13. Publications

13.1 The GMP inspectorate should produce and update, as necessary, a list of authorization holders, together with an outline of the scope of the marketing authorization issued to each manufacturer. The extent to which this list will be distributed should be specified.

13.2 An outline of the inspection and marketing authorization system should be available in published form.

13.3 Other publications, such as GMP guidelines and other guidelines and information brochures, should be available to industry and other interested parties, as appropriate.

Recommended procedure

The quality manual should list the publications issued by the authorization holder and GMP inspectorate. The following information should also be provided:

(a) the name of the person responsible for compiling and updating each publication;
(b) the frequency with which each publication is updated;
(c) how the publications are distributed and to whom;
(d) the procedure for issuing amendments.

14. Appeals

14.1 The GMP inspectorate should have procedures for the consideration of appeals against its decisions.

Recommended procedure

Appeals procedures should be established by the GMP inspectorate and should include:

(a) the method by which an appeal may be lodged;
(b) the method by which an impartial appeals panel, independent of the activity under review, is selected;
(c) the names and positions of the members of the GMP inspectorate to whom appeals are referred, and the procedure for handling them;
(d) a register of all appeals and their outcome.

15. Internal audit and periodic review

15.1 The GMP inspectorate should implement a system of planned and documented internal audits and periodic reviews of its compliance with the criteria of these guidelines.

15.2 There should be procedures for corrective and preventive action whenever faults are detected in the quality system, or in the performance of inspections and the general performance of the inspection service.

15.3 The management of the inspectorate should periodically review the quality system for its continuing suitability and effectiveness.

15.4 Inspectors should be evaluated before being allowed to perform inspections. Periodic reviews should also be undertaken to examine the performance of individual inspectors in order to ensure consistency among them, and in the operations and procedures of the GMP inspectorate.

15.5 A record of all audits and reviews should be kept and should include the findings, conclusions, recommendations and follow-up action. These records should be retained for a specified period of time.

Recommended procedure

Internal periodic review procedures should be documented. The review procedure should include internal audits by staff competent to ensure that all formulated procedures are adhered to. Based on the results of these audits, management must ensure that the GMP inspection system remains effective and that inspections conducted by different inspectors arrive at similar conclusions when the same operation is inspected under the same conditions.

Internal audit procedures should state:

(a) the names or positions of staff members authorized to conduct internal audits;
(b) what is to be examined and how often (a schedule for the examination of the whole organization over a given period should be drawn up);

(c) how the audit will be conducted;
(d) to whom the results will be reported;
(e) who will initiate any corrective action.

Management reviews should take account of the results of internal audits and should include:

(a) consideration of the overall operation of the GMP inspectorate;
(b) uncovering defects or irregularities in the operation of the GMP inspection system;
(c) ensuring that action has been taken to effectively correct defects revealed in previous reviews and audits.

Periodic audit by an experienced person or persons from another national regulatory authority is a useful means of providing an independent review of the GMP inspectorate's operations and procedures.

16. Complaints

16.1 The GMP inspectorate should have documented procedures for dealing with complaints arising from its activities.

16.2 A record should be maintained of all complaints received and the actions taken by the GMP inspectorate. These records should be retained for a specified period of time.

Recommended procedure

The GMP inspectorate should require each authorization holder to keep a record of all complaints received, as well as remedial actions relating to the manufacturing activities and products covered by the marketing authorization.

The GMP inspectorate should have a procedure for recording and investigating complaints received about its inspection activities. The procedure should include a list of those staff members responsible for investigating complaints and those with the authority to take remedial action.

17. Recalls

17.1 The GMP inspectorate should have a documented procedure for dealing with recalls and withdrawals of products from the market.

17.2 Records should be maintained of all recalls and withdrawals registered and dealt with by the inspectorate.

References

1. Provisional guidelines on the inspection of pharmaceutical manufacturers. In: *WHO Expert Committee on Specifications for Pharmaceutical Preparations. Thirty-second report.* Geneva, World Health Organization, 1992 (WHO Technical Report Series, No. 823), Annex 2.

2. *Quality assurance of pharmaceuticals. A compendium of guidelines and related materials. Volume 2. Good manufacturing practices and inspection.* Geneva, World Health Organization, 1999.

3. *Recommendations on quality system requirements for GMP inspectorates of PIC Contracting States.* Geneva, Pharmaceutical Inspection Convention, 1994 (unpublished document PH 7/94; this document forms the basis of the publication *Recommendations on quality system requirements for pharmaceutical inspectorates.* Geneva, Pharmaceutical Inspection Convention, Pharmaceutical Inspection Co-operation Scheme (PIC/S, 2000 (PI 002-1); available from PIC/S Secretariat, PO Box 5695, 1211 Geneva 11, Switzerland).

4. *Quality management and quality assurance standards—guidelines for selection and use. International Standard ISO 9000.* Geneva, International Organization for Standardization, 1990.

5. *Quality systems—model for quality assurance in design/development, production, installation and servicing. International Standard ISO 9001.* Geneva, International Organization for Standardization, 1994.

6. *Quality systems—model for quality assurance in production, installation and servicing. International Standard ISO 9002.* Geneva, International Organization for Standardization, 1994.

7. *Quality systems—model for quality assurance in final inspection and test. International Standard ISO 9003.* Geneva, International Organization for Standardization, 1994.

8. *Quality management and quality system elements—guidelines. International Standard ISO 9004.* Geneva, International Organization for Standardization, 1990.

9. *General criteria for certification bodies operating quality systems certification. European Standard EN 45012.* Brussels, European Committee for Standardization, 1989 (available from CEN Central Secretariat, 36 rue de Stassart, B-1050 Brussels, Belgium).

10. Good manufacturing practices: authorized person—role, functions and training. In: *WHO Expert Committee on Specifications for Pharmaceutical Preparations. Thirty-fifth report.* Geneva, World Health Organization, 1999 (WHO Technical Report Series, No. 885), Annex 4.

Guidance on good manufacturing practices: inspection report[1]

When a site at which pharmaceutical products are manufactured is inspected, the inspector(s) responsible must draw up a report containing the items listed below. Where relevant, the appropriate section of the WHO GMP is indicated.

A. Manufacturer

(a) Name of inspected manufacturer.
(b) Address of inspected manufacturer (including telephone, fax, email and 24 hour telephone numbers).
(c) Address of manufacturing site if different from that given above.
(d) Site number (e.g. site master file or number allocated by the responsible authority).
(e) Manufacturing licence number, if applicable.
(f) Activities.
(g) Pharmaceutical products manufactured.
(h) Key personnel.
(i) Key persons met.

B. Inspection details

(a) Date(s) of inspection(s).
(b) Previous inspection date.
(c) Type of inspection.
(d) Scope of inspection.
(e) The regulatory authority.
(f) GMP guidelines used for assessing compliance.
(g) For foreign inspections, state whether the national regulatory authority (NRA) of the country where the inspection took place was informed and whether it took part in the inspection.
(h) Brief report of inspection activities undertaken.
(i) Samples taken and results obtained.
(j) Assessment of the site master file.
(k) GMP-related recalls from the market of any product in the last 2 years.

---

[1] Guidance on good manufacturing practices (GMP): inspection report. In: *WHO Expert Committee on Specifications for Pharmaceutical Preparations. Thirty-seventh report.* Geneva, World Health Organization, 2002 (WHO Technical Report Series, No. 908), Annex 6.

C. Inspector(s)

(a) Name(s) of inspector(s) and accompanying experts.

D. Introduction

(a) Brief summary of the manufacturing activities.
(b) Other manufacturing activities carried out on the site (e.g. manufacture of cosmetics, research and development).
(c) Use of outside scientific, analytical, or other technical assistance in manufacture and quality control.
(d) Brief description of the quality management system of the firm responsible for manufacture. Reference can be made to a site master file if one is available.

E. Observations

The observations made during the inspection that are considered to be non-compliant with GMP should be listed. Where positive observations are included in the report, clear distinction should be made between "positive" and "non-compliant". Noncompliant observations can be classified, e.g. as "critical", "major" and "minor" if the Member State concerned has defined these terms. The date by which corrective action and completion are requested in accordance with the policy of the national regulatory authority should be given.

E.1 Quality assurance (see WHO GMP, section 1)

(a) Quality system and documented quality policy of the manufacturer, e.g. as described in the quality manual.

E.2 Organization and personnel (see WHO GMP, section 9)

(a) Organizational chart showing the arrangements for quality assurance, including production and quality control.
(b) Qualifications, experience and responsibilities of key personnel.
(c) Outline of arrangements for basic and in-service training and method of keeping records.
(d) Health requirements for personnel engaged in production.
(e) Personnel hygiene requirements, including clothing.

E.3 Premises (see WHO GMP, section 12)

(a) Manufacturing areas (design, location, etc.) used, e.g. for storage and manufacturing (e.g. weighing, production, packaging) and flow of personnel and material.

(b) Special areas for the handling of highly toxic, hazardous and sensitizing materials.
(c) Nature of construction and finishes.
(d) Systems such as drainage, ventilation, air conditioning, and supply of steam and gas. Detailed description of critical areas with potential risks of contamination and cross-contamination.
(e) Classification of the rooms used for the manufacture of products, including clean rooms.
(f) Water systems.
(g) Planned preventative maintenance programme.
(h) Qualification of premises and systems as appropriate.

E.4 Equipment (see WHO GMP, section 13)

(a) Design, location and adaptation of equipment used in production and control laboratories.
(b) Planned preventative maintenance programmes for equipment and records.
(c) Qualification and calibration, including records.

E.5 Materials (see WHO GMP, section 14)

(a) Sourcing of materials.
(b) Control, storage and handling of materials, including:
— starting materials;
— packaging materials;
— intermediate and bulk products;
— finished products;
— returned and rejected materials;
— reagents and culture media;
— reference standards;
— waste material.

E.6 Good practices in production (see WHO GMP, section 16)

(a) Transport, handling and use of starting materials, packaging materials, and bulk and finished products.
(b) Production operations and important parameters (e.g. sampling, quarantine, weighing, process operations and conditions, acceptance limits).
(c) Validation (e.g. process).
(d) Change control and deviation reporting.

E.7 Quality control (see WHO GMP, section 17)

(a) Activities of quality control (including quarantine control, sampling, chemical and microbial analysis).
(b) Organization and personnel.
(c) Premises.
(d) Equipment and instrumentation.
(e) Materials.
(f) Documentation (e.g. specifications, procedures, reports, records).

E.8 Sanitation and hygiene (see WHO GMP, section 3)

(a) Procedures for sanitation and/or cleaning (e.g. of premises and equipment) and records.
(b) Personal hygiene.

E.9 Validation (see WHO GMP, section 4)

(a) Validation master plan.
(b) Validation and qualification protocols and reports for qualification and validation (e.g. of premises, systems, equipment, process, computer, cleaning, analytical methods).
(c) Stages of validation.
(d) Types of validation.

E.10 Documentation (see WHO GMP, section 15)

(a) Documentation (e.g. specifications, procedures, records, protocols, reports).
(b) Preparation, revision and distribution of documentation.
(c) Reports on production, quality control (including environmental control), engineering and other relevant areas.

E.11 Complaints (see WHO GMP, section 5)

(a) Procedure, records and investigation.

E.12 Product recalls (see WHO GMP, section 6)

(a) Procedure, records and investigation.

E.13 Contract production and analysis (see WHO GMP, section 7)

(a) Responsibilities of contract giver.
(b) Responsibilities of contract accepter.
(c) Contract (containing clearly defined responsibilities).
(d) GMP compliance of the contract accepter (initial assessment and continued compliance audited at regular intervals).

E.14 Self-inspection and quality audits (see WHO GMP, section 8)

(a) Procedure, programme and compliance.
(b) Items for self-inspection.
(c) Self-inspection team.
(d) Frequency of self-inspection.
(e) Self-inspection report.
(f) Follow-up action.
(g) Quality audit.
(h) Suppliers' audits.

F. Summary

Brief summary of the findings, and recommendations (where applicable).

G. Conclusions

A statement regarding the GMP status.

Name: ________________ Signature: ________________ Date: __________

Model certificate of good manufacturing practices[1]

A model certificate of Good Manufacturing Practices (GMP) for a manufacturing site is suggested (see below). This is not part of the WHO Certification Scheme on the Quality of Pharmaceutical Products Moving in International Commerce but is intended to serve in situations where a specific GMP certificate is requested by importers, exporters, procurement agencies and regulatory authorities. It is suggested that the certificate should remain valid for a period

[1] Model certificate of good manufacturing practices. In: *WHO Expert Committee on Specifications for Pharmaceutical Preparations. Thirty-seventh report.* Geneva, World Health Organization, 2003 (WHO Technical Report Series, No. 908), Annex 5.

of 2 years from the date of issue, but not exceeding 3 years after the inspection was carried out.

It is recommended that, where possible, GMP certificates should have, e.g. security seals, watermarks or holograms, to help prevent counterfeiting, tampering and other fraudulent activities.

Letterhead of regulatory authority

Model Certificate of Good Manufacturing Practices

This one-page certificate conforms to the format recommended by the World Health Organization (general instructions and explanatory notes attached).[1]

Certificate No: ______________________________

On the basis of the inspection carried out on ____ [date] ____ we certify that the site indicated on this certificate complies with Good Manufacturing Practices for the dosage forms, categories and activities listed in Table 1.

1. Name and address of site:

____

2. Manufacturer's licence number:

____

3. Table 1:

Dosage form(s)	Category(ies)	Activity(ies)

The responsibility for the quality of the individual batches of the pharmaceutical products manufactured through this process lies with the manufacturer.

This certificate remains valid until ____ [date] ____ It becomes invalid if the activities and/or categories certified herewith are changed or if the site is no longer considered to be in compliance with GMP.

Address of certifying authority:

____

Name and function of responsible person:

____

Email: ____________ Telephone no.: ____________ Fax no.: ________

Signature: Stamp and date:

____

[1] This model certificate of GMP is not part of the WHO Certification Scheme on the Quality of Pharmaceutical Products Moving in International Commerce.

Explanatory notes

(1) This certificate, which is in the format recommended by WHO, certifies the status of the site listed in point 1 of the certificate.

(2) The certification number should be traceable within the regulatory authority issuing the certificate.

(3) Where the regulatory authority issues a licence for the site, this number should be specified. Record "not applicable" in cases where there is no legal framework for the issuing of a licence.

(4) Table 1

List the dosage forms, starting materials, categories and activities. Examples are given below.

Example 1

Pharmaceutical Product(s)[1]	*Category(ies)*	*Activity(ies)*
Dosage form(s):		
Tablets	Cytotoxic	Packaging
	Hormone	Production, packaging, quality control
	Penicillin	Repackaging and labelling
Injectables	Cefalosporin	Aseptic preparation, packaging, labelling

Example 2

Pharmaceutical Product(s)[1]	*Category(ies)*	*Activity(ies)*
Starting material(s):[2]		
Paracetamol	Analgesic	Synthesis, purification, packing, labelling

---

[1] Pharmaceutical Products: Any medicine intended for human use or veterinary product administered to food-producing animals, presented in its finished dosage form or as a starting material for use in such a dosage form, that is subject to control by pharmaceutical legislation in both the exporting state and the importing state.

[2] Starting Materials: Any substance of a defined quality used in the production of a pharmaceutical product, but excluding packaging materials.

5. Hazard and risk analysis in pharmaceutical products

Application of hazard analysis and critical control point (HACCP) methodology to pharmaceuticals[1]

1. Introduction

Traditionally, the Hazard Analysis and Critical Control Point (HACCP) methodology has been considered to be a food safety management system. It aims to prevent known hazards and to reduce the risks that they will occur at specific points in the food chain. The same principles are also increasingly being applied in other industries, such as the car industry, aviation and the chemical industry.

This text provides general guidance on the use of the HACCP system to ensure the quality of pharmaceuticals, while recognizing that the details of its application may vary depending on the circumstances (see Appendix 1). It does not provide detailed information on major hazards.

Hazards affecting quality are controlled to a certain extent through the validation of critical operations and processes in the manufacture of finished pharmaceutical products in accordance with Good Manufacturing Practices (GMP). However, GMP do not cover the safety of the personnel engaged in manufacture, while both aspects are covered by HACCP.

Procedures, including GMP, address operational conditions and provide the basis for HACCP. HACCP is a systematic method for the identification, assessment and control of safety hazards. Such hazards are defined as biological, chemical, or physical agents or operations that are reasonably likely to cause illness or injury if not controlled. In the manufacture of pharmaceuticals,[2] these may include the manufacture of certain antibiotics, hormones, cytotoxic substances or other highly active pharmaceuticals, together with operations

[1] Application of hazard analysis and critical control point (HACCP) methodology to pharmaceuticals. In: *WHO Expert Committee on Specifications for Pharmaceutical Preparations. Thirty-seventh report.* Geneva, World Health Organization, 2003 (WHO Technical Report Series, No. 908), Annex 7.

[2] Safety hazards are common in the manufacture of active pharmaceutical ingredients; e.g. dangerous chemical conversions such as catalytic hydrogenation or nitration, or handling reactions with extremely hazardous chemicals such as phosgene or methyl isocyanate require special precaution and control measures.

such as fluid-bed drying and granulation, which are examples of hazard unit operations.

The use of inflammable solvents (solutions) and certain laboratory operations may also constitute hazards.

The following elements of the HACCP methodology are integral parts of the validation master file:

— development of a flow diagram of the process;
— verification of the flow diagram on site.

In addition, HACCP will extend this concept to include an analysis of the critical quality variables as well as the assessment of hazards affecting the safety of workers and environmental pollution hazards directly related to the process (in particular in open systems) concerned.

GMP for pharmaceutical products require the validation of critical processes as well as of changes in the manufacturing process which may affect the quality of the final product. Experience shows that most manufacturing processes contain steps that are "critical" from the point of view of variations in final product quality.

HACCP should not be confused with validation since its approach is broader; it thereby helps to identify matters on which validation should concentrate. It is science-based and systematic, and identifies specific hazards and measures for their control, as well as providing information on environmental protection and labour safety. HACCP is a tool to assess hazards and establish control systems that focus on prevention rather than relying on corrective action based on end-product testing. All HACCP systems are capable of accommodating changes, such as advances in equipment design and processing procedures or technological developments.

HACCP should not replace GMP; however, its application may be used as a first step towards GMP.

In countries where appropriate regulations exist and are enforced, compliance with GMP (including validation), drug regulatory activities and inspections provide good assurance that risks are largely controlled. In countries where control is less effective, however, patients may be put at risk through the production of drugs of inadequate quality. The assessment of individual risks related to specific products and starting materials, and the recognition of hazards at specific stages of production or distribution should permit regulatory authorities to improve drug control by increasing the effectiveness of their activities within the limits of the available resources.

The present guidelines are aimed at assisting industry to develop and implement effective HACCP plans covering activities such as research and development, sourcing of materials, manufacturing, packaging, testing and distribution.

2. Links with other programmes

In each stage of the manufacture and supply of pharmaceuticals, the necessary conditions should be provided and met to protect the pharmaceuticals concerned.

This has traditionally been accomplished through the application of Good Clinical Practice (GCP), Good Laboratory Practice (GLP), GMP and other guidelines, which are considered to be essential to the development and implementation of effective HACCP plans. HACCP plans are focused on hazards, the overall objective being to ensure that pharmaceuticals are safe for use. The existence and effectiveness of GCP, GLP and GMP should be assessed when drawing up HACCP plans.

3. Definitions

The following definitions apply to the terms as used in these guidelines. They may have different meanings in other contexts.

control (noun)
The state wherein correct procedures are being followed and criteria are being met.

control (verb)
The taking of all necessary actions to ensure and maintain compliance with the criteria established in the HACCP plan.

control measure
Any action and activity that can be used to prevent or eliminate a pharmaceutical quality hazard or reduce it to an acceptable level.

corrective action
Any action to be taken when the results of monitoring at the CCP (see below) indicate a loss of control.

critical control point (CCP)
A step at which control can be applied and is essential to prevent or eliminate a pharmaceutical quality hazard or reduce it to an acceptable level.

critical limit
A criterion which separates acceptability from unacceptability.

deviation
Failure to meet a critical limit.

flow diagram
A systematic representation of the sequence of steps or operations used in the production, control and distribution of a particular pharmaceutical.

HACCP plan
A document prepared in accordance with the principles of HACCP to ensure the control of hazards which are significant for pharmaceutical quality in the production and supply chain.

hazard
Any circumstance in the production, control and distribution of a pharmaceutical which can cause an adverse health effect.

hazard analysis
The process of collecting and evaluating information on hazards which should be addressed in the HACCP plan.

monitor
The act of conducting a planned sequence of observations or measurements of control parameters to assess whether a CCP is under control.

pharmaceuticals
All products related to pharmacy, including starting materials (active pharmaceutical ingredients and excipients), finished dosage forms, and biological and other specific products.

validation
The collection and evaluation of data, beginning at the process development stage and continuing through the production phase, which ensure that the manufacturing processes—including equipment, buildings, personnel and materials—are capable of achieving the intended results on a consistent and continuous basis. Validation is the establishment of documented evidence that a system does what it is supposed to do.

verification
The application of methods, procedures, tests and other evaluations, in addition to monitoring, to determine compliance with the HACCP plan.

4. Principles

The HACCP system is based on seven principles. In applying these principles, 12 stages are recommended and are discussed in section 7. Some stages are linked to specific principles while others serve as an introduction to the concept.

The seven principles are:

1. Conduct a hazard analysis.
2. Determine the critical control points (CCPs).
3. Establish target levels and critical limit(s).
4. Establish a system to monitor the CCPs.
5. Establish the corrective action to be taken when monitoring indicates that a particular CCP is not under control.
6. Establish procedures to verify that the HACCP system is working effectively.
7. Establish documentation concerning all procedures and keep records appropriate to these principles and their application.

5. Guidelines for the application of the HACCP system

The following guidelines will be found useful in applying the HACCP system:

- Before HACCP is applied to any sector, that sector should be operating in accordance with the principles of good practices and the relevant legislation.
- Management commitment is necessary if an effective HACCP system is to be implemented.
- HACCP should be applied to each specific operation separately.
- CCPs identified in any given example in any reference document (including GMP guidelines) may not be the only ones identified for a specific application or may be of a different nature.
- The HACCP application should be reviewed and necessary changes made when any modification is made in the product or process, or in any step.
- It is important, when applying HACCP, to take into account the nature and size of the operation.
- There should be a HACCP plan. The format of such plans may vary, but they should preferably be specific to a particular product, process or operation. Generic HACCP plans can serve as useful guides in the development of product and process HACCP plans; however, it is essential that the unique conditions within each facility are considered during the development of all components of the HACCP plan.

6. Training and education

As HACCP is a relatively new concept in the pharmaceutical industry, training of personnel in industry, government and universities in HACCP principles and applications is essential for its effective implementation.

In developing specific training to support a HACCP plan, working instructions and procedures should be drawn up which define the tasks of the operating personnel to be stationed at each critical control point. Specific training should be provided in the tasks of employees monitoring each CCP.

Cooperation between producers, traders and responsible authorities is of vital importance. Opportunities should be provided for the joint training of industrial staff and the control authorities to encourage and maintain a continuous dialogue and create a climate of understanding in the practical application of HACCP.

The success of a HACCP system depends on educating and training management and employees in the importance of their role in producing safe pharmaceuticals. Information should also be provided on the control of hazards at all stages of production and supply.

Employees must understand what HACCP is, learn the skills necessary to make it function properly, and must also be given the materials and equipment necessary to control the CCPs.

7. Application

The application of HACCP principles consists of the following 12 stages, as identified in the logic sequence for application of HACCP.

7.1 Assemble a HACCP team

The pharmaceutical manufacturer should assure that product-specific knowledge and expertise are available for the development of an effective HACCP plan. This may be best accomplished by assembling a multidisciplinary team. Team members should therefore represent all the relevant disciplines, such as research and development, production, quality control, quality assurance, microbiology, engineering and distribution or others as applicable.

Team members should have specific knowledge and expertise regarding the product and process. Where such expertise is not available on site, expert advice should be obtained from other sources.

Team members should be able to:

(a) conduct a hazard analysis;
(b) identify potential hazards;
(c) identify hazards which should be controlled;
(d) recommend controls and critical limits;
(e) devise procedures for monitoring and verification;
(f) recommend appropriate corrective action where deviations occur;
(g) verify the HACCP plan.

The scope of the HACCP plan should be defined. The scope should describe the segment of the process involved and the classes of hazards to be addressed should be identified.

7.2 Describe the product and process

A full description of the product and the process should be drawn up, including relevant quality information such as the composition, physical/chemical properties, structure, pH, temperatures, method of cleaning, bactericidal/bacteriostatic treatments (e.g. heat-treatment), drying, screening, mixing, blending, packaging, and the storage conditions. The method of distribution and transport should also be described, especially where products are thermolabile.

7.3 Identify the intended use

The intended use should be based on the expected uses of the product by the end-user or consumer. In specific cases, vulnerable population groups, e.g. geriatric patients, infants and immunocompromised patients, may have to be considered.

7.4 Construct a flow diagram

The flow diagram should be constructed by the HACCP team, and should cover all operations and decisions in a process.

When applying HACCP to a given operation, the steps preceding and following that operation should also be considered.

A block-type diagram may be sufficiently descriptive.

7.5 On-site confirmation of flow diagram

The HACCP team should confirm the processing operation against the flow diagram during all stages and hours of operation. Amendments to the flow diagram may be made where appropriate, and should be documented.

7.6 List all potential hazards associated with each step, conduct a hazard analysis, and consider any measures to control identified hazards (Principle 1)

When hazard analysis is conducted, safety concerns must be distinguished from quality concerns.

The HACCP team should list all the hazards that may be reasonably expected to occur at each step from production, testing and distribution up to the point of use. It should then conduct a hazard analysis to identify for the HACCP plan which hazards are of such a nature that their elimination or reduction to acceptable levels is essential.

A thorough hazard analysis is required to ensure an effective control point. A two-stage hazard analysis is recommended. During the first stage, the team should review the materials, activities, equipment, storage, distribution and intended use of the product. A list of the potential hazards (biological, chemical and physical) which may be introduced, increased or controlled in each step should be drawn up.

In the hazard analysis, the following should be included wherever possible:

- the probable occurrence of hazards and the severity of their adverse health effects;
- the qualitative and/or quantitative evaluation of the presence of hazards;
- the survival or multiplication of microorganisms of concern;
- the production or persistence in drugs of toxins, chemicals or physical agents;
- the conditions leading to the above.

During the second stage, a hazard evaluation should be conducted, i.e. the severity of the potential hazards and the probability of their occurrence should be estimated.

The team should then decide which potential hazards should be addressed in the HACCP plan, and what control measures, if any, exist that can be applied for each hazard. More than one control measure may be required to control a specific hazard(s) and more than one hazard may be controlled by a specified control measure.

Potential hazards in relation to at least the following should be considered:

- materials and ingredients;
- physical characteristics and composition of the product;
- processing procedures;
- microbial limits, where applicable;
- premises;
- equipment;
- packaging;
- sanitation and hygiene;
- personnel;
- risk of explosions;
- mix-ups.

Examples of common failures are given in Appendix 2.

7.7 Determine critical control points (Principle 2)

A CCP in the HACCP system can be more easily determined by the use of a decision-tree, which facilitates a logical approach. The way that a decision-tree is used will depend on the operation concerned, e.g. production, packing, reprocessing, storage, distribution. Training in the use of decision-trees should be given.

If a hazard has been identified at a step where control is necessary for safety, and no control measure exists at that step, or any other, the product or process should be modified at that step, or at an earlier or later stage, to include such a control measure.

7.8 Establish critical limits for each CCP (Principle 3)

Critical limits must be specified and verified, if possible, for each critical control point. More than one critical limit may sometimes be elaborated at a particular step. The criteria used often include measurements of temperature, time, moisture level, pH, and sensory parameters, such as visual appearance and texture. Critical limits should be scientifically based.

7.9 Establish a monitoring system for each CCP (Principle 4)

Monitoring is the scheduled measurement or observation of a CCP relative to its critical limits. Monitoring should be recorded.

The monitoring procedures used must be able to detect loss of control at the CCP, and this information should ideally be available in time to make adjustments to ensure control of the process and prevent violations of the critical limits. Where possible, process adjustments should be made when the monitoring results indicate a trend towards loss of control at a CCP. These adjustments should be made before a deviation occurs.

Data derived from monitoring must be evaluated by a designated person with the knowledge and authority to carry out corrective actions when indicated.

If monitoring is not continuous, the amount or frequency of monitoring must be sufficient to guarantee that the CCP is under control.

Most monitoring procedures for CCPs will need to be done rapidly because they relate to on-line processes and there will not be time for lengthy analytical testing. For this reason, physical and chemical measurements are often preferred to microbiological tests because they can be done rapidly and can often indicate the microbiological control of the product.

The personnel conducting the monitoring of CCPs and control measures should be engaged in production (e.g. line supervisors, maintenance staff) and, where appropriate, staff from quality control. They should be trained in monitoring procedures.

Where continuous monitoring is possible, a reliable monitoring procedure and frequency should be identified. Statistically designed data collection or sampling systems should then be used.

All records and documents associated with monitoring CCPs must be signed and dated by the person(s) carrying out the monitoring and by a responsible reviewing official(s) of the company.

7.10 Establish corrective actions (Principle 5)

Specific corrective actions should be developed for each CCP in the HACCP system in order to deal with deviations when they occur. These actions should ensure that the CCP is brought under control. Corrective actions should include at least the following:

(a) determination and correction of the cause of non-compliance;
(b) determination of the disposition of the non-compliant product;
(c) recording of the corrective actions that have been taken.

Specific corrective actions should be developed in advance for each CCP and included in the HACCP plan. As a minimum, this plan should specify what is to be done when a deviation occurs, who is responsible for implementing the corrective actions, and that a record will be kept and maintained of the actions taken. Individuals who have a thorough understanding of the process, product and HACCP plan should be assigned the responsibility for the oversight of corrective actions.

As appropriate, experts may be consulted to review the information available and to assist in determining the disposition of non-compliant product. Actions taken must also include the proper disposition of the affected product.

Deviation and product disposition procedures must be documented in the HACCP records.

7.11 Establish verification procedures (Principle 6)

Procedures should be established for verification.

Verification and auditing methods, procedures and tests, including random sampling and analysis, can be used to determine whether the HACCP system is working correctly. The frequency of verification should be sufficient to confirm the proper functioning of the HACCP system.

Examples of verification activities include:

— review of the HACCP system and its records;
— review of deviations and product dispositions;
— confirmation that CCPs are kept under control.

Initial verification of the HACCP plan is necessary to determine whether it is scientifically and technically sound, that all hazards have been identified, and that, if the HACCP plan is properly implemented, these hazards will be effectively controlled.

Information reviewed to verify the HACCP plan should include:

(a) expert advice and scientific studies;
(b) in-plant observations, measurements and evaluations. For example, verification of the moist heat sterilization process for sterile injectables should include the scientific justification of the heating times, pressure and

temperatures needed to obtain an appropriate destruction of pathogenic microorganisms (i.e. enteric pathogens) and studies to confirm that the sterilization conditions ensure that the whole load is kept at the required temperature for the time required.

Subsequent verifications should be performed and documented by a HACCP team or an independent expert, as needed. For example, verifications may be conducted when there is an unexplained system failure, a significant change in product, process or packaging occurs, or new hazards are recognized.

In addition, a periodic comprehensive evaluation of the HACCP system by an unbiased, independent third party is useful. This should include a technical evaluation of the hazard analysis and each element of the HACCP plan as well as an on-site review of all flow diagrams and appropriate records of the operation of the plan. Such a comprehensive verification is independent of other verification procedures and must be performed in order to ensure that the HACCP plan is resulting in the control of the hazards. If the results of the comprehensive verification identify deficiencies, the HACCP team should modify the HACCP plan as necessary.

Individuals doing verification should have appropriate technical expertise to perform this function.

Where possible, verification should include actions to confirm the efficacy of all elements of the HACCP plan.

7.12 Establish documentation and record keeping (Principle 7)

Efficient and accurate documentation and record keeping are essential to the application of a HACCP system and should be appropriate to the nature and size of the operation.

Examples of activities for which documentation is required include:

— hazard analysis;
— CCP determination;
— HACCP plan;
— critical limit determination.

Examples of activities for which records are required include:

— CCP monitoring activities;
— process steps;
— associated hazards;
— critical limits;
— verification procedures and schedule;
— deviations;
— associated corrective actions;
— modifications to the HACCP system.

Appendix 1
Illustrative examples of major industrial hazards that may form part of a HACCP plan

The increasing use of hazardous chemicals in industry and trade further influences the quality and safety of processes and the personnel responsible for production. It is important that both on-site and off-site safety should be considered in all projects involving the storage and use of such chemicals.

This Appendix is intended only as a reminder of the major hazards that may be associated with the production, control and distribution of pharmaceuticals. Other relevant literature should be consulted, depending on the type of pharmaceuticals concerned (e.g. active pharmaceutical ingredients, vaccines).

1. Explosions and fires

Explosions can cause damage to buildings, injuries to personnel and hazards to products. Types of explosions that should be considered include detonations, gas and dust explosions, and confined and unconfined vapour-cloud explosions. Because of the possibility of explosions and fires, industry is required to control operations to prevent such hazards. An appropriate hazard-control system should therefore be in place at each site where such hazards are identified.

2. Workers' safety

3. External environment

3.1 Hazardous waste

3.2 Spillage

Appendix 2
Examples of common failures

Common failures should be identified and suitable control measures implemented.

1. Component failures

Causes of such failures include bad design, pressure, corrosive media, high temperatures, mechanical failure of pumps, blowers and stirrers, failure of control systems, such as sensors, failure of welds and flanges, and failure of safety systems (e.g. valves).

2. Deviations from normal operating conditions

Deviations from normal operating conditions include failures in the monitoring of crucial process parameters (e.g. pressure, temperature), failures in utilities such as steam, cooling, electricity and compressed air, failures in shut-down and start-up procedures, and formation of by-products, residues and impurities.

3. Human and organizational errors

A wide variety of errors can be made by operating personnel. Common errors include operator error, pressing wrong buttons, disconnecting alarms, mix-ups of materials, communication errors, and incorrect maintenance and repairs.

4. Natural forces

External impacts may be caused by natural forces such as wind, water, sunlight and lightning.

Bibliography

HACCP: Introducing the Hazard Analysis and Critical Control Point System. Geneva, World Health Organization, 1997 (document WHO/FSF/FOS/97.2).

Major hazard control: A practical manual. An ILO contribution to the International Programme on Chemical Safety of UNEP, ILO, WHO (IPCS). Geneva, International Labour Organization, first edition 1988; third impression (with corrections) 1993.

Quality assurance of pharmaceuticals. A compendium of guidelines and related materials. Volume 1. Geneva, World Health Organization, 1997.

Quality assurance of pharmaceuticals. A compendium of guidelines and related materials. Volume 2. Good manufacturing practices and inspection. Geneva, World Health Organization, 1999.

6.

Sampling operations

Sampling of pharmaceutical products and related materials[1]

1. Introduction 360
   1.1 General considerations 360
   1.2 Glossary 360
   1.3 Purpose of sampling 363
   1.4 Classes and types of pharmaceutical products and related materials 364
   1.5 Sampling facilities 364
   1.6 Responsibilities for sampling 365
   1.7 Health and safety 365
2. Sampling process 366
   2.1 Preparation for sampling 366
   2.2 Sampling operation and precautions 367
   2.3 Storage and retention 368
3. Regulatory issues 369
   3.1 Pharmaceutical inspections 369
   3.2 Surveillance programmes 369
4. Sampling on receipt (for acceptance) 370
   4.1 Starting materials 370
   4.2 Intermediates in the manufacturing process and bulk pharmaceutical products 371
   4.3 Finished products 371
   4.4 Packaging materials (primary and secondary) 372
5. Sampling plans for starting materials, packaging materials and finished products 372
   5.1 Starting materials 373
   5.2 Packaging materials 375
   5.3 Finished products 375

Bibliography 375

Appendix 1

Types of sampling tools 376

[1] WHO guidelines for sampling of pharmaceutical products and related materials. In: *WHO Expert Committee on Specifications for Pharmaceutical Preparations. Thirty-ninth report.* Geneva, World Health Organization, 2005 (WHO Technical Report Series, No. 929), Annex 4.

Appendix 2
Sample collection form 381
Appendix 3
Steps to be considered for inclusion in a standard operating procedure 382
Appendix 4
Examples of types of containers used to store samples of starting materials and bulk products 386
Appendix 5
Examples of use of sampling plans *n*, *p* and *r* 387

1. Introduction

These guidelines are primarily intended for use by governmental organizations, such as drug regulatory authorities (including inspectorates), quality control laboratories and customs and police officials, but some of the general principles may also be appropriate for application by procurement agencies, manufacturers and customers.

These guidelines should be useful when surveying the national markets for the quality of drug products in accordance with national drug quality surveillance programmes for marketed products, whether registered for sale or compounded in pharmacies.

The choice of a sampling plan should always take into consideration the specific objectives of the sampling and the risks and consequences associated with inherent decision errors. The bibliography at the end of this Annex should be consulted when justifying a sampling plan for a given purpose.

1.1 General considerations

Sampling comprises the operations designed to select a portion of a pharmaceutical product (for definition, see glossary) for a defined purpose. The sampling procedure should be appropriate to the purpose of sampling, to the type of controls intended to be applied to the samples and to the material to be sampled. The procedure should be described in writing.

All operations related to sampling should be performed with care, using proper equipment and tools. Any contamination of the sample by dust or other foreign material is liable to jeopardize the validity of the subsequent analyses.

1.2 Glossary

The definitions given below apply to the terms as used in these guidelines. They may have different meanings in other contexts.

Available sample
Whatever total quantity of sample materials is available.

Batch
A quantity of any drug produced during a given cycle of manufacture. If the manufacturing process is continuous, the batch originates in a defined period of time during which the manufacturing conditions are stable and have not been modified.

Combined sample
Sample resulting from combining all or parts of two or more samples of the material.

Consignment
The quantity of a bulk starting material, or of a drug product, made by one manufacturer or supplied by an agent, and supplied at one time in response to a particular request or order. A consignment may comprise one or more lot-identified packages or containers and may include material belonging to more than one lot-identified batch.

Final sample
Sample ready for the application of the test procedure.

Homogeneity
A material is regarded as homogeneous when it is all of the same origin (e.g. from the same batch) and as non-homogeneous when it is of differing origins.

Original sample
Sample collected directly from the material.

Pharmaceutical product
Any material[1] or product intended for human or veterinary use presented in its finished dosage form or as a starting material for use in such a dosage form, that is subject to control by pharmaceutical legislation in the exporting state and/or the importing state.

Prequalification
The activities undertaken in defining a product or service need, seeking expressions of interest from enterprises to supply the product or service, and examining the product or service offered against the specification, and the facility where the product or service is prepared against common standards of good manufacturing practice (GMP). The examination of the product or service and of the facility where it is manufactured is performed by trained and qualified inspectors against common standards. Once the product is approved, and the

[1] "Material" is used in the document for "pharmaceutical products and related materials".

facility is approved for the delivery of the specified product or service, other procurement agencies are informed of the approval. Prequalification is required for all pharmaceutical products regardless of their composition and place of manufacture or registration, but the amount and type of information requested from the supplier for use in the assessment by the procurement agency may differ.

Production
All operations involved in the preparation of a pharmaceutical product, from receipt of materials, through processing, packaging and repackaging, labelling and relabelling, to completion of the finished product.

Random sample
Sample in which the different fractions of the material have an equal probability of being represented.

Representative sample
Sample obtained according to a sampling procedure designed to ensure that the different parts of a batch or the different properties of a non-uniform material are proportionately represented.

Retention sample
Sample collected as part of the original sampling process and reserved for future testing. The size of a retention sample should be sufficient to allow for at least two confirmatory analyses. In some cases statutory regulations may require one or more retention samples, each of which should be separately identified, packaged and sealed.

Sample
A portion of a material collected according to a defined sampling procedure. The size of any sample should be sufficient to allow all anticipated test procedures to be carried out, including all repetitions and retention samples. If the quantity of material available is not sufficient for the intended analyses and for the retention samples, the inspector should record that the sampled material is the available sample (see *Sampling record*) and the evaluation of the results should take account of the limitations that arise from the insufficient sample size.

Sampler
Person responsible for performing the sampling operations.

Sampling method
That part of the sampling procedure dealing with the method prescribed for withdrawing samples.

Sampling plan
Description of the location, number of units and/or quantity of material that should be collected, and associated acceptance criteria.

Sampling procedure
The complete sampling operations to be performed on a defined material for a specific purpose. A detailed written description of the sampling procedure is provided in the *sampling protocol.*

Sampling record
Written record of the sampling operations carried out on a particular material for a defined purpose. The sampling record should contain the batch number, date and place of sampling, reference to the sampling protocol used, a description of the containers and of the materials sampled, notes on possible abnormalities, together with any other relevant observations, and the name and signature of the inspector.

Sampling unit
Discrete part of a consignment such as an individual package, drum or container.

Selected sample
Sample obtained according to a sampling procedure designed to select a fraction of the material that is likely to have special properties. A selected sample that is likely to contain deteriorated, contaminated, adulterated or otherwise unacceptable material is known as an *extreme sample.*

Uniformity
A starting material may be considered uniform when samples drawn from different layers do not show significant differences in the quality control tests which would result in non-conformity with specifications. The following materials may be considered uniform unless there are signs to the contrary: organic and inorganic chemicals; purified natural products; various processed natural products such as fatty oils and essential oils; and plant extracts. The assumption of uniformity is strengthened by homogeneity, i.e. when the consignment is derived from a single batch.

1.3 Purpose of sampling

Sampling may be required for different purposes, such as pre-qualification; acceptance of consignments; batch release testing; in-process control; special controls; inspection for customs clearance, deterioration or adulteration; or for obtaining a retention sample.

The tests to be applied to the sample may include:

— verifying the identity;
— performing complete pharmacopoeial or analogous testing; and
— performing special or specific tests.

1.4 Classes and types of pharmaceutical products and related materials

The materials to be sampled may belong to the following classes:

— starting materials for use in the manufacture of finished pharmaceutical products;
— intermediates in the manufacturing process (e.g. bulk granule);
— pharmaceutical products (in-process as well as before and after packaging);
— primary and secondary packaging materials; and
— cleaning and sanitizing agents, compressed gases and other processing agents.

1.5 Sampling facilities

Sampling facilities should be designed to:

— prevent contamination of the opened container, the materials and the operator;
— prevent cross-contamination by other materials, products and the environment; and
— protect the individual who samples (sampler) during the sampling procedure.

Where possible, sampling should be performed in an area or booth designed for and dedicated to this purpose, although this will not be possible where samples are required to be taken from a production line (e.g. in-process control samples). The area in which the sample was taken should be recorded in the sampling record and a sequential log should be kept of all materials sampled in each area.

Sampling from large containers of starting material or bulk products can present difficulties. Whenever possible, this work should be carried out in a separate, closed cubicle within the warehouse, to reduce the risk of contamination (e.g. by dust) of either the sample or the materials remaining in the container, or of cross-contamination.

Some materials should be sampled in special or dedicated environments (e.g. when sampling articles for which contamination with dirt or particles from the environment should be avoided, such as aerosol valves, hormones and penicillins).

Generally, taking the original sales pack as a sample from outlets such as pharmacies or hospitals does not present problems. However, the inspector should ensure that the quantity of sample taken is sufficient for the intended analyses and for the retention samples, and that all units sampled are derived from the same batch and preferably from the same location.

1.6 Responsibilities for sampling

Those responsible for sampling procedures include:

- *governmental organizations*, such as drug control authorities (including inspectorates); quality control laboratories; customs and police authorities responsible for the clearance of drug products held in quarantine after manufacture or importation, and for the detection of pharmaceutical products that have deteriorated or have been contaminated, adulterated or counterfeited;
- *customers* such as governmental or nongovernmental agencies involved in the acquisition of drug products; and
- *manufacturers* in the context of good manufacturing practices (GMP).

The samplers need to be adequately trained in the practical aspects of sampling, qualified to perform the sampling operation, and should have sufficient knowledge of pharmaceutical substances to allow them to execute the work effectively and safely. Given that the sampling technique itself can introduce bias, it is important that personnel carrying out the sampling should be suitably trained in the techniques and procedures used. The training should be documented in the individual's training records. Sampling records should clearly indicate the date of sampling, the sampled container and the identity of the person who sampled the batch.

A conscientious approach, with meticulous attention to detail and cleanliness, is essential. The sampler should remain alert to any signs of contamination, deterioration or tampering. Any suspicious signs should be recorded in detail in the sampling record.

If a governmental agency needs to sample a sterile or bulk pharmaceutical product at the manufacturing site, it may be best to have the manufacturer's personnel collect the sample, using their own procedures. The regulatory inspector would observe the procedure in such a way as not to increase the chance of contamination (e.g. for sterile pharmaceutical products, the inspector would observe through a glass window outside the aseptic sampling area) and to preclude the possibility of the inspector inadvertently contaminating the remaining bulk pharmaceutical product through poor procedures, for example.

1.7 Health and safety

It is the responsibility of the sampler to read the relevant health and safety information (e.g. the safety data sheet for a pharmaceutical product and related materials) before sampling the material. The information should include necessary safety precautions and requirements for both the operator and the environment.

The sampler should wear appropriate protective clothing for the task. If specific safety precautions are required, such as the use of respiratory equipment, the sampler should be properly trained in its use.

The sampler should have safe access to and egress from the place where the sample is taken, and the places where the samples are taken for storage. The sample storage areas should have adequate light and ventilation and should be arranged to satisfy the requirements for safety as well as any special ones arising from the characteristics of the material being sampled.

Care should be taken to guard against collapse of stacked containers or solids in bulk.

2. Sampling process

2.1 Preparation for sampling

For the sampling of products, the responsible person should have at his or her disposal all the tools needed to open the containers (e.g. packages, barrels and others). Tools may include knives, pliers, saws, hammers, wrenches, implements to remove dust (preferably a vacuum cleaner), and material to reclose the packages (such as sealing tape), as well as self-adhesive labels to indicate that some of the contents have been removed from a package or container. Containers due to be sampled should be cleaned prior to sampling if necessary.

Sampling of uniform starting materials does not require complicated tools. A variety of pipettes fitted with suction bulbs, cups or beakers, dippers and funnels are needed for liquids of low viscosity. The use of glass should be avoided. A suitable inert rod can be used for highly viscous liquid, and spatulas or scoops are needed for powdered and granular solids. Sterile pharmaceutical products should be sampled under aseptic conditions, and only when deemed absolutely essential, to avoid the risk of loss of sterility.

The tools for sampling non-uniform materials are more complicated and more difficult to clean. For example, a sampling tube with a shutter at the lower end may be used to sample liquids in drums or other large containers and a slotted tube with a pointed end may be used to sample solids. It is important to follow the manufacturer's instructions for the use of sampling devices.

All sampling tools and implements should be made of inert materials and kept scrupulously clean. After use or before reuse, they should be thoroughly washed, rinsed with water or suitable solvent, and dried. They should be stored in clean conditions. Adequate washing facilities should be provided in, or in close proximity to, the sampling area, otherwise samplers will need to bring separate clean sets of implements for sampling each product. The cleaning procedure used for all sampling tools and implements should be documented and recorded. The adequacy of the cleaning procedure for the material from which the sampling tool is made should be demonstrated. The use of disposable sampling materials has distinct advantages.

Examples of sampling tools suitable for each type of material are given in Appendix 1.

2.2 Sampling operation and precautions

There should be a written procedure describing the sampling operation. This should include details of the health and safety aspects of sampling. It should ensure that representative samples are taken in sufficient quantity for testing in accordance with specifications. Closures and labels should preferably be such that unauthorized opening can be detected. Samples should never be returned to the bulk.

The sampling process should be appropriately supervised and documented (see Appendix 2 for an example of a sample collection form).

The sampling procedure should be such that non-uniformity of the material can be detected. During the sampling procedure, attention should be paid to any signs of nonconformity of the material.

Signs of non-uniformity include differences in shape, size or colour of particles in crystalline, granular or powdered solid substances; moist crusts on hygroscopic substances; deposits of solid pharmaceutical product in liquid or semi-liquid products; and stratification of liquid products. Such changes, some of which may be readily reversible, can occur during prolonged storage or exposure to extreme temperatures during transportation. Homogeneous portions of the material or bulk such as those mentioned above should be sampled and tested separately from the rest of the material that has a normal appearance.

Pooling of the samples from the different portions should be avoided, because this can mask contamination, low potency or other quality problems.

Labelling of samples should provide appropriate details, including the batch number and, if known, the container number from which the sample was taken, the amount taken and for what purpose. Labels should be applied at the time of sampling. The container used to store the sample should also be properly labelled with appropriate details such as sample type, name of material, identification code, batch/lot number, code, quantity, date of sampling, storage conditions, handling precautions and container number.

For finished drug products, the sampling procedure should take account of the official and non-official tests required for the individual dosage form (e.g. tablets or parenteral preparations). Non-official tests could include testing for adulteration and counterfeiting. The sampling procedure should also take account of past experience with the pharmaceutical product or related material and with the supplier, and of the number of sampling units in the consignment.

Examples of steps for sampling are given in Appendix 3.

When a container is sampled outside the control of the consignee of the product, the following precautions should be taken. If the tamper-proof seal is broken to obtain a sample, then the consignee of the product should be informed and the container resealed with an appropriate tamper-proof seal, and the consignee of the product informed of its type and its identification. If a bag has been punctured to take a sample, then the sampling hole should be appropriately closed and identified as a sampling hole made by an authorized sampler. Sampled containers should be identified, as they may no longer contain the quantity of product stated on the label. In accordance with national legislation there may be exceptions, e.g. during ongoing investigations of cases related to counterfeit pharmaceutical products.

2.3 Storage and retention

The container used to store a sample should not interact with the sampled material nor allow contamination. It should also protect the sample from light, air and moisture, as required by the storage directions for the pharmaceutical product or related material sampled. As a general rule the container should be sealed and preferably tamper-evident.

Samples of loose materials, whether solid or liquid, should be placed in one or more clean containers. Liquid samples should be transported in suitable bottles closed by screw tops with inert liners that provide a good vapour-proof (moisture-proof) seal for the contents. Suitable screw-top jars in exceptional cases only should be used for solid or semi-solid pharmaceutical products. The container should be inert. Light-sensitive materials should be protected by using amber glass containers or by wrapping colourless glass containers in foil or dark-coloured paper. Headspace should be kept to a minimum to minimize any possible degradation. Any special procedures, for example, nitrogen gassing, should be discussed with the consignee of the material and carried out as appropriate.

Solid dosage forms such as tablets or granules should be protected during transit, either by totally filling the container with the product or by filling any residual space with a suitable material. All containers should be sealed and labelled, and all samples should be packaged adequately and transported in such a way as to avoid breakage and contamination during transport.

For all containers that come apart (e.g. screw-capped jars or metal tins with separate lids) precautions should be taken to avoid any mix-up when they are opened for examination, such as by labelling all parts of each container whenever possible.

If one sample is divided into several sample containers, they should be transported in a suitably sealed box, which should be labelled with the identity of the product, the consignment from which the sample was drawn, the size of the sample, the date and place of sampling, and the name of the inspector.

Security and adequate storage conditions should be ensured for the rooms in which samples are stored. Samples should be stored in accordance with the storage conditions as specified for the respective active pharmaceutical ingredient (API), excipient or drug product. Packaging materials similar to those in which the bulk is supplied should be used for long-term storage.

Examples of types of containers used to store samples of starting materials and bulk products are given in Appendix 4.

3. Regulatory issues

When sampling for regulatory purposes, additional samples for regulatory testing and verification purposes should be provided (e.g. for duplicate testing and parallel testing by different regulatory laboratories and by the consignee of the product). The consignee of the product should be informed that samples have been taken, and should the consignee wish to conduct his/her own testing of the sample taken for regulatory purposes, regulatory authorities should provide a sample to the consignee of the goods.

Sampling of products for prequalification purposes may follow similar procedures.

3.1 Pharmaceutical inspections

Pharmaceutical inspectors may take samples from retail or hospital pharmacies (including samples of preparations manufactured in bulk on the premises), or from industry and wholesalers for a variety of reasons, such as:

— routine monitoring and control;
— following the suspicion or discovery of products that show signs of possible deterioration, contamination, adulteration or counterfeiting; and
— when a particular product is suspected of being either ineffective or responsible for adverse clinical reactions.

For deteriorated dosage forms, the sample should consist of one or more retail containers of the product that shows visual signs of deterioration.

When a complaint has been received about a drug product, the sample should include the original container and, if possible, one or more unopened containers containing the same product and bearing the same batch number. There should be good communication between the regulatory authority and the consignee of the goods concerning the findings and any necessary corrective action.

3.2 Surveillance programmes

National drug regulatory authorities are responsible for monitoring the quality of all drug products marketed in their country and as defined by legislation. The extent to which routine surveillance should be undertaken, as opposed to assessment of suspect products, will depend upon factors such as:

— the capacity of the national quality control laboratory;
— the extent to which the quality of the product has been assessed prior to registration;
— the extent to which the requirements for GMP are implemented; and
— the number of products that are imported from abroad.

A systematic programme of drug quality surveillance should be in place which may include sampling of marketed products, whether registered for sale or compounded in pharmacies, as deemed necessary. Each product should be assessed regularly (e.g. every 2–3 years) for inclusion in the surveillance programme, but particular attention should be accorded to products that are of prime importance to public health programmes or that are potentially dangerous, unstable or difficult to formulate properly.

The responsible laboratory should draw up the sampling programme, if necessary under the guidance of the drug regulatory authority, on a yearly or half-yearly basis. This programme should not only list the products to be sampled during a given period, but should also specify the sampling procedures and the size of the samples to be collected, taking into account the need for retention samples. The programme should state to what extent each brand of a given product will be sampled and which local authority or inspector will be responsible for each sampling operation. It should indicate to which laboratory (if more than one exists) each sample should be sent. Such a programme enables the facilities of each laboratory to be used to best advantage.

4. Sampling on receipt (for acceptance)

4.1 Starting materials

Testing of starting materials should be undertaken using samples collected in accordance with an appropriate procedure.

If the material of a consignment can be regarded as uniform, the sample can be taken from any part of the consignment. If, however, the material is not physically uniform, special sampling tools may be required to withdraw a cross-sectional portion of the material. Alternatively, where applicable, a validated procedure can be followed to restore the uniformity of the material before sampling, based on information concerning the subsequent handling and manufacturing steps. For example, a stratified liquid may be stirred or a solid deposit in a liquid may be dissolved by gentle warming and stirring. Such interventions should not be attempted without adequate knowledge of the properties of the contents and appropriate discussions with the consignee of the goods.

All partially processed natural products, both animal, herbal (dried plants and their parts) and mineral, should be treated as intrinsically non-uniform. Special procedures requiring considerable practice are needed to prepare representative samples from such consignments, including coning and quartering and the treatment of fines. Details of appropriate procedures may be found in the relevant International Organization for Standardization (ISO) documents (see Bibliography). These procedures are not further described in these guidelines.

4.2 Intermediates in the manufacturing process and bulk pharmaceutical products

Pharmaceutical intermediates and products supplied in bulk may need to be examined. These include liquids and semi-solid pharmaceutical products, powdered solids or granulates transported in large containers and intended either for further processing or for direct packaging into final market containers, and unit dosage forms (tablets, capsules) supplied in bulk which are intended for repackaging into smaller containers. There is a risk of segregation of bulk materials during transportation and this should be taken into account when drawing up the sampling plan.

Products of this kind may be assumed to be uniform where the transportation process has been validated, provided that they:

- — are labelled with the name of the manufacturer and a single batch number;
- — have been produced in accordance with GMP; and
- — are supplied with a certificate, issued in the country of origin, according to the WHO Certification Scheme on the quality of pharmaceutical products moving in international commerce.

In these circumstances the collection of a single sample, sufficient for the intended analyses, is adequate.

4.3 Finished products

The quality of finished pharmaceutical products frequently needs to be verified at the time of their importation or purchase. The necessary sampling should be performed using an appropriate method and with regard to the presumed uniformity. A single consignment of a product from a single manufacturer and labelled with a single batch number may be assumed to be uniform.

The minimum size of the samples will be determined by the requirements of the analytical procedure that will be used to test the product. Tests of unit dosage forms for uniformity of weight, volume or content can require a considerable number of units, as can tests for sterility. Depending upon the type of material, the size of the consignment and the way in which the material is packed, a unit to be sampled may be regarded as the transport container, e.g. 20 packs shrink-wrapped or boxed together, rather than an individual container. The required number of unit dosage forms is then withdrawn from any individual container in the selected transit container.

Sampling and testing may be adjusted according to experience with the specific source (e.g. manufacturer or supplier) of the product. If the consignment consists of one very large batch, or if little experience has been obtained with the product to be sampled, it may be prudent to carry out two independent analyses. Two independent final samples should then be taken from different sampling units. Conversely, when a consignment is composed of two or three batches from the same manufacturer, a single sample taken from each batch may suffice, provided that favourable documented experience has previously been gained with the product and the manufacturer, and that there is evidence from the expiry date, or other information, that the batches were produced at approximately the same time.

Note: When sampling finished products, packaging materials may be retained for testing.

4.4 Packaging materials (primary and secondary)

There is a potential for mixing up printed packaging materials during the sampling operations and, therefore, only one material should be handled at a time. Also, samples of packaging materials should never be returned to the consignment.

Adequate protection (e.g. collapsible metal tubes) and identification should be provided for the sample to avoid mixing or damage.

Primary packaging materials should be adequately protected during the sampling operation to avoid environmental contamination. The final use of the packaging should be taken into consideration and appropriate sampling protection afforded (e.g. in the sampling of parenteral ampoules). There are several reasons why a consignment of packaging materials may not necessarily be considered homogenous, for example:

- Materials were manufactured on different days or machines.
- Materials were manufactured on one machine, but on different stations (e.g. 16 printing dye stations or 12 moulding stations).
- Packaging was manufactured with different source materials (e.g. polyethylene from two different sources).
- A change of quality occurred during the process (e.g. container-wall thickness, colour variation, text legibility or change of printing plate).

It is, therefore, important at least to take random samples (e.g. from across the consignment), and to consider focused sampling, taking into account some of the above points.

5. Sampling plans for starting materials, packaging materials and finished products

As stated in the introduction, these guidelines are intended primarily for drug regulatory authorities and procurement agencies. The following sampling plans are, therefore, not necessarily appropriate for manufacturers, although the guiding principles may be useful. The choice of the sampling plan should always take into consideration the specific objectives of the sampling and the risks and consequences associated with inherent decision errors. It should be noted that sampling plans are not recommended for sampling of starting materials for identification tests (see *Quality assurance of pharmaceuticals. A compendium of guidelines and related materials. Volume 2, 2nd Updated edition. Good manufacturing practices and inspection*. Geneva, World Health Organization, 2006; and *WHO Expert Committee on Specifications for Pharmaceutical Preparations. Thirty-ninth report*. Geneva, World Health Organization, 2005 (WHO Technical Report Series, No. 929), Annex 2).

Ideally each sampling unit should be examined to ensure that it is intact and also checked for possible damage to the container. The contents should be inspected for uniformity and appropriately tested for identity. Uniformity should be tested on selected layer samples at different points in the material without previous intermixing. However, in cases when this ideal procedure is not possible or justified by the purpose of sampling, a number of sampling units should be randomly selected for sampling. It is not prudent to open all containers of products, which are liable to deteriorate under the influence of moisture or oxygen when held in a transit warehouse. However, materials in damaged containers or those found to be non-uniform should either be rejected or individually sampled for a complete quality control. Unlabelled sampling units should be rejected.

For random sampling, whenever possible each sampling unit should be consecutively numbered and the required number of random sampling units selected using tables of random numbers.

The number of units to be sampled depends on different assumptions and three possible plans are shown in Table 1. For more comprehensive, statistically-based sampling schemes, see Bibliography.

It is important to recognize that the "*n*-plan" is not statistically based and should be used only as a guiding principle.

5.1 Starting materials

When sampling starting materials proper consideration has to be given to deciding on a sampling plan. The following are examples of sampling plans that could be used.

5.1.1 The n *plan*

The "*n* plan" should be used with great caution and only when the material to be sampled is considered uniform and is supplied from a recognized source. Samples can be withdrawn from any part of the container (usually from the top layer). The *n* plan is based on the formula $n = 1 + \sqrt{N}$, where N is the number

Table 1. Values of n, p, or r for the N sampling units[a]

Value of *n*, *p*, or *r*	Values of *N*		
	n plan	*p* plan	*r* plan
2	up to 3	up to 25	up to 2
3	4–6	26–56	3–4
4	7–13	57–100	5–7
5	14–20	101–156	8–11
6	21–30	157–225	12–16
7	31–42		17–22
8	43–56		23–28
9	57–72		29–36
10	73–90		37–44

[a] An example of how these plans work is given in Appendix 5.

of sampling units in the consignment. The value of n is obtained by simple rounding. A minimum number of containers needs to be sampled, e.g. if N is less than or equal to 4, then every container is sampled. According to this plan, original samples are taken from n sampling units selected at random and these are subsequently placed in separate sample containers. The control laboratory inspects the appearance of the material and tests the identity of each original sample according to the relevant specification. If the results are concordant, the original samples are combined into a final, composite sample from which an analytical sample is prepared, the remainder being kept as a retention sample.

Note: The n plan is not recommended for use by control laboratories of manufacturers who are required to analyse and release or reject each received consignment of the starting materials used to produce a drug product.

5.1.2 The p plan

The "p plan" may be used when the material is uniform, is received from a recognized source and the main purpose is to test for identity. The p plan is based on the formula $p = 0.4\sqrt{N}$, where N is the number of sampling units. The figures for p are obtained by rounding up to the next highest integer. According to this plan, samples are taken from each of the N sampling units of the consignment and placed in separate sample containers. These original samples are transferred to the control laboratory, visually inspected and tested for identity (a simplified method may be used). If the results are concordant, p final samples are formed by appropriate pooling of the original samples.

5.1.3 The r *plan*

The "*r* plan" may be used when the material is suspected to be nonuniform and/or is received from a source that is not well known. The *r* plan may also be used for herbal medicinal products used as starting materials. This plan is based on the formula $r = 1.5\sqrt{N}$, where N is the number of sampling units. The figures for *r* are obtained by rounding up to the next highest integer.

Samples are taken from each of the *N* sampling units of the consignment and placed in separate sample containers. These original samples are transferred to the control laboratory and tested for identity. If the results are concordant, *r* samples are randomly selected and individually subjected to testing. If these results are concordant, the *r* samples are combined for the retention sample.

5.2 Packaging materials

Sampling plans for packaging materials should be based on defined sampling standards, for example, British Standard BS 6001-1, ISO 2859 or ANSI/ASQCZ1.4-1993.

The objective is to ensure that there is a low probability of accepting material that does not comply with the predefined acceptance level.

5.3 Finished products

As for packaging materials, sampling plans for finished products should be based on defined sampling standards such as BS 6001-1, ISO 2859 or ANSI/ASQCZ 1.4-1993.

In some cases it may be sufficient to limit examination of finished goods to visual inspection only. If physical and chemical testing is required, however, the sampling units should consist of whole packs. Individual packs should not be broken open for the purposes of sampling.

An example of the steps to be considered when sampling finished products is given in Appendix 3, based on the sampling plans given in ISO 2859-1.

Bibliography

Good practices for national pharmaceutical control laboratories. In: *WHO Expert Committee on Specifications for Pharmaceutical Preparations. Thirty-sixth report.* Geneva, World Health Organization, 2002 (WHO Technical Report Series, No. 902), Annex 3.

Guidelines on packaging for pharmaceutical products. In: *WHO Expert Committee on Specifications for Pharmaceutical Preparations. Thirty-sixth report.* Geneva, World Health Organization, 2002 (WHO Technical Report Series, No. 902), Annex 9.

Koratochvil B, Taylor JK. Sampling for chemical analysis. Analytical Chemistry, 1981, 53:925A.

Oakland JS. Management tools in the manufacture of chemicals: statistical quality control. Chemistry and Industry, 1981, 16:562–567.

Gy P. Sampling of particulate materials—theory and practice, 2nd edition. New York, Elsevier, 1979.

Sommer K. Sampling of powders and bulk materials. Heidelberg, Springer-Verlag, 1986.

Acceptance sampling plans and procedures for the inspection of bulk materials. Geneva, International Organization for Standardization, 2000. ISO 10725.

Sampling procedures for inspection by attributes. Procedures for assessment of stated quality levels. British Standard BS 6001-5:2000. Geneva, International Organization for Standardization, 1999. ISO 2859-4.

Sampling procedures for inspection by variables. Specification for single sampling plans indexed by acceptable quality level (AQL) for lot-by-lot inspection. British Standard BS 6002-1. Geneva, International Organization for Standardization, 1993. ISO 3951:1989.

Sampling procedures for inspection by attributes. Sampling schemes indexed by acceptance quality limit for lot-by-lot inspection. British Standard BS 6001-1. Geneva, International Organization for Standardization, 1999. ISO 2859-1.

American National Standards Institute/American Society for Quality. Sampling procedures and tables for inspection by attributes. Washington, DC, American Society for Quality, 1993. ANSI/ASQCZ1.4-1993.

Methods for sampling chemical products. Introduction and general principles. British Standard BS 5309-1. London, British Standards Publishing, 1976.

Methods for sampling chemical products. Sampling of liquids. British Standard BS 5309-3. London, British Standards Publishing, 1976.

Methods for sampling chemical products. Sampling of solids. British Standard BS 5309-4. London, British Standards Publishing, 1976.

Appendix 1
Types of sampling tools

Scoops

Small containers of solid materials may be adequately sampled using a spatula or scoop. The samples are then blended to provide a representative sample of that container. Figure 1 shows the recommended designs of scoops, which should preferably be rounded.

If the scoop used is too small for the sizes of particle being sampled, large particles will roll off and testing bias may be introduced. On the other hand, if

Figure 1. Sampling scoops for solids

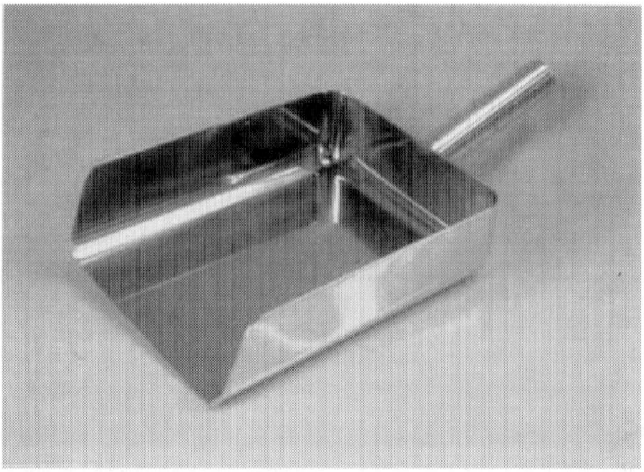

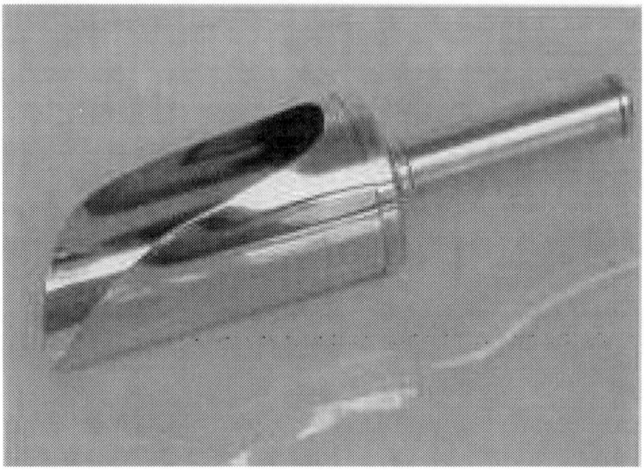

the scoop is too big, an unnecessarily large sample will be obtained for a given number of increments.

A scoopful of sample should be taken in a single movement and transferred to the sample container. Avoid tapping the scoop to remove pharmaceutical product as this is likely to cause segregation of the sample.

Dip tubes

Dip tubes should be used for sampling liquid and topical products and should be made of an inert material, such as polypropylene or stainless steel. A typical dip tube is shown in Figure 2.

Figure 2 Typical dip tube

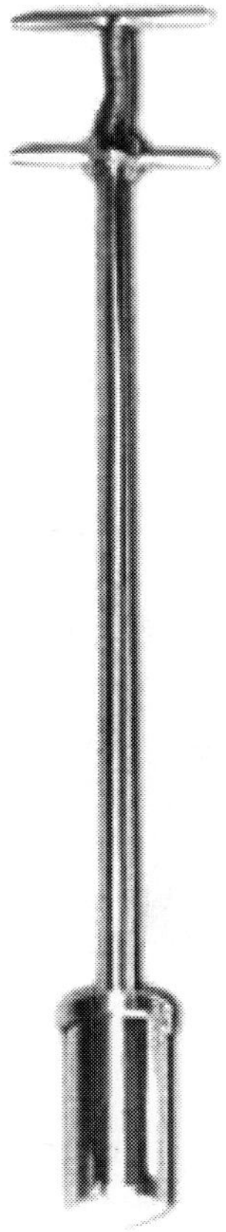

Weighted containers

For taking samples from large tanks and storage vessels, a container in a weighted carrier can be used. The container is designed such that it can be opened at the required depth. Marks on the cord used for lowering the container can be used to determine when the correct sampling depth has been reached. A typical weighted container is shown in Figure 3.

Thieves

Sample thieves should be used when taking samples from deep containers of solids. Typical thieves are shown in Figure 4.

The plug thief typically consists of a hollow tube with an inner rod that has a tip on the end to allow the thief to enter the powder bed in the closed

Figure 3. Typical weighted container

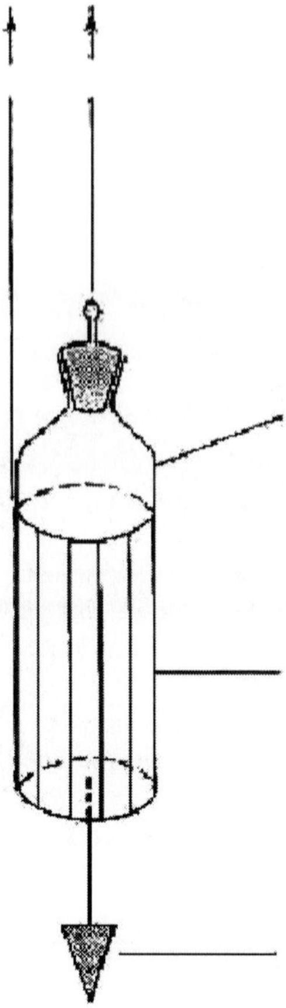

position (see Figure 4.i). The geometry of this tip can influence the sample taken; pointed tips distort the powder bed less than blunt-tipped probes, thereby reducing sampling error. Some thieves have a locking device that allows the sample volume to be set to the required sample weight, thereby reducing the weight variation in the sample population.

A chamber thief generally consists of two concentric tubes (see Figure 4.ii); the inner tube is solid except for the chambers in which the sample is collected. The outer tube is hollow with openings that can be aligned with the chambers in the inner tube. A well-designed thief will have a sharp end to minimize disruption to the powder bed.

When it is inserted into a static powder blend a thief will distort the bed by carrying pharmaceutical product from the upper layers of the blend to the lower layers. The magnitude of this distortion can depend on whether the thief

Figure 4 Typical sample thieves

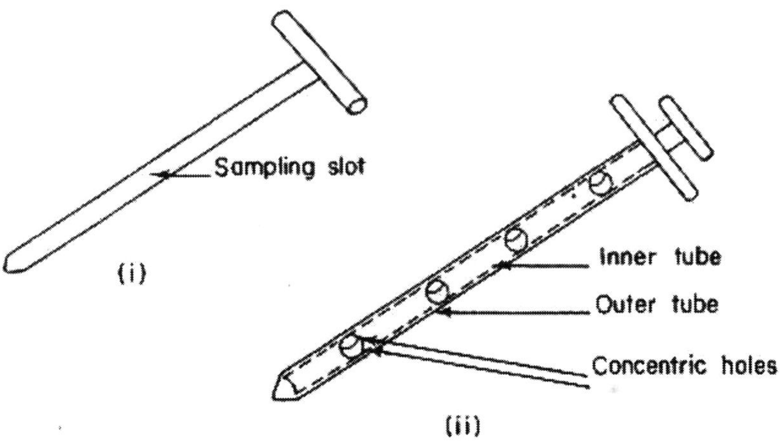

is inserted into the blend with a smooth, jerky or twisting action. Therefore, the correct sampling procedure should be defined and staff trained in using the appropriate technique. Thieves are also sometimes referred to as "double-tube spears".

The angle at which the thief enters the powder bed can also influence sampling error. If a thief is inserted into the powder bed vertically, it can extract samples of different particle size from those that would be obtained using the same thief inserted at an acute angle. In addition the orientation of a chamber thief in relation to the powder bed (i.e. whether the chamber is at the top, the bottom or in the middle of the thief) may also influence the sampling error.

The material from which the thief is constructed, e.g. stainless steel or polypropylene, may also have an effect on sampling error due to static effects.

Sampling error can also be affected by bed depth, as the static pressure of the bulk blend forces the material into the sample chamber(s). This pressure is far greater at the bottom of a large container than it is in the middle or at the top. It is quite possible that the same thief could extract samples of different particle size from the top or bottom of a static powder blend.

Simple bag-sampling spears

Simple bag-sampling spears are the most commonly used instruments for taking samples from bags, because they are relatively cheap, simple and quick. Sampling spears generally have a maximum external diameter of about 12 mm, but can be up to 25 mm in diameter. To obtain a good cross-sectional sample, the spear should be 40–45 cm in length. The tapered type of sampling spear penetrates bags easily. Typical spears are shown in Figure 5.

Figure 5. Typical sampling spears

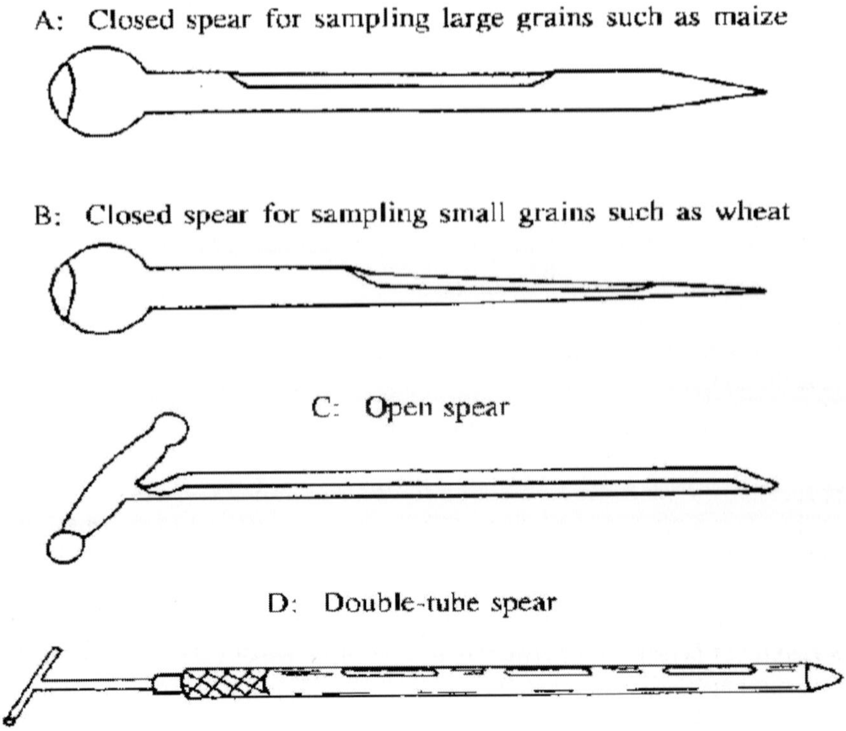

Appendix 2
Sample collection form[1]

Serial number: ___________

Name of location/place where sample was taken:

. . . .

. . . .

. . . .

Address (with telephone and fax number, if applicable):

. . . .

. . . .

Date of sampling: . . . .

[1] This sample collection form should always be kept with the sample collected. Proper sampling procedures should be followed.

Names of people who took samples:
1. . . . .
2. . . . .

Product name of the sample: . . . .
Name of (active) starting material (INN, generic or scientific name) with dosage strength: . . . .
Dosage form (tablet, capsule, etc.): . . . .
Batch/lot number: . . . .
Date of manufacture: . . . . Expiry date: . . . .

Registration or licence number (if applicable): . . . .
Name of the manufacturer: . . . .
Number of sample unit taken (tablet, capsule, etc.: at least 20 but not more than 30 units): . . . .

Brief physical/visual description of sample:
. . . .
. . . .
. . . .
. . . .
. . . .

Signature of person(s) taking samples	Signature of representative of the establishment where sample(s) was taken (optional)
1.	. . . .
2.	

Appendix 3
Steps to be considered for inclusion in a standard operating procedure

The steps for inclusion in a standard operating procedure described below are derived on a purely theoretical basis and are presented for information purposes only.

Bulk liquid products

The steps to be considered when sampling bulk liquid products are as follows.

1. Read and understand the precautions to be observed for the safe handling of the material.

2. Gather together the required sampling equipment (sampling tube or weighted sampling can, sample bottles and labels) and check that all the required items are clean.
3. Locate the batch.
4. Examine the container(s) for signs of contamination of the batch. Record any faults.
5. Examine the labels for obvious differences and signs of changes including obliterations and mislabelling. Record any faults.
6. Investigate and clarify the sources of and reasons for any faults before proceeding.
7. Choose a liquid-sampling tube of size and orifice suitable for the viscosity of the liquid being sampled.
8. Sample the liquid, suspension or emulsion (well stirred, if appropriate) by slowly pushing the open sampling tube vertically downwards through the liquid so that material is collected from each layer.
9. Seal the tube, withdraw it from the bulk liquid, and allow liquid adhering to the outside of the tube to drain. Transfer all the contents of the tube to a clean, labelled sample bottle.
10. Repeat steps 8 and 9 until sufficient samples for analytical and retention purposes have been obtained.
11. Seal the sample bottle.
12. Reseal the container from which the samples were taken and label as "sampled".
13. Clean and dry the sampling tube, observing the relevant safety precautions.
14. Sample other required containers in the same manner following steps 8–12 above.
15. Clean the sampling tube using the recommended cleaning procedure.
16. Deliver the analytical samples to the laboratory and the reserve samples to the retention sample store. Report any aspects of the sampling that should be brought to the attention of the analyst or the inspector.
17. Check supplier certificate versus the specifications, if applicable.

Powdered starting material

The steps to be considered in sampling a powdered starting material are as follows.

1. Read and understand the precautions to be observed for the safe handling of the material.
2. Gather together the required sampling equipment (sampling spear, sample bottles and labels) and check that all items are clean.
3. Locate the consignment and count the number of containers. Record this number.

4. Examine all the containers for obvious differences and signs of damage. Record any faults.
5. Examine all the labels for obvious differences and signs of changes, including obliterations and mislabelling. Record any faults.
6. Segregate any damaged containers and those with suspected spoiled contents for separate examination. These should then be *referred* or *rejected* and dealt with accordingly.
7. Segregate any containers with different batch numbers and treat these separately.
8. Number the remaining containers.
9. Choose the appropriate sampling plan (*n*, *p* or *r*).
10. Choose the containers to be sampled in accordance with the requirements of the chosen plan (by the use of random number tables, by drawing lots or by the use of a random number generator if applicable).
11. Open the containers one at a time and inspect the contents. Record any differences.
12. Choose a suitable, clean sampling spear and plunge this (gates closed) into the powder so that the point of the spear reaches the bottom of the container.
13. Open the gates to allow the powder to enter the spear cavities, then reclose them.
14. Withdraw the spear from the container and transfer the spear contents to a labelled sample bottle.
15. Repeat steps 12–14 until sufficient material has been collected for analytical and retention requirements.
16. Seal the sample bottle.
17. Reseal the container from which the samples were withdrawn and label as "sampled".
18. Wipe clean the sampling spear if required, observing the safety precautions, before sampling the other chosen containers.
19. Repeat steps 12–18 for each chosen container.
20. Clean the sampling spear using the recommended cleaning procedure.
21. Deliver the analytical samples to the laboratory and the reserve samples to the retention sample store. Report any aspects of the sampling that should be brought to the attention of the analyst or inspector.
22. Check the supplier certificate versus the specifications, if applicable.

Packaging materials

The steps to be considered in sampling packaging materials are as follows.

1. Check the consignment against any associated documentation.
2. Check transit containers for the following and report any deviations as necessary:

   2.1 correct identification;
   2.2 integrity of seal, if appropriate; and
   2.3 absence of physical damage.
3. Obtain the required sample from the required number of containers, bearing in mind the special considerations for sampling packaging materials noted in section 4.4 of this Annex.
4. Place the sample units into identified appropriate sample containers.
5. Identify the consignment containers that have been sampled.
6. Note any special situations found during the sampling process (e.g. rogue items or component damage). Report any such observations as necessary.
7. Remove all sampled material pallets or containers from the sampling area together with all documentation.
8. Check supplier certificate against the specifications, if applicable.

Finished products

The following steps should be considered when sampling finished products.

1. Determine the number of pallets per batch in the consignment.
2. Work out as per ISO 2859-1 table level II, the number of pallets to be checked visually.
   2.1 Check condition of pallet and packaging for integrity of outer packaging material.
   2.2 Check outside of goods on the pallets for general cleanliness.
   2.3 Check that the overall labelling of the pallets matches the packing list.
   2.4 Count, categorize and record the number of defects.
3. Count the total number of transport packs on the number of pallets present and verify the total against the packing list.
4. From the number of pallets work out the number of transport packs to be sampled using the ISO table.
   4.1 Check condition of boxes for integrity of packaging material.
   4.2 Check for cleanliness of boxes.
   4.3 Check the labelling of the boxes for damage.
   4.4 Check the boxes for overall damage.
   4.5 Check the labels for spelling mistakes.
   4.6 Check the labels for manufacturing and expiry dates.
   4.7 Count, categorize and record the number of defects.
5. From the number of boxes selected work out the number of unit packs to be examined visually using the ISO table.
   5.1 Check condition of the containers for integrity of packaging material.
   5.2 Check for cleanliness of containers.
   5.3 Check condition of containers for shape and colour.
   5.4 Check the labelling of containers for damage.
   5.5 Check the containers for overall damage.
   5.6 Check the labels for spelling mistakes.

5.7 Check the labels for manufacturing and expiry dates.
5.8 Count, categorize and record the number of defects.

6. From the number of containers selected, determine the number of containers to be taken for physical and chemical testing and for retention.
7. Check the supplier certificate against the specifications, if applicable.

Appendix 4
Examples of types of containers used to store samples of starting materials and bulk products

Figure 1. Bag for storage of samples

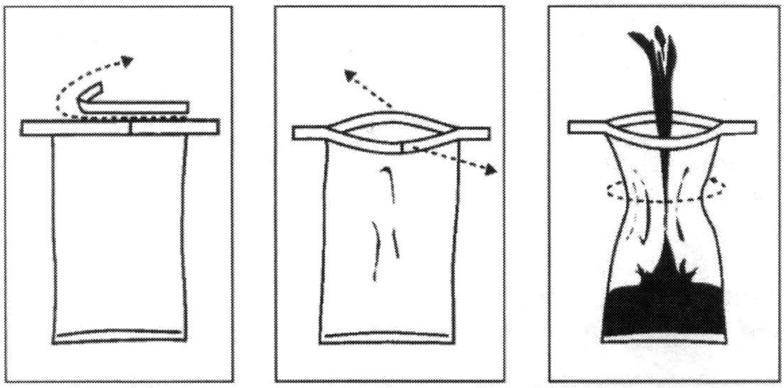

Tear off perforated top.

To avoid contamination to the interior, open bag by spreading pull-tabs apart.

Pour sample into bag (either liquid or solid).

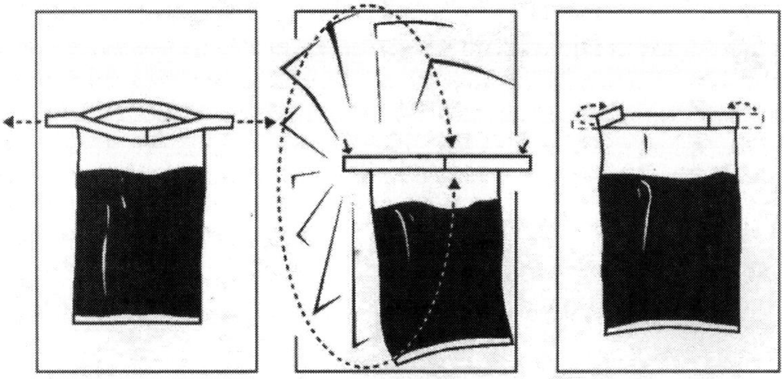

Grab both pull-tabs of the plastic band to close bag.

Twirl the bag 3 or 4 times around the plastic band.

Fold both pull-tabs toward each other, to provide an airtight and leak-proof closure.

Figure 2. Screw-top containers

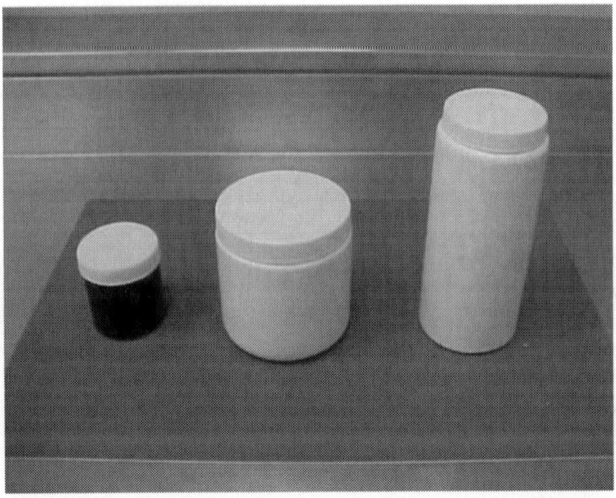

Appendix 5
Examples of use of sampling plans *n*, *p* and *r*

Consider a consignment of 40 containers of a starting material.

n Plan

Assuming a uniform material from a recognized source where there is a high degree of confidence in the source

Using the *n* plan, samples would be taken from seven containers selected at random. The appearance and identity of each of these seven samples is checked. If the results are concordant, the seven samples are combined to produce a single, composite sample from which an analytical sample is prepared for full testing.

p Plan

Assuming a uniform material from a recognized source with the main purpose of checking the identity

Using the *p* plan, samples would be taken from each container. The appearance and identity of each of these samples is checked. If the results are concordant, the samples are appropriately combined to form three final, composite samples to be used for retention (or full testing if required).

r Plan

Assuming the material is non-uniform and/or from a source that is not well-known

Using the *r* plan, samples would be taken from each container. The appearance and identity of each of these samples is checked. If the results are concordant, 10 samples are selected at random and individually subjected to full testing.

Index

Page numbers in **bold** type refer to main discussions; those in *italics* refer to figures or tables.

acceptance criteria
  cleaning validation **127–128**
  definition 61
  HVAC systems 96, *97*
accuracy, analytical methods 131
action limits
  cleanliness of clean areas 219
  definition 61
active ingredients, herbal medicines 256–257, 273–274, 275
active pharmaceutical ingredients **188–196**
  definition 10
  documentation 191–192
  equipment 190–191
  investigational products 247
  packaging 194–196
  personnel 189–190
  premises 190
  production 193–194
  retention of records/reference samples 192–193
  sanitation 191
  sterile 194
adverse drug reactions/events
  herbal medicines 259, 260
  reports 294, 295
air-breathing systems, protective garments 87
air-cleanliness levels 69, *71*, 218–219
air-conditioning
  systems *see* heating, ventilation and air-conditioning (HVAC) systems
  units, central *see* air-handling units
air diffusers
  induction 73, *73*
  non-induction 73, *74*
air filters
  classification 71, *71*
  dust exhaust systems 88
  high-efficiency particulate *see* high-efficiency particulate air (HEPA) filters
  leakage tests *99*
  test standards *72*
air filtration 33, **69–73**
air-handling systems 89–94
  for biological products 237
  clean areas 91, *92*, 230
  for excipients 208
  full fresh-air systems *93*, 93–94, *94*
  low humidity suite *90*, 90–91
  radioactive areas 279
  with return/recirculated air 91–92, *92*
  sterile products 218–219
  see also heating, ventilation and air-conditioning (HVAC) systems
air-handling units (AHU)
  definition 61
  example systems *90*, *92*, *93*, *94*
air pressure differentials
  biological product processing 236–237
  concept 81–84
  sterile product manufacture 230
  testing *98*, *117*
airborne particulate classification systems *218*, 218–219, *219*
airflow
  unidirectional *see* unidirectional airflow
  visualization tests *99*
  volume and velocity readings *98*, *117*
airlocks 82, 230
  bubble 82, *84*
  cascade 82, *83*

changing rooms as 229
definitions 11, 61
pressure cascade systems 82
sink 82, *83*
alert limits
cleanliness of clean areas 219
definition 61
allergens (sensitizing materials) 4, 32, 232
analysis
contract *see* contract production and analysis
suspected counterfeit products 321
analysts
proficiency 130
role in pre-approval inspections 287, 290
analytical methods
characteristics 131–133
for cleaning validation **127**, 203
herbal medicines 258
method validation/verification *see* method validation/verification
non-pharmacopoeial 130
pharmacopoeial 130
pre-approval inspections 290
validation **129–133**, *133*
ancillary areas 31
animal tissues, processing 227–228, 235
animals
care staff 234, 237
quarters and care 31, **237**
antibiotics 32, 190, 346
antigens 4, 232
appeals procedures, GMP inspectorate **335–336**
applications, new drug *see* new drug applications
as-built (condition)
definition 61
HVAC systems 66, *67*
asbestos-containing filters 227
aseptic areas (grade A and B clean areas) 218
clothing 228
personnel 227, 233–234
premises 229, 235
for radiopharmaceuticals 278
for sterile products 220
see also clean areas
aseptic processing *see* sterile pharmaceutical products, aseptic preparation
at-rest (condition)
clean areas 218, 219
definition 61
HVAC systems 66, *67*, 90
audits 292
internal *see* internal audits
quality *see* quality audits
water systems 185–186
authorization holders, list 335
authorized person 26
contractual requirements 22
definitions 11, 323
product recalls 20, 21
role and functions 3, 16, 27–28
autoclaves 224, 279
automated process controls and processing equipment 199

Bacillus anthracis 236
back-ups, computer 136
balances 34
batch(es)
definitions 11, 306, 361
mixing, herbal medicines 269
packaging materials 36
pre-approval 286
process validation 167
recovered, reprocessed and reworked materials 37
release 28, 48, 53
starting materials 35
batch numbers
allocation procedures 47
definitions 11, 307
starting materials 36
batch placebo sampling method 126–127
batch records (documentation) **44–46**
active pharmaceutical ingredients **192**
biological products **239–240**
computerized 41, 192, 206–207
definition 11
excipients **205–207**
investigational products **250**
packaging 45–46
processing 44–45
radiopharmaceuticals **282**
review 56–57
BCG vaccines 234
"biobatch" production 198
bioburden control
before sterilization 222, 223
through cleaning 125

water systems **180**, **182–183**
see also microbiological contamination
bioequivalence 198
biological indicators 223, 226
biological products 4, **232–242**
animal quarters and care 237
in-process controls 241
labelling 238–239
lot processing and distribution records 239–240
personnel 233–234
premises and equipment 235–237
production 32, 238
quality assurance/quality control 240–241
biological tissues, extraction of substances 232
blending/mixing
definition 257
herbal materials 267, **269**
in-process **208–209**
blinding operations, investigational products 250, **252**
blood or plasma derivatives 4, 232, 236, 279
British Standards Institution
BS 5750 standard 292
BS 6001-1 standard 375
building automation system (BAS) 88
building management system (BMS) 88
buildings *see* premises
bulk drug substances *see* active pharmaceutical ingredients
bulk products 37
definition 11
liquid, sampling **382–383**
quality control 54
sampling 364, **371**
specifications 42

calibration **108**
definitions 11, 103
measuring and test equipment 214, 280
campaign manufacture 32, 50
biological products 236
herbal medicines 262–263
investigational products 247
ceilings 32, 229
cell banks, storage 236
cell cultures 232, 233
certificates
of analysis, starting materials 55–56, 241, 283
of destruction 254
of good manufacturing practices **343–345**
Certification Scheme on the Quality of Pharmaceutical Products Moving in International Commerce (WHO Certification Scheme) 2, 5, 9, 10, 292
change control **112–113**, **169–170**
computerized systems 135
definition 61
excipients **207**
HVAC systems 96
changes
inspection after 296–297
qualification and validation 19
requalification after 165
revalidation after 112, 169–170
changing rooms 228, 229
checklist, inspection 296, **315–319**
chemicals, hazardous 357
chromatography
equipment 238, 280
herbal materials 258, 271, 272
clean areas (rooms) **65–69**
air change rates 66, 218
air filtration 69–73
airborne particulate classification systems *218*, 218–219, *219*
aseptic processing 220
classification *69*, 217–219
protective clothing 228–229
tests 66–68, *67–68*
definitions 12, 62
equipment **230–231**
herbal medicines 268
HVAC systems *90*, 91, *92*, *98–99*, 230
microbiological contamination limits 217, *217*
personnel **227–229**, 233–234
premises **229–230**, 235–237
processing procedures 221–222
for radiopharmaceuticals 278
sanitation 216–217
shell-like containment control concept *69*
standards 62
sterile product manufacture 215–216, **217–219**
terminally sterilized products 220
clean-up (recovery)
testing *99*
times 98–99, 117

cleaning
  "bracketing" approach 123–124
  containers, before filling 50
  detergents 124–125
  equipment 34, 124, **202–203**, 263
  herbal materials 268–269
  limits, residual materials 203
  microbiology 125
  personnel 124
  of premises 30, 32
  sampling tools and implements 366–367
  written procedures 48
cleaning validation **120–128**, 202–203
  analytical methods 127, 203
  definition 103
  establishing acceptable methods 127–128
  protocols 122–124
  reports 124
  sampling 125–127, 203
cleanliness *see* hygiene; personal hygiene; sanitation
clinical trials 4
  definition **244**
  dosage forms 243
  investigational products for *see* investigational products
  Phases I–IV 244
clinics, inspection 313, 319
closed systems 198, 201
Clostridium botulinum 236
Clostridium tetani 236
clothing
  changing facilities 31, 228, 229
  clean areas 228–229
  disposable 229
  laundering or cleaning 229
  outdoor 228
  protective *see* protective clothing
coding systems, investigational products **250**
cold storage facilities, inspection 316
commingling, definition 200
commissioning
  definitions 62, 103
  HVAC systems **94–95**, 113–114
  water systems 118, 183
company documents 295
complaints 18, **19–20**
  active pharmaceutical ingredients 196
  drug distribution chain 317
  against GMP inspectorate **337**
  herbal medicines **259–260**
  inspection after 294, 295
  investigational products **246**
  records 20
  site master file 303
computer validation, definition 103
computerized systems
  back-ups 136
  batch records 41, 192, 206–207
  data recording 40–41
  functional specification 135
  hardware and software validation 136–138, *137*
  identification 138–139
  security 136
  system specification 134–135
  validation **133–139**, *137*
concurrent validation 106, 166, **168**
  definition 104
Conference of Experts on the Rational Use of Drugs, Nairobi (1985) 1
confidentiality, inspection activities **334–335**
consignment, definition 12, 361
constituents with known therapeutic activity, definition 257
consultant staff 29
containers
  cleaning before filling 50
  damaged 35, 373, 384
  excipients 204, 206
  labelling *see* labelling
  sample 368, *386–387*
  starting materials 35, 36
  sterile products 231
  water storage 180–181
containment
  definition 62
  displacement concept 80–81
  leakage tests *99*
  physical barrier concept 84
  pressure differential concept 81–84
  shell-like control concept *69*
contamination
  acceptable limits **127–128**
  definitions 12, 62
  GMP guidance 29–30, 34, 39, **49–50**
  HVAC systems 68, *70*, 73
  infiltration **76–80**
  sources 120–121
  water storage vessels 181

see also cross-contamination; microbiological contamination; residues
continuous culture 241
contract 22–23
  acceptor 22
  analysis 22–23
  giver 21–22
  manufacture 22
  staff 29
contract production and analysis **21–23**
  herbal medicines **260**
  site master file 303
control, definitions 348
control measures
  definition 348
  monitoring 354
controlled drugs
  definition 307
  diversion 317
  inspection of distribution chain 313, 316, 317, 318, 319
conveyor belt, in clean area 230
corrective actions **355**
  definition 348
corrosion resistance, water systems 179
cosmetics 228
counterfeit products 1, 5
  complaints 20
  definition 307
  inspection **320–321**
critical control points (CCP) **353–355**
  definition 348
  determination 353–354
  establishing corrective actions 355
  establishing critical limits 353
  monitoring 353
critical limits
  definition 348
  establishing 353
critical parameters/components/ operations 347
  definitions 12, 62
  HVAC systems 96, 114–115
  qualification 139
  validation 166–167
cross-contamination 17
  biological products 236
  definitions 12, 62
  displacement concept 80–81
  excipients **208**
  GMP guidance 30, 32, 33, **49–50**
  HVAC systems 68, *70*, **80–84**
  investigational products 247
  multiple-use equipment 202–203
  physical barrier concept 84
  pressure differential concept 81–84
  radiopharmaceuticals 279
  see also contamination
culture, continuous 241
culture media 38, 238
  sterilization 238
customers, sampling operations 365
customs, sampling operations 365
cytokines 4, 232
cytostatic substances 190
cytotoxic substances 32, 346

data
  checks 135
  electronic recording 40–41, 192
  security 136
defective products 19–20, 196
dehumidification 85, *90*, 90–91
delivery
  definition 12
  excipients 212
design condition
  definition 62
  HVAC systems 96–97, *97*
design qualification (DQ) 19, 110, **141**
  definitions 62, 104
  HVAC systems 115–116
destruction, unused investigational products **253–254**
detection limit, analytical methods 132
detergents 124–125, 217
developing countries, quality assurance needs 1
deviation, definition 348
diagnostic agents for *in vitro* use 4, 232
dip tubes 377, *378*
direct impact system, definition 63
disinfectants 217
dispatch
  areas 31
  see also shipping/dispatch
dispensing
  of drugs, inspection 318–319
  of starting materials 36
displacement concept, prevention of cross-contamination 80–81

distillation 178
distribution
  channels 5
    inspection 5, **303–322**
  establishments, inspection 313, **315–319**
  records 48
    biological products **239–240**
    radiopharmaceuticals **282**
    recalled products 21
  site master file 303
documentation 18, **39–48**
  active pharmaceutical ingredients **191–192**
  biological products 239–240
  on company to be inspected 295
  excipients **205–207**
  GMP inspectorate **328–329**
  HACCP system **356**
  herbal medicines **264–267**
  inspection 296, 316–317
  investigational products **248–250**
  radiopharmaceuticals 282
  required **41–48**
  in site master file 302
dosage forms
  investigational products 243
  new 289
  sample sizes, pre-approval inspections 289
  sampling procedure 371
  solid *see* solid dosage forms
double-tube spears 380, *381*
DQ *see* design qualification
drainage 33
  see also sinks and drains
driers, chemical air 86, *90*, 90–91
drinking-water **173**
  in excipient manufacture 211
  monitoring of quality 176
  production **176–177**
drug distribution *see* distribution
drug inspectors *see* inspectors
drug master file, definition 200
drug regulatory authorities *see* regulatory authorities
drugs
  classification 306
  definition 307
  new *see* new drugs
  side-effects and toxicity 306
  see also pharmaceutical products
drying
  chemical air 86, *90*, 90–91
  equipment 34
  herbal materials 267
dust
  collectors 88–89
  control 30, 49, **86–88**
  in exhaust air 88–89
  extraction systems 82–84, 86–88
  filters 88
  herbal materials 263
  particle count test *98*, *117*
  prevention of cross-contamination 80
  unidirectional airflow systems 73–76, *78–79*, 86–87

eating and drinking 29, 191
education *see* training
effluents
  HVAC systems 89
  infectious or potentially infectious 235, 237
  radioactive 278
  see also sinks and drains; waste materials
electronic data-processing systems 40–41, 192
  see also computerized systems
endotoxins, monitoring 211, 216, 221
energy-recovery wheels 94, *94*
environment
  excipient manufacture 210–211
  protection **88–89**
enzymes 4, 88, 232
equipment (and instruments) **33–34**
  active pharmaceutical ingredients **190–191**
  automated 199
  biological products **235–237**
  calibration 51, **108**, 214, 280
  clean areas **230–231**
  cleaning 34, 124, **202–203**, 263
  component failures 357
  defective 50, 191
  excipients **202–203**
  herbal medicines **263**
  investigational products 247
  labels 41
  multiple use 190, 202–203
  new 289
  qualification *see* qualification
  radiopharmaceuticals **278–279**, 280

records 48
servicing/maintenance 51, 207, 231
site master file 302
standard operating procedures 46
verification **108**
errors, human and organizational 358
escorts, for inspectors 295, 297
ethylene oxide 225–226
eukaryotic cells, growth 232
European Pharmacopoeia, water quality specifications 174, 178
European Standard EN 45012 323
examples
certificate of good manufacturing practice 343–345
inspection report 6
installation qualification protocol and report 142–146
operational qualification protocol and report 148–156
performance qualification protocol 157–164
sample collection form 381–382
sample receipt form 321–322
excipients **196–214**
change control 207
definition 200
delivery 212
documentation 205–207
equipment 202–203
expiry dates 214
glossary 200
good production practices 208–212
ISO 900 series certification 199
materials 203–205
microbial contamination 209–211
packaging operations 211–212
process validation 207
processing steps 199
quality control 212–214
responsibilities of manufacturers 198–200
returned 204–205
safe handling 200
self-inspection and quality audits 201–202
specifications 206
stability studies 213–214
sterile 209–211
storage 205
exhaust air, dust in 88–89
Expert Committees
Biological Standardization 4, 233
Specifications for Pharmaceutical Preparations 1–3, 4, 5–6, 9, 323
expired drugs, in distribution chain 317
expiry dates 57
active pharmaceutical ingredients 195
excipients 214
herbal medicines 272
starting materials 36
see also stability testing
explosions 357
exporters, inspection 310, 311, 318

face masks 228–229
facilities
definition 63
new 288, 289, 311
failures, common **357–358**
fans, air 90
fermentation
herbal medicines 268
products 4, 233
quality control 241
vessels 237
fibres, shedding 221, 227, 228, 229
filtration
air *see* air filtration
sterilization by **226–227**
finished products 37
definitions 12, 307
herbal medicines 257, 266
labels 41
premises for manufacture 30
quality control 54, 56, 57
retention of samples 56–57
sampling plans **375**
sampling procedure 367, **371–372**, **385–386**
specifications 42–43
sterile **231**
fires 357
floors 32
flow diagram 349, 352
follow-up inspection 294, 312
footwear 228
freeze drying 280
fume removal 89
fumigating agents 39
for sterilization **225–226**
fumigation, herbal materials 263, 267

gases, for sterilization **225–226**
GCP *see* good clinical practice
genetically modified organisms 265
GEP *see* good engineering practice
Germany, legal status of investigational products 242
glossaries
distribution channel inspection **306–309**
excipients **200**
GMP **10–15**
HACCP methodology **348–349**
herbal medicines **256–258**
HVAC systems **61–65**
inspection **306–309**
investigational products **243–246**
pre-approval inspections **285–286**
quality systems for inspectorates **323–324**
sampling operations **360–363**
validation **103–106**
gloves 228–229
see also protective clothing
GLP *see* good laboratory practice
GMP *see* good manufacturing practice
good agriculture and collection practices (GACP) 268
good clinical practice (GCP) 16, 243, 348
good engineering practice (GEP)
definitions 63, 104
HVAC systems 96
good laboratory practice (GLP) 16, 348
good manufacturing practice (GMP) **17–18**
active pharmaceutical ingredients **188–196**
compliance 23, 189, 285, 293, 298
definitions 17, 307
and HACCP 348
inspectorate *see* inspectorate
model certificate **343–345**
national and regional guidelines 2
non-compliance 204, 291, 298
record keeping 18
starting materials **188–214**
web page 9
WHO guidelines 2–4
good pharmacy practice, definition 307
government organizations, sampling operations 365
HACCP *see* hazard analysis and critical control point
hair, covering 29, 228
hand washing 29, 230
hardware, computer, validation 136–138, *137*
hazard (and risk) analysis 10, **346–358**
definition 349
procedure 352–353
hazard analysis and critical control point (HACCP) methodology 6, **346–352**
application 350–356
definitions 348–349
documentation and record keeping 356
guidelines for application 350
links with other programmes 348
principles 349–350
training and education 350–351
verification procedures 355–356
hazard analysis and critical control point (HACCP) plan 349, 350
hazard analysis and critical control point (HACCP) team 351
hazards
definition 349
examples 346–347, **357**
see also safety
headgear 228
heads of production and quality control 25, 26–27
health and safety *see* safety
health checks/health status, personnel 228, 234, 277
heat exchangers, water systems 182
heat sterilization **223–224**
heating, ventilation and air-conditioning (HVAC) systems **58–101**, *60*
air filtration 69–73
biological products 235, 236–237
clean areas *90*, 91, *92*, 230
commissioning 94–95, 113–114
cross-contamination 80–84
dust control 86–88
glossary 61–65
infiltration 76–80
maintenance 99–100
operating ranges 96, *97*, 115–116, *116*
production areas 33, 49
protection of environment **88–89**
protection of product and personnel **65–86**
qualification 95–99, **113–118**

quality control laboratories 33
radiopharmaceuticals 278–279
scope of guideline 59–60
systems and components 89–94
temperature and relative humidity 85–86
unidirectional airflow 73–76
validation **113–118**
HEPA filters *see* high-efficiency particulate air (HEPA) filters
hepatitis B vaccination 234
herbal materials 256
definition 257
handling 268–269
sampling 270, 375
specifications 264–266
herbal medicines 4, **254–275**
complaints 259–260
contract production and analysis 260
definition 257
documentation 264–267
equipment 263
glossary 256–258
GMP 258
materials 263–264
personnel 261
premises 261–263
product recalls 260
production 267–269
qualification and validation 259
quality assurance 258
quality control 270–275
sanitation and hygiene 258–259
self-inspection 260
herbal preparations 256
definition 257
specifications 266
herbal products
definition 257
finished 266
mixture, definition 257
herbicides 32, 208
herbs, definition 257
high-efficiency particulate air (HEPA) filters 89–90
air-handling systems 91–92, *92*, *93*, *94*
dust exhaust systems 88
see also air filters
highly purified water (HPW) **174**
applications 174
production **178**
systems *see* water systems for pharmaceutical use
homogeneity, definition 361
hormones 4, 32, 76, 190, 232, 346
hospital pharmacies, inspection 311, 318–319
hospital radiopharmacies 276, 277
hospitals
inspection 313
sample collection 364–365
humidity, relative 59, **85–86**
definition 64
HVAC systems *see* heating, ventilation and air-conditioning systems
hybridoma techniques 232
hydrogen peroxide vapour 225
hygiene **18**
herbal medicines **258–259**
see also personal hygiene; sanitation

identity tests
excipients 206
herbal materials 265, 270–271
sampling plan 374
starting materials 55, 212
immune sera 4, 232
immunoglobulins 4, 232
importers, inspection 310, 311, 318
impurities *see* contamination; cross-contamination
"in operation" condition *see* operational condition
in-process blending/mixing **208–209**
in-process controls 49
biological products 241
definition 12
excipients 212
records 56
vs validation 107
indirect impact system, definition 63
infiltration **76–80**
definition 63
injectable products
quality control 216
water for 175
see also parenteral products
injections
sample sizes, pre-approval inspections 289
water for *see* water for injections
INNs 10
insecticides 39, 208
inserts, package, inspection 318

inspection 4–6, **285–345**
announced 295, 312
comprehensive 311
concise 293, 312
conduct 295–297
of counterfeit, spurious or substandard products **320–321**
drug distribution channels 5, **303–322**
drug distribution establishments **313**, **315–319**
by external body or person 327, 328, 332, 333
facilities required 332–333
follow-up 294, 312, 332
frequency and duration 294–295, 312, 331
glossary 306–309
investigative 312
methods 311–312
of pharmaceutical manufacturers **291–299**
pre-approval *see* pre-approval inspections
premises 316
preparing for 295
procedures **330–332**
process **293–299**
quality systems 5–6, **322–338**
regulatory actions after unsatisfactory 299
routine 293, 311
sampling procedures 297, **319–320**, 364–365, **369**
special 294, 312
team, composition 201, 287, 328
unannounced 295, 312
water systems **185–186**
see also self-inspection
inspection reports 298, 309, 329
confidentiality 330, 332–333
guidance on **339–343**
minimum content 331–332
model lay-out 6, **300–303**
inspectorate 292
administrative structure **324–325**
appeals procedures **335–336**
complaints procedures **337**
confidentiality of information **334–335**
documentation **328–329**
impartiality 324–325
internal audit and periodic review **336–337**
organizational structure **310–311**, **326–327**
personnel **327–328**
see also inspectors
publications **335**
quality systems requirements **322–338**
recalls and withdrawals procedures **337**
records **329–330**
role and functions 306
terms of reference **325**
inspectors **309–312**, 327–328
access to premises, documents, or information 297
checklist for 296, **315–319**
chief/lead 331
cooperation with other agencies 311
employee records 332–333
escorts 295, 297
evaluation 336
numbers 295
qualifications 292, 309–310, 328
reference/information sources 312
role **292–293**
training 10, 292–293, 327, 328
installation qualification (IQ) 19, 107–108, 110, **141**
definitions 63, 104
protocol and report format 142–146
instruments *see* equipment
intermediate products 37
active pharmaceutical ingredients 193
definition 12
quality control 54, 57
sampling **371**
specifications 42
internal audits
GMP inspectorate **336–337**
manufacturing facilities 292, 295
see also self-inspection
International Atomic Energy Agency (IAEA) 4
international border posts 310
International Conference on Primary Health Care, Alma-Ata (1978) 1
International Nonproprietary Names (INNs) 10
International Organization for Standardization (ISO)
2859 standard 375, 385
9000 series standards 5–6, 199, 292, 323
14644-1 standard 62, 90

International Pharmacopoeia 1, 2, 9
  water quality specifications 174
investigational products 4, **242–254**
  complaints 246
  definition 245
  documentation 248–250
  glossary 243–246
  inspections 288
  materials 247–248
  personnel 247
  premises and equipment 247
  production 251–252
  quality assurance 246
  quality control 252–253
  recalls 247
  shipping, returns and destruction 253–254
  validation 246
investigator, definition 245
IQ *see* installation qualification
irradiation, sterilization by 225
ISO *see* International Organization for Standardization

jewellery 228

kits, radiopharmaceutical preparation 276, 280, 281–282

labelling **41**
  active pharmaceutical ingredients 194
  biological products **238–239**
  dispensed drugs 318
  herbal medicines **272–275**
  inspection 318
  investigational products **250**, **252**
  operations, good practice 51–52
  during processing 49
  radiopharmaceuticals 279, **280–282**
  reagents 38
  reference standards 39, 41
  samples 367
  standard operating procedures 46
  starting materials 35, 36
  see also packaging
laboratories
  equipment and instruments 34
  pre-approval inspections 289, 290
  quality control *see* quality control laboratories
laminar airflow systems 218
large-volume parenterals, definition 12
laundry facilities 229
leaching, prevention of 179
licence
  applications *see* new drug applications
  manufacturing *see* manufacturing authorization
  product, definition 13
  see also marketing authorizations
licensing
  drug distribution establishments 315
  manufacturing facilities 292
light fittings 32
lighting 33, 235, 278
linearity, analyte concentrations 132
liquids
  sample containers 368
  sampling 366, 367, **382–383**
  sampling tools 377
lot *see* batch

maintenance
  equipment 51, 207, 230–231
  HVAC systems **99–100**
  personnel, training 227
  premises 30, 32
  water systems 185
  workshops 31
manufacture
  contract 22
  definitions 13, 286
  see also good manufacturing practice; processing; production
manufacturers
  definitions 13, 286
  excipient 198–200
  inspection **291–299**, 310
  licensed 10
  new, pre-approval inspections 287, 289
  responsibility 17
  sampling operations 365
  site master file 301–303
  of starting materials 35
manufacturing authorization (licence) 292, 295
  pre-approval inspection 287
  suspension/revocation 299
markers, definition 257–258
marketing authorizations 295
  applications *see* new drug applications
  definition 13
  holders 304
  publication 335
  suspension/revocation 299
masks, face 228–229

master file
  drug, definition 200
  site **301–303**
master formulae
  active pharmaceutical ingredients **191**
  definition 13
  documentation 43
  investigational products **249**
master record, definition 13
materials **34–39**
  in contact with water systems 180
  excipients **203–205**
  herbal medicines **263–264**
  investigational products **247–248**
  see also packaging materials; starting materials
maternity homes, inspection 319
measuring and test equipment 34
  calibration 214, 280
medicinal plant materials *see* herbal materials
medicinal plants
  definition 258
  production 267–268
  reference samples 264
  see also herbal medicines
method validation/verification 130
  definition 286
  reports 290
microbiological contamination
  excipients **209–211**
  herbal materials 268
  limits, clean areas 217, *217*
  sterile products 220, 223
  water systems 177, 180, 182–183
  see also bioburden control
microbiology, cleaning 125
microorganisms
  airborne dissemination 235
  filtration 222, **226–227**
  growth or propagation 232
  live 32, 221, 236
  processing 227–228, 235
  spore-forming 236
mixing *see* blending/mixing
model examples *see* examples
model product
  approach to stability assessment 213
  definition 200
monitor, definitions 245, 349
monkeys 237
monoclonal antibodies 232, 276
mother liquor
  definition 200
  reuse 209
multi-use areas 208
multiple use equipment 190, 202–203

national inspectorate *see* inspectorate
natural forces 358
new chemical entities 287
new drug applications
  definition 286
  pre-approval inspections 286–291
  refusal 290–291
new drugs 287
  production in existing facility 289
  see also clinical trials; investigational products
new facilities 288, 289, 311
no-impact system, definition 63
non-critical parameters/components
  definition 63
  HVAC systems 96, 114–115
normal operating range, definition 63
nuclear centres and institutes 276, 277
nursing homes, inspection 319

oligonucleotides 276–277
operating conditions, deviations from normal 358
operating limits, definition 63
operating range
  definition 64
  HVAC systems 96, *97*
operational ("in operation") condition
  clean areas 218, 219
  definition 64
  HVAC systems 66–68, *68*
operational qualification (OQ) 19, 107–108, 110, **146–147**
  definitions 64, 104
  protocol and report format 148–156
oral solid dosage (OSD), definition 64
order
  definition 245
  investigational products **248**
"other" ingredients, herbal medicines 275
over-the-counter drugs 306
  definition 308
  inspection of distribution chain 315, 317

package inserts, inspection 318
packaging
  active pharmaceutical ingredients **194–196**
  batch records 45–46
  definition 13
  excipients 211–212
  GMP **51–52**
  instructions 43–44
  investigational products **249–250**, **252**
  premises 33
  see also containers; labelling
packaging materials 36–37
  definition 13
  herbal medicines **272–275**
  quality control tests 55–56
  sampling **372**, **375**, **384–385**
  specifications 42
  storage 31
parallel markets *see* unauthorized markets
parenteral products
  excipients 210–211
  inspection of finished 231
  large-volume, definition 12
  water for injections 175
  see also injectable products
particle count test *98*, *117*
particulate classification systems, airborne *218*, 218–219, *219*
performance qualification (PQ) 19, 108, 111, **157**
  definitions 64, 104
  protocol format 157–164
  water systems 119–120, 183–184
personal hygiene **29–30**, 228, 233–234
  herbal medicines **261**
  see also hygiene
personnel **25–28**
  active pharmaceutical ingredients **189–190**
  biological products **233–234**
  in clean areas **227–229**, 233–234
  expertise and experience 26, 277
  health checks/health status 228, 234, 277
  herbal medicines **261**
  human and organizational errors 358
  inspection **327–328**
  investigational products **247**
  key 25–28
  personal hygiene 29–30, 261
  in pharmacies 317
  protection role of HVAC systems **65–86**
  qualifications and education 26
  radiopharmaceuticals **277–278**
  responsible for cleaning 124
  responsible for validation 106
  safety *see* safety
  site master file 301–302
  training *see* training
  unauthorized/untrained 25, 29, 49
  vaccination 234
  validation and qualification **113**
pest control 30, 262
pesticides 32, 208, 265
pharmaceutical excipients *see* excipients
Pharmaceutical Inspection Convention (PIC) 323
pharmaceutical inspectors *see* inspectors
pharmaceutical products
  counterfeit/spurious/substandard **320–321**
  definitions 13, 245, 307, 361
  licensed 10
  protection role of HVAC systems **65–86**
  sampling *see* sampling
  see also drugs
pharmaceuticals
  definition 349
  see also drugs
pharmacies
  hospital 310, 318–319
  inspection 313, 315, 317, 318–319
  retail 305, 316, 317, 318–319
  sample collection 364–365
  wholesale 317
pharmacists
  definition 308
  as inspectors 309
  registered/licensed 315, 317
pharmacopoeias
  analytical methods 130
  water quality specifications 173, 174, 178
pharmacy-only drugs 306
  definition 308
  inspection of distribution chain 315, 317
photographs, inspection visits 297
physical barrier concept, prevention of cross-contamination 84

pipework 32, 34, 51
clean areas 229, 237
radioactive materials 279
water distribution **181–183**
plant materials *see* herbal materials
plasma derivatives *see* blood or plasma derivatives
point extraction, definition 64
poisons
definition 308
manufacture 32
storage facilities 316, 319
police, sampling operations 365
ports, inspection 310, 311, 313
positive (air) pressure areas 76, 230, 236–237, 279
positron emission tomography (PET) centres 276, 277
post-marketing surveillance 244
powders
sampling 366, 367, 378–380, **383–384**
see also dust
PQ *see* performance qualification
pre-approval batches 286, 289
definition 286
pre-approval inspections **285–291**
carrying out 288–289
follow-up regulatory/administrative decisions 290–291
glossary 285–286
objectives 286
preparation for 287–288
priorities 287
sample collection and testing 289–290
precision 131
intermediate 131
premises
active pharmaceutical ingredients **190**
ancillary areas 31
animal quarters 237
biological products **235–237**
GMP **30–33**
herbal medicines **261–263**
inspection 316
investigational products **247**
labels 41
production areas 32–33
quality control areas 33
radiopharmaceuticals **278–279**
site master file 302
sterile products **229–230**
storage areas 31–32
weighing areas 32
prequalification, definition 361 362
prescription-only drugs 306
definition 308
inspection of distribution chain 315, 316, 317, 318–319
pressure cascades 80, *82*, 82–84
definition 64
see also airlocks
pressure differentials, air *see* air pressure differentials
process validation 19
definition 104
excipients **207**
non-sterile products **165–170**
processing
active pharmaceutical ingredients 193
GMP **50–51**
sterile products **221–222**
processing instructions
herbal medicines **266–267**
investigational products **249**
processing records 44–45
investigational products 250
radiopharmaceuticals 282
see also batch records
product licence, definition 13
product recalls *see* recalls
product specification file(s)
definition 245
investigational products **248–249**
production
active pharmaceutical ingredients **193–194**
biological products **238**
contract *see* contract production and analysis
definitions 14, 362
equipment 34
excipients **208–212**
GMP **48–52**
head of 25, 26–27
herbal medicines **267–269**
investigational products **251–252**
radiopharmaceuticals **280**
site master file 303
production areas 32–33
herbal medicines **262–263**
restriction of access 49
prohibited drugs 306
definition 308
promotional activities, inspection 317
prospective validation 106, **166–168**
definition 104

protection
  environment **88–89**
  levels 69, *71*
  product and personnel **65–86**
protective clothing 29, 191
  clean areas 228–229
  in drug distribution chain 317
  herbal medicines 261
  sampling operations 366
  totally enclosed 87, *87*
protocol, definition 245
pumps, water circulation 182
purified water (PW) **173–174**
  in excipient manufacture 211
  production **177–178**
  systems *see* water systems for pharmaceutical use

qualification (of systems and equipment) 18–19, 107–108, **139–165**
  computerized systems 136, 137–138
  definitions 14, 64, 104
  documentation 141
  herbal medicines **259**
  HVAC systems **95–99**, **113–118**
  "in-use" systems and equipment 165
  personnel 113
  protocols 109
  relationship with validation *95*, 106, *115*
  reports 109–110
  stages 110–111, *140*
  water systems **118–120**, **183–184**
  see also requalification; validation; *specific types of qualification*
quality assurance **16–17**
  biological products **240–241**
  definitions 15, 309
  herbal medicines **258**
  investigational products **246**
  radiopharmaceuticals **282–284**
  system *see* quality system
quality audits **24–25**
  active pharmaceutical ingredients 195
  definition 323–324
  excipients **201–202**
quality control
  active pharmaceutical ingredients **194–195**
  biological products **240–241**
  definition 309
  equipment, calibration 214
  excipients **212–214**
  good practices **52–57**
  head of 25, 26, 27
  herbal medicines **270–275**
  intermediate, bulk and finished products 54
  investigational products **252–253**
  radiopharmaceuticals **282–284**
  records 213
  site master file 303
  starting materials 54
  sterile products **216**
  test requirements 55–56
quality control laboratories 195
  biological products 241
  design 33
  official 297, 319
  radiopharmaceuticals 283
  sampling operations 365, 369–370
quality control unit, responsibilities 194–195, 212
quality management **7–58**
  basic elements 15
  definition 15
  glossary 10–15
quality manual 324–325, **333–334**
  definition 324
quality policy
  definition 15
  excipient manufacture 199–200
  inspectorate 326
quality system 5–6
  definitions 15, 324
  glossary 323–324
  inspectorates 5–6, **322–338**
  review 294, **336–337**
quantitation limit, analytical methods 132
quarantine
  definition 14
  finished products 37
  materials 35
  standard operating procedures 46
  storage areas 31

radiation
  dosimeters 225
  safety procedures 277, 278
  sterilization by **225**
radioactivity
  labelling requirements 281
  measuring equipment 280
radiopharmaceuticals 4, **276–284**
  labelling 279, 280–282
  personnel 277–278

premises and equipment 278–279
production 280
production and distribution records 282
quality assurance/quality control 282–284
radiopharmacies 276, 277
randomization systems, investigational products **250**
range, analyte concentrations 132
rDNA techniques 232, 236
re-evaluation dating, excipients 214
reagents 38
reassessment *see* inspection, follow-up
recalled products 38
storage 31
recalls **20–21**
definition 308
drug distribution chain procedures 317
herbal medicines **260**
inspection after 294, 295
inspectorate's procedures **337**
investigational products **247**
site master file 303
receipt form, sample **321–322**
receipts, records 46
receiving areas 31
recombinant DNA (rDNA) techniques 232, 236
reconciliation, definition 14
record keeping *see* documentation
records
complaints 20
distribution *see* distribution, records
GMP inspectorate **329–330**
retention
active pharmaceutical ingredients **192–193**
biological products 240
excipients 213
inspection activities 330
see also batch records
recovered materials 37
excipients **204**
recovery
definition 14
see also clean-up
reference books, inspection 318
reference samples *see* retention samples
reference sources, for inspectors 312
reference standards **38–39**
chemical and biological **248**
herbal medicines 263–264
labels 39, 41
official 38
secondary or working 39
registration certificate, definition 13
regulatory authorities 304, 305, 306
actions after unsatisfactory inspections **299**
implementation of WHO Certification Scheme 292
inspectorate 292
licensing system 295
pre-approval inspections 287
sampling procedures **369–370**
withholding approval of applications 290–291
reinspection 294, 312, 332
rejected materials 37, 196
excipients **204**
storage 31
rejection, procedures 48
repeatability, analytical methods 131
reprocessed materials 37
reprocessing
definition 14
excipients 204
reproducibility, analytical methods 131
requalification 107, 111, 140, **165**
HVAC systems 117
resampling 125–126
residues
acceptable limits 127–128
cleaning validation 120–121, 127, 128
excipient manufacture 203, 209
retailers, pharmaceutical 310
see also pharmacies, retail
retention samples 53, 56–57, **368–369**
active pharmaceutical ingredients **192–193**
biological products 241
definition 362
excipients 213
herbal medicines 263–264
investigational products 253
pre-approval inspections 290
radiopharmaceuticals 283–284
retrospective validation 106, **169**
definition 105
returned products 38
biological products 240
in distribution chain 317
excipients **204–205**
investigational products **253**
storage 31

revalidation 107, 111, **169**
after change 112
analytical methods 130
computerized systems 135
definition 105
periodic 111–112
reworked materials 37
reworking
definition 14
excipients 204
rinse samples 126
risk analysis *see* hazard analysis
robustness, analytical methods 131
rodent and pest control 30, 262
rodenticides 39, 208
ruggedness, analytical methods 131

safety
manufacturing operations 6, 10, 346–347, 357
radiation 277, 278
sampling operations **365–366**
see also hazards
sale and supply, conditions for 317
sample thieves 378–380, *380*
samplers
definition 362
health and safety 365–366
requirements 365
samples
available, definition 360
collection *see* sampling
collection form **381–382**
combined, definition 361
definition 362
extreme, definition 363
final, definition 361
herbal medicines 263–264
labelling 367
original, definition 361
pre-approval inspections **289–290**
random, definition 362
receipt form **321–322**
representative, definition 362
retention *see* retention samples
rinse 126
storage **368–369**, *386–387*
sampling 6, **359–388**
classes/types of materials sampled 364
cleaning validation **125–127**, 203
drugs in distribution chain 318
facilities 364–365
glossary 360–363
health and safety 365–366
herbal materials 270, 375
HVAC systems 75
operation 367–368
pharmaceutical inspections 297, **319–320**, 364–365, **369**
pre-approval inspections **289–290**
precautions 367–368
preparation for 366–367
procedure, definition 363
process **366–369**
purpose 363–364
quality control 54
radiopharmaceuticals 284
on receipt (for acceptance) **370–372**
record, definition 363
regulatory issues 369–370
responsibilities 365
selected, definition 363
standard operating procedures 47, **382–386**
starting materials *see under* starting materials
sterile pharmaceutical products 216, 366
tools 366, **376–380**
unit, definition 363
water for pharmaceutical use 184
sampling methods
batch placebo 126–127
definition 362
direct surface (direct method) 126
indirect 126
sampling plans **372–375**
definition 363
examples of use 387–388
n plan **373–374**, *374*, 387
p plan **374**, *374*, 387
r plan *374*, **375**, 388
sanitation **18**
active pharmaceutical ingredients **191**
biological products 235–236
clean areas **216–217**
herbal medicines **258–259**
in site master file 302
water system **180**, 183
written procedures 48
scoops, sampling 376–377, *377*
scrubbers, dust and fume removal 89
security, computerized systems **136**
seed lots, storage 236
selectivity, analytical methods 132
self-contained area, definition 15

self-inspection **23–24**, 292
active pharmaceutical ingredients 195
excipients **201–202**
herbal medicines 260
report 24, 292
site master file 303
team 24
see also internal audits
sensitizing materials *see* allergens
shelf-life specifications 57
shipping/dispatch
definition 245
investigational products **253**
sinks and drains
in clean/aseptic areas 229, 235
radiopharmaceuticals 278
see also effluents
site master file **301–303**
smoking 29, 191
software, computer, validation *137*, 138
solid dosage forms
HVAC systems 59
oral (OSD), definition 64
pre-approval inspections 289
sample sizes, pre-approval inspections 289
sample storage 368
solid materials
sample containers 368
sampling procedures 366, 367, 383–384
sampling tools 376–377, 378–380
see also dust
solvents
excipients 206
herbal medicines 267, 274
inflammable 347
recovered 204
residual 206
SOPs *see* standard operating procedures
spears
bag-sampling 380, *381*
double-tube 380, *381*
specifications **41–43**
definition 15
excipients **206**
finished products 42–43
herbal medicines **264–266**
intermediate and bulk products 42
investigational products **249**
starting and packaging materials 42
water quality 173–174, 211
specificity, analytical methods 132
sponsor, definition 245–246
spore-forming organisms, handling 236
spurious pharmaceutical products, inspection **320–321**
stability testing **57**
active pharmaceutical ingredients **195**
excipients **213–214**
herbal medicines **271–272**
inspection 296–297
staff/staffing *see* personnel
standard operating procedures (SOPs)
definitions 15, 65, 105, 324
documentation **46–48**
inspections 313, **320–321**
sampling 47, **382–386**
standards, reference *see* reference standards
starting materials 3, 35–36
active pharmaceutical ingredients 193
biological products 238
certification 9
definition 15
excipients **203–204**, 212
GMP **188–214**
herbal medicines 264–266
identity tests 55, 212
investigational products **247**
pre-approval inspections 289
purchase 35
quality control 54
retention samples 56–57
sampling facilities 32, 364
sampling plans **373–375**
sampling procedures 366, **370–371**, **383–384**
specifications 42
stability studies 57
storage 36, 204
test requirements 55–56
sterile pharmaceutical products **215–232**
active pharmaceutical ingredients 194
aseptic preparation 220, 226–227
excipients 209–211
monitoring 217
processing 221–222
sterilization by filtration 226–227
validation 221
for clinical trials 246, 251–252
excipients 209–211
finishing 231
GMP 3–4

manufacture 190, 217–222
quality control 216
radioactive 279
sampling 216, 366
terminally sterilized 220
processing 221–222
sterilization methods 223–226
see also clean areas
sterility testing 216
sterilization **222–223**
in biological product manufacture 238
by dry heat 224
by filtration 226–227
by gases and fumigants 225–226
by heat 223–224
by moist heat 224
by radiation 225
terminal **223–226**
validation 223
storage
active pharmaceutical ingredients 195
drinking-water 176
excipients 205
facilities 31–32
inspection 313, 316
herbal medicines **262**
materials 35
outdoor 204
samples **368–369**, *386–387*
standard operating procedures 46
starting materials 36, 204
vessels, water **180–181**
waste materials 39
water for pharmaceutical use **178–183**
stores, inspection 311, 313, 316
substandard pharmaceutical products, inspection **320–321**
suppliers
audits and approval 24–25
documentation 316–317
identification 289
new 289
of starting materials 35
surfaces, interior 32, 229, 235
surveillance programmes, sampling procedures 369–370
swabs, sampling 126
system control and data acquisition (SCADA) 88
system suitability testing, analytical procedures 133
systems, qualification *see* qualification

Technical Reports, *WHO* 2
temperature
heat sterilization 223–224
recording devices 224
temperature control
ambient air 33, 59, **85–86**
stored herbal materials 262
water systems 180, 182, 230
see also heating, ventilation and air-conditioning (HVAC) systems
terminal sterilization **223–226**
see also sterilization
terminally sterilized products *see* sterile pharmaceutical products, terminally sterilized
testing
documentation of procedures 41–42, 47–48
pre-approval inspections **289–290**
see also analytical methods
tests
herbal materials 270–271
quality control 55–56
water for pharmaceutical use 184–185
see also identity tests; stability testing
therapeutic activity
constituents with known, definition 257
definition 258
thieves, sample 378–380, *380*
time limits, herbal medicine production 269
toilet facilities 31
toxoids 236
traditional medicines *see* herbal medicines
training
GMP **28–29**
biological products 234
herbal medicines **261**
radiopharmaceuticals 278
sterile products 227
HACCP methodology **350–351**
inspectors 10, 292–293, 327, 328
samplers 365
tuberculosis, testing for 234
turbulent flow, definition 65

ultraviolet irradiation 225
unauthorized markets (parallel markets)
definition 309
inspection 311, 319

unidirectional airflow (UDAF) **73–76**, *77–79*
definition 65
dust control 73–76, *78–79*, 86–87
horizontal and vertical 76, *79*
weighing stations 75, *75*, *77*
uniformity, definition 363
unit operations/processes, excipient manufacture 199
United States of America (USA), legal status of investigational products 242

vaccination requirements 234
vaccines 4, 232, 233
killed 236
processing 221
storage facilities 316
validation **18–19**, **101–170**
analytical method **129–133**, *133*
approaches 106
aseptic processing 221
calibration and verification 108
change control 112–113
cleaning *see* cleaning validation
computerized systems **133–139**, *137*
concurrent *see* concurrent validation
definitions 15, 65, 105, 349
glossary 103–106
and HACCP 347
herbal medicines **259**
HVAC systems **113–118**
identity of starting materials 55
investigational products **246**
personnel 113
before pre-approval inspections 288
process *see* process validation
prospective *see* prospective validation
relationship to qualification *95*, 106, *115*
repeat *see* revalidation
retrospective *see* retrospective validation
scope 106–107
stages 111–112
sterilization methods 223
systems and equipment 139–165
water systems for pharmaceutical use **118–120**, 183–185
WHO guidelines 3
validation master plan (VMP) **108**
definitions 65, 105
HVAC systems 95–96, 114
validation protocols (or plans) (VP) **109**
definition 105
validation reports **109–110**
definition 105
vapour, extraction systems 86, 87
vent filters, water storage vessels 181
ventilation systems *see* heating, ventilation and air-conditioning (HVAC) systems
verification **108**
computerized systems 135
definitions 105, 349
HACCP procedures **355–356**
method *see* method validation/verification
veterinary products, certification 9
videos, inspection visits 297
visitors 29

walls 32
warehouses, inspection 311, 313, 316
washing
equipment 34
facilities 31, 230
hand 29, 230
waste materials
disposal 39
hazardous 357
herbal medicines 259
see also effluents
water
drinking *see* drinking-water
highly purified *see* highly purified water
purification methods **175–178**
purified *see* purified water
quality (grades) **173–174**, 211
requirements and uses 171–172
for sterile product manufacture 221, 231
water for injections (WFI) **174**
applications 175
in excipient manufacture 211
production **178**
water for pharmaceutical use (WPU) 35, **170–187**
application to processes and dosage forms 174–175
in excipient manufacture **211**
water systems for pharmaceutical use **178–183**
continuous monitoring 184–185
distribution pipework 51, 181–183

in excipient manufacture **211**
general requirements 172–173
inspection 185–186
maintenance 185
materials in contact with 180
operational considerations 183–185
qualification 118–120, 183–184
sanitization and bioburden control 180
start-up and commissioning 118, 183
in sterile product manufacture 221, 231
storage vessels 180–181
system reviews 185
validation **118–120**, 183–185
weighing areas 32
HVAC systems 75, *75*, 77
weighted sampling containers 378, *379*
wholesalers, inspection 305, 311, 316
workers *see* personnel
workshops, maintenance 31
World Health Assembly (WHA)
GMP inception 8–9
quality assurance concerns 1
World Health Organization (WHO)
Certification Scheme *see* Certification Scheme
Requirements for Biological Substances 233, 237
Revised Drug Strategy 1
Technical Reports 2
Traditional Medicine Strategy 255
worst case, definition 106
wrist-watches 228